QUALITATIVE INDICATORS OF LABOUR STANDARDS

Social Indicators Research Series

Volume 30

This new series aims to provide a public forum for single treatises and collections of papers on social indicators research that are too long to be published in our journal *Social Indicators Research*. Like the journal, the book series deals with statistical assessments of the quality of life from a broad perspective. It welcomes the research on wide variety of substantive areas, including health, crime, housing, education, family life, leisure activities, transportation, mobility, economics, work, religion and environmental issues. These areas of research will focus on the impact of key issues such as health on the overall quality of life and vice versa. An international review board, consisting of Ruut Veenhoven, Joachim Vogel, Ed Diener, Torbjorn Moum, Mirjam A.G. Sprangers and Wolfgang Glatzer, will ensure the high quality of the series as a whole.

The titles published in this series are listed at the end of this volume.

QUALITATIVE INDICATORS
OF
LABOUR STANDARDS

Comparative Methods and Applications

Edited by

DAVID KUCERA

International Labour Office, Geneva, Switzerland

A C. I. P. Catalogue record for this book is available from the Library of Congress.

ISBN-10 1-4020-5200-6 (HB)
ISBN-13 978-1-4020-5200-2 (HB)
ISBN-10 1-4020-5310-X (e-book)
ISBN-13 978-1-4020-5310-8 (e-book)

Published by Springer,
P.O. Box 17, 3300 AA Dordrecht, The Netherlands.

www.springer.com

Printed on acid-free paper

The designations employed in ILO publications, which are in conformity with United Nations practice, and the presentation of material therein do not imply the expression of any opinion whatsoever on the part of the International Labour Office concerning the legal status of any country, area or territory or of its authorities, or concerning the delimitation of its frontiers.

The responsibility for opinions expressed in signed articles, studies and other contributions rests solely with their authors, and publication does not constitute an endorsement by the International Labour Office of the opinions expressed in them.

Reference to names of firms and commercial products and processes does not imply their endorsement by the International Labour Office, and any failure to mention a particular firm, commercial product or process is not a sign of disapproval.

Contents

CONTENTS

Chapter 1

Introduction and Overview*

DAVID KUCERA
International Labour Office

Recent years have witnessed a rapidly growing interest in the use and construction of "qualitative" indicators of labour standards. This is likely attributable to several factors: the rise of "socially responsible" investment, the aged but still lively debates on the effects of labour standards on international competitiveness, and the sense that traditional quantitative indicators of labour standards (such as unionization rates and gender earnings gaps) are too narrow in scope to adequately capture the wide-ranging and inherently qualitative nature of many aspects of labour stand-ards, both de jure and de facto. Qualitative indicators, while generally having numerical values, are based on such methods as grading by experts, the coding of legislation, and the coding of other textual sources addressing violations of a more de facto nature.

Measuring compliance with labour standards is an undertaking intrinsically fraught with difficulty. This is not because labour standards themselves are neces-sarily difficult to understand or to implement with sufficient resources and will. Rather, the difficulty arises with the act of measurement itself, the act of construct-ing labour standards indicators. For there are a number of possible sources of meas-urement error, both random and non-random, that are unique to such indicators, on top of those that affect qualitative and quantitative indicators alike. The growing use of qualitative indicators of labour standards thus raises a number of questions about comparative methods of construction as well as the appropriateness of particular methods for particular applications.

This volume results from a seminar that was organized by the International Labour Organization (ILO) in the Fall of 2004 to address these and related ques-tions. The seminar brought together ILO colleagues who have worked on these issues with notable outside experts, including Richard Block from Michigan State University, Ludo Cuyvers from the University of Antwerp, Dan Viederman from Verité – all of whom contributed chapters to this volume – as well as Anne Zollner from the U.S. Department of Labor, who presented the seminal report *Monitoring International Labor Standards: Techniques and Sources of Information*, commis-sioned by the U.S. Department of Labor and carried out by the U.S.'s National Research Council of the National Academies (National Research Council, 2004).

The chapters in this volume address a wide range of labour standards, mainly constructed at the country level. Among these are the ILO's four "fundamental

---

* This chapter benefited greatly from insightful comments by Miriam Abu Sharkh, Patrick Belser and Janine Berg.

D. Kucera (ed.), Qualitative Indicators of Labour Standards, 1–25.
© 2007 *by ILO.*

rights at work" – regarding freedom of association and collective bargaining rights, discrimination in the workplace, child labour and forced labour – occupational safety and health, employment protection, minimum wages, working time and unemployment insurance.

The seminar was guided by several main themes, which are taken up by the chapters in this volume. Though this introductory chapter is structured as a chapter-by-chapter summary, it also provides a running comparison of the pros and cons of the methods of each chapter, with these main themes interwoven throughout. In spite of a fair amount of overlap among them, these themes can be grouped into four: 1. Defining labour standards: conceptual definitions and working definitions; 2. Measuring working definitions; 3. Matching construction with application: levels of aggregation and implications of measurement error; and 4. Problems with information sources.

Defining Labour Standards: Conceptual Definitions and Working Definitions

Most of the labour standards indicators presented in this volume are defined with respect to ILO Conventions and jurisprudence and in this sense address *international* labour standards. However, even with a generally agreed-upon definition of what constitutes compliance with a labour standard, there are many ways that a given definition can be used to construct a labour standards indicator. For constructing such indicators requires translating a conceptual definition into a working definition – that is, a set of components or sub-indicators by which a conceptual definition is operationalized. For example, a labour standard can be operationalized by a simple binary variable, such as whether or not a country has ratified a certain Convention. Though simplistic in the extreme, such indicators have in fact been widely used in econometric studies of the relationship between labour stand-ards and international competitiveness. However, even finer methods must decide whether to use either, say, 10 or 100 evaluation criteria to classify different types of compliance with or violations of a given labour standard and thus whether to have 10 or 100 components of a working definition; and though both methods would be based on ILO Conventions and jurisprudence, each will generally yield different relative index values for countries.

Ultimately, the number of components used is fairly arbitrary, to say nothing of the weighting schemes that might be used to aggregate and construct an overall indicator of compliance with a labour standard. Moreover, the information required to assess compliance with certain aspects of a labour standard may simply be unavailable, or not systematically or readily enough available across countries and over time. This creates a tendency for working definitions to be based on the types of information that are more readily available rather than what constitutes compliance in a more *a priori*, conceptual sense.

Constructing a labour standards indicator also requires defining which aspects of a labour standard a method endeavours to measure. Broadly speaking, these can be broken down into de jure and de facto. Most methods presented in this volume address both, with varying degrees of emphasis, though different authors use different words to capture the basic de jure versus de facto distinction. For example, Block distinguishes between "law and legislation" and "labour market outcomes," Cuyvers and Van Den Bulcke between "formal respect" and "real respect," Böhning between "adherence" and "implementation," Abu Sharkh among "input," "process" and "output," and the National Research Council among "legal framework," "government performance" and "output." For indicators combining both de jure and de facto, it should be noted that the relative weight given to each are also ultimately arbitrary but will, all the same, generally change countries' relative index values.

Measuring Working Definitions

Different methods of constructing labour standards indicators may be based on identical working definitions but nonetheless yield different results, for there are any number of ways of measuring the same working definition. For example, different methods may use the dismissal of workers for trade union activities as one component of an indicator of de facto trade union rights and base the measurement of this on exactly the same textual sources and definition of "dismissal," "worker," and "trade union activities." Based on these common starting points, consider four scenarios. The first method counts the number of reported dismissals in a country, evaluated as a proportion of employees in a country. The second method also counts the number of reported dismissals in a country but creates four categories of the number of dismissals and then assigns a whole number score of 1 to 4 depending on the category into which it falls. The third method does not count the number of reported dismissals but rather relies on the judgment of a group of experts to give whole number scores of 1 to 4, depending on what is judged to be the severity of problems in a country. The fourth method simply codes, yes or no, whether any dismissals of workers for trade union activities are reported for a country.

Each of these methods has different strengths and weaknesses. The validity of the first and second methods depends on the number of dismissals of workers for trade union activities being reported with sufficient regularity and accuracy over time, on which different evaluators may disagree, whereas the third and fourth methods do not require that any numbers at all be reported. The third method provides room for more nuanced judgments than the fourth, but it is not strictly reproducible, whereas the other three methods are. It is worth emphasizing that these differences in methods of measurement are not merely hypothetical but rather illustrative of the challenges the authors in this volume face.

These examples also suggest that some methods of constructing labour standards indicators are not purely qualitative but rather take a hybrid approach, using both qualitative information and quantitative information in textual sources as well as traditional quantitative statistics, based on labour force and establishment surveys. There is much to be said for such hybrid approaches, for many aspects of labour standards compliance are countable, at least in principle, such as the number of child labourers or forced labourers or the hourly earnings of male and female workers.

Combining qualitative and quantitative information thus enables an assessment of the intrinsically qualitative nature of many aspects of labour standards while taking advantage of the finer grades of variation and representativeness of traditional quantitative statistics. Within the volume, among those making use solely of qualitative information are Böhning, Kucera and Viederman and Klett. Among those combining qualitative information with quantitative information found in textual sources or with traditional quantitative statistics are Block and Cuyvers and Van Den Bulcke. Belser *et al.* is exceptional in this volume in making use solely of quantitative information – that is, numbers – found in textual sources, though qualitative information from these sources is used to assess the validity of these numbers.

Matching Construction with Application: Levels of Aggregation and Implications of Measurement Error

The usefulness of a labour standards indicator must be evaluated relative to its intended use, and it is therefore important for those wishing to construct such indicators to be clear from the outset about intended use. This is necessary to minimize potential mismatches between intended uses and construction as regards the scope of the indicator, such as regarding how many standards or aspects of a standard are most meaningfully combined in a single indicator, as well as whether an indicator focuses on particular sectors or addresses a country as a whole.

There are several possible uses of labour standards indicators, which can be grouped into three. The first application is for informing direct engagement with countries with the aim of assisting them in improving their labour standards, such as through technical cooperation between the ILO and ILO member countries. The chapter in this volume by Zarka-Martres and Guichard-Kelly provides the clearest example of this application. The second application is for the statistical analysis of *relationships*, such as between trade union rights and such economic outcomes as foreign trade and foreign direct investment, for which Block and Kucera provide examples in this volume. The third application is for the comparison of countries, typically and tellingly through rankings. Though these rankings may be used, for example, to inform foreign investment location decisions, there is also a sense in which these rankings provide results in and of themselves. As such, indicators for this application generally provide overall country scores that aggregate several labour standards, such as the ILO's four "fundamental rights at work." Examples from this volume include Böhning and Viederman and Klett.

For the purposes of directly assisting countries such as through technical cooperation, it is important to have a finely-graded sense of the problems that a country may be experiencing. Indeed, the more detail the better. Zarka-Martres and Guichard-Kelly make an analogy with an automobile in need of repair, for which the owner is best served by having a detailed inventory of what needs fixing, so that the owner can prioritize and make repairs while mindful of budget constraints. For this application, there is no need to aggregate the various components that constitute a working definition of a standard, and thus neither are there the associated problems of devising weights by which to aggregate these components.

For the statistical analysis of relationships, a key consideration is the conceptual coherence of the indicator with respect to hypothesized causal channels, putting upward limits on the level of meaningful aggregation. For example, more child labour may be hypothesized to affect exports positively through the supply of labour as well as negatively through an education effect, whereas stronger trade union rights may be hypothesized to affect exports negatively through a wage share effect and positively through a social stability effect. Given these differences in hypothesized causal channels, it is best to treat child labour and trade union rights as individual variables in the analysis of impacts on exports, as combining them into one indicator would render it impossible to untangle causal channels and meaningfully interpret statistical results.[1] If this holds for child labour and trade union rights, it holds all the more strongly for indicators combining all four ILO "fundamental rights at work" or yet more labour standards. One may also wish, of course, to study relationships among and within various labour standards, such as whether and how trade union rights affect occupational safety and health or employment protection, or whether and how de jure trade union rights affect de facto trade union rights, with attendant implications for the construction of indicators.

For the third application, the comparison of countries, it is imperative that the indicator values for each country are defensible in their own right, particularly when such indicators are used to inform investment decisions or trade policies (such as to determine trade preferences given by richer to poorer countries), for which the inevitable measurement errors of qualitative indicators of labour standards can have very real negative consequences. This differs from the first application, which relies on the carrot rather than the stick, or the second, for which there are a number of techniques for dealing with non-random measurement error and for which the implications of random measurement error are likely to simply be weak econometric results. In this sense, labour standards indicators used for the third application ought to be held to particularly exacting standards, given the higher stakes involved in using them.

Problems with Information Sources

The above three themes address methods of construction. This fourth addresses problems with the information used by different methods, which are perhaps the most fundamental bottleneck to improving qualitative indicators of labour standards. Problems with information sources are discussed at length in *Monitoring International Labour Standards* (National Research Council, 2004) as well as in various papers of this volume and thus can be summarized briefly. Regarding key ILO reports used to construct indicators of labour standards, there are differences in the reporting requirements for countries that have and have not ratified a given

---

[1] One might wish, of course, to include indicators for different labour standards simultaneously in econometric models and also possibly to interact them, if this can be theoretically motivated.

ILO Convention, with some ILO reports referring only to ratifying countries and others only to non-ratifying countries. Since these two types of reports differ in a number of substantive respects, this creates systematic bias between ratifying and non-ratifying countries for indicators based on these reports. In addition, certain ILO reports are based on self-reporting by countries, which may result in bias if countries are not altogether forthcoming in their reporting. Such self-reporting bias can be offset by additionally making use of other more independent information sources. Other ILO reports are based on cases that can be brought forth by ratifying and non-ratifying countries alike, but some countries and regions make consistently greater use of these procedures than others, thus creating systematic information bias in this regard. Other types of regional information bias may result from differences in the openness of the press as well as in the extent to which those constructing indicators or compiling information sources know a region's language. Some methods use the U.S. State Department's *Country Reports on Human Rights Practices*, which one might suspect to be biased to reflect U.S. policy interests and which, in any case, might be considered problematic in that they consist of one ILO member state making assessments of others (though not of itself).

Problems of incomplete information are less acute for solely de jure indicators given that it is possible at least in principle to collect for all countries all legislation relevant to a given labour standard. This is not the case, however, for indicators addressing de facto labour standards, for which information sources will always be incomplete to varying degrees. Another fundamental problem is that information sources have generally not been compiled to construct labour standards indicators and thus it is not obvious that the same detailed working definition of compliance is applied with sufficient consistency across countries and over time. It is striking in this regard that some commonly-used textual sources used to construct labour standards indicators have gotten considerably heftier over time, not because compliance with labour standards has worsened, necessarily, but because interest in and resources devoted to monitoring labour standards compliance have increased over time. Since these sources tend to focus on problems rather than progress, this creates a tendency for indicators based on them to show a worsening of labour standards compliance over time.

What follows in this introduction is a comparative summary of each subsequent chapter in this volume, throughout which it is hoped that the above themes provide unifying refrains. The chapter closes with a brief discussion of lessons learned and ways forward.

Chapter 2: Indicators of Labour Standards: An Overview and Comparison

Richard Block presents a method of constructing labour standards indicators – developed with his Michigan State University colleague Karen Roberts – as well as a critical survey of a number of other such indicators. The stated motivation for creating these indicators is to deepen the understanding of the relationship between labour standards and trade using statistical analysis. A wide range of labour standards indicators are constructed, 13 in all, for 50 states in the U.S., 10 provinces and two territories in Canada, the U.S. and Canada at the national level, and the EU as a whole. The 13 labour standards indicators address minimum wages, overtime and working time, paid time-off, unemployment and employment insurance, workers' compensation for employment injury, collective bargaining, equal employment opportunity and employment equity, unjust discharge, occupational safety and health, advance notice of plant closings and large-scale layoffs, employees' rights to information and consultation, parental and family leave, and transfer of undertaking and ownership. Though these indictors could, in principle, be aggregated into one overall labour standards indicator, they are not. This is consistent with their intended use in statistical analysis, for which such disaggregated indicators more readily enable one to address causally specific relationships.

One noteworthy characteristic of these indicators, which Block refers to as their "relativism" (p. 21), is that they are not defined (at least not directly) with respect to ILO Conventions, but rather with respect to the highest existing standards in the jurisdictions being compared. This differs, by and large, from the other indicators in this volume, which are generally based on ILO Conventions and jurisprudence and in this sense endeavour to measure compliance with *international* labour standards. In large part, Block and Robert's method consists of coding prevailing legislation. This is done by reading laws and deriving from this reading a list of "provisions," or sub-indicators, that constitute a working definition of compliance with each of the 13 labour standards. Each of these sub-indicators is then assigned a weight by which they are aggregated. Some of these sub-indicators are equivalent to yes or no responses, but many of them make use of detailed *quantitative* information within legislation, particularly information expressed in terms of time and money. For instance, as regards the Canada–U.S. comparison for occupational safety and health, the method devises six categories for "maximum penalty for wilful violation of statute," six for "daily penalty . . . until hazard corrected," six "maximum penalty for contravening inspector" (in dollars) and five categories for "maximum imprisonment possible" (in months).[2]

Block and Robert's method addresses not only legislation but also its enforcement, by assessing whether the losing party in a case has a right to appeal "to the judicial system outside the agency dedicated to enforcing labour standards" (p. 9), on the view that this indicates weak enforcement. This information is generally lightly weighted in the construction of the indicators, however, and thus variation in the indicators across jurisdictions is largely driven by de jure differences.

A striking characteristic of these indicators – unique among the chapters in this volume – is that they are constructed for, in a sense, pairwise comparison. More specifically, the indicators for Canada and the U.S. are constructed for comparison with each other and, separately, the indicators for the U.S. and EU are likewise constructed for comparison with each other. This follows logically from the definitional

---

[2] Rather than converting quantitative information into indicators through categories defined by threshold levels, one could also devise a method to convert such information directly, thus enabling finer variation in the indicators.

scope of labour standards addressed by the chapter, satisfying the criteria of what the author describes as "comparability in purpose and administration," "adoption or possibility of adoption in both countries," "governmentally-created and enforced," and "primary effect on workplace transactions." Since these criteria hold differently across different pairs of jurisdictions, indicators for different pairs are constructed from different sets of sub-indicators with different weights. Such pairwise construction does not enable a direct comparison, in this case, between Canada and the EU.

This might seem to indicate a weakness of the indicators, given their intended use to analyse the relationship between trade and labour standards, for which one might hope to evaluate as large a sample of jurisdictions as possible. There are two points worth making in this regard. First, the trade and labour standards debate can be addressed by analysing variation across the jurisdictions of Canada and the U.S., and indeed Block and Roberts produced a study in which they did just this (Block and Roberts, 2003). Second, the basic approach could be adapted by allowing a more general, *a priori* definition of what "provisions" constitute compliance with a labour standard, most obviously by basing these provisions on ILO Conventions. This would more readily enable comparisons among a broader spectrum of countries, certainly countries *within* the EU, for example, but perhaps also countries at more widely different levels of economic development. Block is, of course, well aware of this possibility and squarely addresses the comparative pros and cons of different methods of constructing such indicators, in this and a number of other respects.

Chapter 3: Country-level Assessments of Labour Conditions in Emerging Markets: An Approach for Institutional Investors

Dan Viederman and Erin Klett's chapter presents a method of constructing labour standards indicators developed by Verité, the organization where the authors work.[3] The indicators were constructed to inform the investment decisions of the California Public Employees Retirement System (CalPERS), the largest public pension fund in the U.S. That these indicators have a direct influence on such sizeable investment decisions makes them particularly noteworthy, and illustrates that questions of comparative method in the construction of labour standards indicators are of more than academic interest. From a methodological point of view, moreover, Verité's indicators are particularly impressive in the range of information sources used in their construction and the network of contacts established within countries to obtain and evaluate this information, much of it available only in local languages. Among these sources are proprietary information from Verité's factory audits (more than one thousand) as well as structured interviews with representatives from governments, workers' organizations, employers and NGOs.

---

[3] On its website, Verité describes itself as "an independent, non-profit social auditing and research organization."

Verité began constructing these indicators in 2000 and has continued to update them regularly. They are constructed for 27 "emerging market" countries and address the ILO's four "fundamental principles and rights at work," regarding freedom of association and collective bargaining rights, discrimination in the workplace, child labour and forced labour. The indicators also address other conditions of work, particularly regarding occupational safety and health, wages and hours of work. Countries are scored on how well they do regarding "ratification status of ILO Conventions," "laws and legal system," "institutional capacity," and "implementation effectiveness," weighted respectively to comprise 10, 25, 15 and 50 percent of a country's score. That the heaviest weight is given to implementation of labour standards is consistent with Verité's aim to emphasize de facto labour standards. Though scores are provided for the various sub-indicators, they are also aggregated into a single labour standards indicator, by which Hungary, the Czech Republic and Poland rank the highest and India, China and Pakistan the lowest, for the year 2003.

To provide a flavour of Verité's method, consider its indicator of "implementation effectiveness" for occupational safety and health. A score of 0 is given if the implementation of laws is judged to be "ineffective," 2 if it is judged to be "effective," and 1 for situations falling in between. As regards "laws and legal system," the second most heavily weighted component of Verité's indicators, countries are scored in a similar fashion, depending on what is judged to be the strength of legal protection. For each of the four fundamental rights at work, for example, whole-number scores of 0 to 3 are given to assess the strength of protection for workers by a country's "laws and legal system." Note that Verité's method does not attempt to code legislation, as is done by Block and Robert's method or that of Zarka-Martres and Guichard-Kelly's, described in this volume, but to provide an overall assessment of the strength of protection.

There is thus plainly room for subjectivity in such scoring. Of course, there are elements of subjectivity in any method of constructing any indicator of labour standards. For instance, there is subjectivity in developing weighting schemes as well as defining the specific criteria and their level of detail that constitute compliance with a labour standard. But once these weights and criteria are made explicit, indicators constructed from them can be made to be reproducible. That is, others wishing to exactly duplicate such indicators would be able to do so, providing what is referred to as "intercoder reliability." Some aspects of Verité's method are not obviously reproducible in this sense. The authors are up front about this issue, writing, "our reliance on a range of qualitative sources may make our study less replicable" (p. 7). Yet it is not just Verité's use of information sources that makes some components of its indicators less reproducible but also its method of scoring.

The issue of reproducibility is further discussed in this volume by Kucera, Böhning and Abu Sharkh. Some might hold that a lack of reproducibility is a fatal flaw in such an indicator, but this point is arguable. As regards the use of proprietary and other information sources that are not readily available, there is much to be said for Verité's approach, which is guided by the wise principle that it is best to consider as many sources as possible if one wishes to make an informed judgment about a complex issue. More generally, there is no great challenge in developing an indicator that is perfectly reproducible. Coding the ratification of ILO Conventions comes to mind. The challenge is rather to wrestle fruitfully with the tension between reproducibility and meaningfulness, for which there can be trade-offs, and this Verité's approach does.[4]

Verité's basic approach is also amenable to alterations in a number of respects. For example, regarding the "implementation effectiveness" indicators for child labour and the extent of gender inequality in earnings, whole-number scores of 0 to 2 are given, similar to the scores noted above for occupational safety and health. But since the number of child labourers and male and female earnings can be counted and added (unlike, say, collective bargaining rights) and since there do indeed exist conventional quantitative statistics for these measures (though of varying quality and availability), it is worth considering making use of such statistics to create more finely graded and, indeed, more reproducible indicators. This is basically the approach employed by Cuyvers and Van Den Bulcke, as described in this volume.

Verité's method of assessing "institutional capacity" merits discussion. Most of this score (80 percent) is based on an assessment of government capacity, with the balance an assessment of NGO capacity. It is worth emphasizing that countries with weak institutional capacity by these measures get *deductions* from their scores. It is not self-evident why this should be. For government capacity is surely a determinant of "implementation effectiveness" and it could be argued that this is a form of double counting, unfairly penalizing countries with weak institutional capacity. Moreover, government capacity is determined in part by a country's level of development, particularly as regards the criteria "adequacy of personnel and budgets compared to number of workplaces" and "frequency and adequacy of inspections" (p. 14).

There is a related issue regarding forced labour and child labour. Both forms of labour are caused to a significant extent by poverty. For instance, poverty creates vulnerability to debt bondage and the exploitative nature of debt bondage can in turn further contribute to a worker's poverty. It is not difficult to imagine a scenario in which poorer countries with more forced labour and child labour receive less foreign investment as a result of such indicators. This may in turn hinder economic development in these countries, leading to more poverty and thus more forced labour and child labour. The more general point is that indicators of labour standards can be powerful tools and like all powerful tools should be used with prudence and with a sensibility for unintended consequences. This requires, in turn, an understanding of why labour standards are weak in a country and whether this results because of or in spite of a government's policies.

Chapter 4: Decent Work, Standards and Indicators

Monique Zarka-Martres and Monique Guichard-Kelly of the ILO present a method of constructing labour standards indicators primarily addressing occupational safety and health (OSH) but also the rights of migrant workers. One of the distinguishing

---

[4] This point is further discussed in Kucera in this volume, Chapter 6.

characteristics of their indicators is that there is no attempt to aggregate the individual components, or sub-indicators, that define compliance with a labour standard, even though many of these could be aggregated, being made up largely of yes or no answers. Indeed, the authors argue that such aggregation and particularly the subsequent ranking of countries that often follows can be counterproductive to the ILO's aim of "the promotion and progressive implementation" of labour standards (p. 16).

This view merits serious consideration. There are many facets to implementing labour standards, with respect to law, inspection, enforcement and supporting institutions. In light of these many facets and countries' limited means, the authors' motivation for constructing their indicators is to provide a diagnostic tool for the gradual improvement of labour standards according to a country's priorities. An analogy is made with an automobile in need of repair. The automobile owner is best served by a detailed inventory of the problems with the vehicle, enabling a considered judgment of how to prioritize repairs, based on the budget constraint faced by the owner. In this sense, the indicators are intended to provide a planning tool for ILO member countries as well as for the ILO itself. As the authors write, "The ILO technical departments can use this information to effectively target technical cooperation activities and resources towards those countries most in need" (p. 14). Note the contrast with the intended use of Verité's indicators, in that countries with weakest implementation of labour standards, those "most in need," merit priority consideration in a positive sense, with resources tending to flow towards rather than away from them. But as with the discussion of the use of Verité's indicators, one must also ask why a country "most in need" is as such, and in particular whether this results because of or in spite of a government's policies. Addressing this question is essential to the effectiveness of technical cooperation aiming to improve the implementation of labour standards.

The components of Zarka-Martres and Guichard-Kelly's indicators on OSH are based on a study of 17 ILO Conventions, 24 ILO Recommendations and one ILO Protocol addressing OSH, as well as ILO Conventions on labour inspection. Based on this, a survey was constructed and sent to ILO member states, with invitations for them to consult with employers' and workers' organizations regarding responses, for which 107 ILO member states and 47 employers' and workers' organizations responded. Survey information is complemented by information on national legislation from other sources, in particular the ILO's NATLEX database. The responses of employers' and workers' organizations as well as the assessment of national legislation act to offset possible biases from countries' self-reporting.

The authors' OSH indicators are distinguished by their fine level of detail. Note in this regard that both Block and Verité also have indicators of OSH, as described in this volume. Block's OSH indicator is particularly detailed, with a total of 27 components.[5] By comparison, Zarka-Martres and Guichard-Kelly's OSH indicators consist of 85 components, grouped into 13 categories. This level of detail is, of course, consistent with the intended use of the indicator in guiding

---

[5] Including both the Canada–U.S. and U.S.–EU comparison.

ILO member countries and the ILO itself in the improvement of OSH, again in analogy with a sophisticated machine in need of repair.

It should be emphasized that these indicators go well beyond addressing legislation to address implementation in general, and among the 13 categories developed by the authors are "existence of national OSH infrastructures" and "capacity and functioning of national OSH structures." In addition to yes or no responses for each of the 85 components are a box for comments, references to the relevant ILO Conventions, references to relevant national legislation and comments by the ILO's Committee of Experts on the Application of Conventions and Recommendations.[6] This information is made available on the ILO's internet site. Planned for future development are internet links to related ILO projects undertaken in a country, summaries of best practices, ILO statistics on OSH, and ILO databases on ratification of ILO Conventions and national legislation.

Chapter 5: The Quantification of Respect for Selected Core Labour Standards: Towards a Social Development Index

Ludo Cuyvers and Daniel Van Den Bulcke of the University of Antwerp present a method of constructing indicators addressing the ILO's four "fundamental principles and rights at work," regarding freedom of association and collective bargaining rights, discrimination in the workplace, child labour and forced labour. The authors construct their indicators for 40 countries, based on information for around the year 2000. As with the prior chapters, the authors address both de jure and de facto aspects of labour standards, which they refer to as "formal respect" and "real respect" for labour standards. For each of the four main indicators combining "formal respect" and "real respect," most weight (70 percent) is given to "real respect" and the remainder for "formal respect."

This emphasis on the de facto is akin to Verité's indicators. In contrast with Verité, however, the authors do not create an aggregate indicator across the four fundamental rights at work.[7] To contrast further, whereas Verité's method distinguishes between "ratification status of ILO Conventions" and "laws and legal system," Cuyvers and Van Den Bulcke's indicators of "formal respect" primarily address ratification of the relevant ILO Conventions rather than a country's legislation. The exception is for child labour, for which the authors code various aspects of a country's legislation, such as regards the minimum age for light and hazardous

---

[6] The ILO's website describes its "supervisory bodies" as follows: "the Committee of Experts on the Application of Conventions and Recommendations and the Conference Committee on the Application of Standards – regularly examine the application of ILS in ILO member States. Representation and complaint procedures can also be initiated against states that fail to comply with conventions they have ratified. A special procedure – the Committee on Freedom of Association – reviews complaints concerning violations of freedom of association, whether or not a member State has ratified the relevant conventions."

[7] In prior work, however, the authors do aggregate their indicators into what they refer to as a "social development index" (Wermenbol, Cuyvers and Van Den Bulcke, 1998).

work and for compulsory education. In addition, for freedom of association and collective bargaining rights and for discrimination, the authors address not only ratification of ILO Conventions but also whether non-ratifying countries make a formal report to the ILO on the implementation of these rights, as they are required to do. For the sake of internal consistency, assessing non-reporting could also be extended to child labour and forced labour.[8]

One of the most useful aspects of Cuyvers and Van Den Bulcke's method is the combination of qualitative information based on textual sources with more conventional quantitative statistics. There is nothing to lose and much to gain from such a hybrid approach, since many aspects of labour standards implementation are amenable to counting and thus to being measured by conventional statistics. The best example of this is the authors' "real respect" indicator of gender discrimination, which uses conventional statistics for gender representation in education and employment. For the "real respect" child labour indicator, the authors use the economic activity rate of ten to fourteen year olds. However, this data is constrained by the authors to be a binary variable, equal to 1 for any economically active ten to fourteen year olds and to 0 for none, thus relinquishing the useful variation that conventional statistics can provide. For their "real respect" forced labour indicator, the authors use ILO, U.S. State Department and International Confederation of Free Trade Union (ICFTU) sources to evaluate the types of forced labour reported in a country (up to eight, as defined by the ILO), for which each of these types is scored on a whole-number scale of 1 to 5 based on the authors' judgment as to the extent of forced labour. As with components of Verité's indicators, such scoring leaves room for subjectivity and thus would not appear to be strictly reproducible. This criticism applies only to Cuyvers and Van Den Bulcke's "real respect" forced labour indicator, however, and not to other components of their indicators.

---

[8] Cuyvers and Van Den Bulcke code reporting by non-ratifying countries as per Article 19 of the ILO Constitution. Article 19 reports are thematic, focusing on different labour standards in different years without a preset pattern. Thus from the viewpoint of coding reporting by non-ratifying countries, there is an element of happenstance as to whether Article 19 reports are indeed requested of countries for any given labour standard for any given year. This differs from the coding of reporting for non-ratifying countries undertaken by Böhning, as described in this volume. Böhning rather codes whether non-ratifying countries report to the ILO Declaration on Fundamental Principles and Rights at Work. The Declaration and reporting requirements are defined in the ILO's website as follows: "Adopted in 1998, the Declaration commits Member States to respect and promote principles and rights in four categories, whether or not they have ratified the relevant Conventions. These categories are: freedom of association and the effective recognition of the right to collective bargaining, the elimination of forced or compulsory labour, the abolition of child labour and the elimination of discrimination in respect of employment and occupation. . . . This commitment is supported by a Follow-up procedure. Member States that have not ratified one or more of the core Conventions are asked each year to report on the status of the relevant rights and principles within their borders, noting impediments to ratification, and areas where assistance may be required." Note that for the purposes of coding reporting, Declaration reports have the advantage that non-ratifiers are required to report each year for each of the ILO's four "fundamental rights at work."

The authors' "real respect" freedom of association and collective bargaining indicator uses an approach similar to Kucera (described in this volume) as well as the OECD (1996, 2000).[9] Cuyvers and Van Den Bulcke code violations of freedom of association and collective bargaining rights that are reported in textual sources, in particular the ICFTU's *Annual Survey of Violations of Trade Union Rights* and the U.S. State Department's *Country Reports on Human Rights Practices*. There are three components of this indicator, regarding "reported number of violations vis-à-vis trade union members/leaders," "government interference" and "legal limitations." The "government interference" component is a binary, yes or no variable. The "legal limitations" component consists of four categories, based on the extent to which sectors are excluded from legal protection. The component on "reported number of violations" is of particular interest. Like Kucera's and the OECD's approaches, the authors code various violations of trade union rights. Cuyvers and Van Den Bulcke consider four such violations: the number of murders, wounded, arrests and dismissals. What distinguishes their approach is the word "number," in that the authors actually code the reported number of such violations and then apply a greater weight to higher numbers, based on four categories of the number of reported violations. This method is thus premised on these numbers being available with sufficient accuracy regularly across countries and over time, an issue discussed in Kucera in this volume. Kucera's and the OECD's approaches, in contrast, simply look at whether such violations are reported in a country, yes or no, with weights applied not to categories of numbers but rather to the severity of violations.[10]

Cuyvers and Van Den Bulcke do not elaborate on the intended use of their indicators, and the main motivation they provide for developing them is that while there exist analogous indicators for other aspects of "economic and social life," there is (or at least was) a dearth of indicators for labour standards (p. 3). After descriptions of each of the indicators of fundamental rights at work, however, the authors have a summary section in which they discuss the rankings of countries. There is a sense, then, in which the authors view such ranking as a result in and of itself. In a section titled "sensitivity analysis," the authors also undertake the useful exercise of allowing a number of the key weights used in the construction of their indicators to vary and to see how this affects cross-country correlations.[11] With the exception of the "formal respect" child labour and forced labour indicators, the authors find these correlations to be quite high.

---

[9] This is the lesser-known of the two OECD approaches to constructing indicators of trade union rights. The better-known is discussed in Kucera as described in this volume. The lesser-known is described in annexes of the OECD's reports. Unlike Cuyvers and Van Den Bulcke's and Kucera's method, though, the OECD relies on the ILO's reports of the Committee of Experts on the Application of Conventions and Recommendations (CEACR). This source is problematic for such purposes, as discussed by Kucera and particularly Abu Sharkh in this volume.

[10] One possible amendment to Cuyvers and Van Den Bulcke's method in this regard would be to normalize the numbers of reported violations relative to a base population, such as the number of labour force participants or the number of formal workers.

[11] The authors do this by comparing cross-country Spearman and Pearson correlation coefficients for the various weighting schemes.

This suggests that most of the authors' indicators can be used in cross-country statistical analysis without undue concern that results are driven by a particular weighting scheme. However, if these indicators are used for pure and simple ranking, then even a quite high and statistically significant correlation coefficient can mean that some countries' rankings change a great deal between different weighting schemes, which are ultimately arbitrary. This caution should be borne in mind by those assessing countries on the basis of such rankings, along with the broader question of what one ought to make of such rankings and particularly whether countries with lower rankings merit assistance or opprobrium. This is not, of course, a merely hypothetical question, as suggested by the above discussion of the contrast between the intended uses of the indicators constructed by Verité and Zarka-Martres and Guichard-Kelly.

Chapter 6: Measuring Trade Union Rights by Violations of These Rights

David Kucera of the ILO presents a method of constructing qualitative indicators of trade union rights as well as a comparative critique of similar indicators regarding such properties as reproducibility, evaluator bias and information bias. The author's indicators address only freedom of association and collective bargaining rights, but these rights particularly lend themselves to qualitative approaches, or – perhaps more accurately – are particularly difficult to measure using more conventional statistical approaches.

Kucera uses 37 evaluation criteria for different types of de jure and de facto violations of trade union rights, with an emphasis on de facto violations. These evaluation criteria are grouped into six categories: "freedom of association/collective bargaining-related civil liberties," "right to establish and join unions and worker organizations," "right to bargain collectively," "right to strike," "export processing zones," and "other union activities." The evaluation criteria are derived from reading relevant ILO Conventions and jurisprudence on trade union rights as well as on other violations reported in textual sources. In addition to the ICFTU and U.S. State Department reports that Cuyvers and Van Den Bulcke use, Kucera also makes use of the ILO's Report of the Committee on Freedom of Association. These are arguably the three best sources of textual information for the construction of trade union rights indicators. Each of the 37 evaluation criteria include detailed coding rules addressing such issues as the mutual exclusivity or non-exclusivity of the evaluation criteria, with such rules also contributing to the reproducibility of the method. Indeed because of the intended use of the indicators for econometric analysis and because it was not certain during their constructing whether it would be possible to publish them, reproducibility is the essential condition of their construction.

The author codes violations reported in these three sources for the period from 1993 to 1997 for nearly all ILO member countries. The author's approach is broadly similar to that of Cuyvers and Van Den Bulcke regarding their "real respect" freedom of association and collective bargaining rights indicator,

particularly the component on "reported number of violations." But unlike
Cuyvers and Van Den Bulcke, Kucera codes not the number of reported violations
but rather whether a violation is reported or not reported in a country, yes or no (cf.
OECD, 1996 and 2000 for a similar approach). This is based on the sense that the
textual sources are not systematic enough in reporting numbers of violations and
that, even if they were, it is not obvious that these numbers are accurate. The indicators are constructed in both weighted and unweighted (that is, equally weighted
form), with weights based on the severity of violations. The correlation between
the weighted and unweighted measures is nonetheless very high and their use in
econometric models of wages, foreign direct investment and international trade
yield essentially the same results (Kucera, 2002; Kucera and Sarna, 2006).

The author states that these indicators are not designed for ranking countries
and, moreover, that they are not sufficiently accurate for ranking countries, placing as this does overmuch emphasis on the value of any given country. Rather the
idea is to provide an overall sense of cross-country variation and relationships, for
which the ineluctable measurement errors can be addressed through a variety of
statistical methods. This problem has less to do with the method of construction
than the textual sources on which the indicators are based. Though the three
sources used may indeed be the best existing, they are nonetheless far from perfect.
It is not clear, for instance, whether all the sources consistently apply the same
working definition of what constitutes trade union rights, either across countries or
over time. The increasing volume in recent years of the ICFTU and U.S. State
Department reports, for instance, suggests that they may not. Since these reports
focus on problems rather than progress, this creates a tendency for indicators based
on coding these sources to show an increase in violations of trade union rights over
time when this could simply be a reflection of more complete and detailed reporting. Thus the author urges caution in using this and similar methods to evaluate
change over time and like others argues that the way forward in improving such
indicators depends critically on the improvement of textual sources.

Chapter 7: Taking Labour Laws to the Domestic Dentist:
Measuring Countries' Compliance with International
Labour Non-discrimination Standards

Miriam Abu Sharkh of the ILO presents a method for constructing qualitative
indicators of discrimination, with a focus on race and particularly gender discrimination, and also provides a critical survey of comparable methods and of information sources used to construct labour standards indicators. The author's
definition of discrimination derives directly from ILO definitions – specifically the
Discrimination (Employment and Occupation) Convention of 1958 (Convention
No. 111) – and indeed the "questionnaire" used to construct the indicators is based
on the ILO's reporting forms for member countries for this Convention. The
questionnaire consists of 91 questions that are used to code ILO textual sources.
This level of detail in developing a working definition of a labour standard is
rivalled only by the work of Zarka-Martres and Guichard-Kelly, described in this

volume. Abu Sharkh's indicators are constructed for all ILO member countries going back to their ratification dates for Convention No. 111.

One of the things that makes the author's approach particularly noteworthy is that it represents the first time that labour standards indicators have been constructed by coding the ILO's biannual country reports. These country reports are required to be submitted to the ILO for Conventions that countries have ratified and that provide much of the raw material that is assessed by the ILO's supervisory bodies, particularly the Committee of Experts on the Application of Conventions and Recommendations (CEACR).[12] The reports of the CEACR have been coded to construct labour standards indicators, most notably by Böhning, as described in this volume.

As Abu Sharkh points out, though, there are nontrivial problems in using CEACR reports as well as the ILO database on national legislation (NATLEX) for constructing labour standards indicators. The CEACR reports focus on notable change within countries (whether for better or worse) rather than providing an overall assessment that would be comparable across countries. Moreover, only a fraction of the countries providing biannual country reports are mentioned in CEACR reports, as the CEACR tend to focus on countries experiencing more striking developments. Thus the author argues that any indicators based on these reports would be biased.[13] As regards NATLEX, the author points out that though this database is a "powerful tool," it nonetheless fails to provide a complete record of the legislation that is relevant for assessing implementation of any given labour standard. Of course, the biannual country reports may have their own problems. In particular, they are based on self-reporting by countries that may not be altogether forthcoming in describing their problems, with attendant implications for indicators based on these reports. However, workers' and employers' organizations can also make their own comments on the reports, providing a check on bias that might result from self-reporting. Checks are also provided by an assessment of selected national legislation as well as of United Nations documents addressing discrimination.

The author's questionnaire consists of a detailed set of yes or no questions, with space provided for comments, the year in which the legislation was passed, as well as to indicate when no information is available. Using yes or no questions facilitates the reproducibility of the method, and in this sense is akin to methods

---

[12] As pointed out by Lee Swepston, the ILO's Senior Advisor on Human Rights, the ILO system currently requires biannual reports for the eight ILO Conventions underpinning the ILO's four "fundamental principles and rights at work," regarding freedom of association and collective bargaining rights (ILO Conventions Nos. 87 and 98), discrimination in the workplace (Nos. 100 and 111), child labour (Nos. 138 and 182) and forced labour (Nos. 29 and 105) as well as for four "priority" Conventions (Nos. 81, 122, 129 and 144). Other Convention reports are on a five-year rotation (Correspondence, March 21, 2006).

[13] Though the author's questionnaire does use information from CEACR reports for six of 91 questions in a manner broadly similar to Böhning, this is to supplement the information from the main textual sources the author uses.

developed by Zarka-Martres and Guichard-Kelly and Kucera, as described in this volume. The strategy of each is similar: to ask the simplest of questions but to ask a good many of them, designed to provide a systematic and detailed working definition of what constitutes compliance with a labour standard.

The ILO's biannual country reports and the author's survey address legislation in some detail but also go well beyond legislation to evaluate a number of aspects concerning the implementation of Convention No. 111 on discrimination. The parts of the questionnaire based on coding the biannual country reports address (to use the author's descriptions) "legislation," "judicial aspects," "participatory components" and "technical assistance." Other parts of the questionnaire are based on coding a number of other ILO textual sources. The questions under "judicial aspects" are particularly noteworthy, as some of these questions address court rulings regarding labour legislation, an important aspect of labour standards implementation that few methods of constructing labour standards indicators evaluate, with one notable exception being Bertola, Boeri and Cazes, as described in this volume. To provide a flavour, one such question is, "Of . . . reported decisions, how many found in favour of the claimants?" Akin to Zarka-Martres and Guichard-Kelly's indicators for occupational safety and health (OSH), the author's indicators also evaluate whether there exists a judicial infrastructure addressing discrimination law.

There are a number of possible applications of the author's discrimination indicators. As with Zarka-Martres and Guichard-Kelly's indicators of OSH, they can provide a useful tool for ILO member countries and the ILO itself by identifying gaps in and thus improving implementation. The yes or no responses (or various subsets of them) can also be readily aggregated to construct indicators for cross-country statistical analysis. Indeed the author – being statistically-minded – poses several useful questions that such analysis could address with these indicators, including the effects of legislation on gender outcomes in labour markets (for instance, gender gaps in earnings, female-to-male employment ratios and indicators of job segregation) as well as the processes and timing by which ratifying countries pass laws and establish policies with regard to discrimination in the workplace.

Chapter 8: Towards an Index of Core Rights Gaps

Roger Böhning, formerly of the ILO, presents a method of constructing qualitative indicators of "core rights," that is, the ILO's four "fundamental principles and rights at work," regarding freedom of association and collective bargaining rights, discrimination in the workplace, child labour and forced labour. The author's stated purpose in constructing these indicators is: "(i) to document how well or poorly countries perform, which may shame some of the laggards into making improvements and others to seek bilateral or multilateral technical assistance; and (ii) to monitor progress in the realization of fundamental human rights" (p. 1). The author constructs these indicators for nearly all ILO member countries for four (five-year average) periods, beginning in the mid-1980s and continuing to 2004. The author does not consider each of the four fundamental rights separately (though in principle, one could do so using the same basic approach) but rather all four together. The indicators are broken down, however, into "adherence" and "implementation" indicators, which are intended to basically correspond with the de jure versus de facto distinction, respectively. These two indicators are then aggregated into a single indicator for each country, for which greater weight is given to "implementation."

The "adherence" indicator is made up of three sub-indicators addressing the number of ILO Conventions underlying the four fundamental principles that a country has ratified and the regularity of a country's reporting to the ILO for both ratified Conventions and unratified Conventions. The "implementation" indicator is composed of three sub-indicators based on the reports of ILO's supervisory bodies, specifically the Committee of Experts on the Application of Conventions and Recommendations (CEACR) and the Committee on the Freedom of Association (CFA). The CEACR reports only come into play for Conventions that a country has ratified and thus does not provide information on non-ratifying countries, whereas the CFA is a complaints-driven process that potentially addresses all ILO member countries.

Regarding the "adherence" indicator, coding the regularity of reporting to the ILO is akin to Cuyvers and Van Den Bulcke's method regarding their indicators of freedom of association and collective bargaining rights and discrimination. However, Böhning codes the reporting of both ratifiers (CEACR reports) and non-ratifiers, whereas Cuyvers and Van Den Bulcke code only the reporting of non-ratifiers.[14] In coding the ratification of ILO Conventions, Böhning's method is broadly similar to that of Verité and Cuyvers and Van Den Bulcke. It is worth emphasizing, though, that though the "adherence" indicator is meant to represent de jure aspects of labour standards, it does not directly evaluate a country's legislation.

What makes Böhning's method particularly distinctive is not so much the "adherence" indicator but rather the "implementation" indicator. The "implementation" indicator is constructed from coding the status of ILO member states' exchanges with the ILO's supervisory bodies as embodied in the reports of these bodies – that is whether the CEACR makes a "direct request," an "observation" or expresses "satisfaction" or whether the CFA issues a "definitive" report, an "interim" report or requests "to be kept informed." This method is premised on CEACR "direct requests" and "observations," for example, consistently indicating *problems* within countries rather than progress, a point discussed by Abu Sharkh in this volume. A further point is that what is being coded by the method is not the contents of these reports regarding the specifics of problems within countries, whether de jure or de facto, but more procedural aspects of ILO member states' engagement with the ILO's supervisory

---

[14] A further distinction regarding coding of non-ratifiers is that Böhning codes ILO Declaration reports whereas Cuyvers and Van Den Bulcke code ILO Article 19 reports. See the discussion of Cuyvers and Van Den Bulcke's indicators above for further details on the differences between and comparative suitability of coding Declaration versus Article 19 reports.

bodies. As the author puts it, "It is crucial to understand that it is the formal nature of the outputs of the supervisory machinery – not the contents of either *direct requests* or *observations* or of cases of progress – that is instrumentalized for indicator purposes" (p. 5). The author's rationale for this is that coding the contents of the CEACR or CFA reports would introduce subjectivity into the indicators and thus undermine their reproducibility. By implication, other methods that do attempt to code de jure or de facto violations of labour standards – that is, most methods represented in the chapters of this volume – are not reproducible. But reproducibility is, of course, a testable proposition, and it is not obvious that the substance of labour standards law and practice cannot be coded in a reproducible manner.

In describing desirable properties of an indicator, the author writes, "Key criteria to be respected if human rights indicators are to be credible must include validity, transparency, replicability, use of identical yardsticks and objectivity" (p. 1). The author's method would seem to meet most of these criteria, but a question remains as to how fully valid indicators of labour standards can be constructed without *directly* evaluating either the substance of a country's legislation or its practice. The answer to this question depends, for example, on the extent to which "direct requests," "observations" or expressions of "satisfaction" by the CEACR have similar enough meanings across countries and over time regarding the scope and gravity of labour standards developments. Similar points hold regarding CFA reports.[15] Abu Sharkh provides a thoughtful discussion of these and other concerns regarding the use of the CEACR reports for constructing labour standards indicators.

Chapter 9: Employment Protection in Industrialized Countries: The Case for New Indicators

Giuseppe Bertola of the European University Institute and the University of Turin, Tito Boeri of Bocconi University and Sandrine Cazes of the ILO provide a comparative critique of different qualitative indicators of employment protection as well as several proposals for the construction of new indicators. The authors note that existing indicators of employment protection legislation are both outdated and of limited availability over time.[16] But the authors also make a more fundamental point: that the methods used to construct existing indicators of employment protection do not adequately address the transformations that have taken place in systems of employment protection since the 1980s. One of the more important of these transformations is the

---

[15] Another concern is that the CEACR reports only contain information on ratifying countries for any given ILO Convention. Insofar as these reports focus on problems rather than progress, this creates a systematic scoring bias against ratifiers for the "implementation" indicator. More nuanced types of bias might also exist for ratifiers and non-ratifiers regarding the "adhererence" indicator, given that different information sources are used for each group, though the *a priori* direction of bias is less clear from this indicator.

[16] Two more recent efforts at constructing indicators of employment protection legislation are worth noting, however. These are Heckman and Pagés-Serra (2000) and Djankov *et al*. (2003).

deepening dualism of labour markets resulting from the increased use of fixed-term contracts. The authors also argue that employment protection ought to be evaluated in the context of other labour market institutions, such as unemployment insurance schemes and wage-setting institutions, institutions that may act as complements or substitutes for employment protection, with attendant implications for the use of employment protection indicators. Such a more comprehensive view would provide insights into understanding the de facto nature of employment protection and what this means in practice for workers and employers in a country.

The authors evaluate court records on litigation and judicial outcomes addressing employment protection legislation – that is, the role of the courts in translating de jure into de facto – for a sample of 13 OECD countries. In particular, they look at the number of job dismissal cases brought before courts as a percentage of employees as well as the percentage of such cases won by workers. The authors find that there is substantial variation across the countries according to both these measures. The proportion of cases brought before the courts is highest in France, Germany and Spain and lowest in Austria, Denmark and the U.S. Data on the percentage of cases won by workers are only available for nine countries, but for these, the percentage of cases won by workers is highest in France and Spain and lowest in Ireland and the U.S. The authors make several useful observations regarding this cross-country variation. The authors note that there is a positive correlation between the proportion of cases brought before the courts and the percentage of cases won by workers, that countries with less precise definitions of unfair dismissal tend to have higher caseloads, and that the strength of sanctions and unemployment insurance benefits may also influence caseloads.

The authors' offer these observations as hypotheses for further exploration, yet these preliminary findings suggest the potential value of using court records to deepen the understanding of employment protection legislation and its implementation. The authors' basic approach of evaluating court records might also be extended to other labour standards, and Abu Sharkh provides an example of this for discrimination in the workplace, as described in this volume. This depends, critically, on the availability of relevant court records, which might prove problematic. For the sample of countries considered by the authors, for instance, information on the number of job dismissal cases brought before the courts over time is available only for Germany and Spain, and information on the percentage of job dismissal cases won by workers over time is available only for Spain. The availability of such court records might be even more limited for poorer developing countries, but the sensibility of the authors' approach makes it well worth exploring.

Chapter 10: Measuring Concealed Rights Violations:
The Case of Forced Labour

The final chapter by Patrick Belser, Michaëlle de Cock and Farhad Mehran of the ILO might appear somewhat anomalous in this volume, for rather than addressing qualitative indicators, the authors describe their method of estimating the number of forced labourers. This estimate was developed for the ILO's report *A Global*

Alliance Against Forced Labour (ILO, 2005). Yet in some sense, their approach is similar to Cuyvers and Van Den Bulcke's regarding "reported number of violations vis-à-vis trade union members/leaders," in that both methods involve reading through textual sources to find numbers. What makes Belser *et al.*'s method different and particularly innovative, however, is the use of the 'capture–recapture' method to structure the search for these textual sources and to derive an estimate of the number of reported cases of forced labour based on these searches. One of the virtues of the capture–recapture approach is that it is wide open as regards the textual sources considered and that the approach can be applied to constructing more purely qualitative indicators of labour standards, such as by coding violations of trade union rights.

The basic method underlying the capture–recapture method is that two teams of researchers work independently to search for reported cases of forced labour via whatever means they choose. By comparing the number of overlapping reported cases found by both groups combined with the number found by each, it is possible to estimate the total number of reported cases. The authors' global estimate of forced labour is derived by adding up separate estimates for six regions of the world broken down by broad categories of forced labour: state-imposed, private-imposed for commercial sexual exploitation, and private-imposed for other economic exploitation, as well as the number of private-imposed forced labour resulting from trafficking. These breakdowns by region and type of forced labour are of course interesting in their own right. But the process of separate estimation for a stratified sample also provides a check on differences in the probability of finding a reported case of forced labour depending on the type of forced labour and the region of the world.

One of the more impressive aspects of the authors' estimates is the meticulousness of the validation of textual sources. This is particularly important for the capture–recapture method, given its open-ended nature regarding textual sources. Of the roughly 5,000 reported cases of forced labour, only 2,000 were validated (by the project supervisor of the two teams) and thus used in the final estimates. The other 3,000 reported cases were rejected as invalid because of an insufficiently precise definition of forced labour, concerns about the credibility of the source, and duplication of reported cases in different sources *within* each of the two teams. When multiplied by the average number of victims per case, the authors' methods yielded an estimate for total reported victims of forced labour around the world of just over 12 million (with a margin of error of 2.5 million) over the period from 1995 to 2004. In addition to this estimate, the authors discuss the conditions under which the estimated number of reported victims of forced labour derived from the capture–recapture method represents a minimum estimate of the actual number of victims (both reported and unreported) at any point in time during this ten-year period.

As the authors emphasize, the capture–recapture method estimates *reported* rather than actual victims of forced labour, and the latter may be a considerably greater number than the former. This is of particular concern given the illegal and often hidden nature of forced labour. There may be, for example, many cases of forced labour that are either not reported, not reported in the seven languages used by the teams, or that are reported but do not pass the validation tests. The difference between reported and actual victims is of particular importance in using this method to estimate changes in forced labour over time. Given the growing interest in forced labour, it seems probable that there will be an increasing proportion of reported to actual cases of forced labour. If this is indeed so, then there will be a tendency for the capture–recapture method to estimate increasing numbers of reported victims of forced labour even if the actual number remains unchanged. In such a scenario, what happens is that as reporting improves over time, the capture–recapture method becomes more accurate, which can be expressed as a convergence between the number of reported and actual victims of forced labour. This is essentially the same concern affecting Kucera's method of constructing indicators of trade union rights based on coding reported violations of these rights, as described in this volume. In addition to (and possibly interacting with) this tendency is the possible bias resulting from differences across countries or regions in the probability of actual cases of forced labour being reported, such as resulting from differences in the openness of the press or cultural acceptance of the issue.

There are several ways in which these concerns can be addressed. It might be that reported cases of forced labour will become sufficiently complete over time such that biases in estimates would no longer occur, or at least that the biases would be sufficiently attenuated that broad directions of change in actual number of forced labourers could be reliably estimated using the capture–recapture method for the reported number. In this sense, the capture–recapture method would seem to have time on its side. In addition, it might be possible to derive reliable estimates of the ratio between reported and unreported cases of forced labour and the change in this ratio over time, which could then inform the authors' method of extrapolating from the reported to the actual number of victims of forced labour. Alternatively, one could rely on the judgments of experts in regions around the world who are particularly attuned to whether forced labour is on the rise or decline in a region, thus providing at least a broad qualitative sense of trends. This is basically the approach of Verité, as described in this volume. One might also be able to identify broad trends in forced labour (or violations of trade union rights, for that matter) using more conventional statistical methods, such as through representative surveys, but this too is not without its complications given the often surreptitious nature of forced labour.

Lessons Learned, Ways Forward

Qualitative indicators of labour standards occupy a niche that cannot be readily supplanted by traditional quantitative indicators of labour standards, such as based on labour force or establishment surveys. Qualitative approaches are thus here to stay, in spite of the particular measurement difficulties they pose. It is hoped though that this volume provides some useful guidance in how to manage these difficulties as well as paths by which qualitative indicators of labour standards constructed in the future might be improved. Some of the lessons learned and ways forward are as follows.

Those constructing qualitative indicators of labour standards should be explicit about the intended uses of their indicators and justify how intended uses inform methods of construction. Also useful would be cautions about possible inappropriate uses. This will more readily enable potential users to assess the possibility and extent of mismatch between methods of construction and application.

When it comes to defining the components that provide a working definition of compliance with a labour standard, more detail and disaggregation is generally better than less. This holds not just for the construction of the indicator but also for how the information used in construction is provided to potential users. The more disaggregated the information, the more readily it can be combined into different sub-indicators with different conceptual emphases for use in a range of applications.

Weighting schemes used to aggregate components of an indicator should be justified, whether at the broad level – such as de jure versus de facto – or for detailed components of an indicator, and attention should be paid to the extent to which alternative weighting schemes yield different results, whether these results are country rankings or statistical findings.

Whenever possible, it makes sense to use both qualitative and quantitative information to construct labour standards indicators. This enables one to take advantage of the wide definitional scope made possible by qualitative approaches as well as the precision and representativeness of more traditional qualitative statistics.

Perhaps most importantly, significant improvements in the construction of qualitative indicators of labour standards require improvements in or better use of qualitative information sources. One possible route is suggested by Belser *et al.*, by making open-ended use of a wide range of information sources such as through internet searches backed up by rigorous validation procedures. The other route is to rely on fewer pre-defined sources regarded as generally credible but to improve these sources as regards definitional consistency and comprehensiveness across jurisdictions and over time. Significant improvements in information sources are not difficult to achieve in principle but are rather questions of resources and will.

References

Block, Richard and Karen Roberts. 2003. Do labor standards matter: the economic impact of differences in labor standards across States in the U.S. and Provinces in Canada, presented at The Canada–U.S. business conference. Kelley School of Business, Indiana University, Bloomington, Indiana, April 11–12, 2003.

Djankov, Simeon, Rafael La Porta, Florencio Lopez-de-Silanes, Andrei Shliefer and Juan Botero. 2000. The regulation of labor. NBER Working Paper No. 9756.

Heckman, James and Carmen Pagés-Serra. 2000. The cost of job security regulation: evidence from Latin American labor markets. Economia 1(1): 109–154.

ILO. 2005. A global alliance against forced labour. International Labour Organization, Geneva.

Kucera, David. 2002. Core labour standards and foreign direct investment. Int Labour Rev 141(1–2): 31–69.

Kucera, David and Ritash Sarna. 2006. "Trade Union Rights, Democracy and Exports: A Gravity Model Approach," *Review of International Economics*, 14(5): 859–882.

National Research Council. 2004. Monitoring international labor standards: techniques and sources of information. Committee on Monitoring International Labor Standards. Center for Education, Division of Behavioral and Social Sciences and Education and Policy and Global Affairs Division. The National Academies Press, Washington, DC.

OECD. 1996. Trade, employment and labour standards: a study of core workers' rights and international trade. OECD, Paris.

OECD. 2000. International trade and core labour standards. OECD, Paris.

Wermenbol, G., L. Cuyvers, and D. Van Den Bulcke. 1998. Proposal for a social development index – respect for ILO core labour standards against the background of the implementation capacity of countries. V.L.I.R. Research project, Belgian Administration of Development Co-operation (ABOS). University of Antwerp, Antwerp, Belgium.

DAVID KUCERA,
International Labour Office

Chapter 2

Indicators of Labour Standards:
An Overview and Comparison*

RICHARD N. BLOCK
Michigan State University

I. Introduction

Questions of labour standards and their impact on trade continue to be an important area of debate (Flanagan, 2003; Elliott, 2004; Becker, 2004). The fundamental question continues to be whether, other things being equal, in a globalized economy moving toward free trade, differences in labour standards among trading nations give lower labour-standards countries an (unfair) advantage in trade by providing a cost advantage to producers in those lower standards countries. The assumption in much of this literature seems to be that labour standards did matter; that a country could obtain trading benefits from relatively low labour standards (Block, et al., 2001).

For many years, much of the debate around the relationship between trade and labour standards was based on economic theory and arguments based on social equity, often questioning whether any such "advantage" given to low labour-standards countries is "unfair" (Block et al., 2001). But there had been little empirical work to determine whether labour standards had an effect on trade and related economic phenomena, such as investment, and, if so, how much of an effect. The absence of empirical work was due, in large part, to the absence of measures of differences in labour standards among countries.

Thus, the first step in the process of determining the impact of differential labour standards across countries has been to measure the differences between them. This chapter will discuss the methodology Karen Roberts and I have developed to attempt to fill this measurement gap. Part II of the chapter will discuss the basic principles of the Block–Roberts system, including definitions and scoring methodology and assumptions. Much of this will cite our Upjohn book. As an illustration of the basic principles of the system, Part III of the chapter will focus on the application of the system in a comparison we did in that book of the U.S. with Canada. Part IV will examine our work comparing the U.S. and the EU, including how the basic methodology was modified to adapt it to the U.S.–EU comparison. We will also briefly summarize the U.S.–EU results published elsewhere (Block, et al., 2003a). Part V will compare our methodology with that used by others who have quantified labour standards, focusing on the strengths and weaknesses of the various approaches. Part VI will provide a summary and conclusion.

* The author thanks Jessica Horan-Block for her invaluable research assistance.

27

II. Measuring Labour Standards: Basic Principles and Methodology of the Block–Roberts System

Basic Principles and Concepts

The initial step in the process of quantifiying labour standards on an international basis, or more generally, across political jurisdictions,[1] is to establish a definition of labour standards that will be valid across the jurisdictions. If one defines a "labour standard" as a minimum working condition to which all employers in the affected jurisdiction must adhere, it is clear that there are varying methods of creating labour standards. For example, many European countries use agreements established via corporatist institutions to establish employment standards that apply to all firms and employees within the scope of the institution (Turner, 2002). Similarly, in South Korea prior to the IMF intervention of 1995, an informal, standard for lifetime employment in the *chaebols*, the large conglomerates, had developed through an implied agreement between the government, unions, workers, and the employing *chaebols* (Lee, 1997; Block, Lee, and Shin, 2002). Private organizations, such as Social Accountability International, promulgate labour standards that they hope firms will adopt through market pressure and publicity (Social Accountability International, undated).

While all of these systems create minimum standards for workers, they do not constitute labour standards if that term is used as applying to a standard that affects all workers within the jurisdiction rather than to subgroups of workers. Taking this into account, in order to be considered labour standards for our purposes the standards must be: (1) governmentally created and enforced; (2) designed to affect or regulate workplace transactions for all or almost all employees in the political jurisdictions studied, with any exclusions legislative; (3) generally comparable in purpose and administration across jurisdictions studied such that a fair comparison can be made; and, (4) have been adopted or could reasonably be adopted in all the of the jurisdictions analysed. Thus, we used the following definition of a labour standard:

> a labour standard is any governmentally established procedure, term or condition of employment or employer requirement that has as its purpose the protection of employees from treatment at the workplace that society considers unfair or unjust. The common element across all standards is that they are mandatory – they are governmentally imposed and enforced. Employer failure to comply with the standards brings legal sanctions upon the employer. This provides the universal or potentially universal coverage

---

[1] The term political jurisdiction is used in order to recognize that the national government at the country level is not the only governmental entity that establishes labour standards. In Canada, the provinces, sub-national jurisdictions, have the primary responsibility for establishing labour standards (Block and Roberts, 2000; Block, et al., 2003b). In the U.S., the establishment of labour standards is shared between the national government and the individual states (Block, et al., 2003b). In Europe, standard-setting authority is shared between the super-national European Union and the EU member states (Springer, 1994; Block, et al., 2003a).

that is needed. There may be statutory exclusions, but these can be accounted for and estimated. (Block, Roberts, and Clarke, 2003)

This definition incorporates each of the four components. The rationale for each of the components will be discussed.

Governmentally-Created and Enforced

The requirement that the standards included in our analysis be governmentally created and enforced ensures that they are or could be, if the legislating body so chose, applied to all employers and employees in the political jurisdiction. Although, as will be discussed below, there may be statutory exemptions, these exemptions are created by the choice of the legislating body and could, in principle, be addressed through the value attributed to the standard. Through legislation, government can be seen as establishing a minimum, legally enforceable floor for labour standards (Block and Roberts, 2000; Block, et al., 2003b).

It is acknowledged that there are other sources of benchmarks for practices, such as custom and practice in the locality or industry, the market, and collective bargaining. Thus, in the U.S., custom and practice may determine that employees receive paid days off for holidays, but such paid days are not mandatory. Similarly, collective bargaining may define standards, but the standards are only applicable to the employers and employees covered by the bargain. In addition, exceptions can be negotiated.[2]

Examples of this criterion operating in practice are our consideration of vacations (paid annual leave) in the U.S.–Canada analysis and our exclusion of health care from it (Block and Roberts, 2000; Block, et al., 2003b). We consider the U.S. as not providing vacations because there is no legal requirement on the Federal level or in any state that employees receive vacations, although there is a custom and practice that employees receive vacation pay.[3] Similarly, we exclude health care because there is no legal requirement in the U.S. that employers provide employees with health insurance, although there are equal employment opportunity requirements on employers that choose or are required by collective bargaining agreements to provide their employees with it. In Canada, health care is provided to all citizens indepently of the employment relationship.

Primary Effect on Workplace Transactions

The second major criterion for inclusion in the study as a standard was that the law or regulation was designed to have its primary application at the workplace or its primary effect on workplace transactions in both countries. Matters that may have some linkage to the workplace or work relationship, but do not have the workplace as their primary focus, were excluded.

---

[2] For example, in the construction industry in the U.S. unions and contractor often negotiate project-specific agreements in order to permit unionized contractors to compete with nonunion contractors (Dunlop, 2002).

[3] For example, The U.S. Bureau of Labour Statistics estimates that, in 2003, 79% of all workers in private industry in the U.S. received some paid vacation (annual leave).

An example of using this criterion as the basis for excluding a provision from consideration as a labour standard in the U.S.–Canada analysis is the treatment given to Social Security in the U.S. and the comparable programs in Canada. Although these programs are (at least partially) financed through the employment relationship, their primary purpose is to act as an insurance program for persons who are out of the labour force, either because of retirement or because of a permanent disability. They are not primarily designed to influence workplace transactions.[4] (Block and Roberts, 2000; Block, et al., 2003)

Comparability in Purpose and Administration

This criterion captures the principle that it is important to limit the analysis to those standards that can be fairly compared. This principle was used as a second reason why we excluded from the analysis the public pension systems in the two countries – social security and related programs in the U.S. and Old Age Security and the Canada Pension Plan and related programs in Canada. The system in the U.S. is fully funded by workplace-based (employer, employee, and self-employed person) payments and interest, while the system in Canada is funded by a combination of workplace-based payments, interest, and general tax revenues (Human Resources and Social Development Canada, 2006). In our judgment, this difference made these two programs noncomparable.

Adoption or Possibility of Adoption in Both Countries

The fourth major criterion for including a law or regulation as labour standard in the analysis is that the law or standard could reasonably be adopted in both countries. For example, since the purpose of the U.S.–Canada analysis was ultimately to develop a scoring for and ranking of labour standards in the 63 jurisdictions of the U.S. and Canada, it would have been misleading to "score" a jurisdiction and/or a country lower than it would otherwise be scored on the grounds that it does not have a standard or provision that one could not reasonably expect it to adopt. For example, again using health care, one could not reasonably expect any Canadian jurisdiction to adopt a labour standard requiring health insurance to be provided to all employees, because the state provides health care to all of its citizens through the general tax system of federal and provincial personal and corporate taxes (Health Canada, 2006). In other words, health care is not a workplace issue in Canada as it is in the U.S. While employers in the U.S. could, in principle, be required to provide health care, it would be inappropriate to consider it as a labour standard in a U.S.–Canada comparison in view of the fact that it is not a labour standard in Canada.

---

[4] Of course, to the extent that employers pay social security taxes, such taxes increase the cost of hiring employees and may create disincentives to hire workers. But such taxes do not directly regulate the workplace.

Scoring Methodology

Basic Principles of Scoring

We conceived of labour standards as incorporating (1) the substance of the standard as determined by the enabling legislation and (2) the rigour with which the legislation is enforced. The methodology for comparing the labour standards and for computing a "basic labour standards index" involves three components: (a) an analysis of the substance, that is, the statutory or legislative provisions of each of the standards; (b) development of an index of the strength of the labour standard in a jurisdiction based on the substance of the legislation; and (c) a method of measuring the rigour with which the standards are enforced.[5] (Block, et al., 2003b)

Creation of Numerical Index

Once the components were determined from the legislation, an index was created for each of the standards. The index for each standard consists of a subindex for the provision that is greater when the level of protection given to employees is greater and a weight given to each provision within each standard. Enforcement mechanisms were treated as additional provisions and were assigned a weight. (Block, et al., 2003b)

For each provision, an ordinal scale was constructed. Values were assigned to each relevant statutory provision or enforcement mechanism by assigning to the absence of a provision a score of zero (0), and the strongest provision among all the jurisdictions a score of ten (10). Provisions of intermediate strength were assigned intermediate values in accordance with the number of possible categories in the provision. (Block, et al., 2003b)

Generally,

let s_{pdj} = the score assigned to provision p in standard d in jurisdiction j, where $0 \leq s_{pdj} \leq 10$ and where 10 is the score assigned to the most favourable standard among all j jurisdictions analysed;

let w_{pdj} = the weight assigned to provision p in standard d in jurisdiction j, where $0 \leq w_{pdj} \leq 1$.

Then, the basic index score for standard d for jurisdiction j is:

$X_{dj} = E^n s_{pdj} * w_{pdj}$ where the index consists of n provisions.

The standard scores can be summed to provide an overall labour standards score for a jurisdiction. The labour-standards index for jurisdiction j is denoted as L_j. Then,

$$L_j = E_j^n Xdj.$$

---

[5] We also created a "coverage deflated index" which deflated the basic index by an exclusion from coverage. In the U.S., it is not unusual for a labour standard to exclude specific industries, occupations, employers, or types of employees. For example, the National Labour Relations Act, the statute that governs labour-management relations in the U.S., and protects employees in their rights to unionize, excludes employees who are supervisors, as defined in the law. For a detailed discussion, see U.S. General Accounting Office, 2002.

For example, for collective bargaining laws, jurisdictions in which union recognition could be obtained without an election were assigned a value of 10, and jurisdictions in which an election was required were assigned a value of 0. Thus, for this labour-standard provision, there were no intermediate values. In contrast, advance notice requirements for large-scale layoffs provide an example of a provision that requires an intermediate coding. If the provision of the statute in the jurisdiction required advance notice of greater than or equal to 16 weeks, the jurisdiction was coded as a 10. Notice of 12 to 16 weeks was coded as 7.5; 8 to 12 weeks notice as 5.0; 4 to 8 weeks as 2.5; and no provision was coded as zero.

As indicated above, the jurisdiction which provides the highest level of protection to employees is scored as a 10. Thus, the system is relativistic rather than absolutist. The highest possible score is not based on an absolute standard of protection, but on a standard of protection that is actually provided to employees.

In addition to coding each provision, a weighting scheme was established for provisions within a labour standard, reflecting our assessment of the importance of the provision to the standard. The limitation we used was that the weights of the provisions within a standard must total to 1.[6]

III. Jurisdiction-Specific Issues: Comparing the U.S. and Canada

Levels of Government

Although the scoring principles are uniform, as they are based on the legislated characteristics of labour standards, when adapting the methodology to the comparison of two or more political jurisdictions, one must also take into account the specific characteristics of the standard-setting process in those jurisdictions. When comparing the U.S. and Canada, this meant taking into consideration the fact that different levels of government promulgate standards in the two countries. In the U.S., most labour standards are promulgated on the national level, but some important ones are adopted by the individual states. Moreover, in the U.S., states have the option, for some standards, of adopting a standard that is higher than the federal standard. Canada, on the other hand, has no national labour standards that apply to all workers in the country.

For most workers in Canada, labour standards are adopted at the provincial level, covering all workers in the province. The exception is industries that are primarily

---

[6] Realizing that the indices are a function of the weights given to each relevant provision, and also realizing that weights are based on judgments about which reasonable people may differ, we computed indices with three different sets of assumptions about weights. See, Block, Roberts, and Clarke, (2003).

interprovincial (Block, et al., 2003b).[7] Put differently, within the U.S. and Canada, there were 63 jurisdictions that promulgated, or could promulgate, labour standards – the U.S. federal government, 50 states,[8] 10 provinces, two territories,[9] and the Canadian federal jurisdiction. Thus, in analysing the U.S. and Canada, it was necessary to measure labour standards at both the national and sub-national levels.

Enforcement

Second, in examining the U.S. and Canada, we also considered jurisdiction-specific issues in measuring enforcement. Although an ideal measure would have been enforcement aggressiveness as measured by the budget per covered employee of the enforcing agency, we learned that the agencies in the two countries and the 63 states, provinces, and territories were dissimilar in mission; some had missions beyond labour standards, such as housing, and others did not. Therefore, our measure of enforcement was the right of the losing party in a case to appeal to the judicial system outside the agency dedicated to enforcing labour standards. Our view was that the broader the rights of appeal from the decision of the administrative agency charged with enforcing the labour standards legislation, the weaker the enforcement. In addition to the rationale of "justice delayed, justice denied," the use of appeal rights was also based on the notion that a government agency charged with administering a standard will be expert in administering that standard and will be likely to interpret that standard in a way that is sensitive to the employee beneficiaries of the statute. A court, on the other hand, that enforces all laws, is likely to see its role as interpretation of a statute in the context of other, nonstatutory considerations that may not be consistent with the employee-orientation statute and the specialized agency (Crowley, 1987; Brudney, 1996; Block, 1997; Block, et al., 2003b). Therefore, a broad scope for appeal and judicial review of labour-standards agency decisions is likely to result in interpretations of the statute and standards that are relatively unfavourable to employees. Therefore, for the U.S.–Canada study, the enforcement standard was based on the right of appeal. (Block, et al., 2003b)

Statutory Analysis

Columns II and III in Tables 1-10 contain the components and coding of the indices used to compare the U.S. and Canada (Block, et al., 2003b). In order to minimize the number of tables, and to facilitate a comparison between the U.S.–Canada analysis

---

[7] The labour standards in the following sectors are federally regulated in Canada: air transportation, banking, broadcasting, communications, crown corporations (such as Canada Post), flour, fee mills, grain elevators, longshoring, interprovincial and inter-national railways, interprovincial and international road transport, shipping and navigation, and various miscellaneous industries. See Block, (1997).

[8] For simplicity, we excluded from our analysis the District of Columbia and U.S. territories, such as the U.S. Virgin Islands and Puerto Rico.

[9] Since the study was done, a third territory, Nunavut, was established from the western portion of the Northwest Territories.

and the U.S.–EU analysis in the next section, the presentation is made with dual-purpose tables. For those standards for which we conducted both a U.S.–Canada and U.S.–EU analysis, the tables display the provisions and the coding for both analyses. For those standards for which only one analysis was done, only the coding for that analysis is presented in the tables. Tables 1-3, 6-7, and 9-10 present data for the both the U.S.–Canada and the U.S.–EU analyses. For these seven tables, the relevant columns for the U.S.–Canada analysis are I, II, and III. Tables 4, 5, and 8 contain coding only for the U.S. and Canada. The overall comparison for the U.S. and Canada is presented in Appendix 1.

As can be seen, and as outlined above, each of the standards is divided into provisions, and each of the provisions is assigned a weight such that the total of the provision weights equals 1. Within each of the provisions, a greater weight is assigned to provisions that offer greater protection to workers, with the highest level of protection among all the jurisdictions assigned a value of 10.

Turning to Table 1, within the minimum wage standard, by far the greatest weight was attributed to the level of the minimum wage, with lesser weights for some ancillary provisions. For the overtime/working time standard, the components

Table 1. Minimum wage index: provisions, weights, subindex values.

Provision/language	Provision weight U.S.-Canada	Subindex value U.S.-Canada	Provision weight U.S.-EU	Subindex value U.S.-EU
Minimum Wage Level				
(as of April 1, 1997)	.92		.95	
GT or EQ U.S.$5.00\GT or EQ C$6.90		10.00		
U.S.$4.75 - U.S.$4.99\C$6.55 - C$6.89		8.57		
U.S.$4.50 - U.S.$4.74\C$6.21 - C$6.54		7.14		
U.S.$4.25 - U.S.$ 4.49\C$5.86 - C$6.20		5.51		
U.S.$4.00 - U.S.$4.24\C$5.52 - C$5.85		4.28		
U.S.$3.75 - U.S.$3.99\C$5.17 - C$5.51		2.85		
U.S.$3.50 - U.S.$3.74\C$4.83 - C$5.16		1.42		
Subminimum Wage	.04		.05	
Coded as 10 if province has no subminimum or if subminimum wage would bring wage paid below state minimum,where state minimumis higher than federal minimum, zero otherwise				
Fines Imprisonment	.02			
Coded as 10 if fines or imprisonment a possible sanction on violator, zero otherwise				
Right of Appeal of Agency Decision	.02			

of which are shown in Table 2, the greatest weight was given to the existence of overtime legislation. The paid time-off index, presented in Table 3, was based on a detailed coding of the state and provincial statutes. As paid time-off was regulated at the state and provincial levels, it was important to analyse these details.

Tables 4 and 5 present the components for the employment/unemployment insurance and workers' compensation indices. As these are also regulated at the state and provincial levels in the U.S. in Canada, they were analysed in detail.

Table 6 presents the components of the collective bargaining index for the U.S. and Canada. Although the U.S. regulates collective bargaining at the national level, while Canada regulates collective bargaining at the provincial level, both countries are characterized by majoritarian systems based on majority rule, with administration by a specialized agency. Therefore, the analysis was based on components of the law within a majoritarian system that were thought to strengthen or weaken the rights of employees to unionize.

Table 7 presents the components of the anti-discrimination index. It takes into account protection of the expected classes of employees. Table 8 presents the components of the unjust discharge index. It is based on state level legal

Table 2. Overtime/working time index: provisions, weights, subindex values U.S.–Canada and U.S.–EU comparison.

	II	III	IV	V
	Provision weight	Subindex value	Provision weight	Subindex value
Provision/language	U.S.-Canada	U.S.-Canada	U.S.-EU	U.S.-EU
Overtime	.95		.35	
1.5 × reg rate after 40 hours per week		10		
2 × reg rate after 48 hours per week		8.57		
1.5 × reg rate after 44 hours per week		7.14		
1.5 × reg rate after 48 hours per week		5.71		
1.5 × min wage after 40 hours per week		4.18		
1.5 × min wage after 44 hours per week		2.85		
1.5 × min wage after 48 hours per week		1.42		
Limits on Rights of Appeal of Agency Decisions	.05			
Exemptions in Law			.05	0-10
Employee Right to Refuse Overtime			.05	0-10
Specified Number of Hours of Rest in 24 Hours			.15	0-10
Rest/Meal Required During Day after 5/6 Hrs. Work			.15	0-10
Maximum of 48 Hrs. Average/Week Over 7-Day Period			.15	0-10
Mental or Physical Stress Maximum			.08	0-10
Obligation to Relieve Monotonous or Paced Work			.02	0-10

Table 3. Paid time-off index: provisions, weights, subindex values.

	II	III	IV	V
Provision/Language	Provision weight U.S.-Canada	Subindex value U.S.-Canada	Provision weight U.S.-EU	Subindex value U.S.-EU
Holidays	.165			
13 + days of holiday		10		
12-12.9 days		7.8		
11-11.9 days		6.7		
9-9.9 days		5.6		
8-8.9 days		4.4		
7-7.9 days		.3		
6-6.9 days		.2		
5-5.9 days		.1		
Less Than 5 days		0		
Pay for Holidays not Worked or OT for Holidays Worked Coded 10 if the jurisdiction requires that employees be paid for holidays not worked or be granted overtime for holidays worked, zero otherwise	.335			
Vacation Length/Pay Coding	.45			
3 Weeks Vacation, 6% of Pay or Reg. Pay		10		
2 Weeks Vacation, 6% of Pay		6.67		
2 Weeks Vacation, 4% of Pay or Reg. Pay		3.33		
2 Weeks Vacation, 6% of pay		6.67		
No Vacation, no Pay		0		
When Entitled Coding	.05			
After 10 mos. with employer		10		
After 12 mos. with employer		6.67		
After more than 12 mos. with employer		3.33		
No provision		0		
Holidays Specified			.083	0-10
Pay for Holidays not Worked or Overtime for Holidays Worked			.167	0-10
Paid Vacation/Annual Leave Required			.75	0-10

developments in the U.S. regarding exceptions to the prevailing employment-at-will doctrine as compared with the Canadian legal principles, which generally limit discharge except for just cause.

Table 9 presents the components of the occupational safety and health (OSH) index. It is based on the North American system of standard setting with inspections. It also incorporates the principle of penalties. As shown in Table 10, advance notice provisions are similarly structured in both countries, with notice requirements and notification requirements.

Table 4. Unemployment/employment insurance: provisions, weights, subindex values.

Provision/Language	Provision weight U.S.-Canada	Subindex value U.S.-Canada
Taxable Wage Base, U.S. Dollars	.1	
GT or EQ U.S.$30,000\C$41,100		10
U.S.$25,000 - U.S.$29,999\C$34,250 - C$41,099		8.3
U.S.$20,000 - U.S.$24,999\C$27400 - C$34,249		6.7
U.S.$15,000 - U.S.$19,999\C$20,500 - C$27,399		5.0
U.S.$10,000 - U.S.$14,999\C$13,700 - $20,499		3.3
U.S.$5,000 - U.S.$9,999\C$6,850 - C$13,699		1.7
Employee Tax Rate	.3	
No Employee Tax		10
GT 0 but LT 1%		8.3
1%-2%		6.7
2%-3%		5.0
3%-4%		3.3
4%-5%		1.7
Coding, Avg. Weekly Benefit as a Percentage of Avg. Weekly Wages	.35	
45%-49%		8.3
40%-44%		6.7
35%-39%		5.0
30%-34%		3.3
LT 30%		1.7
Coding, Maximum Total Benefit/Extended Benefits	.25	
45 weeks		10
43 weeks		7.5
39 weeks		5.0
26 weeks		2.5

Note: It is assumed that all employees are entitled to to 13 weeks of federal extended UI benefits.

IV. Labour Standards in the U.S. and the EU

When comparing the U.S. and the EU, as with the U.S.–Canada analysis, we first considered governance differences between the EU and the U.S.[10] We analysed only (a) standards that were regulated at the national level in the U.S. and the community level in the EU, (b) standards that were regulated at the national level in the U.S. but were not addressed at the community level in

[10] An analysis of labour standards in the U.S. and the European Union presumes that it is appropriate to compare the U.S., a sovereign nation, with the EU, a political and economic union of sovereign nations. For the rationale for comparing the U.S. and the EU, see Block, et al., (2003a). For a comparison of governance assumptions in the EU, the U.S, and Canada, see Marleau, (2003).

Table 5. Workers' compensation: provisions, weights, subindex values.

Provision	Provision weight U.S.-Canada	Subindex value U.S.-Canada
Compulsory Coverage		
Compulsory Coverage for Private Employment		.024
No Waivers Permitted		.024
No Exemption Based on Firm Size	.047	
Farmworkers Covered	.047	
Casual and Household Workers Covered	.047	
Mandatory Government Worker Coverage	.047	
No Exemptions based on Employee Class	.047	
Employee Choice over Where to File	.047	
Coverage for All work-Related Diseases	.047	
TTD Benefits = 66 2/3% Wages	.047	
Maximum TTD Benefit at least 100% SAWW	.047	
Retain Prevailing PT Definition	.047	
PT Benefits = 66 2/3% Wages (s.t. maximum)	.047	
Maximum PT Benefit at least 100% SAWW	.047	
Benefit Duration = Disability Duration	.047	
Death Benefits = 66 2/3% Wages	.047	
Maximum Death Benefit at least 100% SAWW	.047	
Continuation of Benefits to Widow(er)		.024
Lump Sum to Widow(er) on Remarriage		.008
Cont. of Benefits to Dep. Children until 18		.008
Continuation of Benefits to Dependent Benefits until 25 if Student		.008
No Statutory $ Limit on Medical or Rehab Svs.	.047	0-10
No Time Limit on Right to Medical or Rehab Svs.	.047	0-10
Right of Appeal		0-10
Internal First Level Agency	.05	0-10
Internal Appeal Process	.05	0-10
Levels of Appeal beyond first	.05	0-10

the EU, and (c) standards that were regulated at the community level in the EU but not regulated at all in the U.S. If a standard was addressed at the community level in the EU but not at the federal level in the U.S., it was presumed that the U.S. made a choice not to regulate. Similarly, if a standard was regulated at the federal level in the U.S. but not at the community level in the EU, it was presumed that the EU made a choice not to regulate. In essence, the country in the U.S. and the community in the EU were treated as comparable subjects for analysis. We did not consider standards that existed in both jurisdictions but were not regulated at the comparable levels. Therefore, standards that were regulated at state level in the U.S. or the country level in the EU were excluded because they were presumed to be regulated at different levels (Block, et al., 2003a).

Table 6. Collective bargaining: provisions, weights, subindex values.

Provision/Language	II Provision weight U.S.-Canada	III Subindex value U.S.-Canada	IV Provision weight U.S.-EU	V Subindex value U.S.-EU
Statutory Protection for Collective Bargaining	.15	0-10		
Election Not Req. if Evidence that Majty. Support Union	.2	0-10		
Unlimited Subjects of Bargaining	.1	0-10		
Conciliation during Negs Compulsory at Request of Gov't or One Party	.2	0-10		
Striker Permanent Replacements Prohibited	.1	0-10		
First Agreement Arbitration Available	.1	0-10		
Limits on Rights of Loser to Appeal	.15	0-10		
Statutory Protection for Collective Bargaining			.67	0-10
Formal Union Involvement in Policymaking			.33	0-10

Based on this, ten standards were analysed. Seven of these minimum wage, overtime/working time ("overtime" in the U.S.–Canada study), paid time-off, collective bargaining, anti-discrimination, occupational safety and health, and large-scale layoffs were included based on their inclusion in the U.S.–Canada analysis, because the U.S regulated these standards at the federal level, and because they were regulated at the community level in the EU. The components and weighting of these indices for the U.S.–EU analysis are shown in Columns IV and V of Tables 1-3, 6-7, and 9-10. Three standards that were included in the U.S.–Canada analysis were excluded because they were regulated at the state level in the U.S.: workers' compensation, unemployment insurance, and unjust discharge.

Three additional standards were included because they were regulated at the community level in the EU but not at that state level in the U.S. These standards were information and consultation, parental leave, and transfer of undertaking ownership. The components and weightings for these standards are presented in Tables 11-13.

In comparison with the U.S.–Canada study, the internal benchmarking principle also required that the provisions within some standards be changed to accommodate matters within the standard that are regulated in the EU but not in the U.S. or Canada. This resulted in changes in the overtime index, which was changed to overtime/working time and the collective bargaining indices, to which was added

Table 7. Equal employment opportunity/employment equity: provisions, weights, subindex values.

	II	III	IV	V
	Provision weight	Subindex value	Provision weight	Subindex value
Provision/Language	U.S.-Canada	U.S.-Canada	U.S.-EU	U.S.-EU
Race, Visual Minorities, Aboriginal				
Peoples	.15		.05	0-10
Gender	.15		.1	0-10
National/Origin/Ancestry	.1		.05	0-10
Religion	.1		.1	0-10
Age	.1		.05	0-10
No Exceptions		10		
Retirement Plan Exceptions		5		
Age Not Covered		0		
Sexual Preference/Orientation	.05		.05	0-10
Disability	.1		.11	0-10
Political Beliefs/Org. Memberships	.05			
Family Leave due to Pregnancy, Illness of Family Member, or Serious Health Problem,				
12-17 weeks unpaid	.05			
Sexual Harassment Covered	.03		.03	0-10
Equal Pay Covered	.03		.03	0-10
Reasonable Accomm. for Disabled				
Employees	.04		.04	0-10
Limits on Rights of Appeal	.05			

a provision on union involvement in policymaking. The overall comparison between the U.S. and the EU is presented in Appendix 2.

Since the U.S. regulates the minimum wage at the national level, and the EU does not, and there is no regulation at the country level in the EU, they were compared based on the U.S. standard. The U.S. index was 9.5, while the EU index was zero (Block, et al., 2003a).

As shown in Table 2, the overtime/working time index was changed substantially for the U.S.–EU analysis. As the U.S. and the Canadian provinces regulate working time only through overtime, that was all that was necessary for the U.S.–Canada analysis. But, under the principle of benchmarking at the highest standards in the jurisdictions studied, the extensive regulation of working time in the EU required the addition of several provisions adopted by the EU that have not been adopted by the U.S. Therefore, regulation of meal periods, rest periods, maximum hours, mental or physical stress was added to the working time index. The overtime provision was reweighted from .95 in the U.S.–Canada analysis to .35 in the U.S.–EU analysis owing to these additional provisions. Because of these additional provisions, the EU index was 5.5 and the U.S. overtime/working time index was 3.5 (Block, et al., 2003a).

Table 8. Unjust discharge: provisions, weights, subindex values.

Provision/Language	Provision weight U.S.-Canada	Subindex value U.S.-Canada
Discharge Prohibited if Employee has Implicit Contract	.05	
Definitive State Ruling in favour of exception		10
No court decision		5
Definitive State Ruling against exception		0
Handbook Exception	.05	
Definitive State Ruling in favour of exception		10
No court decision		5
Definitive State Ruling against exception		0
Public Policy Exception	.1	
Definitive State Ruling in favour of exception		10
No court decision		5
Definitive State Ruling against exception		0
Covenant of Good Faith Exception	.1	
Definitive State Ruling in favour of exception		10
No court decision		5
Definitive State Ruling against exception		0
Limited, except for Misconduct, Incompetence or Negligence/Limited to "Good Cause"	.7	

Table 9. Occupational safety and health: provisions, weights, subindex values.

	II	III	IV	V
Provision/Language	Provision weight U.S.-Canada	Subindex value U.S.-Canada	Provision weight U.S.-EU	Subindex value U.S.-EU
Subject to General Duty Clause	.02		.20	0-10
Inspection Warrant can be Demanded Prior to Inspector Entry	.053			
Maximum Penalty for a Willful Violation of Statue	.053			
3GT or = $100,000		10		
$80,000 -$99,999		8.33		
$60,000 -$79,000		6.7		
$40,000 -$59,999		5.0		
$20,000 -$39,999		3.33		
$1,000 -$19,999		1.7		
No penalty		0		
(All dollar amounts are domestic.)				
Maximum Penalty for a Serious Violation of Statute	.053			

(*Continued*)

Table 9. Occupational safety and health: provisions, weights, subindex values

Provision/Language	II Provision weight U.S.-Canada	III Subindex value U.S.-Canada	IV Provision weight U.S.-EU	V Subindex value U.S.-EU
See coding on "Maximum Penalty for a Serious Violation of Statute."				
Maximum Penalty for Willful Repeat Violation	.053			
For coding, see column entitled "Maximum Penalty for a Willful Violation of Statute"				
Repeat Viol. Penalties may be Increased by Factor of 10	.053			
Penalty for 1st Offense, Willful Violation Causing a Death	.053			
For coding see column entitled "Maximum Penalty for a Willful Violation of Statute"				
Penalty for 2nd Offense, Willful Violation Causing Death	0.53			
For coding see column entitled "Maximum Penalty for a Willful Violation of Statute"				
Daily Penalty for Until Hazard Corrected	0.53			
GT or = $10,000		10		
$8,000 -$9999		8.3		
$6,000 -$7,999		6.7		
$4,000 -$6,999		5.0		
$2,000 -$3,999		3.3		
$1 to $1,999		1.7		
No fine		0		
(All fines in domestic dollars.)				
Reduction in Penalties for Firms with up to 250 Employees	.02			
Reduction for Written Health and Safety Program	.02			
Penalty Reduction if no Violations During a Specified Time	.02			
Recordkeeping Exmptn. for Small Firms/Specified Inds.	.02			
State may set Stricter Standards than Federal Govt.	.053			
Safety Committee or Representative/ Worker Consultation Required	.053		.20	0-10
Maximum Imprisonment Possible	.053			

Table 9. Occupational safety and health: provisions, weights, subindex values. — Cont'd.

24 months		10	
12 months		8	
6 months		6	
3 months		4	
1 month		2	
Maximum Penalty for Contravening			
Inspector	0.53		
= or GT $100,000		10	
$80,000 -$99,999		8.3	
$60,000 -$79,999		6.7	
$40,000 -$59,999		5.0	
$20,000-$39,999		3.3	
$1,000 -$19,999		1.7	
No penalty		0	
Maximum Penalty for any			
Contravention by Anyone	.053		
For coding, see column entitled "Daily Penalty Assessed for Failing to Abate a Hazard Until Corrected."			
Maximum Penalty for Minor Offenses	.053		
For coding, see column entitled "Daily Penalty Assessed for Failing to Abate a Hazard Until Corrected."			
Additional Fines Possible	.053		
Daily Penalty Assessed for			
Failing to Correct a Second Hazard	.053		
For coding, see column entitled "Daily Penalty Assessed for Failing to Abate A Hazard Until Corrected."			
Limits on Appeal of Agency Decisions	.052		
Standards for Chemicals/Contaminants		.15	0-10
Worker Must Be Informed of Job Risks		.20	0-10
Worker Training Requirement		.20	0-10
Working Environment (Psychological			
Factors)		.05	0-10

Unlike the U.S.–Canada analysis, which focused on the lower levels of government and could accommodate detailed differences among the states and provinces, the EU-U.S. analysis was done at the highest governmental level. Thus, broader indicators of the provisions, in this case the existence of certain standards, were analysed, but detail was excluded, as shown in Table 3 for the paid time-off index. The EU paid time-off index was 7.5, while the U.S. paid time-off standard was .83 (Block, et al., 2003a).

Table 10. Advance notice of plant closings/large-scale layoffs: provisions, weights, subindex values.

	II	III	IV	V
Provision/Language	Provision weight U.S.-Canada	Subindex value U.S.-Canada	Provision weight U.S.-EU	Subindex value U.S.-EU
Number of EES	.2		.35	0-10
10+ EES		10		
25+ EES		6.7		
50+ EES		3.3		
NP		0		
Maximum Time Period in Which Layoffs Must Occur	.04			
No Maximum time		10		
4-5 weeks		6.7		
8 weeks		3.3		
NP		0		
Advanced Notice Required	.2		.25	0-10
>\=16 weeks = 10		10		
12 to < 16 weeks = 7.5		7.5		
8 to < 12 weeks = 5		5		
4 to < 8 weeks = 2.5		2.5		
no notice required		0		
Notice to Minister of Labour or Government	.01		.05	0-10
Notice to affected employees	.2		.2	0-10
Notice to Union	.1		.15	0-10
Severance Pay	.2			
Limits on Appeal of Agency Decisions	.05			

Table 11. Employees' rights to information and consultation provisions, weights, subindex values.

	II	III
Provision/Language	Provision weight U.S.-EU	Subindex value U.S.-EU
Right to Information/ Consultation	1	0-10

The collective bargaining index underwent a similar change, as shown in Table 6. The U.S. chooses to provide detailed rights at the national level, while the EU limits its community-level regulation of collective bargaining to the somewhat

Table 12. Parental and family leave provisions, weights, subindex values.

Provision/Language	II Provision weight U.S.-EU	III Subindex value U.S.-EU
Maternity Leave	.25	0-10
Family Leave	.5	0-10
Parental Leave due to Family Illness (14 weeks per year)	.25	0-10

Table 13. Transfer of undertaking/ownership provisions, weights, subindex values.

Provision/Language	II Provision weight U.S.-EU	III Subindex value U.S.-EU
Contracts of Employment	.15	0-10
Collective Bargaining Obligations	.15	0-10
Protection from Dismissal Due Solely to Transfer	.4	0-10
Information Provision to Employees Representatives	.15	0-10
Consultation with Employees in Matters in Relation to Employees	.15	0-10

legally ambiguous Charter of Fundamental Rights. On the other hand, the index was expanded from the narrow legislative focus of the U.S. to include formal participation in policy-making. Nevertheless, the result, based on the level of analysis, was an index that resulted in a higher score for the U.S. than the EU, 6.67 as compared to 3.3, involving a change in the scope and direction of the enterprise.

As can be seen in Table 7, the structure of the anti-discrimination index in the U.S.–EU study was similar to the structure of the index in the U.S.–Canada comparison. Discrimination based on political beliefs was excluded because neither jurisdiction addressed it, as was enforcement. This required a slight reweighting of the components. Nevertheless, both jurisdictions have almost identical scores, 10 for the EU, 9.35 for the U.S., with the difference due to the fact that the U.S. does not prohibit discrimination based on sexual orientation. (Block, et al., 2003a)

Table 9 demonstrates the revision of the occupational safety and health (OSH) index for the U.S.–EU analysis. Rather than focusing on details of standards, as was necessary for the U.S.–Canada comparison, the analysis incorporated broader provisions. Provisions on worker consultation, worker information, worker training, and the working environment were also added to the index because of EU directives. This resulted in substantial reweighting. The EU score on occupational safety and health was 8.0, while the U.S. score was 3.5 (Block, et al., 2003a).

As can be seen in Table 10, advance notice principles are basically the same in the U.S. and the EU. The greatest weight in both countries was given to exclusions, on the grounds that such exclusions reduce the reach of even the broadest set of protections. The EU score on advance notice was 8.75, while the U.S. score was 8.25 (Block, et al., 2003a).

Tables 11-13 were new standards developed for the U.S.–EU study. Table 11 on consultation and Table 13 on transfer of ownership are standards that do not exist in the U.S. and Canada. In the U.S.–Canada study, family leave was included as part of the anti-discrimination index because its origins in both countries were associated with gender equity in employment. Given the importance of these leaves in the EU, and their basis in social equity and broad-based notions of worker health, a separate index was used. This is shown in Table 12. For the information/consultation index, the EU was scored as a 10, the U.S. was scored as 0. For the parental and family leave index, both jurisdictions were scored a 5. For the transfer of ownership obligations, the EU scored 10 and the U.S. scored .75 (Block, et al., 2003a).

V. Other Methods for Measuring Labour Standards

The foregoing discussion highlighted two important characteristics of the Block–Roberts labour standards measure. First, it is relativistic rather than universalistic. The benchmark is not an external standard, but rather the highest standard within the jurisdictions compared. Second, the definition of labour standards used is narrow. It is limited to legislation designed to benefit workers by directly influencing the allocation, hiring, or price of labour.

This part will compare our measures with measures of labour standards used in other studies. As will be discussed, those other measures have components that are universalistic or use a broad definition of labour standards. The advantages and disadvantages of our measure compared with those other measures will be discussed.

Universalism and Relativism

Measures of the levels of labour standards across countries have generally relied on ILO Conventions as a benchmark. Rodrik (1996) uses the number of ILO Conventions and the number of "basic" ILO Conventions ratified. The OECD (1996) also uses ILO Conventions ratified. Mai (1997) used a dummy variable for each of the core labour standards analysed to examine the impact of differences in labour standards on exports in 45 developing countries. Busse (2001) uses the number of "core" ILO Conventions ratified. Ratification, or non-ratification of core (fundamental) ILO Conventions ratified is the largest component of Böhning's (2003) indicator of the worker-rights gap in a country, although he also measures adherence through the ILO's internal complaint procedure. Maskus' (2003) measure of labour standards includes the number of fundamental ILO Conventions ratified. Flanagan (2003) uses the number of core and non-core labour ILO Conventions ratified. All of these studies examined the impact of labour standards in a wide range of countries.

The advantage of using ratification of and/or compliance with ILO Conventions, in some form, is that the Conventions are internationally recognized as benchmarks. Moreover, ratification and compliance are identifiable, voluntary actions by a country that indicate that the country is willing to provide protection to workers. Moreover, given the breadth of countries studied in these studies, a broad-based measure was necessary.

There is, however, a key disadvantage to using data on ILO Conventions as a measure of labour standards across countries. This disadvantage revolves around the question of the universality of the standards. There may be a great range of statutory protections that would be consistent with a ratified Convention (Block, et al., 2001). Moreover, as Böhning (2003) notes, not all countries have similar capacities to implement or enforce ratified Conventions. Thus, there is likely to be substantial measurement error in any variable that considers labour standards to be roughly equivalent in two or more countries that have ratified the same Conventions. Indeed, as Rodrick (1996) points out, Conventions ratified, per se, may not be a valid measure of labour standards. Many less developed countries have ratified more ILO Conventions than the U.S. Yet, even with its low level of labour standards relative to Canada, the EU and other developed countries (Block, et al., 2003a; Block, et al., 2003b), it is not reasonable to believe that that the U.S. has lower standards than many less developed countries that have ratified more ILO Conventions.

The fact that the lack of universality could be associated with measurement error is consistent with Flanagan's (2003) somewhat unexpectedly finding no evidence of a relationship between ILO Conventions ratified and actual labour conditions, operationalized as child labour, civil liberties, and life expectancy. The finding of the absence of a relationship could be due to the fact that ILO Conventions ratified could be due to measurement errors in labour-standards measures that rely heavily on ILO ratifications.

Measures of Labour Standards Used

As noted, a second difference between the Block–Roberts measure of labour standards and the measures used in other research is definitional. What is meant by a "labour standard"? Some researchers use a measure based on law and legislation. Within this category of variables are "pure" measures of labour standards that are limited to laws that regulate the labour market, and broader measures that incorporate political and social rights. Other researchers use a blend of legislative and labour-market outcome measures.

A "pure" measure of labour standards is used by Heckman and Pages-Serra (2000), who measure employment security in Latin American, Caribbean, and OECD countries using a measure based on the period of advance notification and money compensation for dismissal, the probability of remaining on the job, the maximum tenure that an employee can remain with the firm, the probability that economic difficulties will justify dismissal. Thus, the Heckman/Pages-Serra measure is based primarily on legislation.

Galli and Kucera (2004), in their examination of the effect of labour standards on informal employment in Latin America, use Kucera's measure of Freedom of Association and Collective Bargaining (FACB) rights. Neumayer and De Soysa (2006) also use Kucera's measure of FACB rights, albeit as a dependent variable to examine the impact of globalization in FACB rights violations. This measure is based on Kucera's (Kucera, 2001; Kucera and Sarna, 2004) method of evaluating de jure and de facto FACB rights in different countries by the ILO, the International Confederation of Free Trade Unions, and the U.S. Department of State, and the Heckman/Pages-Serra (2000) employment and job security indices. These are fairly pure labour legislation measures. In their correlation analysis, Galli and Kucera also used the Freedom House political and civil liberties index, which can be considered broader legislation, and a measure of unionization, which is an outcome measure.

Similar to the methodology of Galli and Kucera (2001), Cuyvers and Van Den Bulcke (this volume), use a ILO Convention ratification data and other data on enforcement and government actions. The Convention data are used to create a "formal" freedom of association index, while the non-ILO data are added to create a "real" freedom of association index.

Researchers use a combination of legislation-related and outcome-related variables. Rodrik's (2006), this volume model includes both legislative-type measures of labour standards (Conventions ratified, basic – now fundamental – Conventions ratified, child labour standards, statutory hours, granting of leave), and labour-market or institutional characteristics that may be related to labour standards but are not derived directly from labour-standards legislation (unionization, measures of civil and political rights). Busse (2001) uses as a measure of core labour-standards compliance (ratification) with ILO Conventions. But he also uses labour-market measures. His measure of the core labour standard "the degree of discrimination against women in working life," is "the percentages of male and female population ages 15-64 that are working" (Busse, 2001, p. 3). Another measure of a core labour standard, child labour, is defined as the percentage of the population aged 10-14 that is working. The forced labour standard is a measure of the prevalence of forced labour.

Maskus (2003), analysing the labour standards in primarily developing countries, uses as a measure of labour standards a blend of political rights through the Freedom House index, per capita income as a measure of wealth, labour standards based on fundamental ILO Conventions ratified, a capacity to enforce laws, and an assessment of level of compliance with core labour standards. Kucera and Sarna (2004) limit their analysis to the relationship between trade and rights of freedom of association/collective bargaining. But they too estimate a blended model, using the Kucera measure of FACB rights, the Freedom House indices, and unionization.[11]

A middle ground between outcome data and legislation is used by Cuyvers and Van Den Bulcke (this volume) to create a "real" child-labour index to pair with their "formal" child-labour index. Their "real" index incorporates ILO Convention data and data on economically active children 10-14 years of age. On the one hand, the latter can be classified as outcome data, because it is not derived directly from the legal system. On the other hand, it is not likely that the labour force participation of children aged 10-14 would be high without a lack of enforcement.

The advantage of broadening the measure of labour standards used is that the task of analysing the effect of labour standards over a wide range of countries and levels of development is eased. Narrower measures, which are based on precise definitions of legislation, reduce the number of countries that can be studied. The more countries one includes in the model, the greater the variation in legislation that needs to be taken account of.

A disadvantage of broadening the measures of labour standards is that one is not necessarily measuring true *labour standards* or *labour market regulation*. Measures such as unionization and female labour participation are not true measures of labour standards. These measure labour market characteristics which are presumed to be associated with, and more importantly, affected by or affect, labour standards. With respect to labour market characteristics, these variables assume what they hope to show, that labour standards matter. It is assumed, for example, by Maskus, that low labour-force participation by women is due to low anti-discrimination standards. But it might also be the case that other factors besides low levels of anti-discrimination laws affect female labour force participation.

With respect to the political environment variables, it is presumed that greater democracy leads to improved labour standards. While this may be true when analysing labour standards across both developing and developed countries, it may be less true when the analysis is limited to developed countries. The U.S. and Canada, for example, are both free, according to Freedom House (Freedom House, undated), but have different levels of labour standards (Block, et al., 2003b). In addition, it is not always true that democracy means higher levels of labour standards, at least at a point in time and within a country. Democratically elected right-leaning governments may reduce labour standards, within limits.[12]

---

[11] Interestingly, Kucera and Sarna (2004) do not use convention ratification per se as an independent variable.

[12] The Conservative Thatcher government in the UK in the 1980's enacted legislation that restricted union action, although there is a debate about the extent to which the fundamental collective bargaining institutions in the UK were changed. See, for example, Wood (2000). Effective August 23, 2003, the Republican Bush Administration in the U.S. adopted changes in the rules interpreting the provisions of the legislation that requires overtime that, by one estimate, will reduce by 6.7 million the number of employees in the U.S. eligible for overtime (U.S. Department of Labour, 2004; Eisenbrey and Bernstein, 2003).

VI. Summary and Conclusions

This chapter has examined the Block–Roberts methodology for measuring labour standards and has compared it with other research that has measured labour standards. The main characteristics of the Block–Roberts method are its relativism and the narrowness of its definition. It is relativistic in the sense that it does not rely on a universal benchmark, such as ILO Conventions. Rather it uses as a benchmark the most generous provision and standard in the jurisdictions being studied. The advantage of this method is that it is based on a benchmark that is politically feasible, because it has been enacted in at least one jurisdiction. The disadvantage of this method is that it is best for studying countries/political jurisdictions at comparable levels of development and with comparable levels of democracy.

The second major characteristic of the Block–Roberts method is the strictness of its definition. We define a labour standard as being governmentally adopted and enforced (and, therefore mandatory), workplace-oriented, comparable in purposes, and, in a sense adoptable by all the jurisdictions compared. The advantage of this definition is its purity; all of the standards included have similar characteristics. Moreover, if used as an independent variable, the inferences to be drawn from any results are clear.

The disadvantage of strict definition is the narrowness of its application. The stricter the definition, the more difficult it is to bring countries at different developmental levels into the analysis. It does not consider such issues as retirement and social security, issues linked to labour force, but not necessarily to the workplace.

Another important issue that must be addressed involves differences within countries. The U.S.–Canada analysis addressed subnational differences because subnational political jurisdictions in these two countries promulgate labour standards. To the extent subnational political jurisdictions within a country adopt labour standards, ideally the measure of labour standards should account for these differences.

On balance, it is believed that the Block–Roberts methodology for measuring labour standards across political jurisdictions is a potentially useful tool for measuring the effect of labour standards across jurisdictions that are comparable in terms of level of development and democratic institutions. Whether it can be adapted to measure labour standards in less developed countries, or in countries without strong democratic institutions, will be discovered by further research.

The most common alternative to the Block–Roberts relativistic methodology is the methodology of using ILO data and information on convention ratification. While ILO data have the advantage of being generally universalist, they are fundamentally designed for internal ILO purposes – to analyse compliance with ILO Conventions ratified. Thus they are constrained by the nature of the ILO system with its supervisory machinery and the associated dialogue.

Finally, it must be noted that this paper has not attempted to develop a general critique of the overall methodology that researchers have used to analyse the impact of labour standards on trade and trade-related phenomena. Rather, the purpose of this paper is to ask researchers to think clearly about the key variable in such a study – the measure of labour standards used.

Appendix 1. Basic Labour Standards Indices, U.S. and Canada, December 31, 1998.

Standard\Jurisdiction	Standards Requiring Employer Payments					Standards Constraining Employer Allocation of Labour					Sum: Basic Index
	Minimum Wage	Overtime	Paid Time Off	Unemployment\Employment Insurance	Workers' Compensation	Collective Bargaining	EEO\Employment Equity	Unjust Discharge	Occupational Safety and Health	Advance Notice of Plant Closings\Large-Scale Layoffs	
AL	6.84	10.00	1.29	5.12	5.67	1.50	8.35	3.00	3.13	5.03	49.92
AK	9.08	10.00	1.11	5.01	6.64	1.50	8.35	3.00	3.13	5.03	52.83
AZ	6.84	10.00	1.11	5.58	6.02	1.50	8.35	3.00	3.13	5.03	50.55
AR	6.84	10.00	1.11	6.77	5.26	1.50	8.35	2.00	3.13	5.03	49.98
CA	9.60	10.00	1.11	5.02	6.92	1.50	9.35	3.00	3.13	5.03	54.64
CO	6.84	10.00	1.11	6.33	7.07	1.50	8.85	3.00	3.13	5.03	52.85
CT	9.08	10.00	1.11	5.74	7.94	1.50	9.35	3.00	3.13	5.03	55.87
DE	6.84	10.00	1.47	5.58	5.69	1.50	8.35	1.50	3.13	5.03	49.08
DC	10.00	10.00	1.29	5.74	8.65	1.50	8.85	2.50	3.13	5.03	56.68
FL	6.84	10.00	1.11	6.17	5.77	1.50	8.85	1.00	3.13	5.03	49.39
GA	6.84	10.00	1.65	5.58	5.34	1.50	8.35	1.00	3.13	5.03	48.41
HA	7.76	10.00	1.29	8.58	7.91	1.50	9.35	2.50	3.13	5.03	57.04
ID	6.84	10.00	1.29	7.27	5.13	1.50	8.35	3.00	3.13	5.03	51.52
IL	7.24	10.00	1.29	6.17	7.86	1.50	8.35	2.00	3.13	5.03	52.56
IN	6.84	10.00	1.65	5.58	6.13	1.50	8.35	1.50	3.13	5.03	49.70
IA	6.84	10.00	1.29	7.10	8.10	1.50	8.35	2.75	3.13	5.03	54.07
KS	6.84	10.00	1.29	6.77	6.52	1.50	8.85	2.00	3.13	5.03	51.92
KY	6.84	10.00	1.47	6.17	7.55	1.50	8.85	2.25	3.13	5.03	52.78

(Continued)

Appendix 1. Basic Labour Standards Indices, U.S. and Canada, December 31, 1998—Cont'd.

Standard\Jurisdiction	Standards Requiring Employer Payments					Standards Constraining Employer Allocation of Labour					Sum: Basic Index
	Minimum Wage	Overtime	Paid Time Off	Unemployment\Employment Insurance	Workers' Compensation	Collective Bargaining	EEO\Employment Equity	Unjust Discharge	Occupational Safety and Health	Advance Notice of Plant Closings\Large-Scale Layoffs	
LA	6.84	10.00	1.65	5.02	5.38	1.50	8.85	1.25	3.13	5.03	48.64
ME	6.84	10.00	1.29	6.17	7.31	1.50	8.85	1.50	3.13	5.03	51.62
MD	7.24	10.00	1.47	5.58	7.27	1.50	9.35	2.00	3.13	5.03	52.56
MA	7.76	10.00	1.29	7.55	7.31	1.50	8.35	2.75	3.13	5.03	54.66
MI	6.84	10.00	1.47	6.17	5.81	1.50	8.85	2.50	3.13	5.03	51.30
MN	6.84	10.00	1.29	7.10	7.20	1.50	8.85	2.00	3.13	5.03	52.93
MS	6.84	10.00	1.29	5.58	4.76	1.50	8.35	2.25	3.13	5.03	48.72
MO	6.84	10.00	1.29	5.58	7.78	1.50	8.85	3.00	3.13	5.03	52.99
MT	7.24	10.00	1.11	7.10	7.83	1.50	8.85	10.00	3.13	5.03	61.77
NE	7.24	10.00	1.47	5.58	7.15	1.50	8.35	2.25	3.13	5.03	51.69
NV	7.04	10.00	1.29	6.50	6.37	1.50	8.35	2.75	3.13	5.03	51.95
NH	6.84	10.00	1.47	5.58	8.85	1.50	8.35	3.00	3.13	5.03	53.74
NJ	7.24	10.00	1.47	6.50	4.61	1.50	8.35	2.00	3.13	5.03	49.82
NM	6.84	10.00	1.29	5.74	4.70	1.50	8.85	2.50	3.13	5.03	49.57
NY	6.84	10.00	1.29	5.58	5.89	1.50	8.85	1.00	3.13	5.03	49.10
NC	6.84	10.00	1.47	6.33	7.47	1.50	8.35	2.00	3.13	5.03	52.11
ND	6.84	10.00	1.11	6.93	6.95	1.50	9.35	1.75	3.13	5.03	52.58
OH	6.84	10.00	1.11	6.17	8.33	1.50	8.85	2.50	3.13	5.03	53.45

OK	6.84	10.00	1.11	6.93	5.89	1.50	8.35	2.00	3.13	5.03	50.77
OR	9.60	10.00	0.92	6.67	7.70	1.50	8.35	2.50	3.13	5.03	55.40
PA	6.84	10.00	1.29	6.76	7.31	1.50	8.85	1.75	3.13	5.03	52.45
RI	6.84	10.00	1.47	7.66	7.83	1.50	8.85	1.75	3.13	5.03	54.05
SC	6.84	10.00	1.11	6.17	6.13	1.50	8.35	2.50	3.13	5.03	50.75
SD	6.84	10.00	1.29	6.17	7.55	1.50	8.35	2.00	3.13	5.03	51.85
TN	6.84	10.00	1.65	5.58	3.51	1.50	8.35	2.00	3.13	5.03	47.58
TX	6.84	10.00	1.29	6.17	5.26	1.50	8.35	2.50	3.13	5.03	50.07
UT	6.84	10.00	1.29	7.10	7.86	1.50	8.35	2.50	3.13	5.03	53.59
VT	7.76	10.00	1.11	6.17	7.27	1.50	8.85	2.50	3.13	5.03	53.31
VA	6.84	10.00	1.29	6.17	6.26	1.50	8.85	2.25	3.13	5.03	51.31
WA	9.08	10.00	1.29	7.89	7.78	1.50	8.85	2.00	3.13	5.03	56.54
WV	6.84	10.00	1.47	6.17	8.38	1.50	8.35	2.50	3.13	5.03	53.36
WI	6.84	10.00	1.47	6.93	7.86	1.50	8.85	2.00	3.13	5.03	53.60
WY	6.84	10.00	0.92	6.93	4.83	1.50	8.35	3.00	3.13	5.03	50.52
CANADA											
Federal	4.28	10.00	6.27	7.51	6.77	6.00	9.00	7.00	4.33	5.53	66.69
AB	1.52	7.28	7.61	7.51	6.69	6.00	8.10	7.00	3.07	0.00	54.79
BC	7.04	10.00	6.27	7.51	8.58	10.00	8.60	7.00	3.20	7.89	76.10
MAN	2.44	10.00	5.89	7.51	6.54	9.00	9.10	7.00	3.13	6.03	66.64
NB	2.44	3.21	5.38	7.51	5.99	8.00	8.10	7.00	2.11	5.71	55.44
NFL	2.44	4.57	5.53	7.51	7.25	9.00	8.60	7.00	2.08	5.03	59.00
NWT	6.12	10.00	6.27	7.51	8.82	9.00	9.00	7.00	2.18	3.21	66.11
NS	2.44	1.85	5.71	7.51	7.32	6.00	9.10	7.00	2.18	6.37	55.49
ONT	6.12	7.28	6.07	7.51	7.64	9.00	8.50	7.00	3.24	7.03	69.39
PEI	2.44	5.92	5.20	7.51	7.72	9.00	8.60	7.00	1.87	0.00	55.25
QUE	6.12	7.28	7.23	7.51	8.35	10.00	9.00	7.00	2.63	4.50	69.62
SASK	2.44	10.00	9.11	7.51	8.66	9.00	8.60	7.00	3.00	6.87	72.19
YUKON	7.04	10.00	6.27	7.51	8.43	6.00	8.50	7.00	3.17	5.21	69.13

Source: Block, Roberts, and Clarke (2003).

Appendix 2. Summary of Labour Standards Indices, U.S. (Federal) and European Union, Including Unjust Dismissal, December 31, 2001.

Jurisdiction	Minimum wage index	Overtime/ Working time index	Paid-time off	Collective bargaining	Anti discrimination	OSH	Mass layoffs	Information/ consultation	Parental or family leave	Transfer of undertaking	Total
U.S. Federal Law	9.50	3.50	0.83	6.67	9.35	3.50	8.25	0.00	5.00	0.75	47.35
EU	0	5.50	7.50	3.30	10	8.00	8.75	10.00	5.00	10.00	68.05

Source: Block, Berg, and Roberts (2003).

References

Becker, Elizabeth. 2004. Amid a trade deal, a debate over labour. *The New York Times*, April 6, Section C, p. 1.

Block, Richard N., Peter Berg and Karen Roberts. 2003a. Comparing and quantifying labour standards in the U.S. and the European Union. *The International Journal of Comparative Labour Law and Industrial Relations* 19(4): 441–467.

Block, Richard N., Jeong Hyun Lee and Eunjong Shin. 2002. The Korean industrial relations system: from post-independence to post-IMF. In: Eunmi Chang (ed) *Korean business management: the reality and the vision*. Hollyn, Elizabeth, NJ, pp. 309–343.

Block, Richard N. and Karen Roberts. 2000. A comparison of labor standards in the U.S. and Canada. *Ind Relat* 55(2): 273–307.

Block, Richard N. 1997. "Rethinking the National Labor Relations Act and Zero-Sum Labor Law: An Industrial Relations View," *Berkeley Journal of Employment and Labor Law*, 18(1): 30–55.

Block, Richard, Karen Roberts and R. Oliver Clarke. 2003b. *Labor standards in the U.S. and Canada*. W.E. Upjohn Institute for Employment Research, Kalamazoo, MI.

Block, Richard, Karen Roberts, Cynthia Ozeki and Myron Roomkin. 2001. Models of international labor standards. *Ind Relat* 40: 258–292.

Böhning, W.R. 2003. Gaps in basic workers' rights: measuring international adherence to and implementation of the organization's values with public ILO data. Working paper, International Labour Office, May.

Brudney, James J. 1996. "A Famous Victory: Collective Bargaining Protections and the Statutory Aging Process," *North Carolina Law Review* 74(2): 938–1036.

Busse, Matthias. 2001. Do labour standards affect comparative advantage? evidence for labour-intensive goods. Centre for International Economic Studies discussion paper No. 0142.

Crowley, Donald W. 1987. "Judicial Review of Administrative Agencies," *Western Political Quarterly* 40(2): 265–283.

Dunlop, John T. 2002. *Project labor agreements*. Harvard University Joint Center for Housing Studies working paper series, W02–7.

Eisenbrey, Ross and Jared Bernstein. 2003. Eliminating the right to overtime pay: department of labor proposal means lower pay, longer hours for millions of workers. Economic Policy Institute briefing paper, June 26. Available at http://www.epinet.org/content.cfm/briefingpapers_flsa_jun03

Elliott, Kimberly Ann. 2004. Labor standards, development, and CAFTA. Policy brief PB04–2, Institute of International Economics, March.

Flanagan, Robert J. 2003. Labor Standards and International Comparative Advantage. In: Robert J. Flanagan and William B. Gould, IV (eds) *International labor standards: globalization, trade, and public policy*. Stanford University Press, Stanford, CA, pp. 15–59.

Freedom House. undated. Freedom in the world, 2004: table of independent countries comparative measures of freedom. Available at http://www.freedomhouse.org/research/freeworld/2004/table2004.pdf

Galli, Rossana and David Kucera. 2004. Labor standards and informal employment in Latin America. *World Dev* 32(5): 809–828.

Health Canada. 2006. "Canada's Health Care System," at http://www.hc-sc.gc.ca/hcs-sss/medi-assur/index_e.html

Heckman, James J. and Carmen Pages-Serra. 2000. The cost of job security regulation: evidence from Latin American labor markets. *Economia* 1: 109–144.

Human Resources and Social Development Canada. 2006. "Canada Pension Plan," at http://www.sdc.gc.ca/en/isp/cpp/cpptoc.shtml

Kucera, David. 2001. Fundamental rights at work as determinants of manufacturing wages and FDI inflows. International Labour Organization, working paper.

Kucera, David and Ritash Sarna, 2004. "How Do Trade Union Rights Affect Trade Competitiveness?" International Labour Organization, working paper.

Lee, Yeon-Ho. 1997. *The state, society, and big business in South Korea.* Routledge, London.

Mai, Jai S. 1997. Core labour standards and export performance in developing countries. *World Econ* 20: 773–785.

Marleau, Veronique. 2003. Globalization and the Problem of Compound Decentralization: Lessons from the Canadian Labour Relations Setting. paper presented at *The decentralization of labour policies and collective bargaining.* International seminar in commemoration of Marco Biagi, Modena, Italy, March 19–20.

Maskus, Keith. 2003. Trade and competiveness aspects of environmental and labour standards in East Asia. In: Kathie Krumm and Homi Kharas (eds) *East Asia integrates: a trade policy agenda for shared growth.* The World Bank, Washington, DC, pp. 115–134.

Neumayer, Eric and Indra De Soysa. 2006. Globalization and the right to free association and collective bargaining: an empirical analysis. *World Dev.* Available at http://ssrm.com/abstract=604021, 34(1): 31–49.

OECD. 1996. *Trade, employment and labour standards: a study of core workers' rights and international trade.* OECD, Paris.

Rodrik, Dani. 1996. In: Robert Z. Lawrence, Dani Rodrik and John Whalley (eds) *Emerging agenda for global trade.* Overseas Development Council, Washington, DC, pp. 35–79.

Social Accountability International. undated. SA 8000: Overview of SA 8000. Available at http://www.cepaa.org/SA8000/SA8000.htm

Springer, Beverly. 1994. *The European Union and its citizens: the social agenda.* Greenwood Press, Westport, CT.

Turner, Thomas. 2002. Corporatism in Ireland: a comparative perspective In: D. D'Art and Thomas Turner (eds) *Irish employment relations in the new economy.* Blackhall Publishers, Dublin.

U.S. Bureau of Labor Statistics. 2003. *National compensation survey: employee benefits survey.* Available at http://www.bls.gov/ncs/home.htm

U.S. Department of Labor. 2004. FairPay: DOL's FairPay overtime initiative. Employment standards administration, Wage and hour division, August 23. Available at http://www.dol.gov/esa/regs/compliance/whd/fairpay/main.htm

U.S. General Accounting Office. 2002. *Collective bargaining rights: information on the number of workers with and without bargaining rights.* Report to Congressional requesters, U.S. Senate, GAO 02–835, September. Available at http://www.gao.gov/new. items/d02835.pdf

Wood, Stephen. 2000. From voluntarism to partnership: a third way overview of the public policy debate in British industrial relations. In: Hugh Collins, Paul Davies and Roger Rideout (eds) *Legal regulation of the employment relationship.* Kluwer Law International, London, pp. 111–135.

RICHARD N. BLOCK,
Michigan State University

Chapter 3

Country-level Assessments of Labour Conditions in Emerging Markets: An Approach for Institutional Investors

DAN VIEDERMAN AND ERIN KLETT
Verité

I. Introduction

This chapter will outline the approach that Verité has taken to provide an assessment of country compliance with labour standards for institutional investors.

This programme was initiated in 2000 when the California Public Employees Retirement System (CalPERS), the largest U.S. public pension fund, requested assistance in creating a quantitative ranking of 27 emerging markets countries for use in investment decision-making. The assessment has continued until the present. In 2004 an additional U.S. public pension fund began using a slightly modified version of the assessment results, also as an input to decision-making about emerging markets investments.

An emerging market country is classified by the World Bank as having a low/middle income economy. In 2002 these economies were defined as those with Gross National Income per capita below $9,076.

The assessment addresses country performance in defining and enforcing labour protections in the following five areas:

- Freedom of Association and Collective Bargaining
- Forced Labour
- Child Labour
- Equality/Discrimination
- Conditions of Work

The tables at the end of the report present the results of the third year of study, completed in 2003.

The following sections describe the framework, methodology, and findings of this year's study.

II. Framework for Country Assessments

A. Definitions and Benchmarks for International Labour Standards

The core of Verité's assessment is the eight International Labour Organization (ILO) Conventions identified by that agency as the fundamental Conventions. These eight Conventions cover four areas of labour practice, with two Conventions each addressing

57

D. Kucera (ed.), Qualitative Indicators of Labour Standards, 57–81.
© 2007 *by ILO.*

> **Box 1:** Fundamental Conventions of the International Labour Organization.
>
> **The Elimination of Child Labour**
> * Minimum Age Convention, 1973 (No. 138)
> * Worst Forms of Child Labour Convention, 1999 (No. 182)
>
> **The Abolition of Forced Labour**
> * Forced Labour Convention, 1930 (No. 29)
> * Abolition of Forced Labour Convention, 1957 (No. 105)
>
> **Freedom of Association and Collective Bargaining**
> * Freedom of Association and Protection of the Right to Organize Convention, 1948 (No. 87)
> * Right to Organize and Collective Bargaining Convention, 1949 (No. 98)
>
> **Equality/Discrimination**
> * Discrimination (Employment and Occupation) Convention, 1958 (No. 111)
> * Equal Remuneration Convention, 1951 (No. 100)

Freedom of Association and Collective Bargaining, Forced Labour, Child Labour, and Equality/Discrimination. The eight fundamental Conventions, also known as the "core" Conventions, establish international standards for treatment of workers. Box 1 lists the titles of the eight fundamental Conventions that formed the basis of this study.[1]

In addition to examining acceptance of, compliance with and implementation of the ILO fundamental Conventions, Verité researched health and safety; wages and hours of work; status of foreign contract labour; and the impact of export processing zones on labour conditions. These issues, referred to throughout this study as "conditions of work," are not directly related to the fundamental Conventions. But they are vital to an assessment of labour conditions in each country, as they define the direct experience of workers. Particular attention is paid to health and safety and wage issues, which affect substantially all workers and therefore are a broad indication of the effectiveness of a country's labour protections.

Verité considers foreign contract labour to be an issue of concern when workers are imported by formal, legal arrangements either between governments or through formal employment brokers; and when workers' employment contracts are concluded between the worker and a third party. In Verité's experience, these foreign contract workers are frequently denied freedom of movement within the destination country, often illegally. More frequently than the general working population foreign contract workers face wage and hour discrimination, limited job opportunities, sexual harassment, barriers to union formation or affiliation, mandatory pregnancy testing and physical abuse.

B. Focus on the Formal Sector

The assessment focuses on illegal or problematic conditions of employment in formal, legitimate economic sectors in each of the 27 countries of interest to

---

[1] For more on international labour standards, including links to the text of the eight Fundamental Conventions, refer to <http://www.ilo.org/public/english/standards/norm/index.htm>.

CalPERS. The study does not address labour or human rights abuses related to employment in illegal industries.

There are several reasons for this focus. While the informal sector[2] is a major part of the economies in many of the countries studied, the investment of concern to this report will be focused on the formal sector. Furthermore, information on the informal sector is difficult to gather and compare among countries. Country data on the informal sector is a function of how the sector is defined by a particular national statistical agency, and those definitions can vary significantly from one another, which makes data unreliable for comparison. Statistical information that would allow researchers to distinguish between worrisome and acceptable work practices within the informal sector is inconsistent or unavailable.

III. Methodology

Verité's methodology involves gathering information from a wide range of sources, both public and private. The data collected from the range of sources is organized into relevant categories to answer 42 indicator questions.

Our emphasis on a diverse range of sources is a key aspect of our approach. In our experience, no single set of quantitative data exists that could be used effectively to compare labour performance across all 27 countries. As a result we developed a set of indicators for which data was consistently available, and which enabled comparison between countries. Furthermore, it was important that we undertook local inquiries among a diverse range of sectors in order to build support for this type of labour assessment both in investor communities and within the countries themselves. The resulting interviews, with NGO and trade union labour advocates as well as government agencies and private sector institutions, provided useful perspective on local perception of labour issues, as well as an opportunity for representatives of those institutions to comment on the assessment process itself. Lastly, our organizational orientation leads us to include the voices of stakeholders in assessments that affect them.

The integration of information from these diverse sources posed a challenge as well. Assessments derived from information gathered in each of the 27 countries were filtered through the perspective of Verité's project manager. We evaluated each aspect of country performance against a fixed standard. But our reliance on a range of qualitative sources may make our study less replicable, or make our approach less transferable.

The fact-finding and analysis process included:

- Conducting in-country interviews and consultations with key decision-makers in government, business, labour-union and non-governmental sectors, as well as other labour experts, in each of the 27 countries of interest to investors. In-country interviewers used a standardized questionnaire whose purpose was to

---

[2] For a preliminary discussion of the informal sector, see the ILO "Employment: Informal Sector" <http://www.ilo.org/public/english/employment/skills/informal/who.htm>.

ensure uniformity and consistency. Each respondent received the same set of questions and was asked to respond on a common set of issues.

- Using a standard research template, conducting in-country research into local labour conditions, governmental policies, governmental and non-governmental programs, and national laws and regulations. Most of the sources used to identify local conditions were available only in local languages.
- Performing desk research and analysis on country conditions, government policies, laws and compliance with international standards. Carried out by Verité's full-time staff members, the desk research relied on both primary and secondary sources. Primary sources included proprietary information gathered directly by Verité during the course of over 1000 factory audits worldwide. Secondary sources included reports and analyses from governments; international organizations such as the International Labour Organization (ILO) and other UN organizations, the World Bank, and the International Monetary Fund; labour unions and labour union associations; businesses and business associations; and non-governmental organizations involved in workers' issues, human rights, and economic policy.
- Scoring the countries based on the in-country interviews and desk analysis. All information was used to assess country performance against a fixed standard – the relevant ILO core conventions and, for conditions of work, international norms. Verité's assessment relied heavily on qualitative interpretation and comparison to other countries in the study. Where sources disagreed, Verité researchers relied on institutional experience and the opinions of in-country consultants to determine which sources should be given the most weight as the best measures of country performance.

Full information on the scoring and weighting for each indicator is provided below.

A. Scoring and Weighting Overview

Countries have been scored on performance related to standards for freedom of association and collective bargaining, forced labour, child labour, equality/discrimination and conditions of work.

For each of these five areas of concern, countries were rated on:

- Ratification of the eight core International Labour Organization (ILO) Conventions (*Ratification Status of ILO Conventions*)
- Concordance of country laws and regulations with ILO core Conventions and international norms (*Laws and Legal System*)
- Capacity of country enforcement and inspection mechanisms to monitor and enforce laws and policies on labour standards; and capacity of in-country non-governmental organizations to operate in an unrestricted fashion in their involvement in social issues (*Institutional Capacity*)
- Actual level of compliance with or violations of the standards of the eight ILO core Conventions, as well as international norms for conditions of work (*Implementation Effectiveness*)

Categories were weighted in order to give highest importance to the documented presence of problems or violations rather than to laws or institutions that a government has developed to address the problems. Within this weighting framework, a high rate of child labour reduces a country's rating more than a set of excellent child labour laws increases it. Thus on-the-ground impact is more important in this analysis than government action that may or may not result in measurable change. Ratification of ILO core conventions is considered a foundation and represents an important public commitment on the part of governments. But, as is clear from the project findings, ILO ratification frequently coexists with serious problems. For that reason, convention ratifications received the lowest weighting in the scoring system.

In determining a country's final score, categories were weighted as follows:

- *Ratification Status of ILO Conventions*: 10% of the country's final score
- *Laws and Legal System*: 25% of the country's final score
- *Institutional Capacity*: 15% of the country's final score
- *Implementation Effectiveness*: 50% of the country's final score

Box 2 provides details of the weighting among categories.

Box 2: Structure of Scoring.		
Category	Subcategory	Section
ILO Conventions **(10% of total score)**		Each of eight Conventions worth equal amount
Laws and Legal System **(25% of total score)**	Convention-Related Issues (75% of category)	• Freedom of Association (25% of subcategory) • Forced Labour (25% of subcategory) • Child Labour (25% of subcategory) • Equality/Discrimination (25% of subcategory)
	Conditions of Work (25% of category)	
Institutional Capacity **(15% of total score)**	Governmental Capacity (80% of category) Non-Governmental Capacity (20% of category)	
Implementation Effectiveness **(50% of total score)**	Convention-Related Issues (80% of category)	• Freedom of Association (20% of category) • Forced Labour (20% of category) • Child Labour (20% of category) • Equality/Discrimination (20% of category)
	Conditions of Work (20% of category)	• Health and Safety Conditions (50% of subcategory) • Wage Conditions (50% of subcategory)

B. Scoring Criteria

This section contains details on the definition and scoring for the four categories used in this study: Ratification Status of ILO Conventions, Laws and Legal System, Institutional Capacity, and Implementation Effectiveness.

The four categories carried the potential of 40 points in total, with the exception of Taiwan which, ineligible to ratify ILO Conventions, was scored on a 36 point scale. To facilitate comparison among countries, and to streamline presentation of the final ranking, countries were ranked according to the percentage of the total possible points that they received.

1. Ratification Status of ILO Conventions
Percent of Final Score: 10%; Possible Points:[3] 4

For each of the 27 countries in the study, researchers examined whether the eight International Labour Organization (ILO) Conventions considered by the ILO to be fundamental (or "core") Conventions – those that are "fundamental to the rights of human beings at work" – have been ratified.[4] For each Convention ratified, a country received 0.5 points. Countries that ratified all eight Conventions received a perfect score of 4 points. This category represents **Indicators 1-8**.

Table 3 shows the ratification status of the eight core ILO Conventions for each of the 27 countries in the study, as well as the country scores awarded for this category.

2. Laws and Legal System
Percent of Final Score: 25%; Possible Points:[5] 10

For each of the 27 countries in this study, researchers explored in detail the country's labour laws, assessing whether they were in concordance with ILO Conventions and protected the labour rights defined in the Conventions.

Analysis of legal standards was complex, due to the wide variation among national legal systems, as well as within national systems when executive decrees, regional laws and regulations were included. In all cases, Verité's analysis incorporated prohibitions found in national constitutions in addition to those present in legal codes at the national level. Where possible, based on information available, prohibitions and protections provided by regional and local systems or detailed regulations were also evaluated.

In addition, Verité's analysis was complicated by the varying number of legal areas addressed by the different ILO core Conventions. Differing levels of complexity in the various Conventions meant that the number of questions needed to evaluate each area of law varied. For example, the ILO freedom of association and

---

[3] Out of a total of 40 for all four categories.
[4] See Section II.A, "Definitions and Benchmarks for International Labour Standards," for a list of the ILO's eight core Conventions.
[5] Out of a total of 40 for all four categories.

collective bargaining Conventions contain numerous articles addressing the right to organize independently, to bargain collectively, to form federations and to be protected from anti-union discrimination, among others. On the other hand, ILO Conventions on child labour, forced labour and equality/discrimination are more straightforward.

Further complicating the analysis was the general nature of much of the legislation under review. In several countries, for example, forced labour is addressed in the national constitution but not mentioned in the legal code.[6] For most of these countries, forced labour was not found to be a significant problem, which may explain the absence of specific legislation. Full points were awarded where forced labour is outlawed either in the national constitution or in general terms within the legal code.

In addition, scoring laws and legislation needs equitably to assess laws that exist in widely varying social contexts. Of particular difficulty were laws that restrict women's freedom to work in ways that are intended, in a culturally specific manner, to enhance women's security and well-being. In 15 of the countries under study, women are legally excluded from working in certain jobs in situations that legislators identified as socially unacceptable or physically hazardous.[7] Though intended to be protective of women, such laws contravene the broad freedoms that the ILO intended for women to have in choosing their place of work. This study – following the ILO's stated position[8] – considered such laws to be a "minor deficiency" in a woman's freedom to choose her place of work.

After adjusting for the inherent difficulties above, Verité researchers analyzed national laws in detail, and awarded points according to our evaluations.

2a. Convention-Related Topics

Topics related to the ILO core Conventions (i.e., freedom of association and collective bargaining, forced labour, child labour, and equality/discrimination) were treated as one group, *Convention-Related Legislation*. A percentage of the total possible points for each convention area was calculated, and the sums of the percentages for all Convention areas were averaged to obtain an overall percentage for convention-related legislation.

---

[6] In Turkey, for example, where forced labour is prohibited by Article 18 of the Constitution; or in South Africa, where Section 13 of the Constitution outlaws "slavery, servitude or forced labour." In Hungary, similarly, forced labour is prohibited under the Constitution without apparent amplification by the legal code.

[7] Countries whose laws include these restrictions are: China, Colombia, Czech Republic, Egypt, Hungary, Indonesia, Jordan, Korea, Malaysia, Morocco, Poland, Russia, Sri Lanka, Thailand and Turkey.

[8] See Direct Request of the Committee of Experts on the Application of Conventions and Recommendations to the Russian Federation (Convention No. 111), 2000, 71st Session; Direct Request to Jordan (Convention No. 111), 1999, 70th Session; and Direct Request to Morocco (Convention No. 111), 1999, 70th Session. These Direct Requests outline the Committee's findings on laws that, among other things, restrict women's freedom to work in all sectors and jobs. In these three cases the Committee recommended that the restrictions in national legislation be reconsidered. The absence of Direct Requests for other countries can not be taken as evidence that the ILO accepts these specific practices.

Convention-related legislation was then weighted as 75% of the total laws and legal system category score.

Researchers awarded between 0 and 3 points for topics related to freedom of association and collective bargaining, forced labour, child labour, and equality/ discrimination:

- 3 points were awarded to a country whose laws were judged to offer full protection for the labour right defined in the ILO Convention;
- 2 points were awarded to a country whose laws offered protection with only minor deficiencies (partial protection);
- 1 point was awarded to a country whose laws offered protection with significant deficiencies (partial contradiction); and
- 0 points was awarded to a country whose laws offered no protections or whose laws expressly and fully contradicted the labour right.

Freedom of Association and Collective Bargaining. The following issues were considered:

- **Indicator 9**: Workers' organizations have the right to draw up constitutions and rules, freely elect their representatives, organize their administration and activities, and formulate their programs, as defined in ILO Convention No. 87.
- **Indicator 10**: Workers' organizations are protected from governmental interference and from being dissolved or suspended by administrative authority, as defined in ILO Convention No. 87.
- **Indicator 11**: Workers' organizations are freely able to join international labour organizations, as defined in ILO Convention No. 87.
- **Indicator 12**: Workers are protected from discrimination if they join a labour union or participate in union activities outside working hours, as defined in ILO Convention No. 98.
- **Indicator 13**: Workers' organizations are free from interference by and are able to be independent of employers' organizations and businesses, as defined in ILO Convention No. 98.
- **Indicator 14**: Measures are taken to encourage negotiation between workers' organizations and employers' organizations through collective bargaining and the use of collective agreements, as defined in ILO Convention No. 98.
- **Indicator 15**: The right to strike is protected by law. (For this topic, between 2 and 0 points was awarded: 2 points if the country's legal system provided no or few restrictions on the right to strike; 1 point if the legal system provided significant restrictions; and 0 points if the legal system nearly or totally prohibited the right to strike.)

Forced Labour. The following issues were considered:

- **Indicator 16**: Forced labour is illegal, as defined in ILO Convention No. 29.
- **Indicator 17**: Forced labour is illegal as a means of political and labour punishment, as defined in ILO Convention No. 105.

Child Labour. The following issues were considered:

- **Indicator 18**: Child labour is illegal as defined in ILO Convention No. 138.
- **Indicator 19**: Child labour is illegal as defined in ILO Convention No. 182.

Equality of Opportunity and Treatment. The following issues were considered:

- **Indicator 20**: Workers' equality of opportunity and treatment in employment is protected, as defined in ILO Convention No. 111.
- **Indicator 21**: Equal remuneration among women and men for work of equal value is ensured by law, as defined in ILO Convention No. 100.

2b. Conditions of Work

Legislation on conditions of work shows great variation among countries. Verité's approach to scoring for conditions of work legislation was straightforward, not attempting to measure, for example, the adequacy of minimum wages against living wages.[9] Countries received points for the existence of legislation relating to four key areas of concern, listed below. Absence of legislation meant a score of zero points.

Points were awarded on each of the following topics related to conditions of work:

- **Indicator 22**: Laws, legal provisions and/or regulations establishing a minimum wage.
- **Indicator 23**: Laws legal provisions and/or regulations that regulate hours of work and overtime.
- **Indicator 24**: Laws legal provisions and/or regulations protecting the health and safety of workers.
- **Indicator 25**: Laws outlawing sexual harassment.

2c. Deduction: Freedom of Association

The overall score for legislation could be reduced by one additional factor. The suspension of laws related to freedom of association in export processing zones (EPZs, also known as free trade zones or export promotion zones) or in "pioneer" industries, resulted in a deduction of one-half point from the weighted category total.[10]

Points were deducted according to the following indicator:

- **Indicator 26**: Freedom of Association laws suspended (entirely or in part) in Export Processing Zones, or in specified sectors such as "pioneer industries."

The percent compliance levels for Convention Related Topics and Conditions of Work were weighted and combined, to yield an aggregate measure of compliance in the Laws and Legal System category, expressed both in points (see Table 2, Section IV. Findings) and as a percentage (see Table 4).

---

[9] Though comparing minimum wages with living wages is a valuable inquiry, it requires far more resources than were available during this project. We welcome thoughts from reviewers on how to best incorporate wage levels into this assessment.

[10] We have more recently experimented with a fully qualitative approach to Indicator 26, removing it from scoring and instead giving it the status of a 'red flag'.

3. Institutional Capacity
Percent of Final Score: 15%; Possible Points:[11] 6

For each of the 27 countries in the study, researchers examined whether the country has sufficient institutional capacity to monitor and enforce its labour laws and whether non-governmental organizations (NGOs) in the country exist and are able to operate without legal or informal restrictions.

     Countries were awarded between 0 and 3 points based on the assessment of their governmental and NGO capacities.

3a. Governmental Capacity
Points were assessed according to the following indicator:

- **Indicator 27**: Effectiveness of governmental capacity to develop, monitor, correct and implement labour laws.
- 3 points were awarded to a country judged as having strong institutional capacity;
- 2 points were awarded to a country with effective institutional capacity but significant holes in effectiveness;
- 1 point was awarded to a country judged to have institutional capacity of limited effectiveness; and
- 0 points were awarded to a country judged as having seriously limited or ineffective institutional capacity.

To assess governmental capacity, Verité analysts used a variety of sources, including in-country interviews; statistical data regarding budgets, personnel and factory inspections; and proprietary reports from audits carried out by Verité. Among the factors considered were:

- Breadth of administrative coverage within enforcement departments
- Adequacy of personnel and budgets compared to number of workplaces
- Frequency and adequacy of inspections
- Scale and frequency of labour-related corruption
- Severity and frequency of penalties levied for violations
- Adequacy and effectiveness of grievance mechanisms

3b. Non-Governmental Organization Capacity
Points were assessed according to the following indicator:

- **Indicator 28**: Lack of legal and de facto restrictions on involvement of NGOs in social issues, with particular reference to labour issues.

- 3 points were awarded to a country judged as having no significant restrictions on the ability of NGOs to operate in society;
- 2 points were awarded to a country with restrictions that prevent NGOs from addressing some key issues;

---

[11] Out of a total of 40 for all four categories.

- 1 point was awarded to a country with significant restrictions that prevent NGOs from operating freely on many issues, or which put NGOs under undue government control in significant ways;
- 0 points were awarded to a country in which NGOs are almost completely restricted in their operations.

In assessing NGO capacity, Verité researchers did not attempt to evaluate the effectiveness of NGOs at advocating, monitoring, and helping victims or otherwise affecting national policy and practice on labour issues, but rather assessed whether NGOs are legally or informally restricted from doing so.

Countries with strong governmental and NGO capacities received a perfect score of 6 points. Scores were converted to percentages, as shown in Table 6. Percentages for governmental and NGO capacity were each weighted and then combined to arrive at a final percentage for Institutional Capacity, also shown in Table 6. This percentage was applied to the total points possible for the Institutional Capacity category, thus yielding the final score for Institutional Capacity, as shown in Table 2.

4. Implementation Effectiveness
Percent of Final Score: 50%; Possible Points:[12] 20

This last section, worth half of the total score, focuses on the implementation of prohibitions of abusive labour practices. It is likewise divided among several areas of labour practice. The four Convention areas and conditions of work are all are equally weighted at 20% of this category.

In evaluating effectiveness of implementation, the study focused on the nature of the problems and the quality of governmental responses. The most important indicators for this section were the scale of the problems themselves. Scores were reduced where labour violations such as child or forced labour exist in significant numbers; where freedom of association and collective bargaining are curtailed; where discrimination on the basis of gender, religion and/or ethnicity is severe and/or commonplace; or where violations of wage or health and safety laws are frequent. Points were deducted where foreign contract labour was judged to be an issue of significant concern and where non-formal restrictions on labour rights were present in EPZs.

Governmental responses to these problems were examined for the areas of child labour and forced labour. Assessments were made of the number and range of programs that governments supported to address specific problems and of the effectiveness of these programmes. A combined score reflecting the level of activity and effectiveness was derived from these assessments.

Points were assessed for each of the following topics related to freedom of association and collective bargaining, forced labour, child labour, equality/discrimination, and conditions of work.

---

[12] Out of a total of 40 for all four categories.

4a. Freedom of Association and Collective Bargaining
Researchers awarded between 0 and 3 points for the following three topics:

Indicator 29: Independence of trade unions

- 3 points: multiple unions are able to organize workers without government interference.
- 2 points: multiple unions are able to organize workers in most cases without government interference.
- 1 point: unions are closely affiliated with governmental bodies or political organizations.
- 0 points: unions are effectively controlled by government.

Indicator 30: Non-Formal Restrictions

This indicator measures non-formal restrictions (i.e., restrictions not codified in law) on workers' rights to establish and join organizations of their choosing, including non-formal business interference; a lack of enforcement of rights that effectively results in restrictions is also considered.

- 3 points: rare or insignificant non-formal restrictions.
- 2 points: restrictions of limited impact.
- 1 point: moderately significant restrictions.
- 0 points: significant restrictions.

Indicator 31: Collective Bargaining

This indicator measures the extent to which collective bargaining is allowed to occur in the unionized sector without government or business interference.

- 3 points: collective bargaining is widely used and generally effective.
- 2 points: collective bargaining is used in limited circumstances and/or with some limitations.
- 1 point: collective bargaining is used with significant limitations.
- 0 points: collective bargaining is ineffective and/or not widely used.

Researchers deducted points according to the following category:

Indicator 32: Deduction: Freedom of Association

Possible Deductions: 25% of Freedom of Association score
This indicator measures de facto weakening or suspension of freedom of association in EPZs, whether as the result of formal suspensions or informal agreements among tenants of EPZs and government agencies.

- 25% of the total points awarded for Freedom of Association were deducted if a country does not extend freedom of association to its Export Processing Zones (EPZs).

4b. Forced Labour
Researchers awarded between 0 and 2 points for the following two topics:

Indicator 33: Scale of Forced Labour

This indicator measures estimated per capita scale of forced labour overall in the country.

- 2 points: scale of forced labour is small or non-existent.
- 1 point: scale of forced labour is moderate.
- 0 points: scale of forced labour is large.

Indicator 34: Government Activities and Effectiveness: Forced Labour

This indicator measures the level of governmental activity and effectiveness in addressing forced labour.

- 2 points: government is active and effective.
- 1 point: government is somewhat active and effective.
- 0 points: government activity is limited, or inactive and ineffective.

4c. Child Labour

Indicator 35: Scale of Child Labour

This indicator measures estimated per capita scale of child labour overall in the country.

- 2 points: scale of child labour is small or non-existent.
- 1 point: scale of child labour is moderate.
- 0 points: scale of child labour is large.

Indicator 36: Government Activities and Effectiveness: Child Labour

This indicator measures the level of governmental activity and effectiveness in addressing child labour.

- 2 points: government is active and effective.
- 1 point: government is somewhat active and effective.
- 0 points: government activity is limited, or inactive and ineffective.

4d. Equality

Indicator 37: Scale of Unequal Remuneration

This indicator measures estimated scale of unequal remuneration between men and women overall in the country.

- 2 points: scale of unequal remuneration between men and women is small/rare.
- 1 point: scale of unequal remuneration between men and women is moderate/occasional.
- 0 points: scale of unequal remuneration between men and women is significant/common across industries.

Indicator 38: Government Activities and Effectiveness: Non-Gender Discrimination

This indicator measures the level of governmental activity and effectiveness in addressing non-gender discrimination.

- 3 points: government is active in ensuring equality and lack of discrimination in opportunity for employment among demographic groups, not including gender discrimination.
- 2 points: government is somewhat active in ensuring equality and lack of discrimination in opportunity for employment among demographic groups, not including gender discrimination.
- 1 point: government is inactive in ensuring equality and lack of discrimination in opportunity for employment among demographic groups, not including gender discrimination.
- 0 points: government policies have exacerbated and/or provided a framework for the problem of non-gender discrimination in opportunity for employment to persist.

Indicator 39: Government Activities and Effectiveness: Gender Discrimination

This indicator measures the level of governmental activity and effectiveness in addressing gender-based discrimination, including equality of remuneration between men and women.

- 3 points: government is active in ensuring equality and lack of discrimination in opportunity for employment among men and women.
- 2 points: government is somewhat active in ensuring equality and lack of discrimination in opportunity for employment among men and women.
- 1 point: government is inactive in ensuring equality and lack of discrimination in opportunity for employment among men and women.
- 0 points: government policies have exacerbated and/or provided a framework for the problem of gender-based discrimination in opportunity for employment to persist.

4e. Conditions of Work
Indicator 40: Health and Safety

This indicator measures government effectiveness in implementing health and safety laws.

- 2 points: implementation of health and safety laws is effective.
- 1 point: implementation of health and safety laws is effective, with some significant holes in effectiveness (violations common).
- 0 points: implementation of health and safety laws is ineffective (violations widespread).

Indicator 41: Wages and Hours of Work

This indicator measures government effectiveness in implementing laws related to wages and hours of work.

- 2 points: implementation of laws relating to wages and hours of work is effective.
- 1 point: implementation of laws relating to wages and hours of work is effective, with some significant holes in effectiveness (violations common).
- 0 points: implementation of laws relating to wages and hours of work is ineffective (violations widespread).

4f. Deduction: Contract Labour
Possible Deduction: 1 point from the total Implementation Effectiveness score
This indicator measures the extent of contract labour. One point was deducted from the final score for Implementation if a country does not extend labour protections to foreign contract workers. The following benchmark for contract labour was used:

- **Indicator 42**: Significant population of foreign contract labourers with widespread abuses of labour laws and good labour practices. For example, foreign contract workers are frequently denied freedom of movement; and often illegally, and more frequently than the general working population, face wage discrimination, limited job opportunities, barriers to union formation or affiliation, sexual harassment, mandatory pregnancy testing and physical abuse.

Point scores for each of the four categories (Ratifications, Laws and Legal System, Institutional Capacity, and Implementation Effectiveness) were combined to provide a final country total (see Table 2). This score was then expressed as a percentage of the total points possible for that country (see Table 1).[13]

IV. Findings

The following tables present the details of the scoring. For the purposes of country comparison, Table 1 presents the summary most useful for an aggregation of the Labour Protections factor with other Country and Market factors. This is due to Taiwan's ineligibility to ratify ILO Conventions, and subsequent total potential score in our study of 36 points, rather than the 40 point potential for other countries.

List of Sources

Listed below are sources of data that were broadly important for the research in many or all countries. Country-specific sources comprised an additional 140 pages

---

[13] The total points possible for all countries except Taiwan is 40; the total points possible for Taiwan is 36, because Taiwan is not a member of the UN and therefore is not eligible for ILO membership and cannot ratify ILO Conventions. Thus Taiwan was not assessed in the Ratification category.

Table 1. Overall Rank.

Country	Percentage
Hungary	90.6%
Czech Republic	84.8%
Poland	81.7%
Israel	75.3%
Argentina	74.0%
Chile	73.6%
South Africa	73.6%
Korea (Republic of)	73.2%
Taiwan	71.6%
Peru	66.1%
Venezuela	63.6%
Brazil	63.0%
Jordan	61.9%
Philippines	60.6%
Turkey	59.9%
Colombia	58.4%
Sri Lanka	56.4%
Mexico	53.2%
Thailand	52.7%
Morocco	52.6%
Russia	49.7%
Egypt	47.9%
Malaysia	44.8%
Indonesia	44.3%
India	39.8%
China	39.6%
Pakistan	37.1%

This table presents the aggregate percentage compliance scores for each country.

of text, so we have omitted them for convenience. We would be pleased to provide details of the country-specific sources to anyone who is interested.

This study utilized a combination of in-country and desk research. The results of the in-country research were presented in confidential reports to Verité. In-country reports incorporated the findings of confidential interviews with government, business, labour union and non-governmental representatives; as well as document research of publications available at the country level. These documents are listed in the individual country bibliographies.

A further important source for most countries were reports of Verité audits. As these were done confidentially for Verité clients, they are not listed separately as sources. In all countries where Verité has audit experience, these reports are listed as a set.

Table 2. Category Scores.

Country	ILO Conventions Out of 4 points	Laws Out of 10 points	Institutional Capacity Out of 6 points	Implemen- tation Out of 20 points	Contract Labour 1 point deduction	TOTAL Out of 40 points[a]
Argentina	4.0	9.3	2.8	13.5	0	29.6
Brazil	3.5	9.1	2.8	9.8	0	25.2
Chile	4.0	6.4	2.8	16.2	0	29.4
China	1.5	7.1	1.6	5.7	0	15.8
Colombia	3.5	7.6	0.4	11.9	0	23.3
Czech Republic	3.5	8.5	4.4	17.6	0	33.9
Egypt	4.0	6.6	0.4	8.2	0	19.2
Hungary	4.0	9.2	4.4	18.7	0	36.3
India	2.0	7.8	1.2	5.0	0	15.9
Indonesia	4.0	8.4	0.4	4.9	0	17.7
Israel	3.5	8.8	2.4	16.5	−1	30.1
Jordan	3.5	7.9	2.0	12.4	−1	24.8
Korea (Republic of)	2.0	8.8	2.8	16.7	−1	29.3
Malaysia	2.5	4.8	0.4	11.2	−1	17.9
Mexico	3.0	8.7	2.4	8.2	−1	21.3
Morocco	3.5	5.9	2.4	9.3	0	21.0
Pakistan	3.5	4.6	0.8	6.0	0	14.8
Peru	4.0	7.3	2.8	12.4	0	26.4
Philippines	3.5	8.2	2.8	9.7	0	24.2
Poland	4.0	8.2	2.8	17.7	0	32.7
Russia	4.0	8.4	0.4	7.1	0	19.9
South Africa	4.0	9.1	2.8	14.6	−1	29.4
Sri Lanka	4.0	6.0	2.4	10.2	0	22.6
Taiwan	N/A	8.6	2.8	15.4	−1	25.8
Thailand	2.0	8.1	2.4	9.6	−1	21.1
Turkey	4.0	7.4	2.0	10.6	0	24.0
Venezuela	3.5	8.6	2.4	10.9	0	25.5

Countries are listed in alphabetical order. Category totals are provided for each country. Please note that Taiwan's score of 25.8 is derived from a total potential score of 36 rather than 40, making this table inappropriate for comparison among all countries on the basis of total scores.

[a] Taiwan is scored from a total of 36 points because it is not a member of the United Nations and therefore is not eligible to ratify ILO Conventions.

Table 3. Convention Ratifications.

Country	C138	C182	C29	C105	C87	C98	C100	C111	Convention total points (out of 4)
	Each Convention Catification equally weighted at 0.5 points.								
Argentina	y	y	y	y	y	y	y	y	4.0
Brazil	y	y	y	y	n	y	y	y	3.5
Chile	y	y	y	y	y	y	y	y	4.0
China	y	y	n	n	n	n	y	n	1.5
Colombia	y	n	y	y	y	y	y	y	3.5
Czech Republic	n	y	y	y	y	y	y	y	3.5
Egypt	y	y	y	y	y	y	y	y	4.0
Hungary	y	y	y	y	y	y	y	y	4.0
India	n	n	y	y	n	n	y	y	2.0
Indonesia	y	y	y	y	y	y	y	y	4.0
Israel	y	n	y	y	y	y	y	y	3.5
Jordan	y	y	y	y	n	y	y	y	3.5
Korea (Republic of)	y	y	n	n	n	n	y	y	2.0
Malaysia	y	y	y	n	n	y	y	n	2.5
Mexico	n	y	y	y	y	n	y	y	3.0
Morocco	y	y	y	y	n	y	y	y	3.5
Pakistan	n	y	y	y	y	y	y	y	3.5
Peru	y	y	y	y	y	y	y	y	4.0
Philippines	y	y	n	y	y	y	y	y	3.5
Poland	y	y	y	y	y	y	y	y	4.0
Russia	y	y	y	y	y	y	y	y	4.0
South Africa	y	y	y	y	y	y	y	y	4.0
Sri Lanka	y	y	y	y	y	y	y	y	4.0
Taiwan[a]									N/A
Thailand	n	y	y	y	n	n	y	n	2.0
Turkey	y	y	y	y	y	y	y	y	4.0
Venezuela	y	n	y	y	y	y	y	y	3.5

This table provides the details of the ILO Ratification score by identifying which Conventions have been ratified by each country.

[a] Not a UN member, Taiwan is not eligible to ratify ILO Conventions.

Table 4. Laws and Legal System: Sub-Category Percentages.

Subcategory Weights Section Weights Country	Convention-Related Legislation (75% of category)				Conditions of Work Legislation (25% of category)	Total Legal %
	Freedom of Association *25% of subtotal*	Forced Labour *25% of subtotal*	Child Labour *25% of subtotal*	Equality *25% of subtotal*		
Argentina	80.0%	83.3%	100.0%	100.0%	100.0%	93.1%
Brazil	70.0%	83.3%	100.0%	100.0%	100.0%	91.3%
Chile	75.0%	83.3%	100.0%	16.7%	50.0%	64.1%
China	45.0%	16.7%	100.0%	83.3%	100.0%	70.9%
Colombia	70.0%	33.3%	83.3%	83.3%	100.0%	75.6%
Czech Republic	85.0%	50.0%	100.0%	83.3%	100.0%	84.7%
Egypt	35.7%	33.3%	83.3%	66.7%	100.0%	66.1%
Hungary	90.0%	83.3%	100.0%	83.3%	100.0%	91.9%
India	65.0%	83.3%	50.0%	83.3%	100.0%	77.8%
Indonesia	65.0%	83.3%	100.0%	66.7%	100.0%	84.1%
Israel	85.0%	66.7%	83.3%	100.0%	100.0%	87.8%
Jordan	70.0%	66.7%	100.0%	50.0%	100.0%	78.8%
Korea (Republic of)	70.0%	83.3%	100.0%	83.3%	100.0%	88.1%
Malaysia	55.0%	16.7%	83.3%	33.3%	50.0%	47.8%
Mexico	80.0%	83.3%	66.7%	100.0%	100.0%	86.9%
Morocco	80.0%	33.3%	66.7%	33.3%	75.0%	58.8%
Pakistan	55.0%	50.0%	50.0%	16.7%	75.0%	50.9%
Peru	70.0%	83.3%	50.0%	50.0%	100.0%	72.5%
Philippines	70.0%	50.0%	100.0%	83.3%	100.0%	81.9%
Poland	85.0%	50.0%	83.3%	83.3%	100.0%	81.6%
Russia	80.0%	83.3%	100.0%	83.3%	75.0%	83.8%
South Africa	100.0%	83.3%	100.0%	66.7%	100.0%	90.6%
Sri Lanka	70.0%	33.3%	50.0%	33.3%	100.0%	60.0%
Taiwan	60.0%	83.3%	100.0%	83.3%	100.0%	86.3%
Thailand	65.0%	50.0%	100.0%	83.3%	100.0%	80.9%
Turkey	60.0%	50.0%	83.3%	66.7%	100.0%	73.8%
Venezuela	60.0%	83.3%	100.0%	83.3%	100.0%	86.3%

This table includes the percentages for each subcategory, which were weighted and combined to establish the percentage score for the Laws and Legal System category.

Table 5. Laws and Legal System: Deduction and Final Category Score.

Country	Total Legal % (from Table 4)	Deduction for Legal Suspension of Freedom of Association in EPZs	Final Legal Score (out of 10 points)
Argentina	93.1%		9.31
Brazil	91.3%		9.13
Chile	64.1%		6.41
China	70.9%		7.09
Colombia	75.6%		7.56
Czech Republic	84.7%		8.47
Egypt	66.1%		6.61
Hungary	91.9%		9.19
India	77.8%		7.78
Indonesia	84.1%		8.41
Israel	87.8%		8.78
Jordan	78.8%		7.88
Korea (Republic of)	88.1%		8.81
Malaysia	47.8%		4.78
Mexico	86.9%		8.69
Morocco	58.8%		5.88
Pakistan	50.9%	−0.5	4.59
Peru	72.5%		7.25
Philippines	81.9%		8.19
Poland	81.6%		8.16
Russia	83.8%		8.38
South Africa	90.6%		9.06
Sri Lanka	60.0%		6.00
Taiwan	86.3%		8.63
Thailand	80.9%		8.09
Turkey	73.8%		7.38
Venezuela	86.3%		8.63

This table provides the adjustments and deductions (if any) from the laws and legal category.

Table 6. Institutional Capacity: Sub-Category Percentages.

Country	Government Capacity % *80% of total*	NGO Freedom Percentage % *20% of total*	Institutional Capacity Total %
Argentina	33%	100%	46.7%
Brazil	33%	100%	46.7%
Chile	33%	100%	46.7%
China	33%	0%	26.7%
Colombia	0%	33%	6.7%
Czech Republic	67%	100%	73.3%
Egypt	0%	33%	6.7%
Hungary	67%	100%	73.3%
India	0%	100%	20.0%
Indonesia	0%	33%	6.7%
Israel	33%	67%	40.0%
Jordan	33%	33%	33.3%
Korea			
(Republic of)	33%	100%	46.7%
Malaysia	0%	33%	6.7%
Mexico	33%	67%	40.0%
Morocco	33%	67%	40.0%
Pakistan	0%	67%	13.3%
Peru	33%	100%	46.7%
Philippines	33%	100%	46.7%
Poland	33%	100%	46.7%
Russia	0%	33%	6.7%
South Africa	33%	100%	46.7%
Sri Lanka	33%	67%	40.0%
Taiwan	33%	100%	46.7%
Thailand	33%	67%	40.0%
Turkey	33%	33%	33.3%
Venezuela	33%	67%	40.0%

This table details the percentages for subcategories within the Institutional Capacity category, which were weighted and combined to establish the percentage score for the Institutional Capacity category.

Table 7. Implementation Effectiveness: Subcategory Percentages.

Subcategory	Convention-Related Implementation				Conditions of Work Implementation	
Section Points and Weighting	Freedom of Assoc. (out of 4)	Forced Labour (out of 4)	Child Labour (out of 4)	Equality (out of 4)	Conditions of Work (out of 4)	Contract Labour Deduction
Country	*Each section equally weighted at 20% of total*					
Argentina	3.33	4.00	2.60	1.55	2.00	
Brazil	3.33	2.00	1.20	2.23	1.00	
Chile	2.33	4.00	4.00	2.89	3.00	
China	0.25	1.40	2.00	2.00	0.00	
Colombia	2.33	3.40	2.60	1.55	2.00	
Czech Republic	3.67	4.00	4.00	2.89	3.00	
Egypt	1.00	3.40	1.20	1.55	1.00	
Hungary	3.67	4.00	4.00	4.00	3.00	
India	1.75	0.60	0.60	2.00	0.00	
Indonesia	0.75	2.00	0.60	1.55	0.00	
Israel	3.67	4.00	4.00	1.79	3.00	−1
Jordan	1.00	3.40	4.00	2.00	2.00	−1
Korea (Republic of)	2.67	4.00	4.00	2.00	4.00	−1
Malaysia	1.67	3.40	2.60	1.55	2.00	−1
Mexico	0.75	3.40	0.60	2.45	1.00	−1
Morocco	1.67	2.00	2.60	2.00	1.00	
Pakistan	1.75	0.60	0.60	2.00	1.00	
Peru	3.33	3.40	1.20	2.45	2.00	
Philippines	1.75	4.00	1.20	1.79	1.00	
Poland	3.33	4.00	3.40	4.00	3.00	
Russia	2.00	1.40	2.60	1.11	0.00	
South Africa	3.67	3.40	2.60	2.89	2.00	−1
Sri Lanka	2.00	4.00	2.60	1.55	0.00	
Taiwan	1.25	4.00	4.00	3.11	3.00	−1
Thailand	2.00	4.00	0.60	2.00	1.00	−1
Turkey	2.00	4.00	2.60	2.00	0.00	
Venezuela	1.33	4.00	2.60	2.00	1.00	

This category details the points for each subcategory under Implementation Effectiveness, which were weighted and combined to establish the final score for the Implementation category (see Table 2).

Important General Sources of Data Used in the Emerging Markets Research Project

Amnesty International

> *Report 2003*. Available from World Wide Web: (http://web.amnesty.org/report2003/index-eng).

> *Report 2002*. Available from World Wide Web: (http://web.amnesty.org/web/ar2002.nsf/home/home?OpenDocument).

> *Report 2001*. Available from World Wide Web: (http://web.amnesty.org/web/ar2001.nsf/home/home?OpenDocument).

Asia Monitor Resource Center. (http://www.amrc.org.hk/archive.htm).

Bolin, Richard L. and Robert C. Haywood. "World Association of Fair Trade Zones and Export Processing Zones: Comments and Questions." Available from World Wide Web: (http://www.wepza.org/behindthewire/bh001010.htm).

Coalition Against Trafficking in Women. 1999. *The Factbook on Global Sexual Exploitation*. Donna M. Hughes, Laura Joy Sporcic, Nadine Z. Mendelsohn, Vanessa Chirgwin, eds. Coalition Against Trafficking in Women.

Deininger, Klaus and Lyn Squire. 2001. "Measuring Income Inequality: A New Database." Washington, DC: World Bank. Available from World Wide Web: (http://www.worldbank.org/research/growth/dddeisqu.htm).

Freedom House

> *Annual Survey of Freedom 2002*. Available from World Wide Web: (http://www.freedomhouse.org/ratings/index.htm).

> *Annual Survey of Freedom 2001*. Available from World Wide Web: (http://www.freedomhouse.org/ratings/index.htm).

Global March Against Child Labour. 2000. *Out of the Shadows: A Worldwide Report on the Worst Forms of Child Labour*. Available from World Wide Web: (http://globalmarch.org/worstformsreport/index.html).

Human Rights Watch

> *World Report 2003*. Available from World Wide Web: *(http:*//www.hrw.org/wr2k3).

> *World Report 2002*. Available from World Wide Web: (http://www.hrw.org/wr2k2/).

> *World Report 2001*. Available from World Wide Web: (http://www.hrw.org/wr2k1/).

International Confederation of Free Trade Unions

> *Annual Survey of Violations of Trade Union Rights 2003*. Available from World Wide Web: (http://www.icftu.org/survey2003.asp?language=EN).

> *Annual Survey of Violations of Trade Union Rights 2002*. Available from World Wide Web: (http://www.icftu.org/survey2002.asp?language=EN).

> *Annual Survey of Violations of Trade Union Rights 2001*. Available from World Wide Web: (http://www.icftu.org/www/pdf/survey2001en.pdf).

> *Annual Survey of Violations of Trade Union Rights 2000*. Available from World Wide Web: (http://www.icftu.org/www/pdf/survey2000en.pdf).

International Labour Organization

Article 22 Reports. Available from World Wide Web: (http://webfusion.ilo. org/public/db/standards/normes/appl/index.cfm?lang=EN)

ATLAS: Labour Administration Informal System. 2001. Geneva: ILO Available from World Wide Web: (http://www.ilo.org/public/english/dialogue/gov-lab/admitra/atlas/index.htm).

Bureau of Statistics. *Yearbook of Labour Statistics.* 2000. Geneva: ILO

CISDOC/CISILO: The CIS Bibliographic Database. ILO Health and Safety Database. Available from World Wide Web: (http://www.ilo.org/public/english/protection/safework/cis/products/cisdoc.htm).

Committee on the Freedom of Association. Cases. Available from World Wide Web: (http://webfusion.ilo.org/public/db/standards/normes/libsynd/index.cfm?lang=EN)

Committee on the Application of Conventions and Ratifications. Direct Requests and Observations. Available from World Wide Web: (http://webfusion.ilo.org/public/db/standards/normes/appl/index.cfm?lang=EN)

Convention Ratification. Available from World Wide Web: (http://webfusion.ilo.org/public/db/standards/normes/appl/appl-ratif8conv.cfm?Lang=EN).

e.quality@work: An Information Base on Equal Employment Opportunities for Women and Men. Available from World Wide Web: (http://www.ilo.org/public/english/employment/gems/intro/eeo/).

Fundamental Conventions. Available from World Wide Web: (http://www.ilo.org/public/english/standards/norm/whatare/fundam/index.htm).

GLLAD: Government and Labour Law. Available from World Wide Web: (http://www.ilo.org/public/english/dialogue/govlab/).

ILM: International Labour Migration Database. Available from World Wide Web: (http://www.ilo.org/public/english/support/lib/dblist.htm#country).

ILOLEX Legal Database. Available from World Wide Web: (http://ilolex.ilo.ch:1567/public/english/50normes/infleg/iloeng/index.htm).

ILO-CEET: Central and Eastern European Team. Various papers. Available from World Wide Web: (http://www.ilo-ceet.hu/public/english/region/eurpro/mdtbudapest/publication/index.htm).

ILO CONDIT: Conditions of Work Programme. Available from World Wide Web: (http://www.ilo.org/public/english/protection/condtrav/index.htm).

ILODOC: ILO Publications and Documents. Available from World Wide Web: (http://ilis.ilo.org/ilis/engl/ilodoc/eintilo.htm).

International Labour Review. Available from World Wide Web: (http://www.ilo.org/public/english/support/pul/revue/index.htm#SELECTION).

International Migration. "The ILM Statistics Platform." Available from World Wide Web: (http://www.ilo.org/public/english/protection/migrant/ilmdb/ilmdb.htm).

IPEC: International Programme on the Elimination of Child Labour. *Child Labour Statistics.* Available from World Wide Web: (http://www.ilo.org/public/english/standards/ipec/simpoc/index.htm).

LABORSTA Labour Statistics Database. Geneva: ILO, 1998 – 2001. Available from World Wide Web: (http://laborsta.ilo.org/).

Labour Practices in the Footwear, Leather, Textiles and Clothing Industries: Report for discussion at the Tripartite Meeting. Available from World Wide Web: (http://www.ilo.org/public/english/dialogue/sector/techmeet/tmlfi00/tmlfir.htm)

NATLEX: Legal Database. Available from World Wide Web: (http://natlex.ilo.org/).

World Labour Report 2001: Stopping Forced Labour. Geneva: ILO, 2001. Available from World Wide Web: (http://www.ilo.org/public/english/standards/decl/publ/reports/report2.htm).

World at Work. "Export Processing Zones." No. 27, December 1998.

World Labour Report 2000: Income Security and Social Protection in a Changing World. Geneva: ILO, 2000.

Safe Work: Safe Work Programme. Available from World Wide Web: (http://www.ilo.org/public/english/protection/safework/).

International Monetary Fund. "A Role for Labour Standards in the New International Economy?" Seminar and Panel Discussion, September 29, 1999. Available from World Wide Web: (http://www.imf.org/external/np/tr/ 1999/ tr990929.htm).

Internet Law Library. "Laws of Other Nations." Available from World Wide Web: (http://www.lectlaw.com/inll/52.htm).

Law Library of Congress. *Guide to Law Online*. Available from World Wide Web: (http://www.loc.gov/law/guide/).

Population Reference Bureau. "World Population Data Sheets." Available from World Wide Web: (http://www.prb.org/Content/NavigationMenu/Other_reports/2000-2002/2001_World_Population_Data_Sheet.htm).

Transparency International

2002 Corruption Perceptions Index. 2002. Available from World Wide Web: (http://www.transparency.org/documents/cpi/2002/cpi2002.html#cpi).

2001 Corruption Perceptions Index. 2001. Available from World Wide Web: (http://www.transparency.org/documents/cpi/2001/cpi2001.html#cpi).

United Nations Development Program. *2001 Human Development Report: Making new technologies work for human development*. NY: Oxford University Press, 2001. Available from World Wide Web: (http://www.undp.org/hdr2001/ back.pdf).

United Nations Industrial Development Organization. June 2001. Statistics and Information Networks Branch. Available from World Wide Web: (http://www.unido.org).

United Nations Statistics Division. 2000. *United Nations Statistical Yearbook, 44th Edition*. NY: United Nations.

U.S. Bureau Of Labour Statistics. *International Labour Statistics*. Available from World Wide Web: (http://www.bls.gov/bls/international.htm).

U.S. Census Bureau. "Links to International Statistical Agencies." Available from World Wide Web: (http://www.census.gov/main/www/stat_int.html).

U.S. Central Intelligence Agency. *Country Factbooks*. Available from World Wide Web: (http://www.cia.gov/cia/publications/factbook/index.html).

U.S. Department of Labour

2002 Findings on the Worst Forms of Child Labour. Bureau of International Labour Affairs, International Child Labour Program, 2002. Available from World Wide Web: (http://ww.dol.gov/ilab/media/reports/iclp/TDA2002/Findings.pdf).

2001 Findings on the Worst Forms of Child Labour. Bureau of International Labour Affairs, International Child Labour Program. 2001. Available from World Wide Web: (http://www.dol.gov/ilab/media/reports/iclp/TDA2001/Findings.pdf).

Advancing the Campaign Against Child Labour: Efforts at the Country Level. Bureau of International Labour Affairs, International Child Labour Program. 2002. Available from World Wide Web: (http:/www.dol.gov/ILAB/media/reports/iclp/Advancing1/CL%20Advance%20Camp.pdf).

International Labour Assistance Bureau, Office of International Economic Affairs. "Wages, Benefits, Poverty Line, and Meeting Workers' Needs in the Apparel and Footwear Industries of Selected Countries." Available from World Wide Web: (http://www.dol.gov/dol/ilab/public/media/reports/).

By the Sweat and Toil of Children. 1994. Washington, D.C., Available from World Wide Web: (http://www.dol.gov/dol/ilab/public/media/reports/iclp/sweat/main.htm).

Division of Foreign Economic Research. "Foreign Economic Research Staff Papers." Available from World Wide Web: (http://www.dol.gov/dol/ilab/public/programs/oiea/ferstaff.htm).

Public Hearings on International Child Labour: Official Record. 1996. Washington, DC: U.S. Department of Labour: Bureau of International Labour Affairs.

U.S. Department of State

Country Reports on Human Rights Practices 2002. Washington, D.C.: Bureau of Democracy, Human Rights and Labour, March, 2003. Available from World Wide Web: (http://www.state.gov/g/drl/rls/hrrpt/2002/).

Country Reports on Human Rights Practices 2001. Washington, D.C.: Bureau of Democracy, Human Rights and Labour, March 2002. Available from World Wide Web: (http://www.state.gov/g/drl/rls/hrrpt/2001/).

Country Reports on Human Rights Practices 2000. Washington, D.C.: Bureau of Democracy, Human Rights and Labour, February 2001. Available from World Wide Web: (http://www.state.gov/g/drl/hr/).

Country Reports on Economic Policy and Trade Practices. Washington, D.C.: Bureau of Economic and Business Affairs. 1999, 2000, and 2001. Available from World Wide Web: (http://www.state.gov/www/issues/economic/trade_reports/).

Trafficking in Persons Report 2003. Washington, D.C.: Bureau of Economic and Business Affairs, June 2003. Available from World Wide Web: (http://www.state.gov/g/tip/rls/tiprpt/2003/)

Verité. Confidential Factory Audit Reports. 1995–2003.

DAN VIEDERMAN AND ERIN KLETT,
Verité

Chapter 4

Decent Work, Standards and Indicators

MONIQUE ZARKA-MARTRES
International Labour Office

AND MONIQUE GUICHARD-KELLY
International Labour Office Consultant

1. Introduction

1.1. General Remarks

The mandate of the International Labour Organization is to promote social justice. The preamble of its Constitution, established in 1919, begins with these words that are still fully pertinent today:

> Whereas universal and lasting peace can be established only if it is based upon social justice; And whereas conditions of labour exist involving such injustice, hardship and privation to large numbers of people as to produce unrest so great that the peace and harmony of the world are imperilled; and an improvement of those conditions is urgently required.

In 1999, the Director-General of the ILO, Juan Somavia, defined the mission of the ILO in today's world in the following terms:

> The ILO's mission is to improve the situation of human beings in the world of work. Today, that mission finds resonance in the widespread preoccupation of people at times of great change: to find sustainable opportunities for decent work. The primary goal of the ILO today is to promote opportunities for women and men to obtain decent and productive work, in conditions of freedom, equity, security and human dignity.[1]

The international labour standards were the first tool developed by the ILO to implement its mandate. Today, this tool remains the most important means the Organization has at its disposal to achieve its objectives. As stated by the Director-General in 2001,

> firstly, normative action helps to clarify the meaning of decent work: standards provide an authoritative answer to the question of what decent work implies in concrete terms as regards the preconditions (fundamental principles and rights), its content (work that meets certain criteria of

---

[1] ILO, *Decent Work*, Report of the Director-General, International Labour Conference (ILC), 87th Session, Geneva, 1999, p. 3.

83

quality and security) and the process where by it can be achieved (social dialogue). Secondly, it helps to put the Decent Work Agenda into practice: standards are a stern indicator of progress towards the achievement of ILO objectives, not through lip-service but in law and practice.[2]

The strength of the international labour standards, in comparison to other international instruments, is that they are developed and adopted through a tripartite process involving governments, employers and workers. Their adoption at the International Labour Conference (ILC), supreme body of the Organization, to which the 178 member States are invited to be represented by tripartite delegations, guarantees the universality of the values contained in the instruments.

To date, the International Labour Conference has adopted 185 Conventions and 195 Recommendations, which globally cover the following subjects:[3] freedom of association, collective bargaining and industrial relations; forced labour; elimination of child labour and protection of children and young persons; equality of opportunity and treatment; tripartite consultation; labour administration and inspection; employment policy and promotion; vocational guidance and training; employment security; wages; working time; occupational safety and health; social security; maternity protection; social policy; migrant workers; seafarers; fishermen; dockworkers; indigenous and tribal peoples; and specific categories of workers. Conventions and Recommendations in these 21 subject areas provide constituents with a number of detailed provisions enabling them to build a solid platform for regulating decent work.

Given the multi-faceted nature of standards and the differing levels of development and priorities in member States, we cannot expect all countries to be able to immediately, and in all areas, implement the international labour standards. For the standards to have real impact, they must be progressively implemented through national programs, taking into account the institutional and economic capacity of each country as well as national priorities. A tool needs to be developed to assist member States to do this by identifying areas where there are gaps or lacunae in national laws and practices with respect to the principles that underlie decent work as contained in the standards.

1.2. From the Integrated Approach to Standards-related Activities to a Methodology for "Normative" Indicators

Since the 1990's, the ILO has been undergoing a process of modernising and strengthening its standards system. In particular, the Working Party on Policy regarding the Revision of Standards (WPRS) was created in 1995 to examine the contents of each of the Conventions and Recommendations and decide on whether

---

[2] ILO, *Reducing the Decent Work Deficit – A Global Challenge,* Report of the Director General, International labour ILC, 89th Session, Geneva, p. 59.
[3] This classification was followed in the Report of the Committee of Experts on the Application of Conventions and Recommendations, *Application of International Labour Standards 2004 (I),* Report III (Part 1A), International Labour Conference, 92nd Session 2004, Geneva.

they were up-to-date or not. It finished its work in 2002. In 1999 the report of the Director-General, which received wide support at the ILC, pointed out that "the best guarantee of credibility lies in the effectiveness of the ILO's normative activities . . . .Improving the visibility, effectiveness and relevance of the ILO's standard setting system must become a political priority."[4] On the basis of this report and the results of the WPRS, a new approach to standards-related activities called "the integrated approach" was adopted by the Governing Body in November 2000.[5]

The aim of the integrated approach is to improve the impact of standards-related activities through an integrated use of all of the means of action available to the Organization as well as strengthening the coherence and relevance of the standards. It is also intended that this approach assist the constituents in coming up with a consensus on future standard-setting action. Finally, the integrated approach provides a framework for the systematic evaluation of standards and their impact, documenting the positive linkages between families of standards and "encouraging member States to make simultaneous progress on each of the fronts of decent work".[6]

The approach is comprised of three steps. The first is an in-depth study of the standards in a determined subject as well as other instruments (e.g. codes of practices) and means of action (e.g. promotional activities, technical cooperation, development and dissemination of the information and inter-institutional cooperation) that are relevant in the area. The second step is a tripartite general discussion at the ILC, based on the study. The aim of the general discussion is to come up with a consensus on a plan of action in the area being examined. Taking into account the needs and priorities in the area, the plan of action may identify potential new subjects for standard setting, issues that should be the object of more technical instruments, as well as the necessary promotional activities, technical cooperation and inter-institutional cooperation. Thirdly, the Governing Body is invited to make a decision on the specific consequences of this debate by implementing the plan of action adopted at the Conference.

The integrated approach was first applied at the ILC in June 2003 in the area of occupational safety and health (OSH). In 2004, the subject of migrant workers was examined and a third general discussion based on the same approach will take place in 2005 in the area of youth employment.

The idea for developing country profiles evolved after examining the wealth of information received in the responses to the OSH survey, in the context of the preparation for the General Discussion at the ILC in 2003. The purpose was to take a snapshot of the national situation by grouping together all relevant information in a given subject with respect to international labour standards in order to assist member States in implementing the decent work agenda.

The first step was to develop the particular "lens" through which a snapshot could be taken. To take the example of OSH, the standards to be examined were identified and analysed. A survey was then developed based on the main principles

---

[4] *Decent Work*, page 7.

[5] GB/279/4.

[6] *Reducing the Decent Work Deficit – A Global Challenge*, page 60.

in the standards. Taking into account the results of the survey and on the basis of the principles in the standards, a grid containing 13 criteria was identified. These constituted the normative indicators in the area of OSH and can be considered as the ILO "lens" in this area. Secondly, the government, employer and worker responses to the survey were incorporated in the grid along with other relevant information (such as national legislation and comments of the Committee of Experts on the Application of Conventions and Recommendations (CEACR); relevant Internet links will be incorporated into the grid at a later stage). Through this lens, the ILO constituents and the Office can determine the extent to which the principles in a group of ILO standards are applied at the national level, enable member States to identify gaps in their systems and develop national programs for the gradual implementation of standards and assist the Office to better target its technical cooperation activities.

2. Taking a Snapshot of the National Legislative System through the Lens of ILO Standards – Methodology

2.1. Choosing the Standards to be Examined

With respect to OSH, 17 Conventions, 24 Recommendations and one Protocol had been adopted, addressing general OSH issues, specific risks and hazardous occupations. According to the WPRS, of these 12 Conventions and 17 Recommendations were up-to-date. Therefore more weight was put on their provisions. In addition, the Labour Inspection Convention, 1947 (No. 81) and the Labour Inspection (Agriculture) Convention, 1969 (No. 129) as well as their Recommendations and Protocol were examined in this context because of their direct relevance to OSH.

In the area of migrant workers, there were two Conventions and two Recommendations that were considered to be the comprehensive standards in the subject area. In addition to these four instruments, a number of ILO Conventions that contained provisions directly relating to migrant workers were taken into account.

2.2. In-depth Analysis of Standards

Taking the example of OSH, the first step in the process towards selecting the criteria was an in-depth analysis of the contents of the Conventions and Recommendations. Each article or paragraph in the relevant instruments was studied and regrouped into a large document that re-sorted them by theme; i.e. those relating to policy, scope of application, social dialogue, labour inspection etc. were grouped together.[7]

By doing this, the main principles in the subject area became apparent, each of these principles being linked to a number of provisions in two or more instruments. These principles were then used as the basis of the survey questions.

---

[7] An example of one of the areas covered can be found in Appendix 1.

In addition, it assisted in the examination of the relationship between the different instruments and the establishment of a diagram for a model OSH system based on the ILO standards.

2.3. The Survey

In preparation for the General Discussion held at the ILC for the first two subjects, a survey was formulated and sent to member States, inviting them to consult with the most representative employers' and workers' organizations when formulating their response. In the area of OSH, the survey acted as a sort of "checklist" for member States concerning the application of a set of given ILO standards in national law and practice. In the area of migrant workers, even though they were taken into account, the survey did not fully reflect the contents of the standards. For the promotion of youth employment, no survey was undertaken given that employment promotion (in general) had recently been the object of a general survey (*étude d'ensemble*) undertaken by the CEACR.

On the basis of the analysis of the OSH standards, a set of common principles within the instruments were identified. In order to have a functioning OSH system, a country had to have a coherent policy, adequate preventive and protective measures, the necessary organizational frameworks and mechanisms to ensure that the different players had the required powers, rights and duties set out in national law and practice etc.

Each question in the survey was directly linked to one or more of the provisions in the OSH instruments. Annexed to the survey was a table showing the exact Article or Paragraph associated with the question being asked. The questions were formulated to enable yes/no answers with further details being requested where needed.

The survey was sent out to member States with a request to consult with the most representative organizations of employers and workers. In total 107 replies were received from member States, as well as 47 from the most representative employers' and workers' organizations either in addition to or independently from the responses received from governments. The tripartite responses were extremely valuable in assessing the situation in the country. In addition, they provided a valuable amount of detail, not only concerning the legislative and policy framework but also the implementation of these.

The survey served two other purposes. Firstly, it enabled an assessment of, and in fact confirmed, that ILO standards cover the most essential aspects of OSH. Secondly, it provided a general overview on the extent to which the main principles contained in a group of international labour standards were reflected in national legislation. The survey also included questions directly concerning the impact of ILO standards on national law and practice. A large majority replied that they had used the ILO OSH Conventions as models for national law and practice.[8]

---

[8] The results of the analysis of the survey responses can be found in Annex II of Report [VI], *ILO Standards-Related Activities in the Area of OSH*, International Labour Conference 2003, ILO Geneva 2003.

2.4. Choosing Criteria/Normative Indicators for the Country Profiles

The survey responses provided most of the information required to complete the country profiles. Of the 15 questions on national law and practice in the survey, 13 criteria could be distilled. These criteria (listed below) were based on the questions that represented the most important aspects of OSH as indicated by the responses to the survey. Each criterion also has related sub-criteria and together, these constitute a set of normative indicators for OSH.

1. The existence of a national OSH policy formulated, implemented and reviewed on a tripartite basis
2. Coverage of national OSH legislation
3. Existence of national preventive and protective OSH measures
4. Existence of national OSH infrastructures
5. Capacity and functioning of national OSH infrastructures
6. Notification and recording of occupational accidents and diseases
7. Occupational health
8. Existence of measures for consultation, cooperation and communication at all levels
9. Existence of enforcement mechanisms
10. Employer responsibilities
11. Workers' rights and responsibilities
12. Workers' representatives rights and responsibilities
13. Responsibilities of designers, producers, importers and suppliers

The evaluation is based on the above 13 criteria as well as 85 sub-criteria,[9] each of which relates back, in general to two or more provisions in the OSH instruments. In order to evaluate whether a country has implemented the criteria, it is necessary to go back and look at the full text of the relevant standards as set out in the detailed table of ILO OSH standards.[10] This enables a thorough analysis of the situation in a country and avoids over simplification and misleading results. If we take for example the requirements for the implementation of criteria number three (existence of national preventive and protective OSH measures), a country would have to include the following 16 elements in its OSH laws and regulations:

a) The identification and determination of occupational hazards;
b) The prohibition, limitation or other means of control of exposure;
c) The assessment of risks and levels of exposure;
d) Prohibition or limitation of use of hazardous processes, machinery and equipment and hazardous chemical, physical and biological agents;
e) The specification of exposure limits and related criteria including periodic revision and updating of exposure limits;
f) The surveillance and monitoring of the working environment;

---

[9] Appendix 2.
[10] For a short extract of the detailed table, see Appendix 1.

g) The replacement of hazardous chemicals and processes by less hazardous ones;
h) The notification of hazardous work and the related authorization and control requirements;
i) The classification and labelling of hazardous chemicals and the provision of related data sheets;
j) The provision and use of personal protective equipment;
k) Safe methods for the handling, collection, recycling, and disposal of hazardous waste;
l) Working time arrangements (such as hours of work and rest periods, etc.);
m) Adaptation of work installations, machinery, equipment and processes to the physical and mental capacities of the workers, taking ergonomic factors into account;
n) Design, construction, layout and maintenance of workplaces and installations;
o) Design, construction, layout, use, maintenance, testing and inspection of machinery, tools and equipment;
p) The provision of adequate welfare facilities (such as drinking water and sanitary eating and changing facilities).

Each of these sub-criteria is based on a number of provisions in the OSH instruments.[11] Through a comparison of the ILO provisions with national laws and regulations, a detailed and complete picture of the situation with respect to OSH in a country can be obtained.

2.5. The Country Profile Grid[12]

On the basis of the 13 criteria, the above grid was established. The grid is divided up into four parts. The first is the ILO criteria and sub-criteria. Each of these criteria has a box that appears when the cursor of the computer hovers over it in which appears the relevant provisions in the standards.

The second part is the self-assessment section, which is further divided into two parts: a simple yes/no response and a summary of the comments provided by the Government and organizations of employers and workers. In the responses to the OSH survey, the comments section often contained very useful information concerning the implementation of the standards in national law and practice.

The third part is the inclusion of relevant provisions in national law. In some cases, the survey responses provided this information. However, for the majority of countries, it was necessary to analyse national laws and regulations in relation to the criteria with the help of NATLEX, information in the article 22 files,[13] comparative analyses done by the *Normes* Department as well as national legislative and other websites. Where a provision in national law corresponds in whole or in

---

[11] See Appendix 2 for the list of instruments and provisions related to these sub-criteria.

[12] The grid is presented as it is intended to be viewed in its final version. A much simpler grid, without the links, was used for OSH in order to ensure that it was placed on the web without extra delay.

[13] States who have ratified Conventions are obliged to send in reports on their application in national law and practice under article 22 of the ILO Constitution.

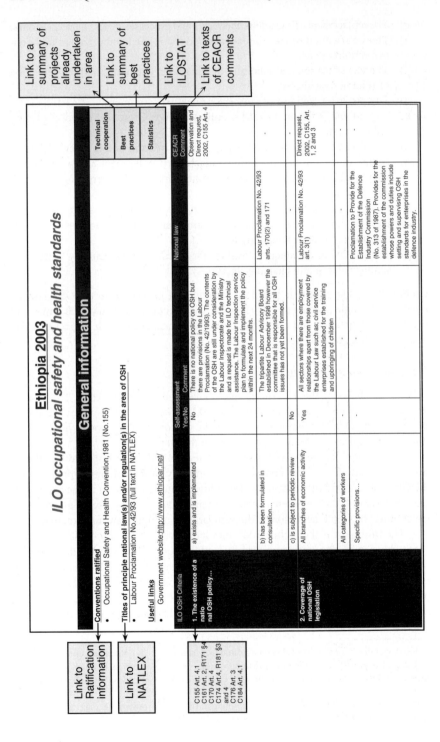

Link to a summary of projects already undertaken in area

Link to summary of best practices

Link to ILOSTAT

Link to texts of CEACR comments

Link to Ratification information

Link to NATLEX

Ethiopia 2003

ILO occupational safety and health standards

General information

	Technical cooperation
	Best practices
	Statistics

Conventions ratified
- Occupational Safety and Health Convention, 1981 (No.155)

Titles of principle national law(s) and/or regulation(s) in the area of OSH
- Labour Proclamation No.42/93 (full text in NATLEX)

Useful links
- Government website:http://www.ethiopar.net/

ILO OSH Criteria		Self-assessment Yes/No	Comment	National law	CEACR Comment
1. The existence of a natio nal OSH policy…	a) exists and is implemented	No	There is no national policy on OSH but there are provisions in the Labour Proclamation (No. 42/1993). The contents of the OSH are still under consideration by the Labour Inspectorate and the Ministry and a request is made for ILO technical assistance. The Labour Inspection service plan to formulate and implement the policy within the next 24 months.		Observation and Direct request, 2002, C155 Art. 4
	b) has been formulated in consultation….	-	The tripartite Labour Advisory Board established in December 1998 however the committee that is responsible for all OSH issues has not yet been formed.	Labour Proclamation No. 42/93 arts. 170(2) and 171	-
	c) is subject to periodic review	No			-
2. Coverage of national OSH legislation	All branches of economic activity	Yes	All sectors where there are employment relationships apart from those covered by the Labour Law such as; civil service enterprises established for the training and upbringing of children	Labour Proclamation No. 42/93 art. 3(1)	Direct request, 2002, C155, Art. 1, 2 and 3
	All categories of workers	-			-
	Specific provisions…	-		Proclamation to Provide for the Establishment of the Defence Industry Commission (No. 313 of 1987). Provides for the establishment of the commission whose powers and duties include setting and supervising OSH standards for enterprises in the defence industry.	

C155 Art. 4.1
C161 Art. 2, R171 §4
C170 Art. 4
C174 Art. 4, R181 §3 and 4
C176 Art. 3
C184 Art. 4.1

part to the criteria, it was noted in this section. If it corresponds only in part, reference to the provision is often followed by the text of the provision. As the criteria may relate to a number of Articles and Paragraphs, the provisions in national law do not always correspond to the exact wording in the instruments.

The CEACR is the competent body for assessing the extent to which member States have respected their obligations under the ratified Conventions. This assessment is articulated in observations and direct requests. These comments make up the fourth part of the grid. A note is made when a country has received one of these along with the Convention and the Article to which it corresponds. The grid provides a link for the reader to go back and read the text of the observation.[14] Although this source of information is limited to countries that have ratified one or more Conventions in the subject area, the information is very useful, in particular as the CEACR often highlights problems in the application of standards or cases where progress has been made. This adds to the overall snapshot of the national situation.

General information is gathered at the top of the profile letting the reader know the Conventions that have been ratified (with a link to the ratification information given on ILOLEX) the titles of up-to-date national laws and regulations (with a link to NATLEX or the relevant national legislative website) and a list of useful websites if the reader wants to get further information from the competent authorities, OSH specialist organizations or other relevant organizations.

This standards-based examination of the de jure national situation is intended to be complemented with links to other information, such as summaries of the technical cooperation activities undertaken by the ILO in this area and their results as well as summaries of best practices, and a link to relevant statistical information available within the ILO.

In the case of OSH, for example, a number of quantitative indicators have been examined (e.g. the number of prosecutions for violations of the law, the number of inspections undertaken, the number of fatal accidents at the workplace etc.). The most frequently used is the number of accidents and deaths at work. It should be kept in mind, however, that while countries often have differing calculation methods for the data, very few developing countries have comprehensive statistical data. This information could be used to complement the qualitative information gathered concerning the legal situation.

2.6. Migrant Workers

As stated above, the range of instruments examined in the context of the integrated approach to migrant workers, was much smaller than for OSH. As with OSH, an in-depth analysis of the four comprehensive instruments and other relevant instruments (ILO as well as UN instruments) was undertaken, as well as an examination of standards-related activities. From this analysis, a draft grid for migrant workers has been established containing normative indicators corresponding to the main principles in relevant instruments.[15]

---

[14] Full texts of the CEACR observations can be found in the ILOLEX website: http://www.ilo.org/ilolex/english/index.htm

[15] Appendix 3.

In comparison to OSH, a different approach was taken concerning the formulation of the survey. Even though standards were taken into account, they were not the only consideration. Instead of being a pure reflection of the standards, questions were formulated in order to obtain information on a broad range of subjects in law and practice, as well as economic and statistical data.

While the survey was not designed to be a "check-list" for States to see whether they implemented the standards or not, as was done for OSH, the responses received provided adequate information that can be used to fill up the grid. A project to create country profiles for the constituents that sent in replies is currently underway, although it will take a little more time to sort through and reformulate the information compared to OSH due to the different approaches taken with respect to the formulation of the migrant worker survey.

2.7. Indicators of Progress Towards Decent Work

The importance role standards have to play in achieving decent work has been highlighted above. Standards provide the framework upon which member States can evaluate their progress towards decent work for all workers. The future goal is to apply the same method used for OSH and migrant workers to all areas in order to establish specific criteria for each subject. These criteria would then make up a group of indicators (or sub-indicators), which would give a global overview of the national situation in a given country with respect to the principles contained in ILO standards.

However, given that each subject may contain a large number of criteria, it would be unrealistic to include all these in the decent work indicators. The criteria in each subject would have to be examined and distilled to establish a set of "supreme" indicators. This should also be backed up by an in-depth analysis of all the standards, as was done for OSH, to identify principles that repeat in a number of Conventions (e.g. the obligation of member States to consult with employers' and workers' organizations).

To illustrate this idea, take the example of a car that is put into the garage to undergo a technical control in order to be registered. In order to give an overall diagnostic of the car, each aspect of the car has to be tested in detail to see whether it passes the criteria set out by the Ministry of Transport. The mechanic will test the safety mechanisms (safety belt, brakes, etc.), the motor (oil, water, radiator, transmission etc.), pollution levels and so on. When the owner comes back at the end of the day to get the car, they will have a list of either minor or major repairs that need to be done. Depending on the cost and inconvenience of the work to be done and his/her resources, the owner will then have to give priorities as to what to do first. In case a part needs to be replaced or repaired, the garage will in stock or will order the precise part for the car in question. On the other hand, they may be handed a clean bill of health for the car and immediately have it registered as a "decent" car.

In the same sense, at the end of the day, a member State will have a full diagnostic of the main aspects of its legislative system based on the criteria of the international labour standards. This diagnostic will give them an idea of where gaps and lacunae exist as well as areas where there are no immediate problems for each subject as well as globally. From this, they will be able to design and implement a national program for the progressive implementation and the possible ratification of ILO standards according to their priorities and resources, thus ensuring the universal application of decent work.

3. Hurdles in Developing the Normative Indicators and Country Profiles

3.1. Basing the Criteria on Standards

National and international opinions and policies change and the ILO standards may become out-of-date or be in need of revision. This puts into question the validity of some or all of the normative indicators chosen as criteria, and the process of deciding what criteria to use will have to be started all over again. Nevertheless, by keeping the criteria as general and universal as possible, it is hoped that this risk has been diminished to a minimum. In addition, experience has shown in the past that international labour standards have a long shelf life and continue to be valid many years after they have been adopted.

Another aspect to take into account is how to address new instruments adopted in the subject area? This may imply that new criteria will need to be created in order to address a new principle introduced in the subject through the instrument. However, the criteria have to be seen as flexible and able to take into account changes in both national and international laws and practices. If not then the country profiles will become only a snapshot of the situation of a country at a certain time in its existence and will soon outrun its usefulness.

3.2. Information Sources

Concerning the collection of information on law and practice related to international labour standards, it should be recalled that the ILO Constitution provides for certain tools. Pursuant to Article 22 of the Constitution, member States are invited to submit reports on a regular basis to the Office on the application of the ratified conventions. In accordance with Article 19, they can – at appropriate intervals as requested by the Governing Body – be called upon to report on the position of their law and practice in regard to the matters dealt with in non-ratified conventions or recommendations. Moreover, pursuant to Article 10, the Office is empowered to collect and disseminate information relating to the international regulation of "industrial life and labour". But most of the time the information received needs to be completed.

As with any project where research needs to be done on national laws, the problem of accessibility to those laws arises. Despite the large number of countries that now have national laws on-line, there are still many, mainly developing countries, that do not. Where no information is available from other sources such as NATLEX, this makes examining the national legislative situation very difficult.

In addition, where texts of the laws can be obtained, these are often in languages not understood by those analysing them and need to be translated before they can be examined. This again poses the problem of resources. In some cases, unofficial translations are available, however using these may put into question the reliability of the data in the profile.

Despite the best efforts in finding the latest information, in some cases the law examined is not the most up-to-date. To diminish the risks of this, a request could be sent out to member States to check their profile before it goes on-line to ensure that the laws and regulations noted under general information are the most recent.

Finally, in certain cases the information is so complex that it takes a lot of time to sort through and come up with a comprehensive country profile. This is the case, in particular, for federal States where the subject area is regulated either at a state, regional, territorial or provincial level. The examination of such countries may take up to ten times longer as each state has to be dealt with individually. This is also the case for countries that have a complex legal system, where there is no general law and instead, the subject area is regulated by a large number of legislative texts. However, the above problems affect the time it takes to complete a profile rather than the quality of the profile once finished.

3.3. Up-dating the Information

In order for the country profiles to be of use beyond the few years following their examination, they will need to be up-dated regularly. This means resources and time will need to be spent in going through and up-dating each country profile.

A number of possibilities exist to make this easier. It is important that dialogue between the constituents and the ILO be maintained to ensure that all changes in national law and practice are notified to the Office. In addition, it would be necessary to establish a network comprised of standards specialists in the field and at headquarters, as well as technical ILO and national experts in the different subject areas. This network of specialists and experts would need to be dedicated to watching out for and analysing the most up-to-date information received from constituents, up-dating the country profiles on subjects that have already been dealt with and implementing the methodology for other subjects.

4. Uses of Normative Indicators

4.1. Snapshot of the National Situation

The main objective of the country profiles based on normative indicators is to allow member States and the Office to obtain an overview of the national situation with respect to international labour standards in a given subject area and identify areas where there are gaps in the application of the principles behind decent work.

For member States, this analysis can be used to formulate and implement a national program for the progressive implementation of the principles in certain areas (as discussed above under section 2.7). The ILO technical departments can use this information to effectively target technical cooperation activities and resources towards those countries most in need.

These indicators also provide a tool to measure the progress each member State has made over time in the implementation of international labour standards through national laws and practices. This assists both member States in implementing and the Office in promoting the standards.

Finally, the normative indicators could be used as a vehicle to gather information on and to highlight best practices in certain countries and make this available to all constituents, conclusions that were drawn from both the general discussion held on OSH (ILO, 2003)[16] and migrant workers (ILO, 2004).[17]

4.2. Promotion of ILO Standards

The country profiles based on normative indicators serve as a promotional tool for the international labour standards concerning not only their ratification but also their implementation. The OSH survey questions used to gather information for the profiles also act as a type of "checklist" for countries. After completion of the survey, countries that have not ratified are able to assess whether they already apply the main components of standards and if they do, they may decide to ratify the relevant Conventions in the subject area. It also allows for the identification of the obstacles to ratification and may encourage member States to make moves to overcome these obstacles and to ratify the Conventions.

4.3. Information Gathering

The country profiles are designed to gather all available up-to-date national legislative and other relevant information, which correspond to a set of criteria based on ILO standards, for each ILO member State. This information has been put on the internet in order to make it available to a wide range of end-users.[18]

The synthetic nature of the country profiles assists those dealing with the supervision of ILO Conventions, saving time researching for information and laws, providing a quick overview of the country situation, showing progress in application when looked at over time or pointing out continuing application problems.

4.4. Qualitative or Quantitative Indicators?

On the basis of the yes/no responses to the survey, it is possible to rank member States according to those that are "good" or "bad". However, doing so would only give a partial and not completely accurate appreciation of the national situation in comparison to other countries. When responding to the survey, member States

---

[16] ILO, *Conclusions concerning ILO Standards-Related Activities in the Area of Occupational Safety and Health – A Global Strategy*, Report of the Committee on Occupational Safety and Health, Provisional Record 22, Record of Proceedings Vol. II, ILC, 91st Session, Geneva 2003, para. 17.

[17] ILO, Conclusions on a Fair Deal for Migrant Workers in a Global Economy, Report of the Committee on Migrant Workers, Provisional Record 22, Record of Proceedings Vol. II, ILC, 91st Session, Geneva 2003, paras. 31 and 33.

[18] http://www.ilo.org/ilolex/english/profileframeE.htm

interpreted the questions more or less strictly. In addition, a number of countries did not respond to all questions. It also does not take into account the fact that application may be good in one area and not in another. Such an analysis would also not take into account the differing economic situations and levels of development within countries. The subjects being addressed are also so broad that more detailed information is needed to fully appreciate the national situation, hence the inclusion of comments from governments, employers' and workers' organizations, national laws, comments from the CEACR as well as other relevant information.

As mentioned in the introduction, standards provide an authoritative answer to defining what decent work is, i.e. they provide a level normative playing field upon which countries can assess themselves. The indicators in the country profiles are based on international labour standards, which fix the objectives that member States should strive to obtain to implement the decent work agenda. The purpose behind the country profiles is the universal implementation of the decent work agenda through national programs adapted to each country's needs as developed by the countries concerned either with or without the assistance of the ILO. They are a self-help tool for member States as well as a tool for the Office to identify gaps so that it can better target technical cooperation and help ILO officials by creating a simple and uniform information base.

To achieve these objectives, the country profiles based on normative indicators contain two types of information. They can be used by member States and the Office to note the progress made towards implementing the decent work agenda in a specific country from one point in time with another. In addition, they provide a detailed appreciation of the national situation with respect to how the indicators are implemented as well as identifying gaps, best practices and possible obstacles. This provides the vital information required to come up with solutions showing how better to go forward towards a workplace where decent work is the central pillar.

In view of the above, using the country profiles based on normative indicators as a ranking system could defeat their purpose, which is the promotion and progressive implementation of the standards. Finally given the complex nature of the standards, if the normative indicators are meant to analyse the legal situation in a country with respect to the objectives outlined in the standards, then the result can only be qualitative and not quantitative.

MONIQUE ZARKA-MARTRES,
International Labour Office

MONIQUE GUICHARD-KELLY,
International Labour Office Consultant

Appendix 1. Example of In-depth Analysis of OSH Conventions and Recommendations.

	General standards		Protection against specific risks						Protection in specific branches of activity				Conventions to-be-revised			
	General	Health services	Radiation	Cancer	Air, noise	Asbestos	Chemicals	Hazard Installations	Offices	Construction	Mines	Agriculture	Benzene	White lead	Machinery	Manual loads
Convention No.	155	161	115	139	148	162	170	174	120	167	176	184	136	13	119	127
Recommendation No.	164	171	114	147	156	172	177	181	120	175	183	192	144		118	128

Infrastructures

Inspection systems

Labour Inspection Convention, 1947 (No. 81) and its Protocol of 1995 to the Labour Inspection Convention, 1947 set out labour inspection requirements including the following:

Article 1:

Each member of the International Labour Organization for which this Convention is in force shall maintain a system of labour inspection in industrial workplaces.

Establishment of a system of labour inspection, scope (to industrial, commercial and other workplaces) and exemptions from scope. It lists the functions of inspection (enforcement of legal provisions, supply of technical information and advices to employers and bringing defects or abuses not covered by existing legal provisions, to the attention of the CA etc). Where possible, the service shall be controlled by a central authority and staff shall be properly qualified and trained and be assured of employment stability and are independent to external changes in the

(Continued)

Appendix 1. Example of in-depth analysis of OSH Conventions and Recommendations. — Cont'd.

	General standards		Protection against specific risks						Protection in specific branches of activity				Conventions to-be-revised			
Convention No.	155	161	115	139	148	162	170	174	120	167	176	184	136	13	119	127
Recommendation No.	164	171	114	147	156	172	177	181	120	175	183	192	144	118	128	

government and have no direct or indirect interest in the undertakings and have to guard confidential information. The number of inspectors should be sufficient and they should be supplied with adequate resources. They are empowered to enter work premises without notice, carry out tests, examinations and enquiries, interrogate the employer or staff, access to information, enforce the posting of notices and remove samples. They must notify the employer or representative of their presence. They can take immediate steps to remedy defects, to make orders requiring alternations if necessary with immediate effect. They are to be notified of accidents and diseases. Workplaces are to be inspected as often and as thoroughly as necessary. Persons who violate legal provisions are liable to prompt legal proceedings; warning and advice on violations from the inspector may be given instead. Inspectors have reporting requirements and the central inspection authority is to publish an annual report (contents of the report are given).

Labour Inspection (Agriculture) Convention, 1969 (No. 129) [C81 adapted to agriculture]

National laws and regulations shall provide for an adequate and appropriate system of inspection — 9.1 (General standards); 5.1 (Protection against specific risks); 6.1 and 5.1 (Protection in specific branches of activity)

Provision	References
The member shall ('undertakes to . . .) provide inspection services for the work place	15* and R 114§ 25 · 6(c)* and R 147 § 22(c) · 16(b) · 5.1 · 14 (c)* & R 144 § 25(c) · 15.2*
The system of inspection provided for in Paragraph 1 of Article 9 of the Convention should be guided by the provisions of the Labour Inspection Convention, 1947, and the Labour Inspection (Agriculture) Convention, 1969. without prejudice to the obligations thereunder of members which have ratified these instruments.	R164 § 5
National laws or regulations shall designate the authority or authorities responsible both for supervising the operation of and for advising occupational health services once they are established	16
The system of inspection provided for in Article 5 of the Asbestos Convention, 1986, should be based on the provisions of the Labour Inspection Convention, 1947. Inspection should be carried out by qualified personnel. The inspection services should be able to obtain from the employer the information referred to in Paragraph 13 above.	R 172 § 21
The competent authority shall have properly qualified and trained staff with the appropriate skills, and sufficient technical and professional support, to inspect, investigate, assess, and advise on the matters dealt with in this Convention and to ensure compliance with national laws and regulations.	18.1
Appropriate measures should be taken, by adequate inspection or other means, to ensure the proper application of laws, regulations or other provisions concerning hygiene	R120 § 83

(Continued)

Appendix 1. Example of in-depth analysis of OSH Conventions and Recommendations. — Cont'd.

	General standards		Protection against specific risks						Protection in specific branches of activity				Conventions to-be-revised			
Convention No.	155	161	115	139	148	162	170	174	120	167	176	184	136	13	119	127
Recommendation No.	164	171	114	147	156	172	177	181	120	175	183	192	144		118	128
Each member shall provide appropriate inspection services to supervise the application of the measures to be taken in pursuance of the Convention and provide these services with the resources necessary for the accomplishment of their task or satisfy itself that appropriate inspection is carried out.									35(b)	16(b)						
Competent persons shall inspect the work place									14.4, 15.1 (d), 17.3, 20.3							
National laws and regulations shall provide for supervision of safety and health in mines											5.2(a) and R183 § 6					

Appendix 2. Thematic Index to the Provisions in the Instruments at Issue.

| Key to the abbreviations in column 4 | C: | Convention |
| | R: | Recommendation |

For the full text of these instruments, please consult the web site www.ilo.org

Grid for OSH

ILO OSH criteria	Subcriteria	Relevant provisions in instruments
1. The existence of a national OSH policy formulated, implemented and reviewed on a tripartite basis	A national OSH policy: (a) Exists and is implemented	C155 Art 4.1 C161 Art 2, R171 Para. 1 C170 Art 4 C174 Art 4, R181 Paras. 3 and 4 C176 Art 3 C184 Art 4.1
	(b) Has been formulated in consultation with the most representative Employers' and Workers' organizations	C155 Art 4.1 C161 Art 2 C170 Art 4 C174 Art 4.1 C176 Art 3 C184 Art 4.1
	(c) Is subject to periodic review	C155 Art 4.1 and 7 C161 Art 2 C162 Art 3.2 C167 Art 5.2 C170 Art 4 C174 Art 4 C176 Art 3 C184 Art 4.1 R164 Para. 4(b) and 19(a)
2. Coverage of national OSH legislation	National OSH legislation covers all branches of economic activity	C119 Art 17.1 C127 Art 2.2 C148 Art 1.1 C155 Art 1.1 C161 Art 3.1
	National OSH legislation covers all categories of workers	C155 Art 2.1 C161 Art 3.1
	Existence of exclusions from the application of OSH provisions in whole or in part of branches of economic activity, or of specific categories of workers	C120 Art 2 C148 Art 1.2 C155 Art 1.2 C162 Art 1.2 C167 Art 1.2 C170 Art 1.2(a) C174 Art 1.4 C176 Art 2.2(a) C184 Art 3.1(a)

(Continued)

Appendix 2. Thematic Index to the Provisions in the Instruments
at Issue. — Cont'd.

ILO OSH criteria	Subcriteria	Relevant provisions in instruments
	National OSH legislation includes provisions applicable to the following branches of economic activity:	
	(a) Construction	C167
	(b) Commerce and offices	C120
	(c) Agriculture	C184
	(d) Mines	C176
		C45
	(e) Major hazard installations	C174
	National OSH legislation includes provisions concerning the following occupational hazards:	
	(a) Air pollution	C148 Art 2.1
	(b) Noise	
	(c) Vibration	
	(d) Ionising radiations	C115
	(e) Chemicals	C170
	(f) Carcinogenic substances and agents	C139
	(g) Asbestos	C162
	(h) Benzene and products of benzene	C136
	(i) Lead	C13
	(j) Machinery	C119
	(k) Manual lifting	C127
3. Existence of national preventive and protective OSH measures	Existence of technical OSH rules and measures including in relation to:	
	(a) The identification and determination of occupational hazards	C139 Art 1
		C148 Art 8.1
		C155 Art 7 and 11(b)
		C161 Art 5(a)
		C170 Art 10
		C174 Art 5, 7 and 9(a)
		C176 Art 7(e)
	(b) The prohibition, limitation or other means of control of exposure	C139 Art 1.1 and 1.3
		C155 Art 11(b)
		C162 Art 9
	(c) The assessment of risks and levels of exposure	C155 Art 11(f)
		C161 Art 5(a)
		C170 Art 13.1
		C174 Art 9(a)
		C176 Art 6 and 7(e)
		C184 Art 7(a)

Appendix 2. — Cont'd.

(d) Prohibition or limitation of use of hazardous processes, machinery and equipment and hazardous chemical, physical and biological agents	C13 Art 1.1 C119 Art 2.1 C136 Art 4.1 C148 Art 12 C162 Arts 10(b), 11.1 and 12.1
(e) The specification of exposure limits and related criteria including periodic revision and updating of exposure limits	C115 Art 5–8 and R114 Para. 4 C139 Art 2.2 C136 Art 6.2, 8.2 and 11.2 C13 Art 1.2 and 2 C148 Art 8 C162 Art 15.1 C170 Art 6 and 12(a)
(f) The surveillance and monitoring of the working environment	C115 Art 11 C136 Art 6.3 C161 Art 5(b) and R171 Art 5–10
(g) The replacement of hazardous chemicals and processes by less hazardous ones	C136 Art 2.1 C139 Art 2 C162 Art 10(a) C170 Art 13.1(a) R164 Para. 3(h)
(h) The notification of hazardous work and the related authorization and control requirements	C139 Art 1 C148 Art 12 C155 Art 11(b) C162 Arts 9, 13 and 17 C170 Art 5 C174 Art 8
(i) The classification and labelling of hazardous chemicals andthe provision of related datasheets	C115 Art 9.1 C136 Art 12 C170 Arts 6, 8, 10–11 C184 Art 12(a) R164 Para. 3(h)
(j) The provision and use of personal protective equipment	C13 Arts 5II (b) and (c) C120 Art 17 C136 Art 8.1 C148 Art 10 C155 Art 16.3 C162 Arts 15.4 and 18 C167 Arts 28(2) and 30 C170 Art 13.1(f) C174 Art 9(c) C176 Arts 5(b), 6(d) and 9(c) R164 Para. 3(n) and 10(e)

(Continued)

Appendix 2. Thematic Index to the Provisions in the Instruments
at Issue. — Cont'd.

ILO OSH criteria	Subcriteria	Relevant provisions in instruments
	(k) Safe methods for the handling, collection, recycling and disposal of hazardous waste	C162 Arts 17.2(c), 19 C170 Art 14 C167 Art 28.4 C184 Arts 12(c) and 13 R164 Para. 3(h)
	(l) Working time arrangements (such as hours of work and rest periods)	C148 Arts 9(b) and R156 Para. 13 C155 Art 5(b) C184 Art 20
	(m) Adaptation of work installations, machinery, equipment and processes to the physical and mental capacities of the workers, taking ergonomic factors into account?	C155 Art 5(b) C161 Arts 5(e), (g) and (i)
	(n) Design, construction, layout and maintenance of work-places and installations	C155 Arts 5(a) and 11(a) C148 Art 9(a) C161 Art 5(c) R164 Para. 3(a)
	(o) Design, construction, layout, use, maintenance, testing and inspection of machinery, tools and equipment	C119 Part III C155 Art 5(a) C167 Arts 15–17 and 30(3) C184 Arts 9 and 10 R156 Paras. 8, 9 and 11 R164 Para. 3(d)
	(p) The provision of adequate welfare facilities (such as drinking water and sanitary eating and changing facilities)	C13 Art 5II(a) C120 Arts 12 and 13 C162 Art 18.5 C167 Art 32 C170 Art 13.1(e) C176 Art 5.4(e) C184 Art 19(a) R102 Paras. 4–15, 18–20, 23(a), 24, 25(a) and 26–28 R115 Paras. 7(b) and (c), 8(c), (d) and (f) R164 Para. 3(o)
4. Existence of national OSH infrastructures	Existence of: (a) Competent authority(ies) responsible for OSH (b) A system of inspection	 C176 Art 5.1 C184 Art 4.2(a) C81 Arts 1, 3–31

Appendix 2. — Cont'd.

	C115 Art 15
	C120 Art 6.1
	C129 Arts 3, 6–27
	C139 Art.6(c)
	C148 Art 16(b)
	C155 Art 9.1
	C162 Art 5.1
	C167 Arts 14.4, 15.1(d),
	17.3, 20.3 and 35(b)
	C176 Arts 5.2(a), (b), 16(b)
	C184 Arts 5.1 and 5.2
(c) Occupational health services	C161 Arts 3.2, 5 and 16
	R171 Para. 8–10
(d) Equipped with qualified	C81 Art 7
and trained staff	C115 Art 13(c)
	C129 Art 9
	C155 Art 5(c)
	C161 Art 11, R171 Para. 36
	C174 Art 18.1
	R183 Para. 4
	R144 Para. 17
	R97 Para. 11
	R31 Para. 14
(e) To establish measures for the	C115 Art 3.2
dissemination and provision	C127 Art 5
of information on OSH	C136 Art 13
matters	C139 Art 4
	R147 Paras. 15–21
	C148 Art 13
	R156 Paras. 21–25
	C162 Art 22
	C167 Art 33(b)
	C174 Art 16
	R183 Paras. 5(a), 19 and 31
	C184 Arts 9.2 and 12(b),
	R192 Para. 8
(f) To establish measures for	C13 Art 5.IV
training and education on	C115 Art 9.2
OSH matters	C148 Arts 7.2
	R156 Paras. 21–25
	C155 Arts 10, 14
	R164 Para. 4
	C161 Arts 5(d) and (i)
	C162 Art 22
	C167 Art 33(b), R175
	Paras. 6, 29, 30, 44 and 40
	C174 Art 20(d)

(*Continued*)

Appendix 2. Thematic Index to the Provisions in the Instruments
at Issue. — Cont'd.

ILO OSH criteria	Subcriteria	Relevant provisions in instruments
		R128 Paras. 5–6
		R147 Paras. 12–21
		R177 Para. 26
		R183 Para. 28
		R192 Paras. 3 and 5
5. Notification and recording of occupational accidents and diseases	The existence of measures for the recording and notification of occupational accidents and diseases including:	
	(a) The establishment and keeping of records of occupationalaccidents and diseases	C162 Art 20
		C170 Art 12(d)
		R164 Para. 15(2)
		R172 Para. 6
		R147 Para. 15
		R172 Paras. 36 and 38
	(b) Notification of occupational accidents and diseases to the competent authorities	C115 Art 13(b)
		C155 Art 11(c)
		C161 Arts 14 and 15
		C167 Art 24
		C162 Art 21.5
		C174 Art 13
		C176 Arts 5.2(c) and 13.1(a)
	(c) Investigation into occupational accidents and diseases	C155 Art 11(d)
		C161 Art 5(k)
		C174 Art 14
		C176 Arts 5.2(c) and 10(e)
	(d) Compilation and periodic publication of statistics on occupational accidents and diseases	C13 Art 7(a)
		C176 Art 5.2(d)
6. Occupational health	Existence of national mechanisms and/or measures:	
	(a) For health surveillance	C161 Art 5(f)
		R171 Para. 11–18
		C162 Part IV, R172 Part IV
		C176 Art 11
		R183 Para. 24
		R164 Para. 3(r)
		R147 Part III
		R156 Part III
		R177 Para. 18
		R192 Para. 4

Appendix 2. — Cont'd.

	(b) For regular medical examinations	C13 Art 5.III(b) C115 Arts 12 and 13 R114 Part VI C136 Arts 9.1 and 10 R144 Para. 15 C139 Art 5, R147 Paras. 11–13 C148 Art 11 R156 Paras. 16–17 C162 Art 21 R128 Part IV R177 Para. 18 R183 Para. 24
	(c) The provision of first aid and emergency treatment	C120 Art 19 R120 Part XVII C155 Art 18 R164 Para. 3(p) C161 Art 5(j), R171 Paras. 23–26 C167 Art 31 R175 Paras. 49–50 C176 Arts 5.4(a), 9(d) C170 Art 13.2(b) R177 Para. 19 R192 Para. 8
	(d) Emergency preparedness and rescue	C115 Art 13 C174 Arts 15–16 R164 Para. 3(q), 4(e) C167 Art 23(b) C176 Art 5.4(a)
7. Existence of measures for consultation, cooperation and communication at all levels	Measures to ensure consultation, cooperation and coordination on OSH between: (a) The various competent authorities and services?	C155 Arts 5(d), 15.1 C161 Art 9.3 C174 Art 16(c) C184 Art 4.2(c)
	(b) The competent authorities and employers' and workers' organizations?	C148 Art 5.1 C161 Art 4, 6(c) C162 Art 3.3, 4, 11.2, 12.2, 22.1 C167 Art 3 C170 Art 3 C174 Art 5, 6 C176 Art 13.3(b) C184 Arts 8.4, 11.1, 16.2, 19
	(c) The employers and workers and their representatives within the enterprise	C148 Art 5.3 C155 Arts 19(e) and 20 C161 Art 8

(Continued)

Appendix 2. Thematic Index to the Provisions in the Instruments
at Issue. — Cont'd.

ILO OSH criteria	Subcriteria	Relevant provisions in instruments
		C162 Arts 6.3, 8, 17.3 and 18.1 C167 Art 6 and 7 C170 Art 16 C174 Art 9(f), 20 C176 Art 5.2(f), 13 and 15 C184 Art 14
8. Existence of enforcement mechanisms	Existence of mechanisms for the imposition of appropriate penalties in cases of infringement of laws and regulations	C81 Art 18 C129 Art 24 C148 Art 16(a) C155 Art 9.1 C162 Art 5.2 C167 Art 35(a) C176 Art 16(a) C184 Art 4.3
	Empowerment of the competent authorities to suspend, restrict or prohibit work where there is a serious threat to the health and safety of workers, until appropriate corrective measures have been implemented?	C148 Art 12 C170 Art 5 C174 Art 19 C176 Art 5.2(e) C184 Art 4.3
9. Employer responsibilities	Employer responsibilities include: (a) Establishment of OSH policies and procedures to implement the preventive and protective measures prescribed by national law and practice	 C162 Art 17.2 C174 Arts 9–12 C176 Arts 5.5 and 7(g) R164 Para. 14
	(b) Monitoring and inspection of the workplace, processes, machinery, tools equipment and other material elements of work	C162 Art 20 C170 Arts 12(c) and (d) C176 Arts 7(e) and 10(b) R164 Para. 10(c) and 15.1
	(c) Establishment of emergency response plans and procedures	C155 Art 18 C162 Art 6.3 C170 Art 13.2(c) C174 Art 9(d) C176 Art 8
	(d) Provision of information to workers and their representatives concerning occupational hazards	C119 Art 10.1 C162 Art 22.3 C170 Arts 10.1, 10.4 and 15(a) C176 Art 9(a) C184 Art 9.3

Appendix 2. — Cont'd.

	(e) Education and training of workers	C155 Art 19(d) C162 Art 22.3 C170 Art 15(d) C176 Art 10(a) C184 Art 7(b)
	(f) Taking of appropriate remedial action after any accident	C115 Art 13(d) C155 Art 19(f) C167 Art 12.2 C174 Art 9(e) C176 Arts 7(i) and 10(d) C184 Art 7(c)
	(g) Establishment of a mechanism for consultation and cooperation on OSH matters between employers where there is more than one employer in a workplace or work site	C148 Art 6.2 C155 Art 17 C162 Art 6.2 C167 Art 8.1 and 8.2 C176 Art 12 C184 Art 6.2
10. Workers' rights and responsibilities	Workers rights and responsibilities include:	
	(a) Access to information relevant to OSH held by the competent authorities and the employer	C148 Art 7.2 C162 Art 20.3 C170 Art 18.3 C174 Art 20(c) C176 Art 13.1(d)
	(b) Being kept informed on workplace hazards and consulted on related OSH measures	C115 Art 9.1 C161 Art 13 C162 Art 21.3 C167 Art 33(a) C174 Art 20(a) and (b) C176 Art 13.1(c) C184 Art 8.1(a)
	(c) Participation in inspection and monitoring activities and the review of OSH measures	C162 Art 20.4 C167 Art 10 C176 Arts 13.1(b), 13.2(b) and (i) C184 Art 8.1(b)
	(d) Selection of a worker safety representative	C176 Art 13.1(f) C184 Art 8.1(b)
	(e) Removing themselves from danger in case of imminent and serious risk to their health	C155 Art 19(f) C167 Art 12.1 C170 Art 18.1 C174 Art 20(e) C176 Art 13(e) C184 Art 8.1(c)
	(f) Being protected from disciplinary measures due to actions taken in accordance with OSH requirements	C155 Arts 5(e) and 13 C170 Art 18.2 C174 Art 20(e) C184 Art 8.1(c)

(Continued)

Appendix 2. Thematic Index to the Provisions in the Instruments
at Issue. — Cont'd.

ILO OSH criteria	Subcriteria	Relevant provisions in instruments
	(g) Incurring no personal cost for the implementation of OSH measures including training and the provisions of personal protective equipment	C136 Art 10.2 C148 Art 11.2 C155 Art 21 C162 Arts 15.4 and 21.2 C176 Arts 9(c) and 10(a)
	(h) Cooperation with the employer and compliance with OSH measures	C148 Art 7.1 C155 Art 19(a) C162 Art 7 C170 Art 17.1 C174 Art 21 C184 Art 8.2
	(i) Taking reasonable care of their personal safety and that of others in the workplace	C119 Art 11 C127 Art 3 C167 Art 11(b) C170 Art 17.2 C176 Art 14(b)
	(j) Making proper use of personal protective equipment	C119 Art11 C167 Arts 11(c) and 30.4 R164 Para. 16(c)
	(k) Immediate reporting to the supervisor of any situation presenting a threat to safety	C155 Art 19(f) C170 Art 18(1) C174 Art20(e) C176 Art 14(c)
11. Workers' representatives rights and responsibilities	Rights and responsibilities of workers' representatives include:	
	(a) Consultation on OSH matters with the employer	C155 Arts 19(c) and (e) C162 Art 17.3 C174 Art 20(c) C176 Arts 13.2(e) and (d)
	(b) Participation in inspections, monitoring and investigations related to OSH with	C148 Arts 5.4 and 7.2 C161 Art 8 C162 Art 20.4 C174 Art 18.2 C176 Art 13
	(c) Access to information on OSH matters held by the competent authorities and the employer	C148 Art 7.2 C155 Art 19(c) C162 Art 20.3 C170 Art 18.3 C174 Art 20 C176 Art 13.2(f)
	(d) The right to appeal to the competent authorities on OSH matters	C148 Art 7.2 C162 Art 20.4
	(e) Cooperation with the employer on OSH matters	C155 Art 19(b) C184 Art 8.2

Appendix 2. — Cont'd.

12. Responsibilities of designers, producers, importers and suppliers	Responsibilities of designers, producers, importers and suppliers include:	
	(a) Taking into account of safety and health requirements and concerns in the design, production, importation, supply and disposal processes	C119 Art 2.3, 2.4 C155 Art. 12(a) C167 Art 9
	(b) Adequate labelling and marking of products	C162 Art 14 C170 Arts 9.1(a) and (c)
	(c) Making available to the user of adequate safety and health information on their products	C155 Art 12(b) C170 Arts 9.1(d) and 9.2 C184 Art 9.2

Appendix 3. Grid for Migrant Worker Country Profile.

ILO migrant worker criteria	Subcriteria	Relevant provisions in instruments
1. Providing assistance in the migration process	Provision of information to migrant workers	C97 Art 2, Annex I Art 5.1(c) and Annex II Art 6.1(c) and R86 Para. 5; C143 Art 12(c) R151 Para. 7; C169 Art 20.3(a) R164, Para. 4(d); R188 Para. 8(b)
	Measures to facilitate the departure, journey, reception and return of migrant workers	C97 Art 4, Annex I, Art 6(c) R86 Paras. 1, 10 and 20; C110 Art 18; C168 Art 26(i)
	Medical services for and prevention of health risks to migrant workers and members of their family	C97 Art 5 R151 Para. 20; C110 Art 11 and 19
2. Recruitment measures	Regulation of recruitment and placement practices	C97 Art 7, Annex I and II; R86 Paras. 13, 14 and 19;
	Measures against misleading propaganda and fraudulent activities	C97 Art 3; C110 Art 17; C181 Art 8

(Continued)

Appendix 3. Grid for Migrant Worker Country Profile. — Cont'd.

ILO migrant worker criteria	Subcriteria	Relevant provisions in instruments
3. Equality of opportunity and treatment between national and regular migrant workers	Employment conditions (remuneration, hours of work, rest periods, overtime, holidays, homework, minimum age, apprenticeship, vocational training, security of employment and OSH measures)	C97 Art 6.1(a)(i); C143 Arts 8.2 and 10; R151 Para. 2; C100 Art 2; C111 Art 2; C169 Art 20.3
	Trade union membership	C97 Art 6.1(a)(ii); C87 Art 2
	Living conditions (housing, social services, educational institutions and health)	C97 Art 6.1(a)(iii) R151 Para. 2(i); R115 Para. 5
	Social security	C97 Art 6.1(b); C143 Art 10; R151 Para. 2(f); C102 Part XII; C110 Art 52; C121 Art 27; C130 Art. 32
	Keeping of acquired rights and receiving benefits abroad	C143 Art 9.1; R151 Para. 34; C118 Arts 4.1, 5.1 and 6; C157 Parts III and IV; C110 Arts 52–53; R157 Para. 69(b)
	Employment taxes	C97 Art 6.1(c)
	Access to legal proceedings	C97 Art 6.1(d)
	Free choice of employment	C143 Arts 14(a) and (c); R86 Para. 16
	Recognition of professional qualifications	C143 Art 14(b)
4. Guarantees in case of termination of employment	Authorization for migrant worker admitted on a permanent basis to stay in case of incapacity to work	C97 Arts 8.1 and 8.2
	Upon loss of employment migrant workers to be allowed sufficient time to find alternative employment and not to be regarded as illegal or in irregular position	C143 Art 8.1 R151 Para. 31
5. Allowing for the transfer of assets	Allow migrant worker to transfer earnings, savings, personal effects, tools, equipment and capital	C97 Art 9, Annex III R86 Para. 10(d)

Appendix 3. — Cont'd.

6. Family reunification	Facilitating family reunification	C143 Art 13 R86 Para. 15; R151 Paras.13–16
7. Preventing abuses of and protecting migrant workers in an irregular situation	Recognition of fundamental rights for all migrant workers	C143 Art 1
	Equality of treatment in respect of trade union membership for migrant workers in an irregular situation	C87 Art 2 R151 Para. 8.3
	Detection of irregular migration and illegal employment	C143 Arts 2 and 4; C182 Art 8
	Measures suppress manpower trafficking and establishment of sanctions against organisers of trafficking	C143 Arts 3, 5 and 6; C97 Annex I Art 8 and Annex II Art 13; C29 Arts 1 and 25; C105 Arts 1 and 2; C182 Arts 3 and 7
	Measures suppress illegal employment and imposition of appropriate sanctions	C143 Arts 3 and 6
	Migrant workers who face expulsion shall have the right to appeal against order and granted a stay of execution of the expulsion order	C143 Art 9.2 R151 Para. 33
	Cost of expulsion not to be borne by migrant worker	C143 Art 9.3
	Possibility to regularize irregular migrant workers	C143 Art 9.4

Chapter 5

The Quantification of Respect for Selected Core Labour Standards: Towards a Social Development Index ?

LUDO CUYVERS AND DANIEL VAN DEN BULCKE

University of Antwerp

1. Introduction

More and more indices to measure and monitor aspects of economic and social life in different countries have been introduced and are now widely used. One of the first such indices, allowing an international comparison by several organisations, was the Human Development Index of UNDP (UNDP, 2003). Other indices were constructed by academics and consultants in order to measure international competitiveness (e.g. IMD, 2004), economic freedom (Heritage Foundation, 2004), corruption (e.g. for Asia: Political and Economic Risk Consultancy, 2001), comparative purchasing power of currencies (e.g. *The Economist*, 2004), etc. Yet, no such index has been proposed to measure social development vis-à-vis the benchmark of international social standards.

By setting up Recommendations and Conventions, the ILO promotes an international environment for labour and labour conditions which is in accordance with specified international standards and therefore aims to create a level playing field in social competition among nations. Eight fundamental standards of the rights of human beings at the working place have been identified. These standards have to be complied with, irrespective of the levels of development of individual Member States, and are called core labour standards. These core labour standards are:

1. Freedom of Association and Protection of the Right to Organize Convention, 1948 (No. 87), Convention No. 87 for short
2. Right to Organize and Collective Bargaining Convention, 1949 (No. 98), Convention No. 98 for short
3. Forced Labour Convention, 1930 (No. 29), Convention No. 29 for short
4. Abolition of Forced Labour Convention, 1957 (No. 105), Convention No. 105 for short
5. Discrimination (Employment and Occupation) Convention, 1958 (No. 111), Convention No. 111 for short
6. Equal Remuneration Convention, 1951 (No. 100), Convention No. 100 for short
7. Minimum Age Convention, 1973 (No. 138), Convention No. 138 for short
8. Worst Forms of Child Labour Convention, 1999 (No. 182), Convention No. 182 for short.

D. Kucera (ed.), Qualitative Indicators of Labour Standards, 115–144.

In previous research (Wermenbol, Cuyvers, and Van Den Bulcke, 1998; Cuyvers, Van Den Bulcke and Wijaya, 2001), we have suggested ways to quantify countries' compliance with some of these core standards, as well as to judge the countries' capacity and willingness to adopt and comply with the core standards. Although in Wermenbol, Cuyvers and Van Den Bulcke (1998) an attempt was made to aggregate the various sub-indices into a social development index, no such exercise was made in Cuyvers, Van Den Bulcke and Wijaya (2001).

This chapter will give an overview of the methodology applied in this quantification of respect for ILO core labour standards, whereas the issue of the capacity of countries to adopt, implement and comply with such standards is left out of the picture for brevity's sake. Compared to Cuyvers, Van Den Bulcke and Wijaya (2001) no update of the quantitative and qualitative information used is carried out, however.

We will concentrate on the freedom of association and collective bargaining, the freedom from child labour, the freedom from gender discrimination, and the freedom from forced labour. For each core labour standard the individual countries' status is measured using an index between 0 and 1, which is constructed by calculating weighted averages of various aspects of the ratification and compliance record of the countries.

In our attempt to measure the core labour standards' status of countries, a distinction has been made between 'formal' and 'real' compliance. The 'formal' social development index of a country refers to any official acceptance toward the core labour standards that takes the form of ratification of these Conventions and consequent reporting. The 'real' social development index takes factual information into account, and refers to the extent of compliance of the mentioned standards, or similar practices consonant with the standards whether the country ratified the standards or not.

In constructing formulas for assessing respect for selected core labour standards, we will use 1 (or 100 %) as maximum compliance. This implies that any aspect or element relating to the lack of respect should diminish this maximum index, so that the index becomes lower than 1. It is as if a "fine" is applied to the maximum score. If various aspects or elements have to be taken into account, they should be weighted using suitable coefficients. As will be seen in the formulas that are put forward in the following sections, this procedure often becomes very tedious and complicated. This seems to be the price that has to be paid for comprehensiveness.

2. Freedom of Association Index

Freedom of Association Index (FAI) in a narrow sense encompasses the freedom to establish trade unions as well as the protection of this right of association and more or less refers to the contents of Convention No. 87. Free association in a broad sense includes not only Convention No. 87 and the right to strike but also the right to collective bargaining as is included in social standard Convention No. 98. At present, there is a discussion about whether or not to include the right to strike in the notion 'freedom of association', since this former right is not explicitly mentioned in Convention No. 87. In this report it was decided to include the right to strike, however.

The FAI is constructed to measure the degree of formal and real respect of a country for the ILO-Conventions Convention No. 87 and Convention No. 98. The degree of formal confidence a country has in Convention No. 87 and Convention No. 98 is measured by whether or not the country ratified the Convention No. 87 and Convention No. 98. The degree of real respect a country has with regard to Convention No. 87 and Convention No. 98 is measured by the type and number of violations of the contents of these Conventions.

2.1 Methodology

The construction of the Freedom of Association Index is confronted by certain constraints, since quantitative data are rarely available. Official records of convention ratification and the reporting history of countries will be used and analysed in order to determine the formal element of a country's compliance. Whenever a country did not ratify a specific Convention, the country legislation compatibility with the Convention substance was taken into consideration instead of ratification.

The other element of the Freedom of Association Index is the degree of real respect of a country for the provisions of Convention No. 87 and Convention No. 98 on the basis of the number of reported violations. Violations such as the number of persons murdered, wounded, arrested or dismissed were classified as 'reported violations' (category A). Whether or not a government intervenes or interferes in trade unions' activities were categorized as 'government interference' (category B). Finally, other kinds of limitations (e.g. legal limitations) with regard to free trade unions were categorized as 'legal and other limitations' (category C). These three categories of violations originated from their frequent and systematic occurrence in the annual ICFTU reports as well as in the Human Rights Practices reports from the US Department of State.

2.2 Formula of the Freedom of Association Index

The Freedom of Association Index (FAI) is based on two elements : the Formal Freedom of Association Index (FFAI) and the Real Freedom of Association Index (RFAI). The components of these element are the following :

FFAI: Formal Free Association Index

- Ratification of Convention No. 87 and Convention No. 98
- Reports requested and received (art. 19) on Convention No. 87 & Convention No. 98

RFAI: Real Free Association Index

- Category A: the reported number of violations vis-à-vis trade union members/leaders
  - ⬦ Number of murders
  - ⬦ Number of wounded
  - ⬦ Number of arrests
  - ⬦ Number of dismissals

- Category B: government interference
- Category C: legal limitations, regarding
  - Formation and/or adherence to an independent union of their own choice
  - Formation and/or adherence to a (con)federation
  - Affiliation with an international trade union organization
  - Right to strike
  - Right to collective bargaining
  - Protection against anti-union discrimination

2.2.1 The Formal Freedom of Association Index (FFAI) Formula

The following formula was constructed, giving the components of the FFAI:

$$\textbf{FFAI}_j = 1 - [(\omega_{87}\,\delta_{87j} - \omega_{art\,19}\,\delta_{\delta 87j\,j}) + (\omega_{98}\,\delta_{98j} - \omega_{art\,19}\,\delta_{\delta 98j\,j})]$$

with

ω_{87} = weighting coefficient (0.5) for Convention No. 87
ω_{98} = weighting coefficient (0.5) for Convention No. 98
$\omega_{art\,19}$ = weighting coefficient (0.125) for article 19 of the ILO constitution
δ_{87j} = a dummy variable which equals 1 in case country j did not ratify Convention No. 87 and equals 0 in case it did ratify the Convention
δ_{98j} = a dummy variable which equals 1 in case country j did not ratify Convention No. 98 and equals 0 in case it did ratify the Convention No. 98
$\delta_{\delta 87j\,j}$ = a dummy variable which equals 1 in case the dummy variable δ87j was 1 (which means that country j did not ratify Convention No. 87, hence article 19 is applicable); AND if the non-ratifying country concerned did however send their report stating their legislation and practice regarding Convention No. 87. On the other hand, $\delta_{\delta 87j\,j}$ equals 0 when the dummy variable δ87j is 0 (which means that country j did ratify Convention No. 87 and hence article 19 is not applicable.
$\delta_{\delta 98j\,j}$ = a dummy variable which equals 1 in case the following two conditions are met. First, in case the other dummy variable δ 98j equals 1 as well (meaning that country j did not ratify Convention No. 98), article 19 of the ILO constitution is applicable. Secondly, when the non-ratifying country j handed in its report stating their legislation and practice regarding Convention No. 98, the dummy variable $\delta_{\delta 98j\,j}$ equals 0 when the dummy variable δ_{98j} amounts to 0 (which means that country j did already ratify the Convention concerned) and thus article 19 is not applicable. The question whether or not a non-ratifying country did send its report then becomes irrelevant.

Consider the situation of China in 2001 as based on the data used in Cuyvers, Van Den Bulcke and Wijaya (2001), China being a country which had ratified neither Convention No. 87 nor Convention No. 98, and was not sending in its reports. In this case, the FFAI = 0. This can be compared with Brazil, which had only ratified Convention No. 98, and does report on that Convention. If Brazil, not having ratified Convention No. 87, would report on that Convention, a different situation would arise. As a matter of fact, the "fine" for not ratifying $-\omega_{87}\,\delta_{87j}$ with $\omega_{87} = 0.5$ and $\delta_{87j} = 1$ – would be reduced with $\omega_{art\ 19}\delta_{887j\ j}$, where $\omega_{art\ 19} = 0.125$ and $\delta_{887j\ j} = 1$. In reality, however, Brazil was not reporting on Convention No. 87 and therefore $\delta_{887j\ j} = 0$. Thus, applying the FFAI to Brazil would lead to the following result: $1-[(0.5^*1 - 0.125^*0) + (0.5^*0 - 0.125^*0)]$.

2.2.2 The Real Freedom of Association Index (RFAI) Formula

To establish RFAI, basically qualitative data have to be transformed into quantitative measures. Therefore scores are attached to various possible situations as reported in the sources that are available. The scores will be higher, the more severe is the violation, as the "fine" applied to such violation should diminish the RFAI. It goes without saying that this introduces a substantial degree of arbitrariness, especially in cases where no information is available. In such cases it was decided to opt for a "fine" equal to 0.3, compared to a maximum "fine" of 1. The lack of information is therefore considered to be equivalent in most cases to information withheld for further scrutiny. The degree of arbitrariness is the price to be paid for quantification. The following scores are applied :

Category A. 'Number of reported violations'

Number of murders		Number of wounded		Number of arrests		Number of dismissals	
Interval	Score	Interval	Score	Interval	Score	Interval	Score
0	0	0	0	0	0	0	0
1–5	1/5	1–10	1/5	1–25	1/5	1–100	1/5
(incl. 5)		(incl. 10)		(incl. 25)		(incl. 100)	
5–10	2/5	10–20	2/5	25–50	2/5	100–250	2/5
(incl. 10)		(incl. 20)		(incl. 50)		(incl. 250)	
10–15	3/5	20–30	3/5	50–75	3/5	250–400	3/5
(incl. 15)		(incl. 30)		(incl. 75)		(incl. 400)	
15–20	4/5	30–40	4/5	75–100	4/5	400–550	4/5
(incl. 20)		(incl. 40)		(incl. 100)		(incl. 550)	
>20	1	>40	1	>100	1	>550	1
N.A.	0.3	N.A.	0.3	N.A.	0.3	N.A.	0.3

Category B. 'Government intervention/interference'

Symbol	Meaning	Score
Y	government interference	1
N	free of government interference	0
N.A.	data not available	0.3

Category C. 'Legal limitations'

Symbol	Meaning	Score
NONE	no legal obstacles	0
S	legal obstacles for a specific sector or a small number of sectors	1/3
APU/APR/A(..)	legal obstacles which exist in all public (APU) or all private (APR) sectors. In case of a legal Limitation that altogether amounts to the overall public or private sector, which is spread out over several public and private sectors, the symbol A(..) is used	2/3
A	legal limitations exist in all sectors of the economy	1
N.A.	data not available	0.3

After having classified the original information into the three types of violations and subsequently converted them into numerical data by attributing scores ranging from zero to one and finally ascribing to them the more or less arbitrary weighting coefficients (see further), the RFAI can be calculated by using the following formula:

$$\text{RFAI}_j = 1 - (\omega_{rv}\, RV + \omega_{gi}\, \delta_{gij} + \omega_{ll}\, LL)$$

with

ω_{rv} = weighting coefficient (0.4) for the number of reported violations
ω_{gi} = weighting coefficient (0.3) for government interference
ω_{ll} = weighting coefficient (0.3) for legal limitations
RV = score of the number of reported violations for the 4 different subcategories
δ_{gij} = a dummy variable with respect to government intervention/interference amounting to 1 in case country j interferes, and to 0 in the case of absence of intervention or interference
LL = legal limitations in 5 sub-categories

The calculation of the RFAI can be illustrated by the following examples based on the data used in Cuyvers, Van Den Bulcke and Wijaya (2001).

Belgium's RFAI = 1, as there are no violations reported and, hence, RV = 0, δ_{gij} = 0 and LL = 0. Consider, however, Argentina with a RV = 0.28. Based on the 2001 data, this figure is arrived at by counting the number of murders (5), the number of wounded (28), the number of arrests (0) and the number of dismissals (0), and applying the attributed score according to the severity of the violation, and the weights for the four types of violations. The penalty score for murders up to five is 0.2 and that for between 21 and 30 wounded, 0.6. The scores for the arrests and the dismissals is evidently 0. By applying the weights, which are 0.5 for murders, 0.3 for wounded, 0.1 for arrests and 0.1 for dismissals, we arrive at: RV = [(0.5*0.2) + (0.3*0.6) + (0.1*0) + (0.1*0)]. In addition, as government intervention in labour issues is reported in Argentina, $\delta_{gij} = 1$. Argentina's LL = 0.3, as information is not available. Therefore: RFAI in Argentina's case is:

RFAI = $1 - [(0.4^*0.28) + (0.3^*1) + (0.3^*0.3)] = 1 - [0.112 + 0.3 + 0.09] = 0.498$.

2.2.3 The Freedom of Association Index (FAI) Formula

Eventually, a composite Freedom of Association Index (FAI) is composed, by weighting the FFAI and the RFAI per country, as follows:

$$FAI_j = \omega_f \, FFAI_j + \omega_r \, RFAI_j$$

with

ω_f = weighting coefficient (0.3) for the FFAI
ω_r = weighting coefficient (0.7) for the RFAI

Again, consider Argentina with a FFAI = 1 (Argentina ratified Convention No. 87 and Convention No. 98 in 2001, and reported in accordance with Article 19) and a RFAI = 0.498, which leads to:

FAI = $(0.3^*1) + (0.7^*0.498) = 0.3 + 0.3486 = 0.6486$

2.3 Analysis

Appendix 1 shows the FFAI, the RFAI and the FAI for a selected number of countries. Table 1 shows the Top 5 worst and the Top 5 best "performers" in terms of freedom of association, based on the calculations of Cuyvers, Van Den Bulcke and Wijaya (2001).

3. Freedom of Child Labour Index (CLI)

The predominant objective of Convention No. 138 is the complete abolition of child labour and the gradual elevation of the minimum age for admission to the labour market in such a way that children have reached their full physical and

Table 1. The top 10 Worst and Best 'Performers' in Terms of their FAI Score, 1999.

Top 10 worst FAI scores	Top 10 best FAI scores
1. Colombia (0.40)	1. Japan, Germany (1)
2. Thailand (0.45)	2. Israel, Namibia (0.99)
3. Morocco (0.47)	3. UK, Slovakia (0.98)
4. Armenia, Kiribati (0.49)	4. Guyana (0.97)
5. Republic Korea (0.58)	5. Bangladesh, South Africa (0.96)
6. China (0.59)	6. Switzerland (0.94)
7. Nepal (0.61)	7. Norway (0.92)
8. Equatorial Guinea (0.62)	8. Russian Federation (0.91)
9. Kenya (0.63)	9. Nicaragua (0.88)
10. India, Mauritania (0.64)	10. Peru (0.87)

mental development before they are employed. At the moment the age limit is set at 15 years. As already mentioned this is not all that fixed and inflexible as it is presumed some relaxation measures have been included (accepted). Besides, there are a number of vague statements and adjectives like 'insufficiently' developed educational facilities, 'light work', 'adequate' instruction or training, etc., mentioned in Convention No. 138 that make such provisions a matter of interpretation. In addition to Convention No. 138, the so-called Worst Forms of Child Labour Convention, 1999 (No. 182), was adopted in 1999.

3.1 Methodology

In order to measure the formal respect of Convention No. 138 and Convention No. 182, a Child Labour Index (CLI) is constructed. Following the same procedure as in the construction of the Freedom of Association Indexes, the CLI consists of two components, viz. the Formal Child Labour Index and the Real Child Labour Index (RCLI), appropriately weighted.

3.1.1 Formal Child Labour Index (FCLI) Formula

With reference to the procedure that was used to set up the FFAI, the following types of violations of Convention No. 138 are considered. Regarding Convention No. 182, the ratification record of the countries at issue are taken into account.
The formula that is used to measure the degree of formal respect for Convention No. 138 uses the same approach as was pointed out in the discussion of the use of weights and scores in the construction of the FFAI, i.e. :

Type A: violation by non-ratification	In case of:
'Strict requirement'	Non-ratification of C-138
'Flexible requirement'	Ratification of less than 4 preceding Conventions
Type B: Violation by a lower stipulated minimum age	In case of:
Type B.1: Violation by lower stipulated basic minimum age	
'Strict requirement'	Basic minimum age of <15 yr.
'Flexible requirement'	Basic minimum age of <14 yr.
Type B.2: violation by a lower stipulated minimum age for light work	Minimum age <13 yr.
Type B.3: violation by a lower stipulated minimum age for hazardous work	
'Strict requirement'	Minimum age <18 yr.
'Flexible requirement'	Minimum age <16 yr.
Type B.4: violation by a lower age than the end of compulsory education	Minimum age <compulsory education age

$$\begin{aligned}
FCLI_j = 1 - [\ &(\delta_{138j}\,(\omega_{138}\,\delta_{4j} + 0.5\,\omega_{138}\,(1 - \delta_{4j}))) \\
+\ &(\delta_{bsj}\,(\omega_{bs}\,\delta_{bfj} + 0.5\,\omega_{bs}\,(1 - \delta_{bfj}))) + (\omega_l\,\delta_{lj}) \\
+\ &(\delta_{hsj}\,(\omega_{hs}\,\delta_{hfj} + 0.5\,\omega_{hs}\,(1 - \delta_{hfj}))) \\
+\ &(\omega_e\,\delta_{ej}) + (\omega_{182}\delta_{182})]
\end{aligned}$$

with

$FCLI_j$ = formal child labour index of country j

δ_{138j} = a dummy variable that equals 1 in the case of a formal violation of Convention No. 138 and equals 0 in the case of a formal respect regarding ratification of Convention No. 138

δ_{4j} = a dummy variable that equals 0 when country j has ratified at least 4 previous Conventions on minimum age and equals 1 when country j has not done so

δ_{bsj} = a dummy variable that equals 0 when country j respects the basic minimum age set at 15 years as stated in Convention No. 138 and equals 1 when it is set at a lower age

δ_{bfj} = a dummy variable that equals 0 when country j has a basic minimum age of 14 years (instead of 15) and equals 1 when it is set at a lower age

δ_{lj} = a dummy variable that equals 0 when country j has, for light work, a minimum age of at least 13 years and equals 1 when country j has a lower minimum age

δ_{hsj} = a dummy variable that equals 0 when country j has, for hazardous work, a minimum age of at least 18 years and equals 1 when a country has set a lower one

δ_{hfj} = a dummy variable that equals 0 when country j has, for hazardous work, set their minimum age at 16 or 17, and equals 1 when it has set a lower age limit

δ_{ej} = a dummy variable that equals 0 when country j has, for compulsory education, set an age limit that at least equals the country's basic minimum age and equals 1 when it is lower

δ_{182j} = a dummy variable that equals 0 when country j has ratified Convention No. 182 and 1 in the case of non-ratification

ω_{138} = weighting coefficient (0.1) for Convention No. 138

ω_{ls} = weighting coefficient (0.1) for the stricter standard regarding the basic minimum age (15 years)

ω_l = weighting coefficient (0.1) for a minimum age of 13 years for light work

ω_{hs} = weighting coefficient (0.1) for the stricter minimum age standard (i.e. 18 years) for hazardous work

ω_e = weighting coefficient (0.1) for the minimum age for compulsory education (that should be at least equal to the country's stipulated basic minimum age limit).

ω_{182} = weighting coefficient (0.5) for Convention No. 182.

It is important to stress that the weighting coefficients add up to one, with the sum of the weighting coefficients applied to provisions of Convention No. 138 representing half of that, and the weighting coefficient relating to formal respect for Convention No. 182 being 0.5.

The rationale for the first part of the formula:

$$(\delta_{138j}\,(\omega_{138}\,\delta_{4j} + 0.5\,\omega_{138}\,(1 - \delta_{4j})))$$

is to increase the penalty or "fine" (i.e. a larger deduction from 1, the maximum FCLI) when a country has ratified previous Conventions, but not Convention No. 138. In such a case $\delta_{138j} = 1$ and $\delta_{4j} = 0$. Therefore, the penalty will be: $(1^*(0.1^*0 + 0.5^*0.1^*1) = 0.05$. The penalty is also increased if neither Convention No. 138 nor four previous Conventions are ratified, in which case $\delta_{4j} = 1$ and the outcome will be : $(1^*(0.1^*1 + 0.5^*0.1^*0) = 0.1$.

Consider e.g., the case of Cambodia, based on the data used in Cuyvers, Van Den Bulcke and Wijaya (2001). This country had ratified Convention No. 138, but not Convention No. 182. This means that its $\delta_{138j} = 0$, but its $\delta_{182j} = 1$. In addition, Cambodia had not ratified at least four previous Conventions on minimum age, so that $\delta_{4j} = 1$. However, as the country had ratified Convention No. 138, the penalty for not having ratified at least four previous Conventions would be zero.

The second part of the formula is :

$$(\delta_{bsj} (\omega_{bs} \delta_{bfj} + 0.5 \omega_{bs} (1 - \delta_{bfj})))$$

which relates to the basic working age of 15 or 14 years. In the case when a country respects 15 years, $\delta_{bsj} = 0$, and it will not be penalized; otherwise it will be equal to 1. If then the basic working age in that country is below 14 years, $\delta_{bsj} = 1$, but $\delta_{bfj} = 1$, as well, and the penalty will be : $(1^*0.1^*1 + 0.5^*0.1^*0) = 0.1$. A country will be penalized only half of that if its minimum working age is 14 years, as $\delta_{bsj} = 1$, but $\delta_{bfj} = 0$, which leads to a penalty of $(1^*0.1^*0 + 0.5^*0.1^*1) = 0.05$.

Again, consider Cambodia, where the basic minimum age, based on the data used in Cuyvers, Van Den Bulcke and Wijaya (2001) was set at 15 years and therefore had a $\delta_{bsj} = 0$, and is not penalized. In Guatemala, however, the strict basic working age was 14 years. Therefore, for that country $\delta_{bsj} = 1$, but $\delta_{bfj} = 1$, and the penalty would be 0.1.

The third part of the FCLI-formula is: $(\omega_l \delta_{lj})$ and relates to a country's legal provisions regarding light work. If the minimum age for light work is set at 13 years, $\delta_{lj} = 0$, and no penalty will be applied. However, if the minimum age for light work is lower than 13 years, $\delta_{lj} = 1$, and as the weighting coefficient $w_l = 0.1$, the penalty will be 0.1.

The fourth part of the formula consists of the following :

$$(\delta_{hsj} (\omega_{hs} \delta_{hfj} + 0.5 \omega_{hs} (1 - \delta_{hfj})))$$

and relates to the working age for hazardous work which should be 18 years, or at least 16 or 17 years. This part of the formula functions in an analogous way as those parts relating to the basic minimum working age and the minimum age for light work.

The fifth part of the formula is : $(\omega_e \delta_{ej})$ and tries to capture the age limit provisions in a country for compulsory education. If that age limit equals the basic minimum age, $\delta_{ej} = 0$, and no penalty is applied. Otherwise, $\delta_{ej} = 1$, and as the weighting coefficient $\omega_e = 0.1$, the penalty for not respecting this part of Convention No. 138 equals 0.1.

The final part of the FCLI-formula only intends to penalize a country if it has not ratified Convention No. 182, in which case its $\delta_{182j} = 1$, and as $\omega_{182} = 0.5$, the penalty applied will be 0.5 as well. On the contrary, if a country has ratified Convention No. 182, $\delta_{182j} = 0$, and no penalty is applied.

3.1.2 Real Child Labour Index (RCLI) Formula

The formula that will be used to measure the degree of real respect for Convention No. 138 and Convention No. 182 is as follows:

$$\mathbf{RCLI_j = 1 - REA_j}$$

with

RCLI$_j$ = Real Child Labour Index of country j
REA$_j$ = the number of economically active (i.e. working) children in country j in the age-group of 10-14 years old as a percentage of the total population in this age group.

Hence, the RCLI ranges from zero to one, where a one refers to an absence of child labour (no children between 10 and 14 years of age working), while a zero would mean that all children between 10 and 14 are working in country j. The REA's were obtained by calculating the ratio of the absolute number of working children in the age group of 10 to 14 years and the total population of 10 to 14 years old.

3.1.3 The (Composite) Child Labour Index (CLI) Formula

Eventually, a (composite) Child Labour Index can be produced from two elements above by using the following formula:

$$\mathbf{CLI_j = \omega_f * FCLI_j + \omega_r * RCLI_j}$$

with

ω_f = weighting coefficient (0.3) for the FCLI
ω_r = weighting coefficient (0.7) for the RCLI
CLI$_j$ = the (composite) Child Labour Index
FCLI$_j$ = the Formal Child Labour Index
RCLI$_j$ = the Real Child Labour Index

Note that the same weights are applied to the formal and the real index as in the calculation of the FAI.

3.2 Analysis

The individual FCLI, RCLI and CLI country scores are presented in Appendix 2. Some conclusions can be drawn from these results. The most serious violations in general, i.e. in the formal and real sense, are apparently to be found in Latin-American developing countries such as Honduras, Guatemala, Colombia and Peru (see Table 2). That Turkey belongs to the Top 5 having the lowest CLI scores is of relevance in view of its application for EU membership. On the other hand, the countries that respect Convention No. 138 and Convention No. 182 most are located in Europe, but also include South Korea, Canada and the USA. It is rather surprising to find also Sri Lanka among the Top 5 with the highest CLI scores.

Table 2. The Top 5 Lowest and Highest CLI Scores.

Top 5 worst CLI scores	Top 5 best CLI scores
1. Ethiopia (0.43)	1. Finland, Ireland, Spain, Switzerland, Malta (1.00)
2. Honduras (0.65)	2. Sri Lanka (0.98)
3. Guatemala (0.66)	3. Croatia, Italy, New Zealand, Republic Korea, Sweden, U.S. (0.97)
4. Turkey (0.73)	4. Bahamas (0.96)
5. Colombia, Cambodia, Iran, Peru (0.76)	5. Canada (0.94)

4. Freedom of Gender Discrimination Index (GDI)

Discrimination is defined in the Discrimination Convention, 1958 (No. 111), as follows: 'any distinction, exclusion or preference on the basis of race, colour, sex, religion, political opinion, national extraction or social origin, which has the effect of nullifying or impairing equality of opportunity or treatment in employment or occupation' (Convention No. 111, art. 1, par. 1(a)).

As in Cuyvers, Van Den Bulcke and Wijaya (2001), only gender discrimination is here considered. The first international standards on discrimination on grounds of gender focused mainly on women's protection and the role of women as mother as is expressed in the following ILO conventions: the Maternity Protection Convention, 1919 (No. 3), the Night Work (Women) Convention, 1919 (No. 4), the Underground Work (Women) Convention, 1935 (No. 45). In addition, equal remuneration as stipulated by Convention No. 100 also focuses on equality of remuneration between men and women.

4.1 Methodology

The factors that should be taken into account when calculating the degree of formal respect a country has for the relevant ILO conventions are :

1. Ratification of all Relevant ILO Conventions

Moreover, the Conventions that deal with discrimination, and which should in any case be ratified (the 'fundamental Conventions') are:

- *The Discrimination (in Employment and Occupation) Convention, 1958 i.e. Convention No. 111,*
- *The Equal Remuneration Convention, 1951 i.e. Convention No. 100, which is part of Convention No. 111.*

However, there are also other Conventions relating to discrimination. The early Conventions on discrimination were focused on the protection of women and their role as mother. These Conventions will be referred to as the 'traditional-Conventions on discrimination':

- *The Maternity Protection Convention, 1919 i.e. Convention No. 3, and Convention No. 103, 1952 (revised)*
- The Night Work (Women) Convention, 1919 i.e. Convention No. 4, and Convention No. 41, 1934 & Convention No. 89, 1948 (revised)
- The Underground Work (Women) Convention, 1935 i.e. Convention No. 45.

Instead of considering the Conventions preceding Convention No. 111, the Conventions that followed the fundamental Convention with respect to discrimination (Convention No. 111) will be considered. These Conventions will be denoted as 'modern Conventions on discrimination' (in short, *'modern Conventions')* :

- *The Workers with Family Responsibilities Convention, 1981 i.e. Convention No. 156,*
- *The Part-Time Work Convention, 1994 i.e. Convention No. 175,*

2. Submission of Reports (in Accordance with Article 19)

In order to overcome the problem of establishing a binary index, where one can only distinguish between countries that did or did not ratify, we will establish a criterion to distinguish within the group of non-ratifying countries. For this Article 19 of the Constitution of the International Labour Organization is relied on. It invites the Member States that have not yet ratified the Convention(s) on discrimination, to submit reports on their legislation with regard to these Conventions. If this report was submitted, the country will be credited for this in accordance with Article 19. Here is a short description of the contents of the formal gender discrimination index (FGDI) with respective weighting coefficients mentioned between brackets.

4.2 Gender Discrimination Index (GDI) Formula

4.2.1 Formal Gender Discrimination Index (FGDI) Formula

The formula for the FGDI was constructed as follows :

$$\mathbf{FGDI}_j = 1 - [\omega_1 \, (\omega_{111} \, \delta_{111j} + \omega_{100} \, \delta_{100j}) + w_2 \, \{\delta_{FGDI(F)j} \, (w_{3/103} \, \delta_{3/103j}$$
$$+ w_{4/41/89} \, \delta_{4/41/89j} + w_{45} \, \delta_{45j}) + (w_{156} \, \delta_{156j} + w_{175} \, \delta_{175j} \,)\}]$$

Or in another way :

$$\mathbf{FGDI}_j = 1 - \omega_1 \, [\mathbf{FGDI(F)}_j + \omega_2 \, \{\delta_{FGDI(F)j} \, (\omega_{3/103} \, \delta_{3/103j} + \omega_{4/41/89} \, \delta_{4/41/89j}$$
$$+ \omega_{45} \, \delta_{45j}) + (\omega_{156} \, \delta_{156j} + \omega_{175} \, \delta_{175j} \,)\}]$$

with

FGDI j   = the formal gender discrimination index of country j

FGDI(F)j= $\omega_{111} \, \delta_{111j} + \omega_{100} \, \delta_{100j}$

ω_1 = a weighting coefficient (0.7) relating to Convention No. 100 and Convention No. 111

ω_2 = a weighting coefficient (0.3) relating to Convention No. 3, Convention No. 4, Convention No. 41, Convention No. 45, Convention No. 89, Convention No. 103, Convention No. 156 and Convention No. 175, when Convention No. 100 and Convention No. 111 have not been ratified

δ_{111j} = a dummy variable which equals 1 in the case of non-ratification of Convention No. 111 with respect to discrimination and equals zero in the case when country j did ratify Convention No. 111

δ_{100j} = a dummy variable which equals 1 in the case of non-ratification of Convention No. 100 with respect to equal remuneration and equals 0 in the case when country j did ratify Convention No. 100

$\delta_{FGDI(F)j}$ = a dummy variable which equals 1 when the two Conventions Convention No. 111 and Convention No. 100 were not ratified and equals 0 if at least one, or both, were ratified. The F between brackets denotes the two fundamental Conventions with respect to discrimination.

$\delta_{3/103j}$ = a dummy variable equals 1 if either Convention No. 3 or Convention No. 103 (or both), about the protection of maternity, were not ratified and equals 0 if they were ratified by country j

$\delta_{4/41/89j}$ = a dummy variable that equals 1 if either Convention No. 4, Convention No. 41 or Convention No. 89 (or all), about night work for women, were not ratified and equals 0 if they were ratified by country j.

δ_{45j} = a dummy variable equals 1 in the case of non-ratification of Convention No. 45 with respect to underground work for women and equals 0 if country j did ratify this convention.

δ_{156j} = a dummy variable equals 1 in the case of non-ratification of Convention No. 156 with respect to workers with family responsibilities and equals 0 if country j did ratify Convention No. 156.

δ_{175j} = a dummy variable equals 1 in the case of non-ratification of Convention No. 175 with respect to part time work and equals 0 if Convention No. 175 was ratified by country j.

ω_{111} = a weighting coefficient (0.7) for Convention No. 111 on discrimination (employment & occupation)

ω_{100} = a weighting coefficient (0.3) for Convention No. 100 on equality of remuneration

$\omega_{3/103}$ = a weighting coefficient (0.2) for Convention No. 3 and Convention No. 103 with respect to maternity protection

$\omega_{4/41/89}$ = a weighting coefficient (0.2) for Convention No. 4, Convention No. 41 and/or Convention No. 89 with respect to night work for women

ω_{45} = a weighting coefficient (0.2) for Convention No. 45 with respect to underground work for women

ω_{156} = a weighting coefficient (0.2) for Convention No. 156 on workers with family responsibilities

ω_{175} = a weighting coefficient (0.2) for Convention No. 175 about part time work

The Formal Freedom of Gender Discrimination Index (FGDI) will be equal to 1 in the case of ratification of both Conventions (and hence refers to a formal non-discrimination), and equals 0 in case one of the Conventions was ratified, which indicates a maximum possible formal degree of discrimination. The FGDI is only higher than 1 if a particular country has ratified the so-called modern conventions on top of Convention No. 100 and Convention No. 111, implying in a sense that these countries are getting a "credit" or "negative penalty" for such ratifications.

The part of the formula: $FGDI(F)j = \omega 111\ \delta 111j + \omega 100\ \delta 100j$ only contains dummies relating to the ratification of Convention No. 111 and Convention No. 100, together with the weights attached. Consider Thailand, which on the basis of the data used in Cuyvers, Van Den Bulcke and Wijaya (2001) had ratified Convention No. 111, but not Convention No. 100. Taking into account the weights $FGDI(F)j = (0.7^*1) + (0.3^*0) = 0.7$, which will be deducted from 1 as a first penalty for non-ratification of the two Conventions. This part of the formula is weighted, however, with $\omega 1 = 0.7$, and therefore the final penalty for Thailand relating to the non-ratification of Convention No. 100 will be $0.7^*0.7 = 0.49$.

The rest of the formula is:

$$\{\delta_{FGDI(F)j}\ (\omega_{3/103}\ \delta_{3/103j} + \omega_{4/41/89}\ \delta_{4/41/89j} + \omega_{45}\ \delta_{45j}) + (\omega_{156}\ \delta_{156j} + \omega_{175}\ \delta_{175j})\}]$$

is weighted with $\omega_2 = 0.3$ and therefore can be considered as consisting of the second and the third part of the formula: $\delta_{FGDI(F)j}\ (\omega_{3/103}\ \delta_{3/103j} + \omega_{4/41/89}\ \delta_{4/41/89j} + \omega_{45}\ \delta_{45j})$ and $(\omega_{156}\ \delta_{156j} + \omega_{175}\ \delta_{175j})$, respectively.

The second part of the formula:

$$\delta_{FGDI(F)j}\ (\omega_{3/103}\ \delta_{3/103j} + \omega_{4/41/89}\ \delta_{4/41/89j} + \omega_{45}\ \delta_{45j})$$

attempts to capture the respect for the Conventions relating to the protection of maternity, and the protection of women from night work and underground work, if Convention No. 111 and/or Convention No. 100 is not ratified. If the country ratified Convention No. 111 and/or Convention No. 100, the dummy $\delta_{FGDI(F)j} = 0$ and no penalty is applied. However if none of the Conventions is ratified, $\delta_{FGDI(F)j} = 1$, and non ratification of the other Conventions (Convention No. 3 and Convention No. 103, Convention No. 4, Convention No. 41, Convention No. 89 and Convention No. 45 will be considered. Thailand, for instance, again on the basis of the data used in Cuyvers, Van Den Bulcke and Wijaya (2001) had not ratified these conventions, hence $\delta_{3/103j} = \delta_{4/41/89j} = \delta_{45j} = 1$, but as the country ratified Convention No. 100, $\delta_{FGDI(F)j} = 0$, and therefore the calculated value of its penalty was $0^*[(0.1^*1) + (0.1^*1) + (0.1^*1)]=0$.

The third part of the formula relates to the ratification of the Conventions about workers with family responsibilities and women and part-time work. The reasoning is the same as before with dummies set at zero in the case of ratification and one otherwise.

The FGDI-scores are presented in Appendix 3.

4.2.2 Real Gender Discrimination Index (RGDI) Formula

The following formula will be used:

$$RGDI_j = 1 - ABS\ [\omega_{ce}\ (1-F/M_{cej}) + \omega_p\ (1-F/M_{pj}) + \omega_{w\ e}(1-F/M_{wej})$$
$$+ \omega_w\ (1-F/M_{wj})]$$

with

$RGDI_j$ = real gender discrimination index of country j

ABS = the absolute value of the result of the calculation between square brackets

ω_{ce} = weighting coefficient (0.333) for access to education by combined enrolment

ω_p = weighting coefficient (0.167) for professions

ω_{we} = weighting coefficient (0.167) for access to waged employment

ω_w = weighting coefficient (0.333) for waged employment

F/M = Number of Females relative to Males

1–F/M = gender gap (number 1 indicates total equality)

F/M_{cej} = ratio of the combined female enrolment percentage to the male pct.

F/M_{pj} = ratio of the pct. of female legislators, senior officers etc., to the male pct.

F/M_{wej} = ratio of the pct. of female professional/technical staff, to the male pct.

F/M_{wj} = ratio of the pct. of females in paid employment among the active female population, to the male pct.

In short, the real freedom of gender discrimination index will vary from 0 to 1. A zero indicates total disrespect for the provisions of Conventions No. 100 and No. 111. Conversely, a 1 refers to total respect for Conventions No. 100 and 111, or in other words, total absence of discrimination.

In the formula, extensive use is made of (1 – F/M) as an indicator of discrimination, with F/M the ratio of female to male employment or education enrolment, respectively. In some cases this F/M ratio is higher than one and therefore (1–F/M) < 0, which consequently would increase the final RGDI of the country at issue. What in fact is measured is a situation of revealed positive discrimination against women, but equally a revealed negative discrimination against men. Therefore, contrary, to the procedure used in Wermenbol, Cuyvers and Van Den Bulcke (1998), Cuyvers, Van Den Bulcke and Wijaya (2001) used instead the absolute value, in which case all, and not only that of women, revealed gender discrimination will lead to a penalty.

The working of the formula is straightforward. Although, as before, the weighting coefficients are chosen arbitrarily. If the case of e.g. the Republic of Korea is used as an illustration, the following values for the respective F/M ratios become apparent :

F/M_{cej} = 0.895
F/M_{pj} = 0.33
F/M_{wej} = 0.918
F/M_{wj} = 0.45

As a result, Korea's RGDI score, based on the data used in Cuyvers, Van Den Bulcke and Wijaya (2001) is: $1 - ABS[0.333^*(1-0.895) + 0.167^*(1-0.33) + 0.167^*(1-0.918) + 0.333^*(1-0.45) = 0.66]$.

The RGDI scores for selected countries are given in Appendix 3.

4.2.3   The (Composite) Gender Discrimination Index (GDI) Formula

Overall performance of a country is calculated from the previous two elements, i.e. the Formal Gender Discrimination Index (FGDI) and the Real Gender Discrimination Index (RGDI) by using the following formula:

$$\mathbf{GDI_j = \omega_f {}^* FGDI_j + \omega_r {}^* RGDI_j}$$

with

ω_f = weighting coefficient (0.3) for the formal gender discrimination index
ω_r = weighting coefficient (0.7) for the real gender discrimination index
GDI_j = the (composite) gender discrimination index for country j
$FGDI_j$ = the formal gender discrimination index for country j
$RGDI_j$ = the real gender discrimination index for country j

Again the same weights are applied for the formal and the real index as in the formulas of FAI and CLI.

4.3 Analysis

As shown in Table 3, developed countries seem to dominate in the list of nations with high GDI scores. There are, however, some noteworthy exceptions like Sri Lanka and the Philippines, which are ranked third and fourth among the "Top Five Best Performers", while Ireland is second among the countries with the lowest GDI scores together with Peru.

5. The Forced Labour Index

In constructing a Forced Labour Index, it is important to clearly define forced labour in advance since it is not identical with low-wage labour as many people may seem to think. According to the ILO Convention No. 29, forced labour should be defined as "all work or service, which is exacted from any person under the menace of any penalty and for which the said person has not offered himself voluntarily". The ILO's Global Report entitled "Stopping Forced Labour" lists the following main forms of forced labour today:

Table 3. Top Five of Selected Countries For Worst and Best GDI Scores.

Top 5 worst GDI scores	Top 5 best GDI scores
1. Togo (0.52)	1. Finland (0.94)
2. Ireland, Peru (0.54)	2. Macedonia (0.93)
3. Guatemala (0.55)	3. Switzerland, Mexico, Spain, Sri Lanka (0.92)
4. Ethiopia (0.58)	4. Philippines (0.91)
5. Indonesia (0.59)	5. Australia (0.90)

1) Slavery and abductions,
2) Compulsory participation in public works projects,
3) Coercive recruitment systems in agriculture and remote rural areas,
4) Certain forms of domestic work,
5) Bonded labour,
6) Forced conscription of both children and adults for non-military purposes,
7) Trafficking of labour under false pretences,
8) Certain types of prison labour and rehabilitation through work in prison.

There have hardly been any countries in the world that have not been involved in the phenomenon of forced labour, one way or another. On the basis of the sources available, it appears that forced labour exists in both developing and developed countries, as well as in the least developed countries.

5.1 Methodology

Like the Freedom of Association Index, the Child Labour Index, and the Gender Discrimination Index, the Forced Labour Index (FLI) consists of two elements: the Formal Forced Labour Index (FFLI) and the Real Forced Labour Index (RFLI). The Formal Forced Labour Index has been developed to assess the legal aspect of a country's compliance in terms of formal respect of the Forced Labour Convention, 1930 (No. 29), and the Abolition of Forced Labour Convention, 1957 (No. 105).

5.1.1 The Formal Forced Labour Index (FFLI)

To construct the Formal Forced Labour Index, the following formula is proposed.

$$\mathbf{FFLI} = 1 - [(\omega_{29} \cdot \delta_{29}) + (\omega_{105} \cdot \delta_{105})]$$

where:

ω_{29} : weight assigned for Convention No. 29, which is set at 0.5,
ω_{105} : weight assigned for Convention No. 105, which is set at 0.5,
δ_{29} : dummy variable which equals 1 if a country has not ratified ILO Convention No. 29, and equals 0 if the country has ratified that Convention,
δ_{105} : dummy variable which equals 1 if a country has not ratified ILO Convention No. 105, and equals 0 if the country has ratified that Convention.

FFLI scores are ranging from 0 to 1. In fact, there are only three possible values that are produced using the above formula: 0, 0.5 and 1. The score of 0 will be produced when a country has not ratified both Conventions; 0.5 if either Convention No. 29 or Convention No. 105 was not ratified; and 1 if both conventions were ratified by the country at issue. Five percent of ILO member States have not ratified either of the forced labour conventions. Consequently, their FFLI score is zero.

5.1.2 The Real Forced Labour Index (RFLI)

The Real Forced Labour Index which follows, is basically constructed as a measure of violations of Forced Labour Conventions as reported in sources whenever available, such as the ILO Global Report 2001, http://www.state.gov/, and http://www.icftu.org/. The formula for constructing the index uses data-counting, combined with some attempt at a quantification of qualitative aspects of the extent of forced labour involved in any particular country.

The following formula for producing the index for a specific country is proposed:

$$RFLI = 1 - [\omega_q . (\Sigma FLQ/40) + \omega_t . (\Sigma FLT/8)]$$

where:

Σ FLQ : the sum of the numerically-converted degrees ("quality") of forced labour from any of the 8 types of forced labour (see above) found in the country

40 : represents the number of numerically converted degrees considered (5, see below) and the number of types of forced labour according to Convention No. 105 (8)

Σ FLT : the sum of types of forced labour that are reportedly found in the country

8 : the number of types of forced labour according to Convention No. 105

ω_q : weight assigned to the quality of forced labour found, which is set at 0.5

ω_t : weight assigned to the number of forced labour types involved, which is set here at 0.5

The numerically converted degrees of forced labour are a conversion of 5 levels of the extent of forced labour found in a particular country into a numerical value set as follows (see Table 4).

It is typical that in the reports on the situation of forced labour in a particular country, no straightforward extent or degree of forced labour is mentioned whatsoever. Therefore a rule of thumb is needed to allow for the determination of the extent of forced labour in the countries at issue, as indicated in Table 5.

The "philosophy" behind the Real Forced Labour Index formula is basically a quantification of the extent of forced labour in a country, combined with the number of types detected in the same country relative to the eight types of forced labour. There are, however, cases in which reliable sources give a different qualification for the same forced labour situation in a specific country. This can happen, e.g., when one source is more keen and specialized in analysing a certain type of forced labour. Whenever this is the case, a mid-value will be constructed by using the simple average of the quantified degrees assigned by the different sources. Consider, for example, a country with the *serious* forced labour violation of practising bonded labour

Table 4. Extent of Forced Labour and Numerical Value Assigned.

Extent	Value assigned
Possible	1
Exist	2
Rather serious	3
Serious	4
Very serious	5

Table 5. Extent of Forced Labour Assigned to Reported Country Situations.

Extent	Condition
Possible	Assigned to a situation, for example where a country has national or local legislation which violates the ILO Conventions (Convention No. 29 & Convention No. 105) but no reported implementation of such legislation
Existing	Assigned to a situation where at least reliable anecdotal evidence is present
Rather serious	Assigned to a situation where forced labour is increasingly becoming a marked trend rather than merely anecdotal evidence
Serious	Assigned to a situation where forced labour cases are spreading out, coupled by poor efforts to eradicate it
Very serious	Assigned to a situation where forced labour is systematically present for instance as a common practice in the country and either no significant progress is seen after efforts are made to abolish it, or no efforts at all are being made

according to source A, but according to another reliable source the situation is deemed to be only *rather serious*. The country will have an RFLI as follows:

Assigned value for "serious"	= 4
Assigned value for "rather serious"	= 3
Sum of forced labour quality (ΣFLQ)	= (4+3)/2
	= 3.5
Sum of type of forced labour involved (ΣFLT)	= 1
So the RFLI score for the country is	= 1 − [0.5(3.5/40) + 0.5(1/8)]
	= 1 − [0.5*0.0875 + 0.5*0.125]
	= 1 − [0.10625]
RFLI	= 0.89

The RFLI calculated scores per country are available in Appendix 8. To illustrate these calculations, consider the following classical instances of forced labour in countries such as India, Bangladesh and Paraguay. According to the sources used in Cuyvers, Van Den Bulcke and Wijaya (2001), India is involved in at least 4 types of forced labour: slavery and abduction, certain types of domestic work, bonded labour and prison labour. The situation seems to be worsened by the apparent extent or degree of forced labour, where the sources are giving qualifications ranging from "existing" (certain types of domestic work and prison labour) to "extremely serious" (bonded labour). This resulted in a low RFLI score of 0.59. Similar situations also seem to occur in Bangladesh and Paraguay that show RFLI scores of 0.58 and 0.56 respectively.

5.1.3 The (Composite) Forced Labour Index

The composite index of forced labour is constructed by calculating a weighted average of both elements, FFLI and RFLI, with weights assigned of ω_{ffli} and ω_{rfli}, respectively. Hence, the Forced Labour Index (FLI) formula can be written as:

$$\textbf{FLI} = \omega_{ffli} \cdot \textbf{FFLI} + \omega_{rfli} \cdot \textbf{RFLI}$$

with :

FLI   : the (Composite) Forced Labour Index
FFLI : the Formal Forced Labour Index
RFLI : the Real Forced Labour Index
ω_{ffli} : weight assigned to the Formal Forced Labour Index, which is set at 0.5
ω_{rfli} : weight assigned to the Real Forced Labour Index, which is set at 0.5

5.2 Analysis of FLI

Appendix 8 presents the FLI scores of the individual countries. The composite FLI scores calculated range between 0.55 and 0.95. Table 6 shows the "Top 10 Worst Cases" of countries showing the lowest Forced Labour Index score.

According to Table 6 some remarkable results come forward. That Myanmar, considered as a notorious violator of the Forced Labour Conventions, is on the list of Top 10 Worst Cases, could be expected. However, it is not revealed as the "number one violator", although the international media normally present it as such. According to the available sources, the country shows only three types of forced labour involved, compared to e.g., Paraguay, which has five types. There exist, however, other countries with a worse revealed forced labour situation. Although Nepal apparently only applies two types of forced labour, it registers the worst FLI score, i.e. 0.55. However, Nepal's RFLI is 0.78, but since the country did not ratify either Convention No. 29 or Convention No. 105, this finally leads to the lowest score of composite FLI. Hence, according to these tentative calculations, countries that have not ratified any of the forced labour conventions do indeed show low FLI scores, even if their RFLI scores are relatively higher. Certainly, countries would have lower FLI scores if they did not ratify any conventions and show many types of forced labour with substantial degrees of seriousness, as demonstrated by e.g., India and Bangladesh.

Table 6. Top 10 of Countries with Lowest FLI.

Rank	Country	FLI
1	Nepal	0.55
2	Vietnam	0.57
3	China	0.58
4	Mongolia	0.58
5	Bolivia	0.59
6	Myanmar	0.61
7	Armenia	0.63
8	Republic of Korea	0.63
9	Equatorial Guinea	0.64
10	Paraguay	0.69

6. Sensitivity Analysis

Referring to the indices in the Appendix 1-8, it will appear that moving down the ranking list of countries in a number of cases leads to more continuous changes of the indices, while in other cases many *ex aequo* are found, and shifts and discontinuities are prevalent. For instance, the FFAI takes only values of 1, 0.5 and 0. The same holds for FFLI. The FGDI seems to be more spread, but still 23 of the 40 countries ranked show a FGDI of 0.88.

On the other hand, for many countries the RFLI shows less discrete changes than FFLI, but 69 of the 175 countries ranked according to RFAI have an RFAI of 0.7. As a matter of fact, neither the ranking according to "formal" indices, nor that according to "real" indices, should be considered, but rather the combination of both into the FAI, the GDI, the CLI and the FLI.

Another issue is, how sensitive the results are for changes in the weights used. In order to check this, the most crucial weights are changed, as summarized in Table 7.[1]
In order to assess, in general terms, the sensitivity of the indices for changes in the weighting coefficients used in their respective formulas, Spearman rank correlation and the Pearson correlation between the relevant alternatives were calculated. These correlation coefficients are shown in Table 8 and Table 9.

With two exceptions, the correlation coefficients are larger than 0.5. These exceptions are Pearson correlation between FCLI and FCLIa, and the Pearson correlation coefficient between FLI and FLIa. In fact, the vast majority of the coefficients in Tables 8 and 9 are larger than 0.7. All, except one, are significant at the 1% level (the significance level is even higher than 0.001 %). The exception here is the Pearson correlation coefficient between FCLI and FCLIbis, but even there the coefficients are significant at the 2.5 % level.

The strange low correlation between FCLI and FCLIa is likely to be due to the fact that the ratification data used in the calculation of the formal child labour index are those of the year 2000, i.e. only one year after the launch of Convention No. 182, when hardly 16 of the 40 countries considered had ratified it, against 38 who had ratified Convention No. 138. Today, the ratification records of Convention No. 138 and Convention No. 182 are much more comparable. But, not surprisingly, if the 2000 data are used and five times more weight is given to the ratification record of Convention No. 182 than to that of Convention No. 138, it will have a large impact on the FCLI.

The relatively lower correlation between FLI and FLIa, however, seems to indicate that that index, in particular the formal forced labour index, needs further refinement. The weights attached to the ratification of Convention No. 29 and Convention No. 105, in combination with the dummies in the FFLI formula, result in a calculated FFLI which takes only three values, i.e., 1, 0.5 and 0, with 1 for 146 of the 175 countries, and 0.5 for only 21 countries.

---

[1] The RCLI was not envisaged here as it contains no weights.

Table 7. Alternative Weighting Coefficients Used in Sensitivity Analysis.

	ω_{87}	ω_{98}	ω_{rv}	ω_{gi}	ω_{ll}	ω_{138}	ω_{bs}	ω_{l}	ω_{ts}	ω_{e}	ω_{182}	ω_{11}	ω_{100}	ω_{ce}	ω_{p}	ω_{we}	ω_{w}	ω_{29}	ω_{105}
FFAI	0.5	0.5																	
FFAI	0.3	0.7																	
RFAI			0.4	0.3	0.3														
RFAI			0.8	0.1	0.1														
RFAI			0.2	0.4	0.4														
FCLI						0.1	0.1	0.1	0.1	0.1	0.5								
FCLI						0.5	0.1	0.1	0.1	0.1	0.1								
FCLI						0.2	0.2	0.1	0.1	0.2	0.2								
FGDI												0.7	0.3						
FGDI												0.3	0.7						
FGDI												0.5	0.5						
RGDI														1/3	1/6	1/6	1/3		
RGDI														1/2	1/4	1/4	1/2		
RGDI														1/4	1/2	1/2	1/4		
FFLI																		0.5	0.5
FFLI																		0.3	0.7
FFLI																		0.7	0.3

Table 8. Spearman Rank Correlation Coefficients Between Social Respect Indices and Their Alternatives.

	FFAI	RFAI	CLI	FCLI	GDI	FGDI	RGDI	FLI	FLI
FFAI	1.00***								
RFAI	0.79***	0.97***							
RFAI		0.72***							
CLI			0.99***	0.97***					
CLI				0.99***					
FCLI				0.70***	0.92***				
FCLI					0.84***				
GDI					0.97***	0.94***			
GDI						0.98***			
FGDI						1.00***	1.00***		
FGDI							1.00***		
RGDI							1.00***	0.91***	
RGDI								0.91***	
FLI								0.58***	0.97***
FLI									0.67***

**   sigmificance level > 0.025
*** significance level > 0.01

Table 9. Pearson Correlation Coefficients Between Social Respect Indices and Their Alternatives.

	FFAI	RFAI	CLI	FCLI	GDI	FGDI	RGDI	FLI	FLI
FFAI	0.98***								
RFAI	0.87***	0.98***							
RFAI		0.74***							
CLI			0.96***	0.90***					
CLI			0.99***						
FCLI				0.40**	0.83***				
FCLI				0.73***					
GDI					0.92***	0.67***			
GDI					0.91***				
FGDI						0.93***	0.98***		
FGDI						0.98***			
RGDI							1.00***	0.94***	
RGDI							0.94***		
FLI								0.50***	0.71***
FLI									0.68***

**   significance level > 0.025
*** significance level > 0.01

With the exception of the FFLI, it can be concluded that varying the weights in the formulas is not having much impact on the ranking of the countries. In all cases, the degree of association between the indices and their variants remains consistently high.

Appendix 1. Freedom of Association Index and its Sub-indices.

Country	FFAI	RFAI	FAI
Australia	1.00	0.70	0.79
Bahamas	1.00	0.70	0.79
Bahrain	0.00	1.00	0.70
Brazil	0.50	0.91	0.79
Cambodia	1.00	0.68	0.78
Canada	0.50	1.00	0.85
Colombia	1.00	0.14	0.40
Costa Rica	1.00	0.66	0.76
Croatia	1.00	0.67	0.77
El Salvador	0.00	0.96	0.67
Ethiopia	1.00	0.65	0.76
Finland	1.00	0.70	0.79
Georgia	1.00	0.58	0.71
Greece	1.00	0.70	0.79
Guatemala	1.00	0.71	0.80
Honduras	1.00	0.78	0.85
Indonesia	1.00	0.52	0.67
The Islamic Republic of Iran	0.00	0.98	0.69
Ireland	1.00	0.70	0.79
Italy	1.00	0.70	0.79
Kazakhstan	1.00	0.70	0.79
Republic of Korea	0.00	0.82	0.58
Lithuania	1.00	0.70	0.79
The former Yugoslav Republic of Macedonia	1.00	0.70	0.79
Malta	1.00	0.56	0.69
Mexico	0.50	0.95	0.82
Morocco	0.50	0.46	0.47
New Zealand	0.00	0.96	0.67
Nicaragua	1.00	0.83	0.88
Peru	1.00	0.81	0.87
Philippines	1.00	0.56	0.69
Slovenia	1.00	0.49	0.64
Spain	1.00	0.70	0.79
Sri Lanka	1.00	0.78	0.85
Sweden	1.00	0.70	0.79
Switzerland	1.00	0.91	0.94
Thailand	0.00	0.64	0.45
Togo	1.00	0.69	0.78
Turkey	1.00	0.73	0.81
U.S.	0.00	0.96	0.67

Appendix 2. Freedom of Child Labour Index and its Sub-indices.

Country	FCLI	RCLI	CLI
Australia	0.45	1.00	0.84
Bahamas	0.85	1.00	0.96
Bahrain	0.75	1.00	0.93
Brazil	0.95	0.83	0.87
Cambodia	0.30	0.95	0.76
Canada	0.80	1.00	0.94
Colombia	0.25	0.97	0.76
Costa Rica	0.40	0.95	0.78
Croatia	0.90	1.00	0.97
El Salvador	0.95	0.88	0.90
Ethiopia	0.35	0.46	0.43
Finland	1.00	1.00	1.00
Georgia	0.30	1.00	0.79
Greece	0.50	1.00	0.85
Guatemala	0.35	0.80	0.66
Honduras	0.25	0.83	0.65
Indonesia	0.95	0.91	0.92
The Islamic Republic of Iran	0.30	0.96	0.76
Ireland	1.00	1.00	1.00
Italy	0.90	1.00	0.97
Kazakhstan	0.40	1.00	0.82
Republic of Korea	0.90	1.00	0.97
Lithuania	0.30	1.00	0.79
The former Yugoslav Republic of Macedonia	0.40	1.00	0.82
Malta	1.00	1.00	1.00
Mexico	0.75	0.89	0.85
Morocco	0.70	0.94	0.87
New Zealand	0.90	1.00	0.97
Nicaragua	0.85	0.89	0.88
Peru	0.30	0.96	0.76
Philippines	0.90	0.92	0.91
Slovenia	0.40	1.00	0.82
Spain	1.00	1.00	1.00
Sri Lanka	1.00	0.97	0.98
Sweden	0.90	1.00	0.97
Switzerland	1.00	1.00	1.00
Thailand	0.70	0.91	0.85
Togo	0.85	n/a	n/a
Turkey	0.40	0.87	0.73
U.S.	0.90	1.00	0.97

Appendix 3. Freedom of Gender Discrimination Index
and its Sub-indices.

Country	FGDI	RGDI	GDI
Australia	0.94	0.88	0.90
Bahamas	0.88	0.72	0.77
Bahrain	0.67	0.61	0.63
Brazil	0.88	0.83	0.84
Cambodia	0.88	0.51	0.62
Canada	0.88	0.89	0.88
Colombia	0.88	0.80	0.82
Costa Rica	0.88	0.73	0.78
Croatia	0.94	0.83	0.87
El Salvador	0.94	0.71	0.78
Ethiopia	0.94	0.42	0.58
Finland	1.00	0.92	0.94
Georgia	0.88	0.65	0.72
Greece	0.94	0.76	0.81
Guatemala	0.94	0.38	0.55
Honduras	0.88	0.62	0.70
Indonesia	0.88	0.47	0.59
The Islamic Republic of Iran	0.88	0.39	0.54
Ireland	0.88	0.82	0.84
Italy	0.94	0.78	0.83
Kazakhstan	0.88	0.86	0.87
Republic of Korea	0.94	0.66	0.74
Lithuania	0.88	0.94	0.92
The former Yugoslav Republic of Macedonia	0.94	0.72	0.79
Malta	0.88	0.64	0.71
Mexico	0.88	0.71	0.76
Morocco	0.88	0.40	0.54
New Zealand	0.88	0.93	0.91
Nicaragua	0.88	0.49	0.61
Peru	0.94	0.61	0.71
Philippines	0.88	0.94	0.92
Slovenia	1.00	0.88	0.92
Spain	0.94	0.77	0.82
Sri Lanka	0.88	0.94	0.92
Sweden	0.94	0.92	0.93
Switzerland	0.88	0.71	0.76
Thailand	0.39	0.70	0.61
Togo	0.88	0.37	0.52
Turkey	0.88	0.53	0.64
U.S.	0.00	0.92	0.64

Appendix 4. Freedom of Forced Labour Index and its Sub-indices.

Country	FFLI	RFLI	FLI
Australia	1.00	0.84	0.89
Bahamas	1.00	n/a	n/a
Bahrain	1.00	0.78	0.84
Brazil	1.00	0.68	0.78
Cambodia	1.00	0.89	0.92
Canada	0.50	0.83	0.73
Colombia	1.00	0.79	0.86
Costa Rica	1.00	0.91	0.94
Croatia	1.00	0.91	0.94
El Salvador	1.00	0.91	0.94
Ethiopia	0.50	n/a	n/a
Finland	1.00	0.91	0.94
Georgia	1.00	0.90	0.93
Greece	1.00	0.81	0.87
Guatemala	1.00	0.71	0.80
Honduras	1.00	0.83	0.88
Indonesia	1.00	0.65	0.76
the Islamic Republic of Iran	1.00	0.93	0.95
Ireland	1.00	0.93	0.95
Italy	1.00	0.90	0.93
Kazakhstan	1.00	0.89	0.92
Republic of Korea	0.00	0.90	0.63
Lithuania	1.00	0.89	0.92
The former Yugoslav Republic of Macedonia	0.50	0.90	0.78
Malta	1.00	n/a	n/a
Mexico	1.00	0.79	0.85
Morocco	1.00	0.81	0.87
New Zealand	1.00	0.83	0.88
Nicaragua	1.00	0.79	0.85
Peru	1.00	0.78	0.84
Philippines	0.50	0.83	0.73
Slovenia	1.00	0.91	0.94
Spain	1.00	0.83	0.88
Sri Lanka	0.50	0.82	0.72
Sweden	1.00	0.91	0.94
Switzerland	1.00	0.91	0.94
Thailand	1.00	0.82	0.87
Togo	1.00	0.65	0.76
Turkey	1.00	0.90	0.93
U.S.	0.50	0.83	0.73

References

Cuyvers, L., D. Van Den Bulcke, and C. Wijaya. 2001. Quantifying respect for selected core labour standards with special emphasis on forced labour. Report prepared for the International Labour Organization, Contract No. 11305, Project Code O.055.10.900.812. University of Antwerp, December 2001.

Heritage Foundation. 2004. 2004 index of economic freedom. Available at http://www.heritage.org/research/features/index/

ILO. 2001. ILO global report – stopping forced labour. International Labour Organization, Geneva.

IMD. 2004. World competitiveness yearbook 2004. Available at http://www01.imd.ch/wcy/ranking/

Political and Economic Risk Consultancy. 2001. Corruption in Asia in 2001. Available at http://www.asiarisk.com/lib10.html

The Economist. 2004. The Big Mac index. Available at http://www.economist.com/markets/Bigmac/Index.cfm

UNDP. 2003. Human Development Report 2003. Available at http://hdr.undp.org/reports/global/2003/pdf/hdr03_HDI.pdf

Wermenbol, G., L. Cuyvers, and D. Van Den Bulcke. 1998. Proposal for a social development index – respect for ILO core labour standards against the background of the implementation capacity of countries. VL.I.R research project, Belgian Administration of Development Co-operation (ABOS). University of Antwerp, Antwerp, January 1998.

LUDO CUYVERS AND DANIEL VAN DEN BULCKE,
University of Antwerp

Chapter 6

Measuring Trade Union Rights by Violations of These Rights*

DAVID KUCERA
International Labour Office

1. Introduction

Constructing qualitative indicators of labour standards is a difficult business. There are several sources of measurement error, both random and non-random, to which such indicators are particularly prone. Perhaps the most important bottleneck in moving toward more definitive qualitative indicators of labour standards is the incompleteness of existing information sources, particularly as regards applying consistent and comprehensive evaluation criteria of labour standards across countries and over time. This is not such a problem for indicators solely addressing legislation, for it is possible at least in principle to collect for all countries all legislation relevant to a given labour standard. The problem is acute, however, for qualitative indicators addressing problems of a more de facto, on-the-ground nature.

These cautions in mind, this chapter describes a method used to construct a country-level indicator of trade union rights based on coding violations recorded in what are regarded as the three best existing textual sources on trade union rights. This indicator was constructed for one purpose only: for use in econometric models of such economic outcomes as wages, foreign direct investment and international trade. Given this end, a certain amount of random measurement error seemed permissible, as such error would tend to lead to attenuated rather than perverse econometric results. Moreover, suspected non-random measurement error, such as by country type, could be addressed to an extent through such econometric methods as specifying models with and without regional dummy variables, dropping a region at a time from samples, incorporating controls for levels of economic development and thus country capacity, and using as many indicators of trade union rights as possible, each having their particular sources of measurement error. Because of the incompleteness of existing information sources and other sources of measurement error, it was never thought that the indicator would be suitable for any application for which each country score must stand on its own, such as for socially responsible investing or monitoring progress in individual countries. The intent in constructing the indicator was, rather, to provide a usable if noisy sense of cross-country variation.

* Many thanks to Githanjali Christian and Ritash Sarna for their excellent research assistance and to Ritash for his coding of the ILO Committee on Freedom of Association reports.

D. Kucera (ed.), Qualitative Indicators of Labour Standards, 145–181.
© 2007 *by ILO.*

This chapter is structured as follows. Section 2 describes the method of construction by coding text and then converting coded text into an indicator. Section 3 presents the indicator and some descriptive statistics with regional breakdowns, both regarding variation across countries and variation across the thirty-seven evaluation criteria that provide the building blocks of the indicator. Section 4 discusses the strengths and limitations of the method, particularly regarding definitional validity, sufficient grades of variation, reproducibility and transparency in the use of sources, evaluator bias, and information bias and other problems with information sources. Section 5 concludes by arguing – no surprise – for improved information sources, in particular for the closer integration of the construction of indicators with the collection and compilation of information, as well as for incorporating new questions into labour force surveys that address violations of trade union rights.

2. Method of Construction

2.1. Coding Text

This statistical indicator is based on thirty-seven evaluation criteria for assessing trade union rights, shown in Table 1 (column A) and grouped into six categories: freedom of association/collective bargaining-related civil liberties; right to establish and join unions and worker organizations; other union activities; right to bargain collectively; right to strike; and export processing zones. The indicator of trade union rights jointly addresses problems regarding legislation as well as more de facto problems, though leaning in emphasis toward the latter. The most fundamental reason for considering both together is that the indicator was intended to evaluate the effects of trade union rights on foreign direct investment and international trade through two main causal channels: through labour costs relative to labour productivity (with higher labour costs hypothesized to have a negative effect) and through stability of labour-management relations and social stability more generally (with greater stability hypothesized to have a positive effect). In this sense, the full range of trade union rights problems were hypothesized to have a stifling effect on the capacity of workers to bargain for wages, with de jure problems not considered to be mutually exclusive from de facto problems. In other words, having a problematic law on the books is taken to signify in and of itself the strength of de facto trade union rights. Consistent with this view, the textual sources used to construct the indicator themselves consider both problems with legislation and problems of a more de facto nature, also leaning in emphasis toward the latter.

These thirty-seven evaluation criteria provide a working definition of trade union rights, insofar as it is possible to define trade union rights by observed violations of these rights, and they were developed in several stages. The first stage involved coming up with a preliminary list of criteria by reading relevant ILO Conventions and jurisprudence. The most relevant ILO Conventions are No. 87 ("Freedom of Association and Protection of the Right to Organise, 1948") and No. 98 ("Right to Organise and Collective Bargaining, 1949"). These are the two

Table 1. Indicator of Trade Union Rights (hypothetical example for a single country).

A	B	C	D	E
Thirty-seven evaluation criteria	Source coding	Dummy variable (0 = no evidence, 1 = evidence)	Weights (1, 1.25, 1.5, 1.75 or 2)	Dummy* weights
Freedom of association/collective bargaining-related civil liberties				
1 Murder or disappearance of union members or organizers	ab	0	2	0
2 Other violence against union members or organizers	a	1	2	2
3 Arrest, detention, imprisonment, or forced exile for union membership or activities	ab	1	2	2
4 Interference with union rights of assembly, demonstration, free opinion, free expression		1	2	2
5 Seizure or destruction of union premises or property		0	2	0
Right to establish and join unions and worker organizations				
6 General prohibitions		0	*default*	*na*
7 General absence resulting from socio-economic breakdown		0	*default*	*na*
8 Previous authorization requirements		0	1.5	0
9 Employment conditional on non-membership in union		0	1.5	0
10 Dismissal or suspension for union membership or activities	abc	1	1.5	1.5
11 Interference of employers (attempts to dominate unions)	a	1	1.5	1.5
12 Dissolution or suspension of union by administrative authority		0	2	0
13 Only workers' committees & labour councils permitted		0	2	0
14 Only state-sponsored or other single unions permitted		0	1.5	0
15 Exclusion of tradeable/industrial sectors from union membership		0	2	0
16 Exclusion of other sectors or workers from union membership	ab	1	2	2
17 Other specific de facto problems or acts of prohibition	a	1	1.5	1.5
18 Right to establish and join federations or confederations of unions		0	1.5	0
19 Previous authorization requirements regarding evaluation criteria 18		0	1	0

(*Continued*)

Table 1. Indicator of Trade Union Rights (hypothetical example for a single country). — Cont'd.

A	B	C	D	E
	Source coding	Dummy variable	Weights	Dummy* weights
Thirty-seven evaluation criteria		(0 = no evidence, 1 = evidence)	(1, 1.25, 1.5, 1.75 or 2)	
Other union activities				
20 Right to elect representatives in full freedom	ab	1	1.5	1.5
21 Right to establish constitutions and rules		0	1.5	0
22 General prohibition of union/federation participation in political activities	b	1	1.5	1.5
23 Union control of finances	c	1	1.5	1.5
Right to bargain collectively				
24 General prohibitions		0	*default*	*na*
25 Prior approval by authorities of collective agreements		0	1.5	0
26 Compulsory binding arbitration		0	1.5	0
27 Intervention of authorities		0	1.5	0
28 Scope of collective bargaining restricted by non-state employers		0	1.5	0
29 Exclusion of tradeable/industrial sectors from right to collectively bargain		0	1.75	0
30 Exclusion of other sectors or workers from right to collectively bargain		0	1.75	0
31 Other specific de facto problems or acts of prohibition	ab	1	1.5	1.5
Right to strike				
32 General prohibitions		0	2	0
33 Previous authorization required by authorities		0	1.5	0

34 Exclusion of tradeable/industrial sectors from right to strike	0		1.5	0
35 Exclusion of other sectors or workers from right to strike	0		1.5	0
36 Other specific de facto problems or acts of prohibition	1	ac	1.5	1.5
Export processing zones				
37 Restricted rights in EPZs	1	a	2	2
Non-scaled (raw) weighted score:			**22**	

Sources:

a: International Confederation of Free Trade Unions (ICFTU), *Annual Survey of Violations of Trade Union Rights.*

b: U.S. State Department, *Country Reports on Human Rights Practices.*

c: ILO, *Report of the Committee on Freedom of Association.*

Note: na indicates not applicable; *default* indicates a minimum scaled country score of 0 on a scale of 0 to 10, where 0 equals worst and 10 equals best possible score.

ILO Conventions providing the foundation of one of the ILO's four "fundamental principles and rights at work" as regards "freedom of association and the effective recognition of the right to collective bargaining" (ILO, 1998: 7). Also important in this first stage of developing these evaluation criteria was a reading of related ILO jurisprudence as embodied in *Freedom of Association: Digest of Decisions and Principles of the Freedom of Association Committee of the Governing Body of the ILO* (1996).

After this first stage, and consultation with ILO colleagues having legal expertise in the field, a pilot stage of coding textual sources with preliminary evaluation criteria was done for a sample of twelve countries from around the world. The three sources were the International Confederation of Free Trade Unions' (ICFTU) *Annual Survey of Violations of Trade Union Rights*, the U.S. State Department's *Country Reports on Human Rights Practices*, and the ILO's *Report of the Committee on Freedom of Association* (CFA). These came to be the same sources used in the final construction of the indicators and indeed are the three main sources of country-level information on trade union rights that are available on a regular basis for a nearly comprehensive sample of countries. These are the same sources referred to as "comprehensive descriptive labour rights reports" in the recent report of the U.S. National Research Council, *Monitoring International Labour Standards: Techniques and Sources of Information* (2004), which also describes the comparative merits and shortcomings of these and other information sources.[1] Problems found regarding the thirty-seven evaluation criteria were coded with letters "a," "b," or "c," indicating each of the different textual sources, respectively, with such coding facilitating the tracing of an observed violation to back a particular textual source.

In order to code the textual sources to satisfy the condition of reproducibility, it was necessary to develop detailed coding rules for each of the evaluation criteria. In particular, coding rules were developed to deal with why an observed problem violated one criterion versus another and whether an observed problem violated more than one criterion. That is, rules for mutual exclusivity and non-exclusivity needed to be developed, as did rules for particular violations that were not specifically referred to in ILO Conventions or jurisprudence. In general, the guiding principle was that an observed problem should be coded as a violation of as many criteria as seemed relevant, just as, by analogy, a given criminal act may lead to multiple counts in an indictment of an accused. These coding rules for each of the thirty-seven evaluation criteria are provided in Appendix 1.[2]

---

[1] Note that the ILO's *Report of the Committee of Experts* was not used. This is because information on Conventions No. 87 and No. 98 are available only for countries that have ratified these Conventions. Since these reports tend to focus on problems in a country, this creates a systematic bias against countries that have ratified these Conventions.

[2] Even with the constraint of using the same thirty-seven evaluation criteria and three of the same textual sources, one could devise different coding rules that might be just as or perhaps more useful. In general, it might be useful to simplify the coding rules and perhaps the evaluation criteria as well, as greater simplicity would facilitate greater reproducibility in the construction of the indicators.

After this pilot stage, the ICFTU and U.S. State Department sources were coded by the author for 169 countries, addressing violations observed over the period from 1993 to 1997. In this process as in the pilot stage, the coding rules were amended and clarified to account for observed violations and issues of mutual exclusivity and non-exclusivity that did not arise during the pilot phase. In this sense, the development of the evaluation criteria and coding rules was highly interactive with the coding itself in this first round for a full sample of countries.

After the ICFTU and U.S. State Department sources, coding was next done for the *Report of the Committee on Freedom of Association*. This proved to be considerably more complicated and time-consuming than coding the other two sources. For the ICFTU reports, for instance, the survey for 1996 is meant to refer to events in 1995 and for the U.S. State Department reports, the survey for 1995 is meant to refer to events in 1995. But the CFA reports are case-driven, and cases may run for years without a definitive decision being made on them (further information on how the CFA works is available at: http://webfusion.ilo.org/public/db/standards/normes/ libsynd/index.cfm?hdroff=1).

The CFA reports were dealt with as follows. All case entries between 1993 and 2000 were read (286th to 322nd report). A total of 611 case entries were reviewed, 217 of them unique cases and the remainder follow-ups to previously filed cases. The only cases considered were those in which the first communication date of the complaint was between 1993 and 1997 (though the actual incidents referred to may have occurred before then). Evidence is then coded only if the CFA makes a recommendation consistent with the complaint in any report of the reports up to 2000.[3] The CFA cases were first coded by a research assistant with the author then reviewing the relevant texts and preliminary coding to move toward the final coding. This process of having two coders for the CFA reports also resulted in some clarification of the coding rules as they now appear in Appendix 1.

Note that only observations of violations are coded, not observations of good conditions and practices for any given evaluation criterion. The textual sources tend to focus on problems in a country, but there are occasional mentions of good (or improving) conditions and practices. By not being coded, however, these good conditions and practices are effectively treated as if there were no mention of them. In this sense, observations and non-observations of good practices and conditions are treated equivalently.

2.2. Converting Coded Text into an Indicator

The basic method of turning the coded text for any given country into an indicator is to add up the number of evaluation criteria, up to thirty-seven, for which violations are observed. This is done in both unweighted (that is, equally weighted) and

---

[3] In addition, cases where the Government makes no reply, even after urgent appeals by the CFA, are coded as violations consistent with the complaint; cases where the Government is still looking into the matter and the CFA has requested to be kept informed are not coded as violations; cases where the statements from the complainant and government are contradictory and the CFA has not made a recommendation consistent with the complaint are not coded as violations.

weighted form, with different weights assigned to the different evaluation criteria. Similar approaches are used by Cuyvers and Van Den Bulcke as well as the OECD (1996, 2000).

As noted, observed violations are coded with letters corresponding to textual sources. A dummy variable is then constructed for each country in which an observation of a problem in any of the three textual sources is given a value of 1 and no observations of a problem in any of the three sources is given a value of 0, for each of the evaluation criteria. For the weighted measures, each of the evaluation criteria is assigned a weight of 1, 1.25, 1.5, 1.75 or 2, with greater weights indicating more severe problems (based in part on the qualitative language used in the *Report of the Committee on Freedom of Association*). Dummy variables for each country are then multiplied by the weights, and then this product is summed across the evaluation criteria to yield, for each country, a non-scaled raw score.

A hypothetical example of this method is illustrated in Table 1. Column A shows the thirty-seven evaluation criteria. Column B shows the coding of problems according to the textual source and column C the dummy variables derived from column B. Within column C, a look at the two shaded rows indicates a value in the dummy variable of 1 for both rows, even though problems were found in all three textual sources for the upper row and only one source for the lower row. The rationale for treating both rows the same (rather than giving more weight to the upper) is to avoid double counting, for the different sources are often describing the same problem in a country. Indeed, some of these reports are partly based on the others (U.S. National Research Council, 2004). Weights are shown in column D. Column E shows the product of the dummy and the weights, the sum of which yields the non-scaled weighted score for a given country. The non-scaled unweighted score is simply the sum of column C. In spite of the differences in construction, the correlation coefficient between the unweighted and weighted measures is 0.99.[4] (For the purposes of statistical analysis, one could of course also construct an index from a subset of the thirty-seven evaluation criteria, with the subset depending on the focus of one's research.)

The non-scaled measures are then normalized to range from 0 to 10, with 10 equal to the maximum observed non-scaled score (not maximum *possible*

---

[4] There is also a difference in construction between weighted and unweighted measures as regards the treatment of excluded sectors. It is assumed that there is a hierarchy of violations, such that the exclusion of a sector from union membership (rows 15 and 16 in Table 1) presupposes exclusion from collective bargaining (rows 29 and 30) which itself presupposes exclusion from the right to strike (rows 34 and 35). For the weighted measures, weights are therefore greater for lower-numbered rows and, for example, if problems are found in rows 29 and 34, only row 29 was coded, since the higher weights of lower-number rows addresses the assumed hierarchy of violations. (This holds even if the violations noted in rows 29 and 34 are for different tradeable sectors.) The unweighted measure also assumes this hierarchy of violations but in a different manner. Here, for instance, if a violation is only observed in row 29, both rows 29 and 34 are coded. In practical terms, these differences between weighted and unweighted measures come to little as regards cross-country statistical analysis, given that the correlation coefficient between the two measures is 0.99.

non-scaled score).[5] The same procedure is used for the unweighted measures, aside from multiplying by the weights. These normalized values are then subtracted from 10 for intuitive reasons, so that 0 equals the worst possible score (most violations observed) and 10 the best possible score (fewest violations observed). In addition, any country for which there are general prohibitions of the right to establish and join unions and worker organizations (row 6), general absence of the above resulting from socio-economic breakdown (row 7), or general prohibitions of the right to collectively bargain (row 24) receive a default worst possible score of 0.

3. Descriptive Statistics

The unweighted and weighted versions of the indicators are shown in Appendix Table 1, with the sample of countries in alphabetical order within eight regions. (Coding of text by evaluation criteria and textual sources and documentation tracing CFA cases is available from the author upon request.) These are the pre-1990s OECD region (excluding Turkey), Latin-America and the Caribbean, the non-OECD East Asia-Pacific, Southeast Asia, South Asia, the transition countries of the former Soviet Union and Eastern bloc, sub-Saharan Africa and Middle East-North Africa (including Turkey).[6]

Also shown in the table for the sake of comparison are the Freedom House civil liberties and political rights indices, based on annual averages for 1993 to 1997, which are available for a similar number of countries. These indicators provide a sense of the broader rights context within which worker rights are situated. Freedom House describes its rating method as follows: "The survey rates political rights and civil liberties on a seven-category scale, 1 representing the most free and 7 the least free. A country is assigned to a particular numerical category based on responses to the checklist and the judgments of the Survey team at Freedom House" (Freedom House, 1999: 549). For Appendix Table 1, the Freedom House indices are normalized to be directly comparable with the trade union rights indicators such that 0 equals least free and 10 equals most free.

Regarding the civil liberties index, the checklist referred to in the above quote consists of fourteen items in four categories: "freedom of expression and belief," "association and organizational rights," "rule of law and human rights" and

---

[5] This means that if these measures are constructed for future periods, the mid-1990s measures might need to be rescaled.

[6] Nine countries were coded but dropped from the sample as it was felt that there was not sufficient textual information to derive an adequate score. These were the nine countries for which there was no ICFTU report (perhaps the richest of the textual sources) and which were 3.0 or more points greater than either the Freedom House civil liberties or political rights indices, on a scale of 0 to 10, with 0 indicating weakest rights and 10 indicating strongest. (Countries that had scores that were 3.0 or more points less than the Freedom House indices were not dropped, as such scores do not suggest that there was not sufficient textual information.) The nine excluded countries are Armenia, Bosnia and Herzegovina, Brunei Darussalam, Kyrgystan, FYR Macedonia, Moldova, Mozambique, Tajikistan and Turkmenistan.

"personal autonomy and economic rights." Under "association and organizational rights," one of the checklist items relates directly to FACB rights: "Are there free trade unions and peasant organizations or equivalents, and is there effective collective bargaining? Are there free professional and other private organizations?" Under the category "personal autonomy and economic rights," another checklist item refers to "freedom from exploitation" regarding employers and union leaders: "Is there equality of opportunity, including freedom from exploitation by or dependency on landlords, employers, union leaders, bureaucrats, or other types of obstacles to a share of legitimate economic gains?" The political rights index addresses questions relating to free and fair elections, the competitiveness of political parties, self-determination, and discrimination.

Also shown in the table are GDP per capita in both current U.S. dollar and PPP terms, both annual averages for 1993 to 1997.

Correlation coefficients between each pair of these six variables are shown in Table 2. Correlation coefficients between GDP per capita (in PPP terms) and the Freedom House indices hovers around 0.60 and for the trade union rights indices around 0.35. This suggests that there may be a developmental aspect to democracy (civil liberties and political rights taken together) and trade union rights, with a tendency for democracy and trade union rights to be stronger in more economically developed countries, though the pattern is clearly less strong for trade union rights. The correlation coefficient between the Freedom House and trade union rights indices is around 0.60.

Table 3 shows descriptive statistics for these six variables broken down into eight regions and then for all regions. Note that in the right-hand panel that there is considerable similarity for all regions among the Freedom House and trade union rights indicators regarding means, standard deviations and coefficients of variation.

The difference between regional means and the mean for all regions is shown in the lower panel of the table. For the Freedom House and trade union rights indices, the most striking differences from the mean for all regions are for the OECD region with scores above average; and the Southeast Asia, South Asia and Middle East-North Africa regions with scores below average. Patterns are more mixed for four other regions, both in terms of differences between the Freedom House and trade union rights indices and differences between regional means and means for all regions.

Also worth noting is variation in observed violations among the thirty-seven evaluation criteria. For all 169 countries coded, the 1,351 observed violations are shown by percent distribution across the thirty-seven evaluation criteria in Figure 1.[7] The most commonly observed violations (above 5.0 percent) are for:

- Arrest, detention, imprisonment, or forced exile for union membership or activities
- Interference with union rights of assembly, demonstration, free opinion, free expression

---

[7] This includes implied violations regarding exclusion of sectors, as per the construction of the unweighted union rights indicator as described above.

Table 2. Correlation Coefficients (Pearson) between GDP per Capita and Freedom House and Trade Union Rights Indices: mid-1990s.

	GDP per capita, USD	GDP per capita, PPP	FH civil liberties index	FH political rights index	Trade union rights index, unweighted	Trade union rights index, weighted
GDP per capita, USD	1.00					
GDP per capita, PPP	0.96	1.00				
FH civil liberties index	0.55	0.64	1.00			
FH political rights index	0.47	0.57	0.94	1.00		
Trade union rights index, unweighted	0.33	0.34	0.61	0.57	1.00	
Trade union rights index, weighted	0.35	0.36	0.64	0.60	0.99	1.00

Note: The critical two-tailed values for 98 degrees of freedom (100 observations) are 0.164, 0.195 and 0.254 at the 10, 5 and 1 percent levels, respectively.

Table 3. Descriptive Statistics for GDP per Capita and Freedom House and Trade Union Rights Indices: Mid-1990s.

Number of countries	No. of obs.	OECD 23	Latin America– Caribbean 27	Non-OECD East Asia-Pacific 8	Southeast Asia 10	South Asia 8	Transition countries 27	Sub-Saharan Africa 45	Middle East-North Africa 21	All regions 169				
				Means						Mean	Std. dev.	Coeff. of var.	Max.	Min.
GDP per capita, USD	161	24,112	3,073	5,489	5,430	521	1,964	741	6,538	5,828	9,049	1.55	40,463	104
GDP per capita, PPP	155	21,383	5,584	7,020	5,373	1,988	5,460	1,905	8,746	7,161	7,475	1.04	32,075	473
FH civil liberties index	168	9.35	6.45	5.00	2.54	2.92	5.06	3.84	2.96	5.03	3.09	0.61	10.00	0.00
FH political rights index	168	9.96	7.10	5.71	2.63	4.22	5.42	3.72	2.92	5.33	3.64	0.68	10.00	0.00
Trade union rights index, unweighted	160	8.41	4.55	4.23	2.38	2.68	6.45	5.27	3.65	5.19	3.24	0.62	10.00	0.00
Trade union rights index, weighted	160	8.62	4.82	4.55	2.70	2.79	6.62	5.43	3.90	5.40	3.17	0.59	10.00	0.00

Difference between regional means and mean for all regions

FH civil liberties index	4.32	1.42	-0.03	-2.49	-2.11	0.03	-1.18	-2.07
FH political rights index	4.63	1.77	0.38	-2.71	-1.11	0.08	-1.61	-2.42
Trade union rights index, unweighted	3.22	-0.64	-0.96	-2.81	-2.51	1.26	0.08	-1.54
Trade union rights index, weighted	3.22	-0.58	-0.85	-2.70	-2.61	1.21	0.03	-1.51

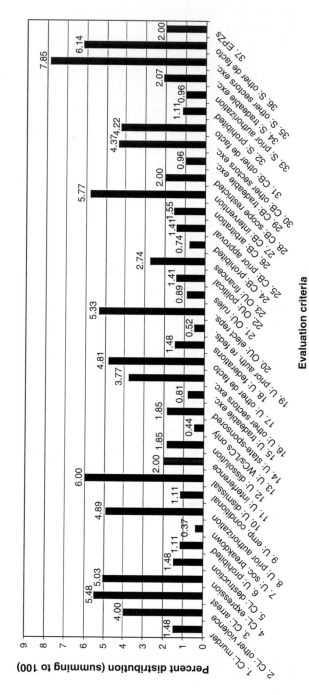

Figure 1. Percent Distribution of Observed Violations of Trade Union Rights for All Regions: Mid-1990s.

- Dismissal or suspension for union membership or activities
- Right to elect representatives in full freedom
- Intervention of authorities [in collective bargaining]
- Exclusion of tradeable/industrial sectors from right to strike
- Exclusion of other [non-tradeable/non-industrial] sectors or workers from right to strike

The least frequently observed violations (below 1.0 percent) are for:

- General absence [of right to establish and join unions and worker organizations] resulting from socio-economic breakdown
- Only workers' committees and labour councils permitted
- Exclusion of other [non-tradeable/non-industrial] sectors or workers from union membership
- Previous authorization requirements [regarding right to establish and join federations or confederations of unions]
- Right to establish constitutions and rules
- General prohibitions [of the right to collectively bargain]
- Exclusion of tradeable/industrial sectors from right to collectively bargain
- Previous authorization required by authorities [regarding the right to strike]

Percent distributions of observed violations among the thirty-seven evaluation criteria are show broken out by the eight regions in Figures 2 and 3.

4. Strengths and Limitations of the Method

There are several criteria that are useful in assessing qualitative indicators, which together provide a sense of the limitations and accuracy (or conversely measurement error) of an indicator (Cf. Bollen and Paxton, 2000). Among these are:

- **Definitional validity:** Is the definition used to construct the indicator consistent with the phenomena it aims to measure?
- **Sufficient grades of variation:** Is the indicator sufficiently finely graded to capture important dimensions of variation?
- **Reproducibility and transparency in the use of sources:** To what extent are different evaluators able to consistently arrive at the same results? How well can a score and its constituent elements be traced back to individual information sources?
- **Evaluator bias:** To what extent do scores reflect the bias of evaluators, with, for example, evaluators favouring countries that are more like their own?
- **Information bias and other problems with information sources:** For example, do textual sources contain systematically more information on some groups of countries than others, such as by region or language? Is there systematically more information on some sectors within a country, such as the formal sector? Are textual sources consistent across countries and over time in the criteria by which they evaluate countries?

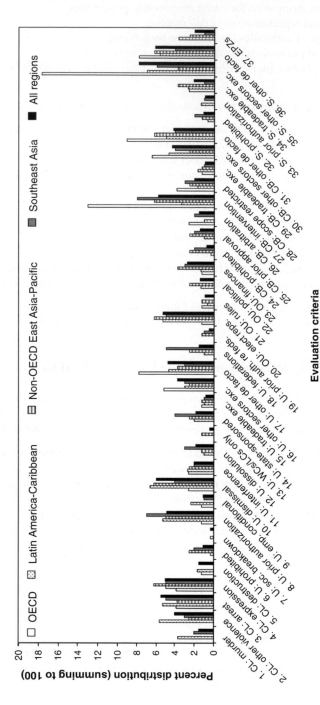

Figure 2. Percent Distribution of Observed Violations of Trade Union Rights by Region: Mid-1990s.

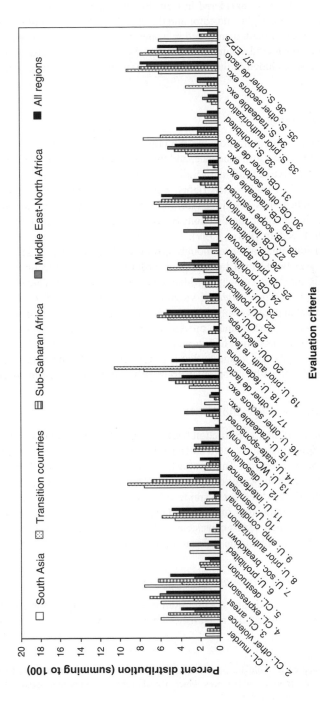

Figure 3. Percent Distribution of Observed Violations of Trade Union Rights by Region: Mid-1990s.

Each of these criteria is considered in turn. Because comparisons are made with the OECD trade union rights indicator and the Freedom House civil liberties index, a schematic survey of them is included in Appendix 2, categorized by method, definition, period considered, country coverage and information sources. To facilitate comparison, also included in this schematic survey are our own trade union rights indicators.

Definitional Validity

The trade union rights indicators are directly based on ILO Conventions No. 87 and No. 98 and related jurisprudence, and thus from the viewpoint of international labour standards have definitional validity. This is not necessarily the case for other indicators related to trade union rights. For instance, whereas the OECD trade union rights indicator is based on essentially this same definition, this does not appear to be the case for the Freedom House civil liberties index (OECD, 1996; OECD, 2000; Freedom House, 1999).

Another fundamental issue, though, is how well the strength of de facto trade union rights can be defined by observed violations without accounting for the latent, underlying rights context in which these violations occur. There are clearly cases, for instance, when observed violations are a reflection of a vibrant trade union movement and, conversely, where violations are not observed and indeed do not occur because the trade union movement is suppressed and under threat. This reveals an intrinsic limitation to any method based solely on observed violations of trade union rights and suggests that a fuller sense of the strength of de facto trade union rights must be complemented by other approaches and measures.

Sufficient Grades of Variation

Given the nature of their construction based on thirty-seven evaluation criteria, the trade union rights indicators seem sufficiently finely graded to capture important differences among countries. This contrasts to an extent with the OECD trade union rights indicator, with its scores of 1, 2, 3 or 4 (OECD, 1996; OECD, 2000). For the pre-1990s OECD countries, for example, all countries but Turkey get the best possible score. By our indicators, in contrast, Japan, the U.K. and the U.S. get scores of fair to middling, which seems consistent with a more impressionistic sense of the de facto strength of trade union rights in these countries in the mid-1990s.[8]

Reproducibility and Transparency in the Use of Sources

In constructing these indicators, a premium was put on satisfying the condition of reproducibility, or "intercoder reliability." There were two linked reasons for this:

---

[8] The OECD approach could be modified, though, along the lines of the Freedom House approach, by having more possible scores, which would probably require more clearly delineated and thus more transparent scoring criteria.

first, because it was not clear whether it would be possible to make the indicators publicly available; and, second, because the indicators were constructed not as ends in themselves but rather for use in econometric models of wages, foreign direct investment, and international trade (Kucera, 2001; Kucera and Sarna, 2006). Therefore, the credibility of the econometric results depended on the reproducibility of the indicators. Reproducibility is, of course, a testable proposition, and the construction of these indicators has not been fully tested in this regard, such as via a comparison of the results of two evaluators working independently. However, the detail and explicitness of the coding rules as well as the comparison of the results of two coders of the Committee on Freedom of Association reports suggests that the method of construction does indeed lend itself to attaining reproducible results.[9]

When it comes to addressing intrinsically qualitative phenomena such as the de facto strength of trade union rights, however, reproducibility may trade off against accuracy. That is, the method is reproducible because it is rigid, but this very rigidity forecloses the sorts of nuanced judgements that may result in greater accuracy. Consider the problem of dismissal for union activities. This method treats one dismissal the same as a thousand (and the textual sources do not come close to providing such information systematically), whereas such approaches as the OECD's and Freedom House's need not.[10] Rather than coding with a binary dummy variable, one could alternatively code observed violations using a three-or four-point system. But then different evaluators may well disagree on how to make these assessments, which are no longer a question of no or yes but rather of no or what sort of yes. This too illustrates the potential trade-off between reproducibility and accuracy.

Last, the method is transparent in its use of sources in that the components of country scores can be readily traced back to a *particular* textual source, rather than just to the set of sources used.

---

[9] There may be a difference with Compa's assessment of the method in this regard (Compa, 2002). Compa writes, for instance: "No purely quantifiable system for assessing countries' compliance with freedom of association standards is possible. Even the three most sophisticated efforts at quantifying labour rights compliance – the OECD, Kucera, and Verité schemes – acknowledged that in the end someone sitting in a room in Paris or Geneva or Boston said '2 points? 3 points? Let's give it a 3,' or something like that, in constructing their country scores. One had to read closely to find these admissions. Kucera used the passive voice to describe his scoring method: 'with greater weights indicating what are judged to be more severe problems" (ibid: 55). However, the mention of the severity of problems refers not to the coding as such, but rather to the weighting scheme of the evaluation criteria, which is in a sense prior to the coding. Different evaluators could, of course, use different weighting schemes, and while such a choice is ultimately subjective, this does not imply that the scores would not be reproducible by different evaluators for any given weighting scheme.

[10] Because they leave room for more nuanced judgments, the OECD and Freedom House approaches might also enable one to better assess the broader underlying rights context in which violations of trade union rights are observed.

Evaluator Bias

In an important study, Bollen and Paxton provide evidence that evaluator bias is a significant source of systematic measurement error for a number of indicators of democracy, including the Freedom House indices (2000). That is, evaluators are biased by what Bollen and Paxton call "situational closeness," the extent to which the countries being scored are more or less like the evaluators' own countries. But because it appears to do well in terms of reproducibility, this indicator of trade union rights does not seem problematically vulnerable to evaluator bias.

Information Bias and Other Problems with Information Sources

As the U.S. National Research Council report notes, the information used in the three textual sources tends to focus on the formal sector and is thus not representative of trade union rights in the economy as a whole (National Research Council, 2004: 120). However, these indicators were constructed and used to evaluate the effects of trade union rights on primarily formal sector phenomena, such as wages in registered manufacturing establishments, foreign direct investment and international trade, and so such sectoral bias does not appear a serious concern in this regard.

The National Research Council report also notes that there is a regional bias in the ILO Committee on Freedom of Association reports, stating that "Approximately half of all CFA complaints come from Latin American countries, in part reflecting the fact that Latin American unions have grown accustomed to using this mechanism" (ibid.: 123-124). This regional bias is suggested as well by the figures in Table 4, which shows that for the Latin America–Caribbean region, 41 percent of observed violations from the three textual sources originate from the Committee on Freedom of Association reports. This is a higher share than for any of the other seven regions considered. However, this and other regional biases can be and indeed were addressed in econometric analysis by such methods as specifying models with and without regional dummy variables, dropping a region at a time from the sample, and using indicators related to trade union rights that do not rely on the Committee on Freedom of Association reports, such as the Freedom House civil liberties index.

There is also a likely problem using this method in attempting to assess variation over time. This is because country write-ups in our textual sources have tended to become longer and more detailed over time. Because these sources tend to focus on problems, this creates a systematic tendency for indicators based on coding these sources to show a weakening of trade union rights over time, which might simply be a reflection of better reporting of violations of trade union rights. One consequence is that it would seem prudent that panel data analyses using an indicator constructed by this method (or an indicator using these sources) focus on cross-country variation rather than variation over time.

These points aside, a fundamental source of measurement error for this indicator and those based on the same sources derive from the shortcomings of existing information sources. The basic problem is that existing sources do not consistently apply, by and large, a systematic and detailed definition of what

Table 4. Regional Comparison of Number of Observed Violations from Committee on Freedom of Association (CFA) Reports versus Other Information sources.

	OECD	Latin America–Caribbean	Non-OECD East Asia-Pacific	South-east Asia	South Asia	Transition countries	Sub-Saharan Africa	Middle East-North Africa
Number of observed violations from CFA reports	21	124	17	20	19	20	68	20
Number of observed violations from all three information sources	77	300	80	100	66	153	380	195
Percentage of observed violations from CFA reports	27.3	41.3	21.3	20.0	28.8	13.1	17.9	10.3

constitutes trade union rights as well as violations of these rights, either across countries or over time. Neither is it clear to what extent those involved in constructing the sources have access to relevant information even if they did endeavour to apply a consistent and detailed definition of trade union rights. The sources are, in many respects, anecdotal in nature, and it is not clear how telling and representative these anecdotes are. It is not difficult to imagine, for instance, that there might have been in nearly every country in the world at least one dismissal of an employee for union-related activities in the 1993 to 1997 period, while such violations are only reported for a smaller share of countries in our three sources. More generally, it is unclear to what extent the report of violation in a country is indicative of what actually occurred in that country as compared to a country for which no such violation is reported. A similar assessment of existing information sources is made in the U.S. National Research Council's report *Monitoring International Labor Standards: Techniques and Sources of Information* (2004). Indeed the opening sentences of the report's "conclusions and recommendations" are,

> The committee [responsible for the report] concludes that the informational base for assessing compliance with international labor standards is very far from ideal. This chapter has presented examples, which can be multiplied, indicating why it is difficult for an observer to decide on the severity of a problem or its evolution (*ibid.*: 29).

Moreover, all five general recommendations of the committee are about improving information sources on labour standards.

5. Moving Forward

A key bottleneck in moving toward more definitive qualitative indicators of trade union rights is improved information sources. The above and similar methods could be amended by adding information from additional sources that are less comprehensive by country coverage. But using these sources comes with its own set of problems, such as possibly introducing bias depending on country selection in these additional sources. It would be better, if anything, to have fewer but more definitive sources. This could provide the basis for qualitative indicators constructed by a number of plausible methods, and from the viewpoint of econometric analysis and assessing the robustness of results, the more reasonable indicators the better. It would be useful, in particular, if the construction of such indicators were more closely integrated with the collection and compilation of information so that country reports provided well-defined, consistent, detailed and clearly structured information regarding what constitutes trade union rights and violations of these rights, in both the negative and positive senses and addressing the latent, underlying rights context. A welcome initiative in this regard is the WebMILS Monitoring International Labour Standards website, an outcome of the U.S. National Research Council project on monitoring international labour standards.[11] The ultimate usefulness of this initiative depends, however, on how the templates for country reports come to be filled out and how this information is updated.

Another potentially promising route for improving the measurement of the strength of trade union rights is through incorporating a small number of carefully designed questions into labour force surveys – that is, by developing quantitative indicators of trade union rights.[12] Labour force surveys have of course the tremendous advantage of providing a more precise sense of how representative violations of trade union rights are in the context of a relevant population. One such question might be *"Have you been* negatively affected for being a union member or for trying to organize a union?" Such a question might constitute a problematically rare event, particularly in countries having low union membership or small shares of formal employees. As such, it might be preferable to modify the question to ask, *"Do you know of anyone who has been* negatively affected for being a union member or for trying to organize a union?" The challenge in this approach would be to have such questions introduced into labour force surveys for a sufficiently large sample of countries and for such questions to continue to be asked over time.

---

[11] Available: http://www.trikat.com/WEBMILS/

[12] Thanks to Farhad Mehran and the participants in an ILO Turin Center workshop in July 2004 for valuable discussions on such use of labour force surveys.

Appendix 1. Textual Sources and Coding Rules

Textual Sources

a. International Confederation of Free Trade Unions (ICFTU), *Annual Survey of Trade Union Rights* for 1996 (referring to developments in the year 1995) or nearest available year when no country report was available in 1996.

b. U.S. State Department, *Country Reports on Human Rights Practices* for 1995 (referring to developments in the year 1995), based on sections 6a and 6b of these reports and other relevant sections referred to in Sections 6a and 6b.

c. ILO, *Report of the Committee on Freedom of Association* for 1993 to 2000, reports 286-322.

Coding Rules

Note: For the sake of documenting the construction of the trade union rights indicator, these coding rules are presented as they were used in coding. They could, however, be edited for clarity and simplicity without substantively changing their content.

Freedom of association/collective bargaining-related civil liberties

1–5   As defined in chapter 2 on "Trade Union Rights and Civil Liberties" of *Freedom of Association: Digests of Decisions and Principles of the Freedom of Association Committee of the Governing Body of the ILO* (1996).

1 Murder or disappearance of union members or organizers
   - Includes violence to family members.

2 Other violence against union members or organizers
   - Includes violence to family members.
   - Includes coercion under threat of force (other than for **3** regarding forced exile or flight from country under threat) but not threats themselves or unspecified harassment. Does not include use of tear gas unless this results in injury.
   - Double counts with **1** in cases of murder or disappearance but not other violence.

3 Arrest, detention, imprisonment or forced exile for union membership or activities
   - Includes prosecution and flight from country under threat.
   - Includes laws that indicate sanctions for participating in union activities that may be illegal but that should not be illegal according to ILO Conventions.

4 Interference with union rights of assembly, demonstration, free opinion and free expression
   - Includes interference with freedom of movement, except as regards **5**, and also includes surveillance.
   - Includes problems with "access of trade union representatives to workplaces" (CFA 295th Report, p. 141).
   - Includes search or entry without warrant and search or entry with warrant unless the latter is for illegal non-union related activities;
   - Search or entry with warrant for illegal union related activities are also included for activities that should not be illegal according to ILO Conventions.
   - Includes interference with general, protest and solidarity strikes when these involve assembly or demonstrations (otherwise included under **36**, with double-counting allowed between **4** and **36**, for such strikes involving assembly and demonstrations).

5 Seizure or destruction of union premises or property

Right to establish and join unions and worker organizations

6–23 As defined in articles 2 to 7 of Convention No. 87, with unions broadly defined to
        include all independent workers' organisations, as per Article 10 of Convention No. 87.

6   General prohibitions

7   General absence resulting from socio-economic breakdown

8   Previous authorization requirements
    - Including that the "acquisition of legal personality by workers' . . . organisations,
      federations and confederations shall not be made subject to conditions such as to
      restrict the application of the provisions of Articles 2, 3 and 4" of Convention No.
      87 (Article 7 of Convention No. 87), e.g., includes problems with registration or
      official recognition of unions and workers organizations by authorities.
    - Also including regulations regarding the minimum number of members being
      set at "obviously too high a figure," as per paragraph 255 of *Freedom of
      Association* (1996).
    - Deregistration of an already existing union is included in **12** and not **8**.

9   Employment conditional on non-membership in union
    - As defined in Article 1 (2a) of Convention No. 98. Involves new hires and non-
      union membership as an express condition (by employers) of continued employ-
      ment. Double counts with **10** if dismissal results from these conditions.

10 Dismissal or suspension for union membership or activities
    - As defined in Article 1 (2b) of Convention No. 98.

11 Interference of employers (attempts to dominate unions)
    - As defined in Article 2 of Convention No. 98, particularly regarding attempts
      by employers to place unions "under the control of employers or employers'
      organisations . . ." (not noted under other evaluation criteria).
    - Includes the establishment or attempted establishment of parallel unions by
      employers.
    - Includes the government when it is an employer.

12 Dissolution or suspension of union by administrative authority
    - Deregistration of an already existing union.

13 Only workers' committees & labour councils permitted
    - Refers only to economy as a whole, not particular sectors/workers. (Do *not* also
      check **8** for a problem regarding **13**).

14 Only state-sponsored or single unions permitted
    - Refers only to economy as a whole, not particular sectors/workers. As per para-
      graph 277 of *Freedom of Association* (1996) regarding single union structure.
      Analogous restrictions on national federations or international confederations
      are included in **18** but not **14**. In cases of state sponsored single unions/union
      structures associated with an absence of independent unions, this is counted in
      both **14** and **6**. (Do *not* also check **8** for a problem regarding **14**).

15 Exclusion of tradeable/industrial sectors from union membership
    - Refers to when sectors/workers are generally excluded, not to other more inci-
      dental problems involving these sectors/workers.
    - Tradeable/industrial sectors defined to include manufacturing, mining, con-
      struction, utilities (industrial sectors) and agriculture, forestry, and fishing
      (additional tradeable sector).

16 Exclusion of other sectors or workers from union membership
    - Refers to when sectors/workers are generally excluded, not to other more inci-
      dental problems involving these sectors/workers. Except regarding armed
      forces and police.

- "Essential services" not specifically defined are included. If evidence of excluded sectors does not allow one to distinguish between "tradeable/industrial" and "other" sectors, it is included in "other" sectors.

17 Other specific de facto problems or acts of prohibition
- Includes problems/prohibitions for general union activities not specifically related to collective bargaining or right to strike.
- Includes blacklisting and unspecified interference in a worker organization's internal affairs.
- Double counts with **37** regarding EPZs, in part since the latter is used as a stand-alone measure. This effectively gives more weight to problems in EPZs if the information for all four evaluation criteria is used in a single measure.
- Other than noted in evaluation criteria under *same* headings (right to establish . . . for **17**, right to collectively bargain for **31**, right to strike for **36**). Note: for **31** and **36**, not other than noted in **1-5, 10** or **12**. **31** and **36** indicate prohibited act and **1-3, 5, 10** or **12** indicate sanctions for act, de jure or de facto. **17, 31** and **36** also indicate lesser sanctions, such as transfers and fines, but not threats themselves nor unspecified harassment.

18 Right to establish and join federations or confederations of unions
- As per paragraph 613 of *Freedom of Association* (1996) regarding single union affiliation with national or international federations or confederations of unions; or regarding single federations or confederations as per paragraph 277 of *Freedom of Association* (1996). If there are problems with the registration or official recognition of a federation or confederation resulting from restrictions regarding single federations or confederations, this is included in **18** but not **19**.

19 Previous authorization requirements regarding evaluation criteria 18
- As per paragraph 613 of *Freedom of Association* (1996) regarding single union affiliation with national or international federations or confederations of unions; or regarding single federations or confederations as per paragraph 277 of *Freedom of Association* (1996). If there are problems with the registration or official recognition of a federation or confederation resulting from restrictions regarding single federations or confederations, this is included in **18** but not **19**.

Other union activities
20 Right to elect representatives in full freedom
- Including the absence of eligibility requirements for union leaders, as per paragraphs 350-367 of *Freedom of Association* (1996).
- Includes dismissal or suspension of union leaders and representatives for union-related activities (which counts under both **10** and **20**), but not general civil liberties violations under **1-3**.

21 Right to establish constitutions and rules
22 General prohibition of union/federation participation in political activities
23 Union control of finances
- Including collection of union dues.

Right to bargain collectively
24–31 As defined in chapter 14 of *Freedom of Association* (1996).
24 General prohibitions
- As defined in chapter 14 of *Freedom of Association* (1996).
25 Prior approval by authorities of collective agreements
- For non-government employees only.

26 Compulsory binding arbitration
- As per paragraphs 860-865 of *Freedom of Association* (1996) and applying to right to strike as well, but excepting when problem is exclusively for sectors excluded from collective bargaining and right to strike (**29, 30, 34, 35**).
- Includes cases where compulsory arbitration is or can be used to prevent a strike from occurring altogether or to end an ongoing strike (even if only for the period of arbitration) as this is taken to imply "binding."
- Does not include cases where compulsory arbitration not indicated as binding is required prior to a strike's occurrence. Not double-counted with **27** or **28**.

27 Intervention of authorities
- As per paragraphs 866-903 and 806 & 811 of *Freedom of Association* (1996), particularly regarding "wages, working hours, leave and conditions of work . . . ."
- For **27**, includes when the government is the employer and unilaterally sets wages (including maximum wages or wage increases), working hours, etc. (which is *not* double-counted with **25**) or when prior approval by authorities is required when the government is the employer.
- For **27**, includes de facto exclusion of public sector from collective bargaining, as when government unilaterally sets wages; this is not included under **30**, for which public sector employees are included only for general de jure exclusion of the sector from collective bargaining (this is the only case for which de jure and de facto problems are treated differently regarding excluded sectors or groups of workers).
- Regarding **28**, if the scope of collective bargaining is restricted by non-state employers as a result of the intervention of the state or by legislation, this is included in **27** but not **28**.

28 Scope of collective bargaining restricted by non-state employers
- As per paragraphs 866-903 and 806 & 811 of *Freedom of Association* (1996), particularly regarding "wages, working hours, leave and conditions of work . . . ."
- Regarding **28**, if the scope of collective bargaining is restricted by non-state employers as a result of the intervention of the state or by legislation, this is included in **27** but not **28**.

29 Exclusion of tradeable/industrial sectors from right to collectively bargain
- Refers to when sectors/workers are generally excluded, not to other more incidental problems involving these sectors/workers.
- Tradeable/industrial sectors defined to include manufacturing, mining, construction, utilities (industrial sectors) and agriculture, forestry, and fishing (additional tradeable sector).

30 Exclusion of other sectors or workers from right to collectively bargain
- Refers to when sectors/workers are generally excluded, not to other more incidental problems involving these sectors/workers. Except regarding armed forces and police.
- "Essential services" not specifically defined are included. If evidence of excluded sectors does not allow one to distinguish between "tradeable/industrial" and "other" sectors, it is included in "other" sectors.

31 Other specific de facto problems or acts of prohibition
- Includes failure to recognize existing bargaining agreements and refusal of employer to bargain or participate in mediation, but not other or unspecified delay or non-payment of earnings.
- Double counts with **37** regarding EPZs, in part since the latter is used as a stand-alone measure. This effectively gives more weight to problems in EPZs if the information for all four evaluation criteria are used in a single measure.

- Other than noted in evaluation criteria under *same* headings (right to establish ... for **17**, right to collectively bargain for **31**, right to strike for **36**). Note: for **31** and **36**, not other than noted in **1-5, 10** or **12**. **31** and **36** indicate prohibited act and **1-3, 5, 10** or **12** indicate sanctions for act, de jure or de facto. **17, 31** and **36** also indicate lesser sanctions, such as transfers and fines, but not threats themselves or unspecified harassment.

Right to Strike
32–37 As defined in chapter 9 of *Freedom of Association* (1996).
33 General prohibitions
33 Previous authorization required by authorities
34 Exclusion of tradeable/industrial sectors from right to strike
  - Refers to when sectors/workers are generally excluded, not to other more incidental problems involving these sectors/workers.
  - Tradeable/industrial sectors defined to include manufacturing, mining, construction, utilities (industrial sectors) and agriculture, forestry, and fishing (additional tradeable sector).
35 Exclusion of other sectors or workers from right to strike
  - Refers to when sectors/workers are generally excluded, not to other more incidental problems involving these sectors/workers. Except regarding armed forces and police.
  - "Essential services" not specifically defined are included. If evidence of excluded sectors does not allow one to distinguish between "tradeable/industrial" and "other" sectors, it is included in "other" sectors.
36 Other specific de facto problems or acts of prohibition
  - Double counts with **37** regarding EPZs, in part since the latter is used as a standalone measure. This effectively gives more weight to problems in EPZs if the information for all four evaluation criteria are used in a single measure.
  - Other than noted in evaluation criteria under *same* headings (right to establish ... for **17**, right to collectively bargain for **31**, right to strike for **36**). Note: for **31** and **36**, not other than noted in **1-5, 10** or **12**. **31** and **36** indicate prohibited act and **1-3, 5, 10** or **12** indicate sanctions for act, de jure or de facto. **17, 31** and **36** also indicate lesser sanctions, such as transfers and fines, but not threats themselves nor unspecified harassment.

Export processing zones
37 Restricted rights in EPZs

General Coding Rules

Regarding year of problem in source, all de facto problems evidence occurring between 1993 and 1997 (inclusive) are included.

Contrary evidence within a source is excluded. For contrary evidence across sources, evidence of problems is included if it seems credible on its own terms.

When a violation of trade union rights occurs but is remedied, it is nonetheless still coded as a violation. There are several reasons for this approach. For instance, union premises are destroyed and then, afterwards, there is a process through which there is compensation to the union: this is not equivalent to the union premises not having been destroyed in the first place. This approach seems reasonable in light of the main causal channels through which trade union rights are hypothesized to affect foreign direct investment and trade – through labour costs and through social stability. Violations of trade union rights, even when afterwards remedied, are likely to contribute to social instability. And even eventually remedied violations of trade union rights are likely to hinder workers' sense of strength and thus their willingness and ability to bargain for higher wages. An alternative approach would be to double the number of evaluation criteria to account for remedied versus non-remedied violations of trade union rights. In addition to being unwieldy, however, the information sources tend to be anecdotal rather than systematic in reporting whether a violation was remedied and thus this alternative approach was not adopted.

Evaluation criteria **1, 2, 3, 5, 10** and **12** indicate sanctions, for which double-counting of a problem is likely. E.g., dismissal for strike activity counts in both **36** (prohibited act) and **10** (sanction for the act, de jure or de facto). In general, such double-counting is done throughout, with evaluation criteria generally not mutually exclusive, unless specifically indicated otherwise.

Sanctions and violations against non-unionized workers are also included, if these workers are wrongfully prevented from unionizing and are punished for carrying out union-like activities or for providing worker voice (except of military and police). Particularly relevant for **1-3, 5, 10** and **12**. Includes sanctions and violations against excluded sectors/workers noted in **15, 16, 29, 30, 34** and **35**.

Appendix 2. Schematic Survey of Three Qualitative Indicators Pertaining to Freedom of Association and Collective Bargaining Rights.

- OECD trade union rights indicator
- Freedom House civil liberties index
- Kucera trade union rights indicator

OECD Trade Union Rights Indicator

Method:

The OECD created three tables with up to one paragraph of text on three aspects of FACB rights:
"Restrictions on the right to establish free unions"
"Restrictions on the right to strike"
"Protection of union members and collective bargaining rights"
"[B]ased on [OECD] Secretariat judgment," an overall score of 1, 2, 3 or 4 is given for each country based on text in tables (in OECD 1996, 1 = strongest rights, 4 = weakest rights, with order reversed in OECD 2000).

Definition:

Based on ILO Conventions No. 87 and No. 98 and related ILO jurisprudence.

Period considered:

Mid-1990s (OECD 1996) and late-1990s (OECD 2000).

Country coverage:

Available for up to 79 countries.

Information sources:

ILO, various sources.
International Confederation of Free Trade Unions (ICFTU), *Annual Survey of Violations of Trade Union Rights.*
U.S. State Department, Country Reports on Human Rights Practices.

Freedom House Civil Liberties Index

Freedom House is a non-profit organization based in the U.S. that describes itself as follows: "Non-partisan and broad based, Freedom House is led by a Board of Trustees composed of leading Democrats, Republicans, and independents; business and labour leaders; former senior government officials; scholars: writers; and journalists."

Method:

Freedom House describes its method as follows: "The survey rates political rights and civil liberties on a seven-category scale, 1 representing the most free and 7 the least free. A country is assigned to a particular numerical category based on responses to the checklist and the judgments of the *Survey* team at Freedom House."

Regarding the civil liberties index, the checklist referred to in the above quotation consists of 14 items in four categories: "freedom of expression and belief," "association and organizational rights," "rule of law and human rights" and "personal autonomy and economic rights." Under "association and organizational rights," one of the checklist items relates directly to FACB rights:

> "Are there free trade unions and peasant organizations or equivalents, and
> is there effective collective bargaining? Are there free professional and
> other private organizations?"

Under the category "personal autonomy and economic rights," another checklist item refers to "union leaders":

> "Is there equality of opportunity, including freedom from exploitation by
> or dependency on landlords, employers, union leaders, bureaucrats, or
> other types of obstacles to a share of legitimate economic gains?"

Each of the 14 items is assigned 0 to 4 "raw points," with more points indicating a judgment of stronger civil liberties. These "raw points" are then summed across the 14 checklist items and the civil liberties index based on the total number of "raw points" as follows:

Raw points	Civil liberties index
50 to 56	1
42 to 49	2
34 to 41	3
26 to 33	4
17 to 25	5
9 to 16	6
0 to 8	7

Note that the score on the checklist item relating to FACB makes up only 1/14 of the overall civil liberties index and that scores are not available for individual checklist items.

In explaining its judgments in the construction of the civil liberties index, Freedom House writes:

> When analysing the civil liberties checklist, Freedom House does not mistake constitutional guarantees of human rights for those rights in practice. For states and territories with small populations, particularly tiny island nations, the absence of trade unions and other types of association is not necessarily viewed as a negative situation unless the government or other centres of domination are deliberately blocking their formation or operation.

Definition:

Definitions are not made explicit except insofar as noted above under "method." No reference is made to ILO Conventions or related ILO jurisprudence.

Period considered:

Annual data from 1972 to present, updated annually.

Country coverage:

Available for 201 countries and territories.

Information sources:

Approximately 120 publications and 120 organizations are consulted. These are listed in the "Sources" section of *Freedom in the World*. However, none of these are ILO publications and the ILO itself is not consulted.

Kucera Trade Union Rights Indicator

Method:

Established 37 evaluation criteria providing classification of types of FACB violations. See Table 1. Each of the evaluation criteria are based on a detailed set of definitions and decision rules, indicating relevant ILO Convention articles and jurisprudence passages; how to classify the diverse range of problems noted in the information sources; and how the various evaluation criteria relate to each other. The aim is to have a sufficiently detailed set of definitions and decision rules that different evaluators would arrive at the same results.

Assign value of 0 for no evidence found and 1 for evidence found for each of 37 evaluation criteria, creating a country dummy variable.

Constructed in two versions: **unweighted** (that is, equally weighted) and **weighted**. Weights purport to indicate the severity of violations (weights: 1, 1.25, 1.5, 1.75, 2, with 1 = least severe and 2 = most severe).

For the weighted version, country dummy variable is multiplied by weighting scheme.

Overall country score (non-normalized) is given by summing across 37 evaluation criteria (unweighted and weighted).

"Default" worse possible scores are given to countries for which sources indicate general prohibitions of the right to establish and join unions and other worker organizations or general prohibitions of collective bargaining.

Definition:

Based on ILO Conventions No. 87 and No. 98 and related ILO jurisprudence and violations observed in information sources.

Period considered:

Mid-1990s (based on violations occurring between 1993 and 1997 inclusive).

Country coverage:

Available for 160 countries.

Information sources:

ILO, *Report of the Committee on Freedom of Association.*
International Confederation of Free Trade Unions (ICFTU), *Annual Survey of Violations of Trade Union Rights.*
U.S. State Department, *Country Reports on Human Rights Practices.*

Appendix Table 1. GDP per Capita and Freedom House and Trade Union Rights Indices: Mid-1990s.

OECD	GDP per capita, USD	GDP per capita, PPP	FH civil liberties index	FH political rights index	Trade union rights index, unweighted	Trade union rights index, weighted
Australia	20,649	21,272	10.00	10.00	7.62	7.44
Austria	26,357	22,384	10.00	10.00	10.00	10.00
Belgium	24,425	22,683	9.58	10.00	9.05	9.10
Canada	19,810	23,122	10.00	10.00	8.57	8.65
Denmark	31,420	23,257	10.00	10.00	8.10	8.20
Finland	22,151	19,184	10.00	10.00	9.52	9.55
France	24,689	20,753	8.33	10.00	9.05	8.95
Germany	26,952	21,660	8.33	10.00	9.05	9.47
Greece	10,689	13,318	6.67	10.00	9.05	9.10
Iceland	25,433	23,624	10.00	10.00	9.05	9.10
Ireland	17,987	17,734	9.17	10.00	10.00	10.00
Italy	19,260	20,499	7.92	10.00	9.52	9.55
Japan	36,556	23,879	8.33	9.17	5.71	6.39
Luxembourg	40,463	32,075	10.00	10.00	9.52	9.55
Netherlands	24,364	21,025	10.00	10.00	9.52	9.55
New Zealand	15,589	17,318	10.00	10.00	9.05	9.10
Norway	32,038	25,297	10.00	10.00	8.57	8.65
Portugal	10,126	13,767	10.00	10.00	10.00	10.00
Spain	14,063	15,375	8.33	10.00	7.14	8.05
Sweden	25,870	20,089	10.00	10.00	9.52	9.55
Switzerland	38,633	25,758	10.00	10.00	9.52	9.55
United Kingdom	19,183	19,629	8.33	10.00	3.33	4.14
U.S.	27,871	28,116	10.00	10.00	2.86	4.74

Latin America-Caribbean	GDP per capita, USD	GDP per capita, PPP	FH civil liberties index	FH political rights index	Trade union rights index, unweighted	Trade union rights index, weighted
Argentina	7,585	11,264	6.67	8.33	2.38	2.56
Bahamas	12,389	14,869	8.33	10.00	8.10	8.95
Barbados	7,116	12,446	10.00	10.00	8.57	8.65
Belize	2,711	4,730	10.00	10.00	3.81	4.59
Bolivia	908	2,177	6.25	8.33	0.48	1.43
Brazil	4,101	6,625	5.00	7.92	3.33	3.83
Chile	4,287	7,635	8.33	8.33	4.76	5.86
Colombia	2,251	5,863	5.00	6.25	0.00	0.00
Costa Rica	3,360	6,714	8.33	10.00	2.38	2.56
Cuba			0.00	0.00	0.00	0.00
Dominican Republic	1,544	4,381	6.67	5.83	4.76	4.29
Ecuador	1,530	3,198	6.25	8.33	2.38	2.78

El Salvador	1,624	3,923	6.67	6.67	2.38	2.78
Guatemala	1,452	3,378	3.75	5.42	2.86	2.48
Guyana	740	3,332	8.33	8.33	8.57	8.65
Haiti	341	1,441	2.50	2.92	6.67	6.24
Honduras	696	2,392	6.67	6.67	2.38	3.08
Jamaica	1,930	3,688	6.67	8.33	8.57	8.50
Mexico	4,051	7,453	5.42	5.00	1.90	2.63
Nicaragua	430	2,292	4.58	5.42	6.19	6.09
Panama	3,020	5,167	6.67	7.92	4.76	5.19
Paraguay	1,778	4,501	6.67	5.42	1.90	2.33
Peru	2,107	4,237	5.00	3.75	1.43	2.03
Suriname	876	2,394	6.67	6.67	9.52	9.55
Trinidad and Tobago	4,196	6,958	8.75	10.00	9.52	9.55
Uruguay	5,624	8,141	8.33	8.75	8.57	8.65
Venezuela	3,251	5,986	6.67	7.08	6.67	6.92

Non-OECD East Asia-Pacific	GDP per capita, USD	GDP per capita, PPP	FH civil liberties index	FH political rights index	Trade union rights index, unweighted	Trade union rights index, weighted
China	563	2,639	0.00	0.00	0.00	0.00
Fiji	2,502	4,598	6.67	5.00	4.29	5.19
Hong Kong (China)	23,039	22,162			4.76	5.04
Korea, Dem. People's Republic of			0.00	0.00	0.00	0.00
Korea, Republic of	9,928	13,515	8.33	8.33	1.43	2.93
Mongolia	373	1,485	6.67	8.33	7.14	7.14
Papua New Guinea	1,166	2,521	5.00	8.33	8.57	8.65
Solomon Islands	850	2,221	8.33	10.00	7.62	7.44

Southeast Asia	GDP per capita, USD	GDP per capita, PPP	FH civil liberties index	FH political rights index	Trade union rights index, unweighted	Trade union rights index, weighted
Brunei Darussalam	16,702		2.50	0.00		
Cambodia	255	1,269	2.50	3.33	6.19	5.94
Indonesia	1,010	2,879	2.08	0.00	0.48	0.98
Lao People's Democratic Republic	357	1,213	1.67	0.00	0.00	0.00
Malaysia	4,182	7,461	3.33	5.00	0.48	2.18
Myanmar			0.00	0.00	0.00	0.00
Philippines	1,047	3,619	5.42	7.50	1.90	1.95
Singapore	22,410	19,001	3.33	3.75	8.10	8.20
Thailand	2,629	6,060	4.58	6.67	4.29	5.04
Vietnam	273	1,486	0.00	0.00	0.00	0.00

South Asia	GDP per capita, USD	GDP per capita, PPP	FH civil liberties index	FH political rights index	Trade union rights index, unweighted	Trade union rights index, weighted
Afghanistan			0.00	0.00	0.00	0.00
Bangladesh	314	1,273	5.00	7.92	1.43	1.73
Bhutan	444	1,168	0.00	0.00	0.00	0.00
India	374	1,846	5.00	5.83	5.71	5.34
Maldives	1,131	4,003	1.67	1.67	0.00	0.00
Nepal	203	1,136	5.00	6.67	6.67	6.39
Pakistan	476	1,730	3.33	6.25	1.43	2.78
Sri Lanka	703	2,759	3.33	5.42	6.19	6.09

Transition Countries	GDP per capita, USD	GDP per capita, PPP	FH civil liberties index	FH political rights index	Trade union rights index, unweighted	Trade union rights index, weighted
Albania	658	2,659	5.00	6.67	4.76	5.49
Armenia	568	1,940	5.00	5.42		
Azerbaijan	460	2,233	2.08	1.67	9.05	9.10
Belarus	2,166	5,746	3.75	3.33	4.29	3.98
Bosnia and Herzegovina	648		2.08	2.08		
Bulgaria	1,277	5,225	7.92	8.33	6.19	6.24
Croatia	3,457	5,955	5.00	5.00	6.19	6.77
Czech Republic	4,624	12,268	8.33	10.00	7.14	7.29
Estonia	2,931	6,751	8.33	7.92	8.10	8.05
Georgia	515	2,169	3.75	4.17	9.52	9.55
Hungary	4,218	9,465	8.33	10.00	6.67	6.84
Kazakhstan	1,381	4,673	3.75	1.67	6.19	6.24
Kyrgyzstan	626	2,287	5.83	4.58		
Latvia	2,098	5,142	7.92	7.50	9.05	9.10
Lithuania	1,929	5,836	7.50	10.00	6.67	6.84
Macedonia, The Former Yugoslav Republic of	1,388	4,361	6.67	5.42		
Moldova, Republic of	642	2,512	4.58	5.00		
Poland	2,993	6,746	8.33	9.17	8.10	8.20
Romania	1,346	6,290	6.25	5.83	3.33	4.29
Russian Federation	2,574	7,403	5.00	6.67	3.33	3.98
Slovakia	3,210	8,640	5.83	7.92	8.10	8.20
Slovenia	8,353	13,147	8.33	10.00	8.10	8.05
Tajikistan	283		0.00	0.00		
Turkmenistan	772	3,422	0.00	0.00		
Ukraine	1,122	4,044	5.00	6.25	5.24	5.04
Uzbekistan	814	2,115	0.42	0.00	9.05	9.10
Yugoslavia			1.67	1.67	0.00	0.00

Sub-Saharan Africa	GDP per capita, USD	GDP per capita, PPP	FH civil liberties index	FH political rights index	Trade union rights index, unweighted	Trade union rights index, weighted
Angola	542	1,872	0.83	0.83	6.67	6.69
Benin	364	842	7.50	8.33	8.10	8.20
Botswana	3,210	5,878	7.50	8.33	5.71	7.44
Burkina Faso	224	841	5.00	3.33	7.62	8.50
Burundi	153	644	0.00	0.83	6.67	7.44
Cameroon	697	1,464	3.33	0.83	2.38	3.08
Cape Verde	1,188	3,788	8.33	10.00	7.62	7.44
Central African Republic	325	1,071	4.58	6.67	6.67	6.69
Chad	215	815	3.33	1.67	2.86	3.23
Comoros	435	1,601	5.00	5.00	7.14	6.84
Congo	863	916	5.42	5.42	6.67	6.24
Côte d'Ivoire	711	1,535	3.33	1.67	5.71	5.34
Democratic Republic of Congo	146	907	1.67	0.00	2.38	2.93
Equatorial Guinea	600	1,930	0.00	0.00	0.00	0.00
Eritrea	155	764	4.17	1.67	9.52	9.55
Ethiopia	104	572	3.33	3.33	1.90	2.33
Gabon	4,498	6,104	5.00	3.33	9.05	9.10
Gambia	344	1,464	3.33	2.08	7.62	8.20
Ghana	373	1,702	5.00	4.58	8.10	7.89
Guinea	548	1,742	3.33	1.67	7.14	6.99
Guinea-Bissau	233	846	4.58	5.42	8.57	8.35
Kenya	305	1,023	1.67	1.25	3.81	4.44
Lesotho	472	1,563	5.00	5.42	4.29	5.19
Liberia			1.67	0.42	0.00	0.00
Madagascar	256	792	5.00	8.33	7.62	8.35
Malawi	198	535	5.83	6.67	5.24	5.04
Mali	249	670	6.67	8.33	7.62	7.59
Mauritania	451	1,523	1.25	0.83	5.71	5.34
Mauritius	3,394	7,588	8.33	10.00	5.71	6.39
Mozambique	167	661	4.17	5.42		
Namibia	1,968	5,209	6.67	8.33	7.62	7.59
Niger	194	723	3.75	5.00	7.14	6.99
Nigeria	260	831	1.67	0.00	1.43	2.03
Rwanda	209	765	1.67	0.42	0.00	0.00
Senegal	542	1,277	3.75	5.00	6.19	5.94
Sierra Leone	193	646	2.08	1.25	7.62	7.59
Somalia			0.00	0.00	0.00	0.00
South Africa	3,630	8,598	7.08	7.92	5.71	5.49
Sudan	306		0.00	0.00	0.00	0.00
Swaziland	1,300	4,097	3.33	1.67	3.33	3.23
Tanzania, United Republic of	190	473	2.92	2.50	6.67	6.69

Sub-Saharan Africa (Cont'd)	GDP per capita, USD	GDP per capita, PPP	FH civil liberties index	FH political rights index	Trade union rights index, unweighted	Trade union rights index, weighted
Togo	316	1,342	3.33	1.25	5.71	5.49
Uganda	264	982	4.17	3.33	5.71	6.09
Zambia	385	793	5.00	5.83	2.86	2.48
Zimbabwe	688	2,604	3.33	3.33	3.81	4.44

Middle East-North Africa	GDP per capita, USD	GDP per capita, PPP	FH civil liberties index	FH political rights index	Trade union rights index, unweighted	Trade union rights index, weighted
Algeria	1,626	4,649	1.25	0.83	6.19	5.79
Bahrain	9,383	14,129	1.67	1.25	7.14	7.14
Cyprus	10,965	16,377	10.00	10.00	8.57	8.65
Egypt	1,040	2,933	1.67	1.67	3.81	4.59
Iran, Islamic Republic of	1,460	5,109	0.00	1.67	0.00	0.00
Iraq			0.00	0.00	0.00	0.00
Israel	15,417	17,142	6.67	10.00	6.19	6.69
Jordan	1,582	3,887	5.00	5.00	5.71	6.69
Kuwait	16,939	18,438	3.33	3.33	2.86	3.53
Lebanon	2,784	3,941	3.33	1.67	4.76	5.34
Libyan Arab Jamahiriya			0.00	0.00	0.00	0.00
Malta	8,156	13,027	10.00	10.00	9.52	9.55
Morocco	1,214	3,253	3.33	3.33	3.81	3.68
Oman	6,151		1.67	1.67	8.10	7.89
Qatar	16,125		1.67	0.00	0.00	0.00
Saudi Arabia	7,184	11,091	0.00	0.00	0.00	0.00
Syrian Arab Republic	1,114	3,143	0.00	0.00	0.00	0.00
Tunisia	1,937	5,041	3.33	1.67	6.67	6.54
Turkey	2,814	6,022	3.75	4.17	0.00	0.68
United Arab Emirates	18,012	19,784	3.33	1.25	0.00	0.00
Yemen	320	718	2.08	3.75	3.33	5.04

References

Bollen, Kenneth and Pamela Paxton. 2000. Subjective measures of liberal democracy. Comp Polit Stud 33(1): 58–86

Compa, Lance. 2002. Assessing assessments: a survey of efforts to measure countries' compliance with freedom of association standards. Paper prepared for the National

Research Council workshop on international labour standards: quality of information and measures of progress. Available at http://www7.nationalacademies.org/internationallabor/Dqworkshop.html

Freedom House. 1999. Freedom in the world: the annual survey of political rights and civil liberties 1998–1999. Freedom House, New York.

ILO. 1993–2000 (reports 286–322). Report of the Committee on Freedom of Association. ILO, Geneva.

ILO. 1996. Freedom of Association: digest of decisions and principles of the freedom of association committee of the governing body of the ILO. ILO, Geneva.

International Confederation of Free Trade Unions. Various years. Annual survey of trade union rights. ICFTU, Brussels.

Kucera, David. 2001. The effects of core worker rights on labour costs and foreign direct investment: evaluating the 'conventional wisdom', International Institute for Labour Studies Working Paper No. 130. Available at http://www.ilo.org/public/english/bureau/integration/download/publicat/4_3_172_wp19.pdf

Kucera, David and Ritash Sarna. 2006. "Trade Union Rights, Democracy and Exports: A Gravity Model Approach," *Review of International Economics,* 14(5): 859–882.

National Research Council. 2004. Monitoring international labor standards: techniques and sources of information. Committee on Monitoring International Labor Standards. Center for Education, Division of Behavioral and Social Sciences and Education and Policy and Global Affairs Division. The National Academies Press, Washington, DC.

OECD. 1996. Trade, employment and labour standards: a study of core workers' rights and international trade. OECD, Paris.

OECD. 2000. International trade and core labour standards. OECD, Paris

U.S. State Department. 1995. Country reports on human rights practices. U.S. Government Printing Office, Washington, DC.

DAVID KUCERA,
International Labour Office

Chapter 7

Taking Labour Laws to the Domestic Dentist: Measuring Countries' Compliance with International Labour Non-discrimination Standards

MIRIAM ABU SHARKH
International Labour Office

Introduction: Beyond the Confines of the Toothless-tiger Talk

Despite the enormous amount of resources devoted to the production of International Labour Organization (ILO) Conventions, there is remarkably little evidence showing if and how the manner in which such international treaties are implemented contributes to the desired socio-structural effects. The reason is simple: there is a lack of valid and reliable indicators drawing on unbiased, comprehensive sources to address these important questions. This paper seeks to contribute to the recent efforts by Kucera (2001), the National Research Council (2004), Cuyvers and Van den Bulcke (this volume), Zarka-Martres and Guichard-Kelly (this volume) and others to close this void and shift the current country-compliance discourse to more fertile ground based on a Labour Standards Indicator Project (hereafter referred to as the "project") the present author directed.

This chapter argues that the value of any indicator is only as good as the source it is based on. Thus, the first focus of this article is to show that among all the sources available for the construction of valid and reliable country compliance indicators regarding labour law, the ILO's bi-annual[1] in-house *Country Reports* constitute the most unbiased, comprehensive reference. Using the Discrimination (Employment and Occupation) Convention, 1958 (No. 111) as an example, this article delineates the types of variables and values (dichotomous) addressing compliance that these Reports can yield. Third, the article gives a short, descriptive overview of the data, or lack thereof, accrued via this coding exercise. Lastly, possible academic and social policy data application scenarios are discussed.

Much of the country-compliance discourse currently takes place within the confines of the toothless-tiger talk: can or should the World Trade Organization (WTO) or ILO be able to force countries to comply (*complying* often being falsely conflated with *applying)* with international labour law treaties? The underlying unitary, rational actor and *Realpolitik* assumptions are that countries purposefully avoid committing to labour laws that enhance everyone's long-term well-being,

---

[1] The reporting cycle is bi-annual for Fundamental Conventions; see explanation later on.

D. Kucera (ed.), *Qualitative Indicators of Labour Standards,* 183–210.
© 2007 by ILO.

in order to attain short-term benefits.[2] These benefits are accrued by everyone according to the unitary actor assumption, but according to more left-leaning authors they are reaped only by a small stratum of society (for the latter position see Greven and Scherrer, 1998).

There are manifold practical and ethical concerns bound up with force mechanisms such as a WTO-linked social clause: unintended side effects, injustices and inconsistencies. Thus, such measures of force fall prey to suspicions of hurting precisely those whom they should help (see also Abu Sharkh, 2000; Charnovitz, 1994; Frank, 1999; Langhammer, 1999; Van Liemt, 1989; Malanowski, 1997; OECD, 1995; Piepel, 1995; Sapir, 1995; Windfuhr, 1999; Wet, 1998; Zeeb, 1994). The social clause debate has thus reached a stalemate in which the ILO retains healthy gums but no teeth. The history of the discourse on the problem of how to motivate countries to sign, which is often framed in terms of game theory, is a literature in its own right (for an overview see Abu Sharkh, 2000, 2002; Langille, 2006) to which the indicators developed in this chapter do not seek to contribute for several reasons. First, motivations are hard to decipher, often even by a unitary actor him or herself (Stroebe and Jonas, 1996). Second, the motivation-action nexus is frail (Stroebe and Jonas, 1996; Stahlberg and Frey, 1996). Third, even conceding good intentions, to equate signing with effective compliance leading to structural labour market change presupposes the influence of powerful and effective governments that may not exist in many developing countries where the government hovers like a hot air balloon far above real existing conditions on the ground (for a classic discussion see Jackson and Rosberg, 1982).

Rather, this chapter takes another angle. Once countries have ratified a Convention, for whatever reason, they retain much leeway in how to implement it on paper and in practice. The assumption in this chapter is that a way forward in the country-compliance discussion would be to assess, in detail, the de facto domestic fleshing-out of the international labour law skeleton and to ascertain the domestic effectiveness (domestic teeth) of country compliance.

The purpose of this chapter is thus to outline the development of indicators that can help contribute to this specialized debate, a debate focussing on the extent and effects of compliance at the nation-state level. Motivating this effort was the problem that despite the substantial interdisciplinary literature available on the spread and effect of international standards, only a small subset of this debate concerns countries' concrete labour standard compliance. Although measuring "commitment to development" or "transparency" has become increasingly popular, the assessment process is opaque and may be subject to political pressures

---

[2] According to Hathaway (2002), the general literature on treaty adoption and compliance of States in international relations and legal scholarship is much broader than this rather narrow debate, and can be grouped into rational actor models and normative models. Among the rational actor models, compliance is seen as "coincidence" (realism), "strategy" (institutionalism), or "by-product" (liberalism). In the normative models, "compliance is due to a norm of compliance fostered by persuasive discourse" (managerial model), "occurs when rules are legitimate and just" (fairness model), or because "norms are internalized" (transnational legal process model) (ibid.: 1944-1962).

(National Research Council, 2004). Valid and reliable measures of social development are scarce. Where they do exist, they are often rather limited to so-called "input" (e.g. ratified Conventions) and "output indicators" (e.g. unemployment rate) rather than "process indicators" such as alignment and application of domestic law to international law, with the possible exception of the legal literature on the European Union (see ILO, 2004).[3]

To recapitulate, leaving behind speculation about the motivation (or lack of thereof) to pledge allegiance to the international labour standard regime, two questions on the domestic level arise: (1) once countries have ratified labour Conventions, which actions do they take, *in practice*, to live up to their on-paper commitments? (2) How do these real-world actions and their interactions with country-specific institutional frameworks impact socio-structural outcomes? The answers to these questions carry important social policy implications, such as suggesting country-specific implementation strategies or modifications in the way and the degree to which Conventions are set out and applied.[4] However, in order to address these questions, valid and reliable indicators drawing on an unbiased, comprehensive source need to be developed. The evolution of this effort at the ILO is the topic of this chapter.

For the first time, the International Labour Organization's (ILO) Programme on Socio-Economic Security has undertaken to code the wealth of information available in the country reports on fundamental Conventions in order to establish numerical process indicators (ILO, 2004), or what are also called "compliance indicators" (National Research Council, 2004). The construction of these indicators places them among the so-called "qualitative indicators" or "subjective indicators" because they are "constructed from assigning numerical values to qualitative information, usually text" (Kucera, 2001:127). As mentioned above, the validity and reliability of such qualitative indicators depend on how and by whom the indicators are constructed. Thus, the context and methods of construction including, most crucially, the source are addressed in detail.

While developing the questionnaire on which the indicators are based was an easy deductive exercise – as it mirrors the reporting form countries need to submit to the ILO on their Convention implementation measures, the choice of data source was subject to more debate (see appendix for questionnaire). The argument

---

[3] "Formal" acceptance, or what the ILO (2004) calls "input", signifies a symbolic acceptance on the international level expressed by ratification. It is symbolic insofar as ratification of human rights treaties does not necessarily mean implementation, and failure to implement typically does not entail any material sanctions (Hathaway, 2002). "Implementation", or what the ILO (2004) calls "process", refers to the integration of the Conventions' stipulations into national law, in other words, legislation or setting up other implementation machineries. In this context, it also encompasses judicial decisions. "Structural change", or what the ILO (2004) calls "outcome", in the context of the non-discrimination regime, refers to a declining of the "vice" targeted by the labour Convention. "Socioeconomic development" is defined more broadly than in the Human Development Index and refers to: (1) the improvement of workers' welfare, i.e. the reduction of unemployment; (2) reducing poverty and inequality.

[4] Conversation with Lee Swepston, April 2005, and Werner Sengenberger, October 2005.

espoused here is that ILO Country Reports, as mandatory self-assessments of countries' efforts to implement a particular Convention, are the most promising option. The Country Reports on the Discrimination (Employment and Occupation) Convention, 1958 (No. 111) (hereafter referred to as Convention No. 111), with a special focus on race and gender issues, serve as a paradigm.

The following pages outline the context and outcome of the coding enterprise to establish valid and reliable indicators of domestic law implementation efforts and grip (teeth) across time.

Analytical Framework: Examining the Role of International Organizations

What prompted the coding of the implementation indicators was the effort to widen the scope of gender and race studies and advance the literature on the practical application of international law. The goal of the project was to use a reliable and comprehensive source to track, cross-nationally, *when* countries introduced *which* procedures or mechanisms to advance non-discrimination measures in "labour law", that is, the laws regulating individual employment relations.

Convention No. 111 covers seven grounds of discrimination:[5] race, colour, sex, religion, political opinion, national extraction and social origin. The purpose was to establish indicators regarding each of the seven grounds of discrimination. However, since discrimination on the grounds of the ascriptive characteristics of race and sex are among the most universal, and since domestic law often focuses on these dimensions, the questionnaire paid special attention to these issues. As René Robert, the lawyer entrusted with the actual coding, pointed out, "Also, from a practical point of view, there was more information on race and sex discrimination in the country reports than on any of the other grounds, meaning that there would be more information and of better quality than for the remaining grounds."[6] In the context of the substantive framework of this project, discrimination on the grounds of sex is taken as paradigmatic, that is as an example not only regarding information on sex discrimination, but also concerning discrimination in general, and how government action (implementation) effects social change.

Research on the effects of international treaties has been rightly criticized for not examining whether transnational norms[7] are implemented and yield the desired outcomes.

---

[5] Article 1. of the Convention stipulates:
"1. For the purpose of this Convention the term discrimination includes–
(a) any distinction, exclusion or preference made on the basis of race, colour, sex, religion, political opinion, national extraction or social origin, which has the effect of nullifying or impairing equality of opportunity or treatment in employment or occupation".
[6] René Robert, e-mail February 26th, 2006.
[7] See Keck and Sikkink (1998) on norms and "frames".

As Hathaway argues:

> Until fairly recently, the question of international law compliance fell by
> the wayside of both international law and international relations scholar-
> ship. Legal scholars examined and explicated the rules of state interna-
> tional behaviour, generally taking as a given that the rules would have
> impact. International relations scholars, for their part, had little interest in
> international law. The centrality in international relations of realist think-
> ing . . . discouraged careful examination of the role of transnational insti-
> tutions and hence of international law. (Hathaway, 2002: 1942)

The literature has also paid scant attention to gender issues in the labour market
(Ostner, 1987; Gottschall, 1998; Abu Sharkh, forthcoming-a). Gender issues are of
special interest in this project due to their universality; but a second reason is a practical one: labour market data are available by sex across time and nations, whereas,
lamentably, no such wealth of information exists for race or the other grounds of
discrimination, thus hindering any concrete cross-national impact studies.

The indicators can thus ultimately also substantively contribute to the toothless-tiger talk and other concerns regarding a fairer globalization. Much opposition
to globalization rests on the assumption that globalization will lead to a race to the
bottom, thereby lowering core labour standards, including anti-discrimination
measures, through so-called "social dumping" (Alber and Standing, 2000), following the logic of the familiar prisoners' dilemma.[8] However, it is questionable
whether a stag hunt may not be the more appropriate game-theoretical analogy.[9]
Yet in fact, more countries subscribe to more human rights conventions, declara-
tions, and treaties than ever before. But what does this paradox mean? Are the
endorsements merely symbolic and not translated into national law and policies?
Or does none of the former make a difference for workers on the ground? As long
as valid and reliable indices to measure labour standard implementation and social
development are lacking, these questions will remain unanswered.

Coding Implementation Indicators: The Literature

There have been various attempts to code labour standard implementation indicators. Major drawbacks have included the small number of countries surveyed, the
sources employed or the time frames captured.

Among *governmental* approaches to monitoring, the largest-scale attempt was
made by the U.S. under the Clinton administration. The U.S. Department of Labor
mandated the National Research Council to design a database on monitoring and
enforcement with experts on a scientific basis on issues pertaining to international
labour standards (National Research Council, 2004). To assess compliance, the
Committee developed three sets of indicators at the country level in a database

---

[8] While all countries benefit when they all adhere to core labour standards, every individual country has an incentive to defect and disregard those standards to attain short-term benefits.
[9] E-mail by Kara Contreary, March 2006.

named WebMILS, delineating the (1) legal framework; (2) government's implementation performance regarding both effort and effectiveness; and (3) overall outcome.

Although the list of indicators is a comprehensive and thoughtful wish list, WebMILS, for political reasons, has remained an empty matrix. Even if the matrix were filled, problems would remain. The matrix was not specified to include the dates of legislative enactment. A more potent drawback still is the trio of sources the project aims to rely on: the ILO supervisory machinery, the *Follow-up to the Declaration on Fundamental Principles and Rights at Work* (the *Follow-up*), and the U.S. Department of State's Country Reports on Human Rights Practices. Officials from the U.S. Department of Labor would undertake the assessment.

There are several drawbacks to this approach. The problem of relying on the ILO supervisory machinery, primarily the *Committee of Experts on the Application of Conventions and Recommendations* (CEACR), is the gravest and is therefore discussed at length later in the chapter. Focussing on the *Follow-up* also means relying on a fairly cursory assessment of countries, spanning little more than five years let alone five decades, as some Country Reports do where countries have been long-time ratifiers of a given Convention. If the assertion of Bollen and Paxton (2000, see also Kucera, 2001) is accurate that evaluators are biased by situation closeness, a multilateral organization may be in a better position to converge on unbiased assessments than U.S. officials. Even if the ILO assessment is subject to human inaccuracy, a United Nations (UN) institution has more global credibility than the U.S. Government in undertaking this kind of analysis.

Non-governmental efforts have included those of Verité, an independent, not-for-profit social auditing, research and training organization. Verité explored thoroughly whether countries' laws were in accord with ILO standards, although it did this for only 27 countries (Viederman and Klett, this volume).[10] Furthermore, effort and effectiveness often seem to be conflated in Verité's measurement, for example when taking the level of government activity as a proxy for equality and lack of discrimination. Block (this volume) confines his academically rigorous application of labour-standard-methodology-measurement to the U.S., Canada and the EU. Bertola *et al.* (this volume) examine only OECD countries but, unique to this examination, judicial decisions were taken into account to assess the threat level to noncompliant employers by measuring the percentage of cases won by employees.

Organizational Framework: The ILO

The ILO, being the oldest specialized agency in the UN system, has a long history of receiving Country Reports on the efforts made by member States to implement

---

[10] Note, their interesting observation that a lacking law may also be the sign of a "lack of problem", for instance in respect to forced labour.

ratified Conventions. The source of this reporting obligation is found in Article 22 of the ILO Constitution and reads:

> Each of the Members agrees to make an annual report to the International Labour Office on the measures which it has taken to give effect to the provisions of Conventions to which it is a party. These reports shall be made in such form and shall contain such particulars as the Governing Body may request.

Today, countries are required to report at two-year intervals (assuming ratification) on 12 of the ILO Conventions, including eight Fundamental Conventions[11] and four Priority Conventions.[12] Given that Convention No. 111 is itself a Fundamental Convention dating back to 1958 and boasts one of the highest rates of ratification,[13] there is a wealth of individual country information available for study, often spanning decades. In addition, faithful to the tripartite structure of the ILO, comments are, from time to time, submitted by employers' and workers' organizations with respect to a given Convention, thereby supplementing the information provided by governments in their reports.[14]

Measuring Compliance: The Project

The labour standards project launched by the ILO's Programme on Socio-Economic Security aimed to create numerical indicators covering various aspects of the Non-Discrimination Convention. The project was conceptualized in 2004 and executed in 2005. The implementation of the Convention both in law and in practice was to be captured. The latter is important because many Conventions of the ILO actually leave considerable leeway for countries to exercise their particular implementation method.

---

[11] These eight Conventions cover four labour standards dimensions that the ILO declared in 1998 to be the most fundamental among the almost 200 Conventions adopted by the Organization since 1919 (Kellerson, 1998). The Declaration on Fundamental Principles and Rights at Work covers four areas:
Freedom of association and the right to collective bargaining;
The elimination of forced and compulsory labour;
The abolition of child labour, and;
The elimination of discrimination in the workplace.

[12] For all Conventions other than the 12 priority Conventions, the reporting interval is every five years. Uniquely, however, under the follow-up to the 1998 Declaration, countries that have not ratified all eight fundamental Conventions are required by their mere membership in the Organization to report annually on their efforts to do so in accordance with the Declaration.

[13] As of December 2005, 163 out of a possible 178 countries had ratified Convention 111.

[14] Under Article 23, paragraph 2, of the ILO Constitution, governments must communicate to the representative employers' and workers' organizations copies of the information and reports supplied to the ILO. The organizations concerned have an opportunity to comment on their country's position with regard to these matters.

The Methods: Sources and Questionnaire

General Criteria for Indicators

When coding indicators there are two major areas of concern. The first has to do with the source used for indicator construction, the second with the indicators themselves. Regarding the source, Böhning (this volume) advocated unbiased sources (neutrality) that collect data on a recurrent, systematic basis (temporal and content consistency) for, in principle, all countries (universalism).

The indicator construction should be transparent and reproducible, allowing for objective judgments (Böhning, this volume). *Transparency*, also referred to as *reproducibility* or *reliability*, concerns the rating methods, which should be systematic and obvious, thus optimally guaranteeing inter-coder reliability over time (Kromrey, 1995; Kucera, 2001; and Bollen and Paxton, 2000). Kromrey (1995) and Kucera (2001) add two more criteria: *Variation*: Since variables need to vary, indicators need to be sufficiently graded to capture varying manifestation intensities. *Validity*: This criterion denotes that the concept that is supposed to be measured is really captured by the indicators. Note that different types of indicators have distinct implications for the likeliness of validity (Kromrey, 1995).

Following Kromrey (1995), and developing the work of Nowak (1963), there are definitional indicators, which are indicators defined by their dimensional characteristics, e.g. if "education" is defined as years of formal schooling. Correlative indicators are not defined as dimensional characteristics and usually fall into two groups: internally correlative and externally correlative indicators.

Regarding internally correlative indicators, one or more aspects are by definition part of the concept. For instance, a classic part of the multidimensional concept "socio-economic status" is "years of formal education". Not so for externally correlative indicators. An externally correlative indicator for socio-economic status might be the type of floor material used in a house. Pietschman (2004) discussed this at length in her work about poverty indicators, pointing out that, for instance, a sand floor is not a good indicator of poverty; many Indonesians keep a sand floor for religious reasons, to avoid losing touch with the ground, rather than out of economic necessity. Taking the type of floor as a sign of poverty is like taking a Zen stone garden as a sign of poor soil fertility. The validity is therefore not guaranteed.

Even more problematic from a validity perspective are deductive indicators. Only theoretically grounded correspondence rules allow the inference from empirically observable manifestations to the theoretical concept of interest. A classic example is "alienation" that cannot be measured directly but only via such indicators as "alienated behaviour". The validity is therefore tentative and always dependent on the veracity of the theoretical construct.

Criteria for Labour Standard Implementation Indicators

In order to ensure validity and reliability, simple dummy variables based on "yes" or "no" questions were constructed. After a wide consultation within the International

Labour Office, various experts in the International Labour Standards Department[15] agreed that any attempt to assess the degree of a country's implementation of the principles of the Convention No. 111 would be unlikely to succeed given the character and quality of the information on hand.

Aside from the fact that such detailed information is often not available, answers to "degree questions" introduce a possibly unacceptable level of subjectivity (see Swepston, 2004). We therefore opted to prepare simple questions that would yield either a factual "yes" or "no" answer in order to assess, for instance, if relevant legislation had been passed or not, despite the various contraindications for dichotomous (0/1) variables, such as their lower probability of extracting statistically significant results. The "extent" of implementation was measured by additional variables rather than by an intensity scale. So, "which grounds do the statutes cover?: race? . . . colour? . . . sex?" replaced a question that asks "to what degree is the Convention implemented".

Possible Sources

The ILO boasts a vast collection of member State labour laws, policy documents and programme details on the implementation of certain Convention principles, but "analyzing compliance with ILO standards is simply not easy, and the ILO has never undertaken it as a systematic exercise" (Swepston, 2004: 2). Although existing ILO databases contain a wealth of information, they were not designed to assess Convention implementation.[16]

Two ILO databases, both textual, deal specifically with the implementation of labour conventions and labour law. The first is constituted by the annual *Report of the Committee of Experts on the Application of Conventions and Recommendations*. The second is NATLEX, a database of national legislation and bi- and multi-lateral agreements. Both databases have severe drawbacks concerning their applicability, reliability, interpretability and representativeness, as the following discussion shows.

Annual Report of the Committee of Experts on the Application of Conventions and Recommendations

The most obvious source, though severely flawed, for determining a country's compliance with ratified ILO Conventions is the Annual Report of the Committee of Experts on the Application of Conventions and Recommendations (CEACR) and has served as a source for various Labour Standard coding efforts (Böhning,

---

[15] The primary consultants in 2004 were Lee Swepston, Constance Thomas and René Robert.
[16] Prominent examples include databases on Social Security Systems, Inventory of Social Protection Schemes for the Informal Sector, Conditions of Work and Employment Database on maternity and other issues, LABORSTA database and other data bases on occupational injuries.

this volume). This Committee, composed of 20 independent experts, meets annually in late November to review the Country Reports that have come in during the year.

The Governing Body appoints the 20 CEACR experts to three-year terms upon the recommendation of the ILO Director-General. The Committee's role is to provide an impartial and technical evaluation of the state of application of international labour standards. In its work, the Committee prepares two kinds of comments: (1) observations, which contain comments on fundamental questions raised by the application of a particular convention by a state, and (2) direct requests, which are not published but rather sent directly to the governments concerned and which relate to more technical questions or requests for further information.[17]

In preparing its comments, the CEACR relies not only on reports submitted by the governments but also on other official UN documents associated, for example, with the work of the Committee on the Elimination of Discrimination Against Women (CEDAW), or the Committee on the Elimination of Racial Discrimination (CERD). Information from other reputable human rights sources such as Amnesty International or Human Rights Watch may also be consulted. However, such materials are only considered so as to assist the Committee's understanding of human right issues in a given country and are not relied upon as authoritative sources in the preparation of its comments. Reports by international non-governmental organizations such as Human Rights Watch are also consulted but may not be cited. The way to weave those observations in would be to state: "The Committee understands that . . ."

The observations of the Committee also serve as the basis for the work of the tripartite *Conference Committee on the Application of Conventions and Recommendations* (*"Committee on Application of Standards"*). This Committee meets every June during the *International Labour Conference*.

The report of the Committee of Experts (hereinafter referred to as the "Committee Report") has the advantage of being available to the public and, for someone with no legal background, reasonably accessible and comprehensible. A typical technical excerpt from a CEACR comment on Convention No. 111 would read something like the following one on Greece:

> Article 3(c) of the Convention. Repeal of legislative provisions discriminating on the basis of sex. The Committee notes with satisfaction the adoption of Act No. 3103 of 2003, section 20 of which provides that section

---

[17] The Committee also approves what the International Labour Office in Geneva researches and writes, namely a General Survey each year dealing with a topic decided upon by the Governing Body. For this survey, reports are solicited from all Member States on a given Convention and Recommendation regardless of ratification. This serves as a supplementary, more inclusive universal assessment of the implementation of the chosen aspects, especially if the convention is not widely ratified. Of course, this approach too falls prey to the same problems that beset the regular reporting cycle: not all countries follow the request to submit reports and the quality of submitted self-assessments varies. For a list of these surveys see following link: http://www.ilo.org/ilolex/english/surveyq.htm. The most recent General Survey relevant to Convention No. 111 appeared in 1996, entitled "Equality in Employment and Occupation".

1(2)(a), paragraphs 2, 3 and 4 of Act No. 2226 of 13 December 1994, as amended by section 12 of the Act No. 2713 of 1999, imposing restrictions on women's admission to the police academies have been replaced by the following: "Both men and women are admitted to the academies concerned and the qualifications and preliminary tests of the candidates will be the same for both sexes."

This excerpt, while indicating progress and containing the Committee's signature expression of *satisfaction*[18] (see below for explanation), does not allow one to judge the extent of policy implementation at any given point in time. Norway, in principle one of the more progressive countries in terms of eliminating discrimination, is another case in point: "The Committee notes with interest the wide range of measures recently taken by the Government to promote gender equality . . ." including policy measures and apologies to the Roma people.

From individual CEACR comments it is difficult to judge *when* concrete measures to expand the intensity or extent of compliance were undertaken. In the words of Lee Swepston (2004: 2):

> While the ILO does have the most complete supervisory process in the international system, and a very large volume of information is available as a result, the supervisory process does not yield any consolidated assessment of compliance. Instead, after an initial evaluation following ratification, the supervisory mechanism examines steps towards – or even away from – implementation without ever again doing a complete evaluation, and without publishing [the] original analysis.

Thus there is a veritable consensus among different experts at the ILO that merely reporting on the interactions that the Committee has had with countries does not give an adequate picture of the degree of Convention implementation. To outline the problems:

(1) The *window of time is too small*. Typically, the Committee only addresses the most recent developments in a country's efforts or failings to implement the principles of the Convention. Court decisions or policies that are either dated or no longer worthy of the Committee's attention are not mentioned. However, if the goal is to assess every effort made by a country since ratification, or even before, the CEACR's comments, especially when only looking at a subset of them, are not suitable for coding the actual state of the labour law in the country for comparative purposes or to gauge when and why these legislative changes were introduced.

---

[18] Although CEACR comments are written in paragraph form and vary widely in content from one country to the next depending on the issues being addressed, the Committee does employ a number of "stock" words and phrases to convey a more or less consistent meaning across all of its comments. In this example, "satisfaction" is used to express the Committee's pleasure at the adoption of a legislative measure which the Committee likely requested in a previous comment. The term "satisfaction" then, is used to express the Committee's pleasure when a country complies with an earlier Committee request.

(2) Another disadvantage of these reports is that the Committee by and large *benchmarks countries against the progress they have achieved relative to their starting point* and not exclusively against the principles as contained and understood in the Convention itself. Not only do the reports only measure progress or regress, not the actual state of the art, they also do not adequately capture the *degree* of change that has taken place. There are also different scales used for different countries depending on the development level.[19] As René Robert, who has been involved in reading and commenting the Country Reports for the Committee, stated: In practice, if not theory,

> those preparing the comments have to understand the context of countries who do not have the same resources (fiscal or human) to implement policies, programs etc. to apply the Convention. Essentially then, the Committee tries to be realistic, criticising where appropriate and admonishing where justified, but not pretending that a Burkina Faso can be held to a Sweden standard, for example.[20]

The CEACR reports also typically focus on noteworthy issues within a country whether positive or negative, thereby not yielding a representative overview of the entire situation in the country. Again according to René Robert: "Comments are a distillation of a country's report, which primarily focus on noteworthy progress or failure".[21]

(3) Related to the second point, not all ratifying countries are studied every year. In 2005, the Committee in respect to Convention No. 111 mentioned 32 countries in its report. Only "observations" are published in the report; but this does not indicate that the Committee only considered reports from 32 countries. Usually, because of the two-year reporting cycle, countries are staggered to allow for more even reporting. However, the relatively low number published reflects that often only more noticeable cases are included as observations. The number of countries requested by the committee of experts to submit a report in 2005 (between June and September) was 112. It is unlikely that all 112 reports requested were received and dealt with by the Committee, whether as an observation or direct request. Unfortunately, the exact number of countries treated by the Committee in 2005 is not public information.[22]

Thus, relying on the CEACR reports means relying on a possibly systematically biased sample. However, the CEACR reports do yield insight on the interactive compliance with the Committee. What can be gauged are questions such as: if the report is available, how many reporting cycles does a country take to rectify

---

[19] Lee Swepston, personal interview Sept. 14th, 2004.

[20] René Robert, e-mail Jan. 12th, 2006.

[21] Personal interview Dec. 6th, 2005.

[22] There is some discussion in the house, though, about publishing all the Committee's comments in its report – direct requests as well – which would allow for complete transparency in terms of comments, but would nonetheless not solve the fact that comments remain a distillation of the country's report file.

aspects admonished by the CEACR? Examining the number of repeated requests yields a ratio of fulfilled requests to unfulfilled or further requests. None of this, however, allows the researcher to gauge how serious the non-fulfilment is when comparing across countries.

On a positive note, the Committee tries to address de jure and de facto discrimination, going beyond labour law in a strict sense. For example, in Turkey, the 1991 Terrorism Act and its effects are reprimanded. In Sudan it addressed general societal problems not specifically pertaining to labour: "The Committee recalls that under the Public Order Act 1996, Muslim women are liable to be beaten and whipped if their dress is deemed improper." This overlapping focus of conventions by different UN bodies indicates that, as a whole, they may reinforce each other.

NATLEX

NATLEX is an ILO database containing information on national laws including labour, social security and related human rights issues. It provides a powerful tool to investigate if countries have tried, via legislation, to implement ILO Conventions they have ratified. NATLEX is an electronic database containing bibliographic references and in some cases the actual text of national laws on labour, social security and related human rights by category (Graphic 1: NATLEX: Structure and Search Example). It contains a large volume, some 50,000 pieces of legislation (according to NATLEX coordinator Oliver Liang, November 2005). However, the database has the disadvantage of not being representative regarding the laws enacted.[23] Due to the somewhat *ad hoc* way NATLEX gathers information, many relevant pieces of legislation enacted by a country within the labour field are not featured. These gaps in NATLEX's legislative record render it a sub-optimal source.

Country Reports

ILO Country Reports are mandatory (bi-annual for fundamental Conventions) self-assessments of a government's implementation efforts. These reports contain more information than the Committee of Experts' comments reveal. "This is because the Committee usually focuses on the most problematic or positive elements of a report and, in cases where a country report contains exhaustive information, the Committee will not address a variety of issues that may be of interest in the development of implementation indicators," according to René Robert.[24] He cautions, however:

> One 'problem' with the country reports is the fact that they are self-reported. Some countries are in fact candid about the challenges and failings of their government in implementing the principles of a Convention or in the impact of their policies on actual social outcomes. But one must always be wary of

---

[23] Personal conversation with Oliver Liang, May 2004.
[24] René Robert, e-mail February 26th, 2006.

the potential for governments to present a positive picture that might not correspond to reality. This is why employee and employer comments can be valuable, yet are often an insufficient counterweight to the government's assessment because these groups typically do not have the information or resources to dispute the government's claims.[25]

In this project, we relied most heavily on the country reports, supplemented by the Committee's comments. While the comments are a distillation of a country's reports, they sometimes also include novel information from other UN sources such as CEDAW and CERD. The Committee's comments are also "important for understanding where a country has succeeded, failed or needs improvement with respect to the standards laid out in ILO Conventions (an important interpretive filter)".[26]

The Questionnaire

The following discussion is intended to illustrate both the scope and depth of the questionnaire. It also assesses how far the quality measures discussed above could be applied. The questionnaire is available in full in the appendix. The discussion also conveys an assessment of the availability and accuracy of the existing data (see Table 1 in the appendix for an overview).

To counter criticisms, discussed below, of focusing on the purely legal aspects, the questionnaire was designed to cover more than simply the *legislative dimension*. It also touches on *participatory mechanisms*, that is, to what extent workers and employers were involved in a consultative way, as well as *judicial aspects*, including measures on the utilization and results attained through courts. Outcomes of judicial decisions as an expression of the effective enforcement of the laws and compensation or restitution of the victims were addressed in the questionnaire by asking for the powers awarded to non-discrimination machineries. According to René Robert:

> The number of reporting countries each year is also affected by the fact that some countries fail to submit their reports on time and are thereby requested to report in the following year, which, if they do, changes the sequence of reporting for that country. Also, a country may be required to report in successive years upon the request of the Committee. So although the idea is to have half of the ratifying countries report each year, this pattern can quickly change based on the reporting record of a given country. It is correct though to say that many more countries are analysed (particularly under Convention No. 111) than appear in the Committee's published report.[27]

Lastly, the assessments of the CEACR and the International Labour Conference were measured.

The following section gives a brief overview of the questionnaire regarding its content, not the way in which the questions were asked, which excludes

---

[25] René Robert, e-mail February 26th, 2006.
[26] René Robert, e-mail February 26th, 2006.
[27] René Robert, e-mail February 26th, 2006.

double-barreled questions. Since the goal is to measure the application of the Convention, the questionnaire was modeled after the Convention No. 111. The full text of Convention No. 111 is attached in the appendix; Articles 1 through 5 contain the substantive provisions of the Convention.

Legislation

The first clusters of questions in the questionnaire concern formal legal instruments. The goal was to cover laws on different levels of abstraction. Legal instruments on a norm-setting level were coded, such as the integration of a non-discrimination clause in a country's constitution, as well as their translation into statutes, regulations or judicial decisions.

What is the coverage of the law or statute[28] by: (1) ascriptive characteristics mentioned in the Convention: Do the country's laws cover all seven grounds of discrimination enumerated under the Convention (race, colour, sex, religion, political opinion, national extraction and/or social origin). Additional questions assessed if national legislation covers any ground beyond those listed in the Convention, such as age or sexual orientation or sexual harassment, the latter of which has come to be understood as covered by Convention No. 111 under the ground of sex discrimination; (2) aspect of employment: Whether prohibitions on discrimination apply to vocational training, access to employment and to particular occupations, and/or terms and conditions of employment.

The questionnaire also accounted for not only the passing of new legislation but also the modification or elimination of prior legislation: In the last two reporting cycles, has the Government repealed any statutory provisions or modified any administrative instructions that were inconsistent with the Convention?

It also covers *policies* which, in contrast to formally adopted pieces of legislation, are an additional and variegated tool at the disposal of governments to pursue the goal of non-discrimination: Has the Government developed national policies to promote equal opportunity and treatment in employment and occupation per Article 2 of Convention No. 111? The questionnaire only captures *national* policies as well as legislation, however, which poses a challenge when evaluating federal countries such as Canada or Germany where a significant role is given to the local levels of government with respect to labour legislation and policy development.

Concerning the two dimensions that have engaged the most interest and for which there is the most information – race and sex – the exact date of the adoption of legislation, which included the prohibition of discrimination on these two grounds, was surveyed. Establishing the temporal sequence of ratification of laws and policies is especially pertinent if underlying causal mechanisms are of interest.

However, criticisms of only focussing on the legal aspect are mounting. Frequently cited drawbacks of an exclusive focus on legal measures are centred on two main criticisms:

---

[28] Laws or statutes as well as acts or, more commonly in the civil law traditions, decrees or codes denote similar kinds of legislative enactments.

(1) The first is an enactment problem: interpretation and enforcement vary greatly among different legal systems, for example common and civil law or customary and religious law, and also according to the development status of a country. Thus any *de jure* indicator is a very biased indicator of what happens *de facto* (for a differing opinion see Botero et al. 2003).

(2) The second issue is a *specification* problem: if the interest lies on functional outcomes, formal legal indicators may not be the right route to uncover the characteristics and requirements corresponding to a functional outcome. For example, there is disagreement about the extent to which labour law is statutory. Botero *et al.* (2003: 9) concede that critics argue that:

> in French civil law tradition, the practice is just to 'write-it down', leading to a greater measured formalism and intervention. In the present context, this argument would hold that the greater protection of workers in civil law countries that we might identify is fictitious – the common law countries regulate just as much through court decisions which are never 'written-down' in statues.

However, they maintain that "virtually all of law is statutory, even in common law countries, and deviations from statutes are an exception, not the rule" (ibid.). Furthermore, if and how legislation and court decisions complement each other or coincide is an empirical question, especially since law can be conceptualized in a much broader sense beyond how a government imposes its will or pursues certain outcomes through legal texts enacted by elected officials. This assertion thus calls for indicators able to address this question.[29]

Judicial Aspects

To assess enforceability, the questionnaire asks if there is machinery specific to race/sex discrimination and if it has the power to award remedies and/or impose sanctions. This was a particularly difficult area in which to elicit "objective" answers. The informational material often did not suffice and the reliability of the coding is lower than in other segments of the questionnaire. For instance, "Is the judicial machinery in which individuals can exercise their rights in relation to Convention No. 111 accessible?" involves quite a subjective assessment and was generally not answerable using only the information provided.[30]

---

[29] René Robert, e-mail Jan. 12th, 2006.

[30] In other cases, more subjective framing of accessibility such as "Do persons invoke their rights to equality of opportunity and treatment in employment and occupation in credible numbers (i.e. are there a significant number of cases brought forward)?" was replaced with a number of more reliable questions: "How many decisions involving questions of principle did the Government identify in its most recent/second most recent report? Of those reported decisions, how many found in favour of the claimants? But this strategy also did not yield the targeting information, as there was only sporadic information. No cases brought may be a sign that there are no judicial resources devoted to the issue of discrimination or that the principle of discrimination is poorly publicized to those individuals who are the target of unequal treatment or may merely reveal that a government does not keep track of such information and therefore has no means of reporting the number of cases that have been considered which deal with discrimination.

Participatory Components

Since the Convention addresses the co-operation of the two other ILO constituents, workers' and employers' organizations, the questionnaire further considers the inclusion of these social partners in a government's efforts to promote the acceptance and observance of its national policy on non-discrimination. And because the social partners are entitled under the ILO Constitution to submit comments on a country's implementation of its Convention obligations, the questionnaire also addresses these communications on the part of workers' and employers' organizations.

Technical Assistance

The comments of the Committee of Experts, while not relied upon exclusively for the above-mentioned reasons, was integrated to assess the more fine-tuned application of law. Examples include:

> Does the Committee of Experts identify exceptions to coverage under the law or outstanding discriminatory provisions in law which it considers incompatible with Convention No. 111? Has the Committee of Experts encouraged the Government to seek technical assistance from the ILO with respect to the implementation of the Convention in the last two reporting cycles? If yes, has the Committee encouraged technical assistance with respect to discrimination on the basis of race? . . . or sex?

To assess the impact of ILO projects, closer attention should be paid in the future to recording the date, amount and type of technical assistance provided to a country by the Office for a given Convention. Questions such as "Has technical assistance in fact been provided by the ILO to the Government concerning the application of the Convention in the last two reporting cycles?" had a large number of responses missing because information to satisfy this question was seldom contained in the Country Reports.

Committee of Experts

The language used in the annual Report of the Committee of Experts is, though highly formalized and designed to be consistent across the years, vague. To give but a few examples, according to Lee Swepston, the term "satisfaction" means "we asked you to do something and you did it – thank you". "Interest" can connote that a measure of the government has attracted the attention of the Committee but the Committee is "not quite sure what to make of it"[31], as the Committee may not yet have enough information on a given government initiative to state confidently whether it is in conformity with the principles of the Convention or not. It can also

---

[31] Conversation with Lee Swepston, November 24, 2004.

connote that there has been a positive development in the implementation of the Convention that the supervisory machinery did not ask for (Swepston, 2004: 2).

A request for "more information" can be a subtle reprimand or a genuine petition. Considering that 50 per cent of requests centre on soliciting more information (Liang, 2004), the ambiguity entailed in the language is not trivial.

The questions in the questionnaire mimicked the vocabulary employed by the Committee: "Has the Committee of Experts expressed "interest" or "satisfaction" in its comments during the past two reporting cycles? . . . on the basis of race? . . . on the basis of sex?"

To provide "redundancy", test questions included:

> Does the Committee of Experts identify exceptions to coverage under the law or outstanding discriminatory provisions in law which it considers incompatible with Convention No. 111? Has the Committee of Experts encouraged the Government to seek technical assistance from the ILO with respect to the implementation of the Convention in the last two reporting cycles? . . .

Sheer formalities regarding compliance with the reporting cycle were also addressed: "Did the Government submit its most recent report and its *second* most recent report according to its reporting obligations? Were there worker and employer submissions?"

Article 24 Representations

Article 24 of the ILO Constitution allows any national or international workers' or employers' organization to make a Representation alleging that any ILO member State has failed to secure the effective observance within its jurisdiction of any Convention (see appendix for procedure).[32] If utilization were a measure of utility, the conclusion would be that the Representation mechanism under Article 24 of the ILO Constitution was a failure.

The questions surrounding this mechanism were layered:

> In the past 5 years, has a Representation under Article 24 of the ILO Constitution been submitted alleging the Government's non-observance of the Convention? . . .addressing discrimination on the basis of race/sex? . . . did the Governing Body conclude that there was a violation of the Convention?

---

[32] According to article 24 of the ILO Constitution a trade union or an employers' organization may file a representation if a State "has failed to secure in any respect the effective observance within its jurisdiction of any Convention to which it is a party". The ILO Governing Body handles the representation, which must refer specifically to Article 24 of the ILO Constitution and should contain details concerning the alleged violation. The government concerned is invited to comment on the allegations. The Committee presents its and the government's report to the Governing Body, which decides on the publication of the representation and notifies the parties and government concerned. Issues raised in the representation are followed-up by the ILO's supervisory machinery, CEACR and the tripartite Conference Committee on the Application of Conventions and Recommendations ("Committee on Application of Standards").

By most accounts, there was virtually no use made of Article 24 in respect of Convention No. 111 for the relevant period considered by the questionnaire. Further investigations would be needed to better appreciate why this is the case and suggest user-friendly improvements.

International Labour Conference[33]

Similar measures may be appropriate regarding the consideration of individual country cases by the International Labour Conference. The questions "Has the ILC Committee on the Application of Conventions and Recommendations made an individual observation about the country with respect to the Convention in the past five years? If yes, does the observation address discrimination on the basis of race/sex?" yielded virtually no answers.

The lacuna of data on this issue again suggests that perhaps this fundamental Convention has not received its share of attention by the Conference Committee. The Conventions receiving the most attention by the ILC Committee were the Forced Labour Convention, 1930 (No. 29), and the Freedom of Association and Protection of the Right to Organise Convention, 1948 (No. 87) and the Right to Organise and Collective Bargaining Convention, 1949 (No. 98). Whereas this attention may be justified due to the gravity of the issue of forced labour and because Conventions Nos. 87 and 98 immediately affect trade unions, a constituent of the ILO, the discussion on these issues seems to crowd out all other fundamental Conventions, possibly pointing to problems with the supervisory machine.

Conclusion: Using the Data

This chapter outlines one attempt to construct indicators measuring countries' reported efforts to comply with the ILO Discrimination (Employment and Occupation) Convention, 1958 (No. 111). Most attention in this chapter focuses on two crucial issues currently debated in the expanding literature on treaty implementation.

To reiterate, the first major theme of the chapter addresses the *sources* used for coding. No construction of indicators can circumvent the "garbage-in garbage-out" predicament. No sophistication in construction or coding can redeem a coding source that is non-representative, politically biased or otherwise skewed due to its mandate. The paper argues that the Country Reports of the ILO are the most comprehensive and temporally consistent source for constructing implementation indicators.

---

[33] Article 24 of the ILO Constitution states that complaints may be submitted by any delegate (government, worker or employer) of an ILO Member State which has ratified the same convention to the International Labour Conference, or by the ILO Governing Body if a Member State has failed to observe an ILO Convention to which it is party.

However, even though the ILO Country Reports are an excellent source, their usefulness depends on the reporting discipline of countries. While typically 70 to 80 per cent of countries fulfil their reporting obligations within a couple of months of the official deadline, some submit incomplete or no reports for many reporting cycles.[34] Even if governments do submit, they may (systematically) withhold information. In such cases, the Committee notes with regret that, for example, for the second year in a row a government's report has not been received and therefore repeats its previous observation. This potentially introduces a systematic bias into the data in favour of compliant countries.

A second problem is the uneven focus of the constituents, even among Fundamental Conventions, with Convention No. 111 receiving comparably little attention compared to the Conventions dealing with freedom of association and collective bargaining. This exercise has flagged the lack of awareness among workers' and employers' organizations of the need to report violations of Convention No. 111, or any other Article 22 reporting obligations, even though they are invited to do so according to ILO rules, possibly due to the inaccessibility or perhaps invisibility of the ILO machinery or simply a lack of technical expertise or resources. This flags a broader systemic challenge within the ILO-supervisory machinery.

The third concerns the type of *operationalization*. This paper argues that there are grounds for going beyond purely legal indicators. It has done so using the Convention as a guideline. However, due to the limited access to socio-economic data and the legal orientation of the Committee of Experts, legal information is more readily available and accessible than other relevant information on the implementation of Convention No. 111. The Country Reports could be more consistently employed as a repository for gathering and localizing relevant information on a country, especially within the Office.[35]

The actual development of the indicators is linked to the questions posed at the beginning of this paper: *when* do countries introduce *what* procedures or

---

[34] Conversation with Lee Swepston, April 2005.

[35] As René Robert, who has worked in the ILO department responsible for the Reports, commented: "This is a situation of which the staff . . . are acutely aware. Efforts are being made to encourage the collection and communication of data on workers disaggregated by the various grounds of discrimination (which poses its own problem in some developed countries where privacy laws restrict employers from asking questions of such a personal nature, i.e. race, religion). In some cases, Norway to give an obvious example, the Office receives an enormous volume of statistical materials relevant to the socio-economic situation of workers of different ethnic backgrounds or gender for instance, yet the department is not equipped nor does it really have the time to sift through all this material in an exhaustive way except perhaps to note broad trends in the employment of minorities etc." However, perhaps due to the personnel structure, being composed of lawyers, not quantitative-oriented social scientists, the is no systematic quantitative approach of analysing this material. (Correspondence with René Robert, March 27th, 2006.)

mechanisms to *which* effect regarding the advance of equality in law and practice?

The ultimate uses of the data gathered are numerous. One popular use may involve ranking countries. While some may oppose ranking on the basis of cross-national incomparability, it seems nothing interests and motivates actors like their position *relative* to others (see Kahneman *et al.*, 1999, and Layard, 2005: 42, for explanations from the hedonic literature). As Sengenberger pointed out, any systematic use of the data, including assigning ranks, may lead countries to take their reporting more seriously.[36]

However, it is questionable if implementation variations are linearly distributed, or perhaps similar to Esping-Anderson's (1990) argument concerning welfare regimes more generally, clustered by regime types.[37] Using this data to find and analyse clusters may yield a more finely-graded, successful approach to policy prescription than simplistic rankings that may stretch the quality of the data (Abu Sharkh, forthcoming-b. On the logic of clustering see Wolfson *et al.* (2004) and McKernan *et al.* (2005).

Uses of the data go beyond identifying different country implementation strategies and their labour market effects. Good data can help address and define the larger discourse on the impact of labour standard institutions on trade and foreign direct investment.

With the data yielded by this project, at a later stage three crucial questions in the cross-national gender discrimination literature can be addressed concerning:[38] (1) Formal acceptance of domestic non-discrimination legislation: what influences the length of time countries take to ratify this specific Fundamental Convention? (2) The nexus between ratification and national implementation: when and why do countries adopt national laws and policies or set up mechanisms to apply international labour standards on non-discrimination? (3) Effects of legislation on structural change, specifically labour market discrimination and worker welfare: how and when does international or national law impact on the wage gap,[39] employment ratio of men to women and/or the segregation of women in the labour market?

These questions are currently addressed in quantitative studies using the data gathered in the context of this project together with other cross-national,

---

[36] Conversation with Werner Sengenberger, December 2005.

[37] As Esping-Anderson (1990: 26) demonstrates, there are "qualitatively different arrangements between state, market, and the family."

[38] While the sequencing of these questions draws on the familiar typology of input, process and outcome (e.g., see ILO, 2004), the sequencing does not suggest causality necessarily runs that way.

[39] Note, although Convention No. 100 is the "wage equality Convention", large wage gaps may be an indicator of discrimination, it can also be used as a structural, dependent variable in the content of 111.

longitudinal data through the post-World War II period covering all existing nation states (see Abu Sharkh, forthcoming-c and forthcoming-a).[40] At a later stage, cases flagged by the quantitative results can be followed up with case studies in the field.

Together, this body of work could function as a virtual domestic dentist, permitting a more thorough examination of the teeth and hence possible bite of international conventions and national laws.

Appendix I: Questionnaire Template

COUNTRY	
CONVENTION	*111 – Discrimination (Employment and Occupation)*, 1958

A. Application at the National Level

1. Are the grounds of the Convention consecrated in law? In the Constitution? In statutes (laws and regulations)? In courts of law or other tribunals?
2. Coverage of the law –
   - i. What grounds does the Constitution cover? Race? Colour? Sex? Religion? Political Opinion? National Extraction? Social Origin?
   - ii. In what year was discrimination on the basis of race prohibited by the Constitution, if at all?
   - iii. In what year was discrimination on the basis of sex prohibited by the Constitution, if at all?
   - iv. What grounds do the statutes cover? Race? Colour? Sex? Religion? Political Opinion? National Extraction? Social Origin?
   - v. In what year was discrimination on the basis of race prohibited by statute, if at all?
   - vi. In what year was discrimination on the basis of sex prohibited by statute, if at all?
   - vii. Does the Committee of Experts identify exceptions to coverage under the law or outstanding discriminatory provisions in law which it considers incompatible with Convention No. 111?

---

[40] The underlying hypotheses for the quantitative study are that the long-term, increased symbolic enactments of global (that is, ratification by states) are driven also driven by macro-level global societal forces such as links to the world society that create or intensify internal pressures to proclaim attachment to the international human rights regime, rather than merely by day to day contingencies of domestic politics. The coupling between legal enactment and structural change, however, is determined on the micro-level by conflicting actors such as non-governmental organizations (NGOs), unions and social movements. In developing this argument, the project links the macro-sociological theories, such as the world society theory, with micro-level social movement theories, and thus addresses common criticisms of macro-studies (Esser, 1993).

viii. Do the country's laws cover other grounds of discrimination beyond those listed in Article 1(1)(a) of Convention No. 111? (e.g. HIV/AIDS, disability, age, sexual orientation, union membership or activity, nationality, language, marital status etc.)

 ix. Does the country prohibit discrimination in employment and occupation on the basis of age?

3. Do prohibitions on discrimination apply to: Vocational training? Access to employment and to particular occupations? Terms and conditions of employment?

4. National Practice

  i. Has the Government developed national policies to promote equal opportunity and treatment in employment and occupation per Article 2 of Convention No. 111?

 ii. What grounds do these policies cover? Race? Colour? Sex? Religion? Political Opinion? National Extraction? Social Origin?

iii. In the last two reporting cycles, has the Government sought the co-operation of employers' and workers' organisations in promoting the acceptance and observance of these policies?

iv. In the last two reporting cycles, has the Government repealed any statutory provisions or modified any administrative instructions that were inconsistent with the Convention?

 v. In what year did the Government adopt a policy (apart from legislative enactment) with respect to racial discrimination, if at all?

vi. In what year did the Government adopt a policy (apart from legislative enactment) with respect to sex discrimination, if at all?

5. Invoking the Rights Under the Convention –

  i. Is the judicial machinery in which individuals can exercise their rights in relation to Convention No. 111 accessible?

 ii. Do persons invoke their rights to equality of opportunity and treatment in employment and occupation in credible numbers (i.e. are there a significant number of cases brought forward)?

iii. How many decisions involving questions of principle did the Government identify in its *most recent* report?

iv. Of those reported decisions, how many found in favour of the claimants?

 v. How many decisions involving questions of principle did the Government identify in its *second* most recent report?

vi. Of those reported decisions, how many found in favour of the claimants?

vii. Does the machinery find in favour of claimants in credible numbers?

viii. Is there machinery specific to the grounds under the Convention (not necessarily a dispute resolution mechanism)?

 ix. Is there machinery specific to race discrimination?

 x. If yes, does this specific machinery have the power to: Award remedies? Impose sanctions?

 xi. Is there machinery specific to sex discrimination?

xii. If yes, does this specific machinery have the power to: Award remedies? Impose sanctions?

B.   Application at the International Level

6. Reporting -
    i.   Did the Government submit its most recent report according to its reporting obligations (i.e. in form and in substance)?
    ii. Did the Government submit its *second* most recent report according to its reporting obligations (i.e. in form and in substance)?
7. Worker and Employer Submissions
    i.   Have employers' or workers' organizations submitted comments in the last two reporting cycles on the Government's implementation of the Convention?
    ii. If comments have been submitted, are they *critical* of the manner in which the Government has implemented the Convention?
    iii. If yes, are the comments critical with respect to discrimination on the basis of race?
    If yes, are the comments critical with respect to discrimination on the basis of sex?
8. Technical assistance -
    i.   Has the Committee of Experts encouraged the Government to seek technical assistance from the ILO with respect to the implementation of the Convention in the last two reporting cycles?
    ii. If yes, has the Committee encouraged technical assistance with respect to discrimination on the basis of race?
    iii. If yes, has the Committee encouraged technical assistance with respect to discrimination on the basis of sex?
    iv. Has the Government requested the ILO's technical assistance for the implementation of the Convention in the last two reporting cycles?
    iv. If yes, has the Government requested technical assistance with respect to discrimination on the basis of race?
    v.   If yes, has the Government requested technical assistance with respect to discrimination on the basis of sex?
    vii. Has technical assistance in fact been provided by the ILO to the Government concerning the application of the Convention in the last two reporting cycles?
    vii. If yes, has the technical assistance related to discrimination on the basis of race?
    viii. If yes, has the technical assistance related to discrimination on the basis of sex?
9. Other Conventions relevant to discrimination -
    i.   Has the Government ratified C. 97 the Migration for Employment Convention (Revised), 1949 (No. 97)?
    ii. Has the Government ratified C. 100 the Equal Remuneration Convention, 1951 (No. 100)?
    iii. Has the Government ratified C. 118 the Equality of Treatment (Social Security) Convention, 1962 (No. 118)?
    iv. Has the Government ratified C. 122 the Employment Policy Convention, 1964 (No. 122)?

    v. Has the Government ratified C. 143 the Migrant Workers (Supplementary Provisions Convention, 1975 (No. 143)?

    vi. Has the Government ratified C. 156 the Workers with Family Responsibilities Convention, 1981 (No. 156)?

    vii. Has the Government ratified C. 159 the Vocational Rehabilitation and Employment (Disabled Persons) Convention, 1983 (No. 159)?

    viii. Has the Government ratified C. 183 the Maternity Protection Convention, 2000 (No. 183)?

10. Committee of Experts

    i. Has the Committee of Experts expressed "interest" in its comments during the past two reporting cycles?

    ii. If yes, has the Committee expressed interest with respect to discrimination on the basis of race?

    iii. If yes, has the Committee expressed interest with respect to discrimination on the basis of sex?

    iv. Has the Committee of Experts expressed "satisfaction" in its comments during the past two reporting cycles?

    v. If yes, has the Committee expressed satisfaction with respect to discrimination on the basis of race?

    vi. If yes, has the Committee expressed satisfaction with respect to discrimination on the basis of sex?

11. Sexual Harassment

    i. Has the Government enacted legislation or adopted a policy prohibiting sexual harassment in the workplace (as discussed by the Committee of Experts in its 2002 General Comment)?

    ii. If the Government enacted legislation on sexual harassment, when did it do so?

    iii. If the Government adopted a policy on sexual harassment, when did it do so?

12. Article 24 Representations

    i. In the past 5 years, has a Representation under Article 24 of the ILO Constitution been submitted alleging the Government's non-observance of the Convention?

    ii. If yes, does the Representation address discrimination on the basis of race?

    iii. If yes, does the Representation address discrimination on the basis of sex?

    iv. If yes, was the Representation receivable?

    v. If it was receivable, did the Governing Body conclude that there was a violation of the Convention?

13. International Labour Conference

    i. Has the ILC Committee on the Application of Conventions and Recommendations made an individual observation about the country with respect to the Convention in the past five years?

    ii. If yes, does the observation address discrimination on the basis of race?

    iii. If yes, does the observation address discrimination on the basis of sex?

References

Abu Sharkh, Miriam. 2000. Wachstum contra Gerechtigkeit? Basispapier zu Sozialstandards in der Technischen Zusammenarbeit. GTZ, Eschborn.

Abu Sharkh, Miriam. 2002. History and results of labour standard initiatives. An event history and panel analysis of the ratification patterns, and effects, of the international labour organization's first child labour convention. Berlin.

Abu Sharkh, Miriam. forthcoming-a. International labour standards: how effective are they in reducing sex discrimination world wide?

Abu-Sharkh, Miriam. forthcoming-b. "Worlds of Welfare Integration and Their Effect."

Abu-Sharkh, Miriam. forthcoming-c. "All the Honeys Earning (Un)equal Monies?"

Alber, Jens and Guy Standing. 2000. Social dumping, catch-up, or convergence? Europe in a comparative global context. J Eur Social Policy 10(2): 99–119.

Block, Richard. 2004. Indicators of labour standards. ILO, Geneva.

Bollen, Kenneth and Pamela Paxton. 2000. Subjective measures of liberal democracy. Comp Pol Studies 33: 58–86.

Botero, Juan, Simeon Djankov, Rafael La Porta, Florencio Lopez-de-Silanes and Andrei Shliefer. 2003. The regulation of labour. ILO, Geneva.

Charnovitz, Steve. 1994. The World Trade Organisation and social issues. Presentation made at the Conference on 'The future of the trading system'. University of Ottowa, Ottowa.

Esping-Anderson, Gosta. 1990. *The Three Worlds of Welfare Capitalism*. New Jersey: Princeton University Press.

Esser, Hartmut. 1993. Soziologie: allgemeine grundlagen. Campus, New York.

Frank, Volker. 1999. Die Durchsetzung internationaler standards – erfolgsbedingungen von sozialklauseln. Peripherie 75: 66–82.

Gottschall, Karin. 1993. Doing gender while doing work? Erkenntnispotentiale konstruktivistischer perspektiven für die analyse des zusammenhangs von arbeitsmarkt, Beruf und Geschlecht. In: B.F. Maier and B. Pfau-Effinger Geissler (eds) FrauenArbeitsMarkt: sozialwissenschaftliche arbeitsmarktforschung neue folge 6. Sigma, Berlin.

Greven, T. and Christoph Scherrer. 1998. Die soziale flankierung des weltmarkts – eine einführung. Sozialklauseln. Westfälisches Dampfboot, Münster.

Hathaway, Oona. 2002. Do human rights treaties make a difference? Yale LJ 111: 1935–2020.

International Labour Office (ILO). 2004. Economic security for a better world. ILO, Geneva.

Jackson, Robert and Carl Rosberg. 1982. Why West Africa's weak states persist. World Politics 35: 1–24.

Kahnemann, Daniel, Ed Diener and Norbert Schwarz. 1999. Well-being: the foundations of hedonic psychology. Russell Sage Foundation, New York.

Keck, Margaret and Kathryn Sikkink. 1998. *Activists Beyond Borders: Advocacy Networks in International Politics*. Ithaca: Cornell University Press, 1998.

Kellerson, Hilary. 1998. "The ILO Declaration of 1998 on Fundamental Principles and Rights: A Challenge for the Future," *International Labour Review*, 137(2): 223–227.

Kromrey, Helmut. 1995. Empirische sozialforschung. Leske und Budrich, Opladen.

Kucera, David. 2001. Decent work and rights at work. In: R. Blanpain and C. Engels (eds) The ILO and the social challenge of the 20th century. Kluwer Law School, Great Britain.

Langille, B. 2006. Core labour rights – the true story. Social Issues, globalization and international institutions: labour rights and the EU, ILO, OECD and WTO. Koninklijke Brill NV, Leiden, The Netherlands.

Layard, Richard. 2005. Happiness: lessons from a new science. Allen Lane, London.

Liang, Oliver. 2004. Informational dimensions of the ILO's Committee of Experts. ILO, Geneva.

Liemt, Gijsbert. 1989. Minimum labour standards and international trade: would a social clause work? Int Labour Rev 128: 433–448.

Malanowski, Norbert. 1997. Social and environmental standards in international trade agreements: links, implementations and prospects. Westfälisches Dampfboot, Münster.

McKernan, Signe-Mary, Jen Bernstein and Lynne Fender. 2005. "Taming the Beast: Categorizing State Welfare Policies," *Journal of Policy Analysis and Management* 24(2): 443–460.

National Research Council. 2004. Monitoring international labor standards. The National Academies Press, Washington, DC.

Nowak, Stanley. 1963. Correlational, definitional and inferential indicators in social research and theory.

Organisation for Economic Co-operation and Development (OECD). 1995. Trade and labour standards: a review of the issues. OECD, Paris.

Ostner, Illona. 1987. Scheu vor der Zahl? die qualitative erforschung von lebenslauf und biographie als element einer feministischen wissenschaft. Leske und Budrich, Opladen.

Piepel, Klaus. 1995. Sozialklauseln im welthandel 3/4 ein instrument zur förderung der menschenrechte. Misereor, Aachen.

Pietschmann, Ina. 2004. "Between Tradition and Modernity: A Survey on Poverty in East Lombok (Indonesia)," GTZ Working Paper.

Sapir, Andre. 1995. The interaction between labour standards and international trade policy. World Economy 4: 791–803.

Stahlberg, Dagmar and Dieter Frey. 1996. Einstellungen: struktur, messung und funktion. Springer, Berlin.

Stroebe, Wolfgang and Klaus Jonas. 1996. Grundsätze des einstellungserwerbs und strategien der einstellungändersanderung. In: M. Hewstone and G. Stephenson W. Stroebe (eds) Sozialpsychologie: Eine Einführung. Springer, Berlin.

Swepston, Lee. 2004. Indicators of core labour standards. ILO, Geneva.

Wet, Erika de. 1998. Labour standards in the globalized economy: the inclusion of a social clause in the general agreement on tariff and trade/World Trade Organization. Hum Rights Quart 17(3): 143–462.

Windfuhr, Michael. 1999. Durchsetzung sozialer menschenrechte: problemdimensionen und vergleich der reichweite zivilgesellschaftlicher kampagnen und initiativen. Peripherie 6–25.

Wolfson, Murray, Zagros Madjd-Sadjadi and Patrick James. 2004. "Identifying National Types: A Cluster Analysis of Politics, Economics, and Conflict," *Journal of Peace Research* 41(5): 607–623.

Zeeb, Matthias. 1994. Gegen einseitige verbote. EPD-entwicklungspolitik 29–30.

MIRIAM ABU SHARKH,
International Labour Office

Chapter 8

Towards an Index of Core Rights Gaps*

W. R. BÖHNING[1]

Formerly International Labour Office official; now private consultant

1. Introduction

A year after drafting the initial version of this chapter as a contribution to an ILO seminar, I published a book presenting the full methodology to measure the achievement of fundamental human rights in the world of work (Böhning, 2005a). The main purposes of this revised version are to outline the structure and workings of the new indicator system, to include the 2004 data and to refine the measurement of the implementation dimension.

Which fundamental rights and principles are the object of measurement? Those that the Anglo-Saxons refer to as 'core labour standards'. They comprise the eight core Conventions of the International Labour Organization[1] and the four general subject matters enunciated in the Organization's 1998 Declaration on Fundamental Principles and Rights at Work, and its Follow-up (hereafter Declaration) that underpin them.[2]

Two broad advocacy aims inspire the setting up of the new system: (i) to document how well or poorly countries perform, which may shame some of the laggards into making improvements and others to seek bilateral or multilateral technical assistance; and (ii) to monitor progress in the realization of fundamental human rights.

---

* I am most grateful to David Kucera and Peter Peek for their unflinching support of my work on indicators in the labour field.

[1] Forced Labour Convention, 1930 (No. 29), here referred to for short as Convention No. 29; Freedom of Association and Protection of the Right to Organize Convention, 1948 (No. 87), referred to for short as Convention No. 87; Right to Organize and Collective Bargaining Convention, 1949 (No. 98), referred to for short as Convention No. 98; Equal Remuneration Convention, 1951 (No. 100), referred to for short as Convention No. 100; Abolition of Forced Labour Convention, 1958 (No. 105), referred to for short as Convention No. 105; Discrimination (Employment and Occupation) Convention, 1958 (No. 111), referred to for short as Convention No. 111; Minimum Age Convention, 1973 (No. 138), referred to for short as Convention No. 138; and Abolition of the Worst Forms of Child Labour Convention, 1998 (No. 182), referred to for short as Convention No. 182.

[2] Freedom of association and the effective recognition of the right to collective bargaining; elimination of all forms of forced or compulsory labour; effective abolition of child labour; and elimination of discrimination in respect of employment and occupation.

211

D. Kucera (ed.), Qualitative Indicators of Labour Standards, 211–236.
© 2007 *by ILO.*

2 Construction of the Gap System

2.1 Basic Considerations

The key criteria to be respected if human rights indicators are to be credible must include validity, transparency, replicability, use of identical yardsticks and objectivity. Objectivity does not obtain where a group of self-selected people from the same geo-political or cultural background gets together to grade countries – usually putting their own at the top – whether it be in New York (e.g. Freedom House) or, say, Shanghai. The objectivity requirement makes me turn to existing ILO data associated with core labour standards and the supervisory or complaints machinery established to hold countries to their obligation to comply with their international commitments. For heuristic reasons the new indicator system measures the *non-achievement* of rights, which I refer to as a *gap*.

The conceptual structure of the new indicator system is set out in Box 1, which is adapted from Adcock and Collier (2001). Briefly, two dimensions are

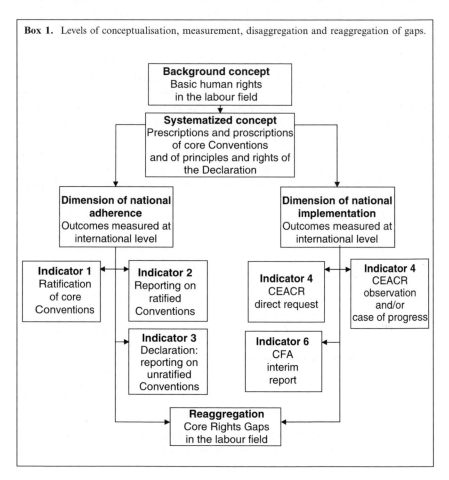

Box 1. Levels of conceptualisation, measurement, disaggregation and reaggregation of gaps.

constructed, the first is the *adherence* dimension, the second the *implementation* dimension. The two are additive, although later weighted, and pulled together in a single notion called the *Core Rights Gap* (CRG). When used as specifications of the new indicator system, the terms *adherence*, *implementation* and *gap* or variants thereof are italicized. Scores are established on a binary basis (Yes/No) and calculated in the form of country-years, that is, every country is assigned a *gap* or the absence of a *gap* each year on all indicators. Of course, the smaller the *gap*, the better a country's – or a region's or the world's – performance.

Each dimension is built up of three indicators. Unfortunately, I have been compelled to drop a seventh indicator foreseen in the book, the Declaration progress indicator, because the ILO, while it had inscribed in its last-but-one programme and budget that it would henceforth assess each year whether countries that had not ratified one or several core labour standards had taken significant strides to promote, respect and realize the principles and rights inspiring the Conventions in question (ILO, 2003, para. 143), apparently cannot set out countries' achievements in detail and, by default, expose those whose status quo is unchanged (see ILO, 2006).

2.2. Adherence Dimension

The first indicator is non-ratification of core Conventions, which constitutes an *adherence gap*. Ratification in year X makes this gap disappear as from that year. Ratification is the system's lynchpin because all other indicators are calculated as a percentage of the value of adhering to a core Convention. The reason for adopting such a simple but innovative approach is that, whether one is concerned with reporting on ratified Conventions or with assessing the importance of implementation problems, failure to report or to implement can call into question no more than a proportion of the commitment a country makes when it ratifies a core Convention.[3]

Logically, when all other indicators are fixed as a proportion of the value of ratification, their sizes vary in unison with that initial number, and its value is not an analytical issue. Whether ratification is set at 1, 50 or whatever becomes a question of convenience – to make it easy to comprehend derivatives. I opted for a value that adds up to a maximum adherence gap of 100 when no Convention is ratified, irrespective of how many Conventions form part of the system (seven during the period 1985-99 and eight thereafter). Moreover, although the system's construction proceeds with absolute numbers at the first stage in order to enable readers to follow things easily, the data are normalized at the second stage, which is to say they are compressed into a 0-1 range.

---

[3] One might put that proportion as high as 100 per cent in extreme cases when the International Labour Organization's annual conference asks its member States to consider sanctioning a country for continued grave disregard of a ratified Convention, as happened in the case of Myanmar in relation to Convention No. 29 in 2000. However, highly exceptional data of this kind should not be a constituent element of an indicator system that is meant to apply potentially to all countries at any time.

The second indicator records whether or not governments report on ratified Conventions when they are supposed to do so. Governments are constitutionally held to report to the ILO every other year on how they apply ratified core labour standards in law and in practice. Reporting is important, politically and for the indicator system (it feeds the main component of the implementation dimension with data); but the act of reporting is not by any means as important as the decision to adhere to a Convention. Indicator 2 is given a weight of 25% of a Convention's value. However, the effective weight of this indicator for most countries is about half its postulated size because the system can score the fulfilment of reporting obligations only during the years when governments are requested to report on ratified Conventions, normally once in two years. On an annual basis, the effective weight of this reporting indicator in the gap system is thus 12.5%.

The third indicator of the adherence dimension instrumentalizes the Declaration that emerged from the discussions surrounding globalization and which was meant to encourage the ratification of core labour standards. A reporting procedure on unratified Conventions was instituted that requests concerned governments to inform the ILO each year whether they have moved forward on promoting, respecting and realizing the principles and rights underpinning those of the core Conventions they have not ratified. Indicator 3 is given a weight of 12.5% of a Convention's value, which is equivalent to the reporting indicator on ratified Conventions that normally feeds data into the system every other year. The Declaration reporting indicator is integrated into the new system in the form of bonus points. If a country reports when it should, its existing adherence gap that is due to non-ratification is reduced by 12.5%. If it does not report, no such reduction occurs. Declaration-reporting data accrue only as from 1999.

2.3. Implementation Dimension

Validity, transparency, replicability, use of identical yardsticks, objectivity and regularity are evidently not in question as far as adherence data are concerned. But how is one to measure national implementation by heeding these criteria? My answer is (a) by drawing on the evaluations carried out by the Committee of Experts on the Application of Conventions and Recommendations (hereafter Committee of Experts or CEACR) of how countries apply ratified core Conventions, and (b) by considering certain reports of the Committee on Freedom of Association (CFA) regarding allegations concerning infringements of freedom of association and collective bargaining. Among the many ILO supervisory and complaints procedures these two are the most valid, transparent, replicable, identically applied, least culture bound and geo-politically the most dilute – they beat all others in the ILO and in the world at large as far as objectivity is concerned. Furthermore, given the high degree of ratification of core Conventions, the Committee of Experts covers practically all countries on a regular basis.

2.3.1. CEACR Component

Four of the Committee of Experts' comments are turned into numbers for the purpose of measuring the extent to which countries realize in law and practice the commitments they entered into by ratification. Two are of a substantive 'negative' nature in respect of a country's implementing laws and practices. They are called direct requests and observations.[4] The other two comments are 'positive' in that the CEACR lauds countries when it identifies cases of implementation progress. They takes the form of notes of interest and expressions of satisfaction. The four terms have a specific meaning given to them in the new indicator system.

As regards direct requests and observations, the Committee of Experts recently and succinctly reiterated the distinction between them in a note to readers, as follows: '[T]he observations contain comments on fundamental questions raised by the application of a particular Convention . . . The direct requests usually relate to more technical questions or questions of lesser importance' (CEACR, 2004, p. 2). *Observations* are published, *direct requests* not. *Observations* are clearly more important than *direct requests*.

As regards cases of progress, I have previously taken into account only expressions of *satisfaction* but am now persuaded that the Committee of Experts' noting of *interest* constitutes a valid and pertinent refinement when measuring the implementation of human rights in the labour field. Expressions of satisfaction are set out by the Committee of Experts in the form of an observation where a government responds to a negative comment or situation and the CEACR judges the measures taken as amounting to significant and definite progress. One can, therefore, relate negative *observations* and positive *satisfaction* to each other on the same scale.

Notes of interest have been used by the Committee of Experts consistently for decades but have been given more publicity since its 2001 report where, as for expressions of satisfaction, a table now provides summary data and statistics (CEACR, 2001, pp. 66-8). The gap system scores not from this table because it also lists *interest* that is conveyed in unpublished direct requests but only when notes of interest are contained in a published comment.

Interest and satisfaction are integrated into the gap system in a way that is akin to the bonus-points approach under the Declaration reporting component – they reduce gaps associated with observations. Interest data have been added ex post facto beginning in 1987, two years after the starting year of the system, because of the time lags involved in reporting on each ratified Convention (about which more will be said later).

A weight of 20% is attached to each *direct request*. For most countries this is effectively equivalent to 10% during each of the two-year reporting-cum-evaluation cycles. *Observations*, which represent a more critical view of countries' situations, call into question 40% of a Convention's value per comment, which for the great majority of countries corresponds effectively to 20% on an annual basis. When the Committee of Experts has reason to be interested or even to be satisfied in one respect but at the same time finds that there remain doubts

---

[4] Non-substantive or procedural observations are not scored as gaps. Examples are acknowledgements of a trade union's observations on a governmental report that the CEACR asks the government to comment on next time, or when the CEACR records in a formal observation that it suspends its examination while an ILO Commission of Inquiry examines the same subject matter.

about implementation or that other parts of the implementation problems have not been dealt with or that new ones have cropped up, it puts forward simultaneously a 'negative' *observation* and a 'positive' note of *interest* and/or expression of *satisfaction*, which the indicator system scores by reducing the gap deriving from an observation proportionately.

As Table 1 spells out, the basic weights of CEACR single-form comments in the first four rows give rise to 11 combinations. Together with the absence of any comment, a total of 16 variations of comments grade the implementation of human rights in law and in practice. Taking into account that several possibilities yield identical proportions, there can be up to seven different implementation scores per Convention or a multiple of this number if several or all Conventions have been

Table 1. CEACR Component: 16 Possibilities of Comments per Convention Yield Seven Distinct Implementation Gaps.

	Size of implementation score measured as % of value of single Convention	
Possibilities of CEACR comments	Weight during normal two-year reporting cycle	Effective annual weight for 'normal' countries
1. Only *direct request*	20%	10%
2. Only *observation* of a critical substantive nature	40%	20%
3. Only *interest* noted (scored if in a formal observation)	0%	0%
4. Only *satisfaction* expressed in relation to prior *observation*	0%	0%
5. *Direct request* and *interest* noted in formal observation (1 – 3)	20%	10%
6. *Direct request* and *satisfaction* expressed in formal observation (1 – 4)	20%	10%
7. *Direct request* and *interest* and *satisfaction* (1 – (3+4))	20%	10%
8. *Observation* and *interest* (2 – 25% or 3/4 of 2)	30%	15%
9. *Observation* and *satisfaction* (2 – 50% or 1/2 of 2)	20%	10%
10. *Observation* and *interest* and *satisfaction* (2 – 75% or 1/4 of 2)	10%	5%
11. *Observation* and *direct request* (2 + 1)	60%	30%
12. *Observation* and interest plus *direct request* (8 +2)	50%	25%
13. *Observation* and satisfaction plus *direct request* (9 + 2)	40%	20%
14. *Observation* and *interest* and *satisfaction* plus *direct request* (10 + 2)	30%	15%
15. *Interest* and *satisfaction* without a negative *observation* (3 + 4)	0%	0%
16. Neither critical comment nor case of progress	0%	0%

ratified, and this under the CEACR component alone (but, of course, a country can have only one number as a score in any single year). One could make these grades still more variable by choosing odd numbers. But not only are the selected basic weights easier to follow as they stand; what counts is that they are both reasonable in themselves and when one compares the various indicators' weights. They should be seen as averages that apply to all countries across all core Conventions at any point of time. They are the identical yardsticks that human rights assessment systems must apply if they are to be credible.

It is crucial to understand that it is the formal nature of the outputs of the supervisory machinery – not the contents of either direct requests or observations or of cases of progress – that is instrumentalized for indicator purposes. The Committee of Experts itself makes the distinctions that matter, and it does so in the most objective way possible. To go deeper into each direct request, observation or case of progress in order to determine which direct request is 'more important' than another or which observation incriminates a country 'more strongly' than another or which case of progress deals with a 'more important' subject than another would inevitably add subjectivity; personal preferences would creep in; and superhuman efforts would be required to maintain identical yardsticks for all countries at all times. The Committee of Experts itself grades countries validly, transparently and identically.

2.3.2. CFA Component

Quantitatively speaking, the Committee of Experts component feeds the implementation dimension with most of its data. The CFA component comes on top and enlarges the number of possible grades, albeit only as far as Convention Nos. 87 and 98 or the achievement of the principles and rights of freedom of association and collective bargaining are concerned.

Inclusion of the CFA's complaints machinery bestows two advantages on the gap system. First, it potentially extends the assessment of implementation problems to countries that have not ratified either or both of the freedom of association and collective bargaining Conventions, which matters because 30 of the 159 gap countries had not adhered to the prescriptions and proscriptions of Convention Nos. 87 and/or 98 by the end of 2004. Second, it gives freedom of association and collective bargaining greater importance than the areas of forced labour, child labour and discrimination when combined or overall CRGs are estimated, which reflects the central role of this most fundamental of all human rights in the labour field.

How, then, should one measure non-achievement? One should not be tempted by the incidence of complaints lodged at the input stage of the CFA procedures because allegations of infringement of freedom of association and collective bargaining may turn out to be unjustified. I instrumentalize outputs, that is, a certain kind of report which the CFA issues. There are in essence three kinds of CFA reports: (i) 'definitive' reports, (ii) reports where the CFA asks 'to be kept informed' and (iii) 'interim' reports. 'Definitive' reports cover quite heterogeneous situations; it would require interpretation to determine how to score them; and one's political culture and geo-political preferences would fail the test of objectivity. The same applies where the CFA issues a 'to be kept informed' report, in which case it considers that it has had sufficient information to adopt its findings but prefers to follow the manner in which the government gives effect to its conclusions and recommendations in order to encourage their full implementation before closing the case. Interim reports are issued either when the CFA needs further information in order to come to its assessment in knowledge of all the facts or when the problems raised, because of their gravity, should continue to be subject to an in-depth examination – and the two are usually interrelated. Interim reports (italicized in the context of the system) are an acceptable indicator of the worst implementation problems in the area of freedom of association and collective bargaining (for empirical confirmation, see Böhning, 2005a, Chapter 5.3.5); and they are thus the one category of CFA reports retained for the purpose of measuring implementation gaps.

Interim reports are given a weight of 20% of a Convention's value, which is the same level as annualized CEACR observations. However, I cap the CFA component at the first stage of the system's construction at 15 points, which means that a country can accumulate no more than 15 CFA points during any year. Why 15? Because it is equivalent to the Committee of Experts' maximum charge on the implementation dimension were it to issue simultaneously two direct requests and two observations on the two freedom of association and collective bargaining Conventions.[5] Therefore, the complaints procedure cannot entail a larger implementation gap than the supervisory procedure. The ceiling is reached when, during any year, six different cases give rise to six different interim reports. Two gap countries' scores reach 15 CFA points: Peru in 1993 and Guatemala in 1995, 1996 and 1997.

The CFA figures are not, as such, annual data, because complaints are lodged with the ILO *ad hoc* rather than according to time slots predetermined by receivability procedures or other factors. They are annual data in a factual sense because the CFA has to deal with numerous cases during the three sessions that it holds each year – some 2,500 cases in the CFA's over 50 years of existence. If during any single year it were to put out two or three interim reports on the same case, only one would be counted by the system as an implementation gap because the country–year format of the system's data corresponds to a case–year format in the context of the CFA component.

It is worthwhile pointing out that here, too, it is the formal nature of interim reports – not their contents – which provides the yardstick for the measurement of implementation gaps. The weight, again, should be seen as an average that applies to both Conventions and all countries during all years.

Box 2 summarizes the construction and weights of the new indicator system. The bottom rows refer to the second stage of construction, which comprises re-weighting of the adherence dimension and normalization of the estimates.

---

[5] In the period starting with the year 2000, I disregard the slightly higher maximum up to 1999 and fix a uniform ceiling for 1985-2004.

Box 2. Logical Structure and Method of Calculating Countries' Gaps (Rounded Figures).

	1st stage	
Dimension	Adherence to fundamental labour rights in principle	Implementing basic labour rights in law and practice
Measurement Component	International expression of national adherence	International verification of effect given nationally
	Core Conventions component — Core Conventions (Nos. 29, 87, 98, 100, 105, 111, 138 up to 1999 plus No. 182 as from 2000) / Declaration comp. — Reporting on unratified Conventions	CEACR component — Critical comment on each ratified Convention (direct request and/or observation) and/or case of progress (note of interest and/or expression of satisfaction) / CFA component — Interim reports
Indicator	1 = Annual (a) Ratification of seven or eight Conventions or (b) lack of ratification / 2 = Biannual (a) Reporting on each ratified Convention or (b) failing to report / 3 = Annual (a) Reporting on up to four principles and rights since 1999 or (b) failing to report	4 = Biannual (a) Direct request or (b) no direct request / 5 = Biannual (a) Observation with or without note of interest and/or expression of satisfaction or (b) no such observation / 6 = Ad hoc (a) Interim report or (b) no such report

(Continued)

Box 2. Logical Structure and Method of Calculating Countries' Gaps (Rounded Figures).—Cont'd

	(a) No gap	(b) Gap = points per unratified Convention	(a) No gap	(b) Gap = 25% of Convention points	(a) 12.5% bonus points per principle and right	(b) No bonus points	(a) Gap = each direct request equal to 20% of Convention points	(b) No gap	(a) Gap = each observation equal to 40% of Convention points. Interest and/or satisfaction reduce gap by 25%, 50%, 75% or by 100% if no critical comment	(b) No gap	(a) Gap = each such report is equal to 20% of Convention points	(b) No gap
Mode of calculating gaps under each indicator												
1985-99	0	14.3	0	3.6	*1.8*	0	2.9	0	5.7, 4.3, 2.9, 1.4, 0	0	2.9	0
since 2000	0	12.5	0	3.1	*1.6*	0	2.5	0	5.0, 3.8, 2.5, 1.3, 0	0	2.5	0
Maximum gap of component	100 points each year		25 points in 2 years or 12.5 annually		*Reduces ratification gaps each year*		20 direct request + 40 observation points = 60 points every two years, half on an annual basis				Cap of 15 points in any year	
Maximum gap of dimension	Adherence gap = interaction among indicators 1 to 3 = 100 points						Maximum implementation gap if all Conventions are ratified = interaction between indicator 1 and indicators 4 to 6 = 75 points. Maximum implementation gap if no Convention is ratified = 15 points					
CRG	CRG = adherence gap + implementation gap = scores range from 0 to 115 points											

2ⁿᵈ stage

Reweighting	CRG = (adherence gap)/4 + implementation gap = scores range from 0 to 81.25 points
Normalization	CRG = Actual first stage gap/maximum gap = scores range from 0 to 1

2.3.3. Time Lags and Second-stage Changes

Three features of the gap system combine to render recent CRG and implementation scores of quite a few countries more favourable than one might expect – though only temporarily. First, ratification in year X lowers the adherence gap strongly, immediately and forever, which reduces the CRG commensurately. Second, because the Convention enters into force for the country concerned one year after ratification and the first governmental report on its laws and practices is requested to arrive a year later, the Committee of Experts will be able to assess the country's implementation at best in year X+2. This assumes that the government fulfils its reporting obligation on time, which is not always the case, and that the Committee of Experts has the time to examine the sometimes voluminous first report, which is sometimes impossible. The Committee of Experts many times gets to grips with the first report only in year X+3. Therefore, while an instant drop occurs in the adherence gap and CRG, a potential implementation gap can be recorded and feed through to the CRG – leaving aside the special case of the CFA – only two or three years after the ratification was recorded. Third, the Committee of Experts has the understandable habit of commenting on a government's first report, if justified, by way of a lightly weighted direct request, asking for additional information and giving it time to put its house in order, rather than to inflict a heavily weighted observation on it. Should the Committee of Experts exceptionally perceive well documented and highly significant deviations from the Convention's stipulations, it might opt for an observation straight away. Such a comment usually appears only one reporting cycle later when the next implementation report is examined, which would be year X+4 or more likely X+5.

The second and third factor stretch the time before a charge may appear on implementation indicators 4-5 and be transmitted to CRGs, putting countries in a seemingly good light for several years. The impact of the time lag is most pronounced when a country had previously not ratified any or many core Conventions; it is less noticeable when a number of Conventions had already been ratified much earlier. Time-lag effects impact on a sliding scale according to the extent of preceding ratifications and the spacing of new ratifications.

Time lags can best be exemplified by choosing a pair of Conventions, such as Gambia's ratification of Convention Nos. 87 and 98 in 2000. The first report on the application of the Conventions were due in 2002 but not received. They were received in time for the Committee of Experts' session of 2003, and the CEACR promptly addressed two direct requests to the government on each Convention that charged the implementation dimension and the country's CRG with a total of 5 points. As far as the two freedom of association and collective bargaining Conventions are concerned, Gambia has a CRG of 0 points in 2000-01, 5 points in 2002 and again has a CRG of 0 points in 2003-04 because the next reports on the two Conventions are not due until 2005. The average for the five-year period 2000-4 would thus be 1 point. Comparing the pre-ratification average of 1995-9 (14.3 points) with the average of 2000-4, Gambia's CRG dropped by 13.3 points on account of two ratifications. This effect would be multiplied by four if the country ratified all core Conventions in one fell swoop. In Gambia's case, seven Conventions were ratified in 2000, the eight in 2001 and, as the later Table 2 shows, time-lag effects catapulted it from a very low rank in 1995-9 to CRG rank 1 in 2000-4 – probably not the rank it really deserves and probably not the one it will occupy in years ahead.

Theoretically, if all countries ratified core Conventions at about the same time, they would all be subject to similar time lags and enjoy huge drops in CRGs; and countries' ranking would not be jumbled greatly. Reality is quite different. Compare Gambia with, for example, Sweden. Gambia's wholesale ratification occasioned a drop in its adherence gap of 87.5 points in 2000 and of another 12.5 points in 2001, moving it from near the back of the CRG ranking to up front. Sweden, on the other hand, had ratified seven core Conventions by 1990 and adhered to the eighth, Convention No. 182, in 2001. Sweden benefited from a reduction in its CRG of 12.5 points in that year, everything else being equal. This did not even have a positive effect on its CRG rank (4 in 1995-9 and 12 in 2000-4) because six extensive recent ratifiers rushed past it (Gambia, St. Kitts and Nevis, South Africa, Namibia, Switzerland, Seychelles), benefiting as they did from the cumulative time-lag effects associated with the recent ratification of Conventions; and three other countries improved their scores (Ireland, Hungary and Senegal) while Sweden actually scored a little worse in 2000-4 than in 1995-9.

The normal workings of the new indicator system are blown out of proportion by a further factor, which is the ratification campaign launched by the ILO's Director-General in 1995 and the adoption of the Declaration in 1998 that occasioned a large jump in ratifications of core Conventions between the mid-1990s and the beginning of the 21st century. The most striking example is Convention No. 182 that, adopted in 1999, was adhered to by 89% of the countries in the gap system by December 2004, a phenomenal rate for the Organization. Where a country ratifies several or all core Conventions at once or within a very short period of time, its CRGs undergo dramatic improvements. Gambia is an example.

The time lags can be expected to dissipate during the second half of the current decade because the spurt in new ratification has ebbed off and there will be relatively few ratifications in years hence (see Section 4 below). The Committee of Experts will now get a handle on how countries implement the Conventions that they recently ratified, and this will be reflected in more realistic CRGs in future years for extensive recent ratifiers. While ratification is the lynchpin of the new indicator system and, through the adherence dimension, is the biggest single determinant of the size of CRGs at the first stage of its construction, over time CRGs emancipate themselves a little from adherence and are influenced progressively by the implementation dimension.

Adherence is a necessary factor, for without commitment in principle there is no assurance of political willingness to embrace in their full scope and lastingly the fundamental human rights in the labour field. But formal adherence does not by itself suffice to realize rights. It has to be followed up by concrete implementation measures in law and in practice. The proof of the human rights pudding lies not in the recipe but in its realization. It follows that the importance of adherence in the calculation of CRGs should be downgraded somewhat, which happens at the second stage of the gap system's construction. Downgrading is carried out after completion of the first stage because the weights of (a) reporting on ratified Conventions, (b) the Declaration component and (c) the three implementation indicators are expressed as a proportion of the value of ratifying a Convention and must be introduced in a transparent and easy-to-follow manner. Following sensitivity tests, the weight of the whole of the adherence dimension in the estimation of CRGs is reduced to one quarter of its first-stage weight.

In the case of the overall scores that cover all Conventions and the principles and rights of freedom of association and collective bargaining, the first stage maxima were 100 points for *adherence*, 75 for *implementation* and 115 for CRGs.[6] After re-weighting, they become 25 for *adherence* and 81.25 for CRGs.[7] *Implementation* is not re-weighted, and its maximum of 75 points stays unchanged.

Moreover, the reweighted gaps are normalized for each country each year. Normalization amounts to a rescaling of the calculations carried out at the first stage and compresses scores into a 0 to 1 point scale. Normalization must be carried out separately for adherence gaps, implementation gaps and CRGs because, unlike at the first stage, a normalized CRG is not the sum of the normalized adherence gap and of the normalized implementation gap (summing the two could yield values in excess of 1 point).

As regards the formula to be applied, I simplify UNDP's normalization method (actual points–minimum points)/(maximum points–minimum points) on the ground that gaps can be more variable in the short term – up and down – than the indicators chosen by UNDP, that is, life expectancy, education and economic success. Due to both the reporting-cum-CEACR cycles and the volatility of political developments, variations of the minima or maxima would unnecessarily force the gap data into different ranges in different years. My simplifications apply to both the minimum and the maximum points. As regards the lowest number of points attained by any country, given that the minimum of 0 adherence, 0 implementation and 0 CRG points are attained by a number of countries in each area of freedom, I put all minima at 0, even at the level of overall data that are the focus of this contribution. This enables me to drop the minimum altogether and use the intuitively comprehensible formula actual gaps/maximum gaps, where the actual points are those estimated at the first stage. As regards the highest number

---

[6] Which is the sum of the *adherence* maximum (due to non-ratification of Conventions, 100 points) and of the CFA maximum (15 points). In this 'worst-case scenario', non-reporting and the CEACR component are inactive, and no bonuses are generated under the Declaration component.

[7] A CRG of 81.25 points presupposes that all Conventions are ratified, all reports on ratified Conventions are due in the same year and the Committee of Experts has no reason to record progress during that year. In these circumstances, 6.25 points could derive from (re-weighted) non-reporting; a further 60 points could be due to seven or eight direct requests plus seven or eight observations, depending on the year; and the CFA component could generate a maximum of 15 points. The Declaration component is inactive in the 'worst-case scenario' because all Conventions are ratified. It should be noted that the Committee of Experts can and does formulate direct requests and observations even if the government has not sent a report. For example, it may remind the government of its reporting obligations or, because workers' and employers' organizations have a constitutional right to inform the ILO of their on views on how the government applies a ratified Convention, the Committee of Experts may formulate a critical substantive observation if the views put forward by non-governmental organizations justify it.

of points or largest gaps, I use the maxima foreseen by the system (see Box 2). The advantage of choosing identical lower and upper limits in normalization throughout the system's review period is that the reference points are always the same. Thus, a country's normalized gaps are strictly comparable over different periods of years, even over the longest periods.

2.3.4. Further Specifications

While the Committee of Experts analyses a country's situation in principle every other year, it may ask for a report within a year where it finds a country's laws and practices to deviate strongly from the prescriptions and proscriptions of a core Convention. The standard two-year reporting cycle and the associated implementation data thus forestall valid annual comparisons of a country's scores for an individual Convention. As a rule, a minimum of two two-year scores is required for comparisons to be undertaken. But because governments' reports are not infrequently delayed, an even longer period is more appropriate to assess a country's evolution in the course of time and to compare scores among countries. The gap system prefers five-year averages.

Of the International Labour Organization's member States, the new indicator system covers 159. Non-functioning or non-independent States are excluded when one or the other of three criteria applies: (i) their governments lack the authority to administer their territories because a large part of their territories is in the hands of secessionists or foreign powers, (ii) they depend on foreign governments, or (iii) they are for other reasons incapable of implementing international commitments. Seventeen are left aside altogether (Afghanistan, Angola, Armenia, Colombia, the Democratic Republic of Congo, Georgia, Haiti, Iraq, Liberia, Moldova, Montegnegro, Nepal, Somalia, Solomon Islands, Tajikistan, Sudan and Serbia, including those that became non-functioning or non-independent toward the end of the review period (Iraq and the Solomon Islands are cases in point). If the government of a non-functioning or non-independent State manages to establish normal, continuing autonomous control, the State will be scored after a grace period of two years. Albania is scored starting 2003, Bosnia-Herzegovina starting 1997, Cambodia starting 1995, Lebanon 1994 and Sierra-Leone starting 2002. Averages or trends are not produced where they would be based on endpoints without data in the middle. New member States, Timor-Leste, Vanuatu and Samoa, will be scored after a grace period and, therefore, do not figure in the data up to 2004.

3. Results

3.1. Introduction

The *gap* system generates a spread and depth of country-level, regional and global data that cannot be tapped here. Only the most challenging will be presented – ranks – in full knowledge of the fact that the time-lag effects due to the recent bout in ratifications affect the system's averages of 1995-9 and 2000-4 for quite a

Table 2. Countries' normalized overall core rights gaps since 1985 (averages sorted by 2000–2004 order of best to worst performers).[1]

Countries by groups	1985–1999 Score	1990–1994 Score	1995–1999 Score	2000–2004 Core rights gaps Score	Rank	Adherence gaps Score	Rank	Implementation gaps Score	Rank
124 High ratifiers[2] including 41 extensive recent and 18 long-standing ratifiers									
GAMBIA	0.308	0.308	0.300	0.061	1	0.030	78	0.027	7
San Marino	0.182	0.160	0.040	0.065	2	0.013	49	0.053	14
Italy	0.171	0.136	0.087	0.074	3	0.000	3	0.080	25
ST. KITTS and NEVIS	–	–	0.308	0.079	4	0.054	109	0.013	4
SOUTH AFRICA	–	–	0.178	0.079	5	0.002	16	0.083	27
NAMIBIA	0.308	0.308	0.281	0.087	6	0.033	83	0.050	11
Ireland	0.193	0.184	0.139	0.089	7	0.005	20	0.090	32
SWITZERLAND	0.204	0.197	0.141	0.096	8	0.000	9	0.103	36
Hungary	0.176	0.185	0.118	0.100	9	0.006	23	0.100	35
Senegal	0.183	0.202	0.293	0.105	10	0.000	8	0.113	49
SEYCHELLES	0.250	0.295	0.255	0.106	11	0.006	24	0.107	43
Sweden	0.116	0.202	0.090	0.107	12	0.009	36	0.103	37
Nicaragua	0.277	0.188	0.127	0.108	13	0.000	4	0.117	51
Austria	0.190	0.202	0.159	0.108	14	0.005	21	0.110	46
The Netherlands	0.213	0.155	0.152	0.110	15	0.012	44	0.103	40
Portugal	0.167	0.139	0.174	0.111	16	0.000	6	0.120	54
Poland	0.218	0.158	0.098	0.113	17	0.012	45	0.107	44
Iceland	0.148	0.163	0.114	0.118	18	0.003	18	0.124	57
Romania	0.228	0.215	0.224	0.121	19	0.000	7	0.131	62
Malta	0.169	0.139	0.123	0.122	20	0.006	32	0.124	58
Finland	0.144	0.099	0.095	0.123	21	0.000	2	0.133	66
KAZAKHSTAN	–	0.308	0.299	0.126	22	0.063	125	0.053	13
Luxembourg	0.093	0.074	0.094	0.127	23	0.023	67	0.107	42
Israel	0.091	0.058	0.098	0.127	24	0.036	89	0.090	31
Germany	0.190	0.225	0.164	0.129	25	0.012	43	0.124	59
SLOVAKIA	–	0.123	0.101	0.131	26	0.011	41	0.127	61
Togo	0.171	0.181	0.170	0.132	27	0.000	10	0.143	76
CAMBODIA	–	–	0.253	0.133	29	0.058	118	0.067	19
EQUATORIAL GUINEA	0.241	0.252	0.259	0.137	31	0.061	123	0.067	17
Jordan	0.259	0.250	0.185	0.138	32	0.027	74	0.113	48
Guyana	0.179	0.213	0.093	0.138	33	0.013	46	0.133	64
Ukraine	0.156	0.121	0.180	0.139	34	0.000	11	0.150	81
BAHAMAS	0.241	0.243	0.256	0.140	35	0.029	77	0.113	47
Benin	0.151	0.181	0.185	0.140	36	0.014	51	0.133	68
Norway	0.171	0.141	0.095	0.142	37	0.000	5	0.154	87
LESOTHO	0.232	0.228	0.192	0.143	38	0.029	76	0.117	50

(Continued)

Table 2. Countries' normalized overall core rights gaps since 1985 (averages sorted by 2000–2004 order of best to worst performers).[1] — Cont'd.

Countries by groups	1985–1999 Score	1990–1994 Score	1995–1999 Score	2000–2004					
				Core rights gaps		Adherence gaps		Implementation gaps	
				Score	Rank	Score	Rank	Score	Rank
PAPUA NEW GUINEA	0.327	0.317	0.288	0.144	39	0.017	59	0.133	65
Belgium	0.160	0.130	0.127	0.146	41	0.013	50	0.140	74
Croatia	–	0.167	0.190	0.147	42	0.006	28	0.151	82
Panama	0.308	0.269	0.267	0.149	43	0.003	19	0.157	88
Argentina	0.199	0.229	0.230	0.149	45	0.006	25	0.154	86
ST. VINCENT and GRENADINES	0.308	0.308	0.253	0.150	46	0.057	116	0.087	28
GRENADA	0.256	0.204	0.176	0.152	48	0.074	127	0.067	18
ALBANIA	–	–	–	0.153	49	0.016	55	0.144	77
Lebanon	–	0.088	0.179	0.153	50	0.049	98	0.100	34
ZIMBABWE	0.299	0.278	0.214	0.153	51	0.020	61	0.140	72
Barbados	0.219	0.214	0.251	0.154	53	0.020	62	0.140	73
Mali	0.114	0.161	0.203	0.156	54	0.014	53	0.150	79
MOZAMBIQUE	–	–	0.191	0.158	55	0.051	104	0.103	39
Honduras	0.189	0.204	0.162	0.159	56	0.006	30	0.163	93
Greece	0.299	0.298	0.125	0.162	57	0.006	29	0.167	99
Lithuania	–	0.220	0.127	0.163	58	0.017	58	0.153	83
BOTSWANA	0.308	0.308	0.138	0.163	59	0.033	80	0.133	63
MALAWI	0.234	0.271	0.213	0.165	60	0.006	31	0.170	101
Costa Rica	0.143	0.197	0.234	0.165	61	0.006	27	0.171	103
Tunisia	0.237	0.216	0.178	0.165	62	0.009	37	0.167	97
Belarus	0.119	0.130	0.155	0.169	64	0.000	1	0.183	112
Uruguay	0.171	0.114	0.117	0.171	65	0.006	34	0.177	106
Spain	0.134	0.155	0.144	0.171	66	0.006	33	0.177	108
Cape Verde	0.269	0.224	0.184	0.172	67	0.057	115	0.110	45
Slovenia	–	0.079	0.115	0.173	68	0.020	63	0.160	92
Russian Federation	–	0.167	0.134	0.174	70	0.019	60	0.164	94
Ivory Coast	0.160	0.230	0.241	0.175	71	0.047	96	0.127	60
Cyprus	0.148	0.169	0.184	0.176	72	0.017	57	0.167	100
CHILE	0.281	0.246	0.230	0.177	73	0.011	38	0.177	107
Macedonia	–	0.044	0.083	0.178	74	0.080	131	0.087	29
UK	0.250	0.281	0.275	0.179	75	0.000	12	0.194	122
BURKINA FASO	0.284	0.266	0.226	0.180	76	0.006	26	0.187	113
France	0.126	0.159	0.139	0.180	77	0.011	39	0.181	111
Cuba	0.179	0.285	0.162	0.182	79	0.028	75	0.160	91
Rwanda	0.185	0.223	0.358	0.182	80	0.005	22	0.190	119
Yemen	–	0.265	0.243	0.188	81	0.013	47	0.187	114

Table 2. Countries' normalized overall core rights gaps since 1985 (averages sorted by 2000–2004 order of best to worst performers).[1] — Cont'd.

ZAMBIA	0.266	0.171	0.145	0.188	82	0.025	70	0.170	102
FIJI	0.285	0.229	0.281	0.188	83	0.075	128	0.103	38
ERITREA	–	0.308	0.300	0.192	84	0.036	88	0.160	89
Egypt	0.248	0.276	0.222	0.196	87	0.012	42	0.197	123
St. Lucia	0.194	0.221	0.342	0.196	88	0.059	121	0.133	69
Dominican Republic	0.391	0.283	0.197	0.196	89	0.002	13	0.211	129
Syrian Arab Republic	0.247	0.241	0.241	0.202	91	0.022	64	0.190	117
CONGO	0.306	0.279	0.275	0.203	92	0.050	100	0.153	84
TANZANIA	0.383	0.389	0.388	0.206	93	0.034	87	0.177	105
Libyan Arab Jamahiriya	0.316	0.278	0.353	0.206	95	0.013	48	0.207	127
Peru	0.263	0.442	0.296	0.206	96	0.025	71	0.190	118
MAURITIUS	0.279	0.220	0.245	0.208	97	0.049	99	0.160	90
Bulgaria	0.135	0.147	0.164	0.214	100	0.003	17	0.227	136
INDONESIA	0.293	0.309	0.269	0.215	101	0.002	15	0.231	139
Brazil	0.243	0.292	0.311	0.217	102	0.033	81	0.191	120
Ecuador	0.316	0.307	0.322	0.217	103	0.002	14	0.233	140
Bosnia-Herzegovina	–	–	0.168	0.219	104	0.055	110	0.164	95
Kyrgyzstan	–	0.073	0.191	0.219	105	0.078	129	0.133	67
COMOROS	0.179	0.197	0.247	0.220	106	0.089	136	0.120	53
Swaziland	0.215	0.213	0.255	0.223	107	0.041	91	0.187	115
SRI LANKA	0.269	0.299	0.292	0.223	108	0.026	72	0.207	128
Antigua and Barbados	0.135	0.242	0.175	0.227	112	0.059	119	0.167	96
Niger	0.118	0.138	0.169	0.231	115	0.017	56	0.227	134
Gabon	0.264	0.302	0.220	0.232	116	0.053	108	0.180	109
KENYA	0.319	0.276	0.323	0.234	118	0.045	95	0.194	121
BURUNDI	0.346	0.255	0.271	0.234	120	0.025	68	0.220	131
Ghana	0.322	0.292	0.386	0.236	121	0.044	93	0.197	124
Azerbaijan	–	0.097	0.191	0.236	122	0.037	90	0.207	126
Denmark	0.215	0.169	0.156	0.242	125	0.023	65	0.231	138
Morocco	0.246	0.364	0.357	0.244	126	0.033	82	0.221	132
MAURITANIA	0.336	0.384	0.325	0.249	129	0.027	73	0.234	142
BELIZE	0.183	0.190	0.266	0.257	130	0.023	66	0.247	144
MADAGASCAR	0.332	0.312	0.328	0.259	133	0.043	92	0.223	133
NIGERIA	0.310	0.272	0.312	0.261	134	0.052	105	0.214	130
Central African Republic	0.422	0.356	0.230	0.263	135	0.014	52	0.267	150
Czech Republic	–	0.123	0.189	0.264	136	0.044	94	0.227	135
Philippines	0.253	0.288	0.294	0.272	138	0.033	84	0.250	146
ETHIOPIA	0.288	0.288	0.335	0.273	139	0.047	97	0.234	141
Jamaica	0.375	0.381	0.332	0.274	140	0.050	101	0.230	137
Dominica	0.124	0.261	0.175	0.277	141	0.025	69	0.267	149
Algeria	0.239	0.251	0.286	0.284	143	0.016	54	0.287	152
Cameroon	0.288	0.303	0.381	0.286	145	0.034	86	0.263	148

(Continued)

Table 2. Countries' normalized overall core rights gaps since 1985 (averages sorted by 2000–2004 order of best to worst performers).[1] — Cont'd.

Countries by groups	1985–1999 Score	1990–1994 Score	1995–1999 Score	2000–2004 Core rights gaps Score	Rank	Adherence gaps Score	Rank	Implementation gaps Score	Rank
Bangladesh	0.355	0.250	0.308	0.291	146	0.034	85	0.270	151
Chad	0.227	0.302	0.319	0.293	147	0.051	103	0.250	145
Paraguay	0.316	0.332	0.342	0.299	148	0.059	120	0.244	143
TRINIDAD and TOBAGO	0.324	0.320	0.287	0.300	149	0.051	102	0.257	147
Venezuela	0.217	0.165	0.277	0.323	152	0.030	79	0.310	156
Guinea	0.315	0.237	0.400	0.330	153	0.053	107	0.287	153
Bolivia	0.209	0.230	0.302	0.332	154	0.052	106	0.290	154
TURKEY	0.280	0.250	0.224	0.333	155	0.009	35	0.348	157
Pakistan	0.470	0.426	0.400	0.343	157	0.058	117	0.294	155
Guatemala	0.273	0.244	0.368	0.384	158	0.011	40	0.401	159

21 Medium ratifiers[3] including six extensive recent and eight long-standing ratifiers

Countries by groups	1985–1999 Score	1990–1994 Score	1995–1999 Score	2000–2004 Core rights gaps Score	Rank	Adherence gaps Score	Rank	Implementation gaps Score	Rank
TURKMENISTAN	–	0.308	0.163	0.133	28	0.108	141	0.000	1
ESTONIA	–	0.264	0.175	0.136	30	0.060	122	0.067	20
New Zealand	0.244	0.248	0.214	0.152	47	0.078	130	0.060	16
Uzbekistan	–	0.132	0.121	0.154	52	0.120	148	0.007	3
Guinea-Bissau	0.240	0.297	0.249	0.168	63	0.087	135	0.067	21
MALAYSIA	0.299	0.298	0.244	0.181	78	0.082	133	0.087	30
Iran	0.357	0.211	0.268	0.194	85	0.098	139	0.080	26
Kuwait	0.268	0.258	0.238	0.196	86	0.056	114	0.137	71
EL SALVADOR	0.364	0.381	0.204	0.200	90	0.055	112	0.143	75
THAILAND	0.325	0.368	0.270	0.210	99	0.113	145	0.077	22
Saudi Arabia	0.195	0.290	0.227	0.225	110	0.090	138	0.123	55
Latvia	–	0.103	0.276	0.225	111	0.090	137	0.123	56
Djibouti	0.211	0.169	0.312	0.230	114	0.109	142	0.103	41
Mexico	0.172	0.176	0.188	0.234	117	0.055	113	0.180	110
Mongolia	0.194	0.230	0.188	0.234	119	0.100	140	0.120	52
Canada	0.286	0.308	0.260	0.240	123	0.082	132	0.150	80
Australia	0.149	0.128	0.148	0.240	124	0.055	111	0.187	116
UNITED ARAB EMIRATES	0.280	0.280	0.199	0.248	127	0.069	126	0.177	104
Japan	0.262	0.255	0.297	0.258	132	0.062	124	0.197	125
Uganda	0.281	0.249	0.266	0.306	150	0.124	150	0.167	98
Sierra Leone	–	–	–	0.432	159	0.082	134	0.359	158

14 Low ratifiers[4] including four extensive recent and two long-standing ratifiers

Countries by groups	1985–1999 Score	1990–1994 Score	1995–1999 Score	2000–2004 Core rights gaps Score	Rank	Adherence gaps Score	Rank	Implementation gaps Score	Rank
KIRIBATI	–	–	–	0.144	40	0.117	147	0.000	2
Suriname	0.174	0.153	0.157	0.149	44	0.111	144	0.013	5
BAHRAIN	0.296	0.280	0.255	0.174	69	0.116	146	0.033	9
VIETNAM	–	0.308	0.251	0.206	94	0.138	153	0.040	10

Table 2. Countries' normalized overall core rights gaps since 1985 (averages sorted by 2000–2004 order of best to worst performers).[1] — Cont'd.

China	0.315	0.294	0.271	0.208	98	0.149	155	0.027	8
KOREA,									
REPUBLIC OF	–	0.319	0.272	0.223	109	0.121	149	0.080	23
Singapore	0.317	0.307	0.283	0.229	113	0.126	151	0.080	24
USA	0.308	0.280	0.278	0.248	128	0.164	156	0.050	12
Qatar	0.289	0.294	0.262	0.258	131	0.137	152	0.097	33
Oman	–	–	0.290	0.266	137	0.171	157	0.060	15
India	0.281	0.455	0.269	0.278	142	0.111	143	0.154	85
Lao PDR	0.305	0.289	0.275	0.285	144	0.217	159	0.020	6
Sao Tome and									
Principe	0.273	0.241	0.280	0.312	151	0.144	154	0.147	78
Myanmar	0.283	0.365	0.357	0.337	156	0.171	158	0.137	70

[1] Eight groups of countries are highlighted in this table.
- Three groups by categorizations reflected in subheadings and defined in notes 2–4.
- Three groups by shading, which grades countries' performance on the 2000–2004 CRG scale. Good performers' CRGs, whose scores are <25% of the worst score (Sierra Leone's), are not shaded. Medium performers are lightly shaded, with scores ranging from 25 to 50% of the worst score. Poor performers' CRGs, which exceed 50% of the worst score, are strongly shaded.
- CAPITAL LETTERS identify 51 extensive recent ratifiers.
- Italicizing identifies 28 long-standing ratifiers, defined as countries that adhered before 1985 to such core Conventions as were listed as having been ratified by them on 31 December 2004.
- All other countries are presented in ordinary print.

[2] Countries that had ratified seven or eight core Conventions by 31 December 2004.
[3] Countries that had ratified five or six core Conventions by 31 December 2004.
[4] Countries that had ratified four or less core Conventions by 31 December 2004.

number of countries. I expect that the time-lag distortions will have worked their way out of the system in the second half of the current decade and that the next full five-averages, 2005-9, will be free from notable distortions.

Much information and several categorical distinctions are packed into Table 2, which presents normalized rather than 'raw' data. As each dimension and the combined CRGs are normalized separately, the adherence and implementation scores do not, as such, add up to CRGs; but one can perceive the relationship that exists between the constituent dimensions and the summary index.

The central column, CRG averages for 2000-4, is the table's backbone in that it ranks countries from best to worst overall performer. To render visible the pivotal role of the ratification of fundamental standards, countries are grouped into high, medium and low ratifiers. High ratifiers (7-8 Conventions) tend to have small *adherence gaps*, medium ratifiers (5-6 Conventions) middle-size adherence gaps and low ratifiers (4 or less Conventions) large adherence gaps. For example, among high ratifiers, Italy (which can be found under 2000-4 CRG rank 3), Switzerland (rank 8) and Senegal (rank 10) have no adherence gaps during

2000-4. Among low ratifiers, the US rank 156 out of 159 on the adherence scale (2000-4 CRG rank 128).

In the ideal world portrayed by the International Labour Organization's Conventions, fundamental principles and rights, there should be no implementation problems after ratification. The scores on the right side of Table 2 tell a mixed story – at each level of ratification. Illustrations of good and not-so-good implementation performers, starting with a selection of high ratifiers who adhered to all eight core Conventions, could refer to Italy's fairly good 25th implementation rank and Ireland's 32nd rank (2000-4 CRG ranks 3 and 7, respectively). By contrast, two generally well-regarded European countries occupy low implementation ranks at the beginning of the 21st century: France rank 111 and Denmark rank 138 (2000-4 CRG ranks 77 and 125, respectively). Among Asian medium ratifiers that adhered to six core Conventions, local political differences account for, on the one hand, New Zealand occupying a good 16th implementation rank in 2000-4 but Australia the much poorer 116th rank (2000-4 CRG ranks 47 and 124, respectively). When one looks at low ratifiers one might expect implementation gaps to be small because the Committee of Experts cannot address as many direct requests and observations to low ratifiers as it can, potentially, to medium and high ratifiers – though the CFA component can weigh in and add up to 15 'raw' points even in the absence of ratification of Convention Nos. 87 and 98. But low ratification is no assurance against sizeable implementation gaps. While, for example, the 8th implementation rank of China, which had ratified two core Conventions by 1999 and added a third in 2002, and the 12th implementation rank of the US, which had ratified two Conventions by 2000, conform to such considerations (2000-4 CRG ranks 98 and 128, respectively), much worse performances are turned in by Sao Tome and Principe (four ratifications) at implementation rank 78 and India (also four ratifications) at implementation rank 85 (2000-4 CRG ranks 151 and 142, respectively).

A brief look is in order at countries that are benefiting from the time-lag effects of ratification on implementation. To make them visible, Table 2 capitalizes the 51 extensive recent ratifiers that are defined as having ratified three or more core Conventions since December 1995 after the ILO's Director-General had launched a ratification campaign. Two examples of time-lag effects among high ratifiers at the top of Table 2 are Gambia, whose wholesale ratifications have already been referred to and which ranks 7th on the implementation scale in 2000-4; and St. Kitts and Nevis, which ratified seven core Conventions in 2000 and scores 4th on the implementation scale. Among medium ratifiers, Turkmenistan is a striking example that at present, after having ratified six of the eight Conventions in 1997, has had no charge on its implementation dimension. Among low ratifiers, Kiribati ratified four of the eight core Conventions in 2000 upon becoming a member State of the International Labour Organization. Scored as from 2001, time-lag effects give it, for now, an unblemished implementation score; but its remaining adherence gap feeds through to the CRG and puts it temporarily on CRG rank 40 in 2000-4.

Extensive recent ratifiers are not only a minority but, once the Committee of Experts has had an opportunity to assess during two or three post-ratification reporting cycles how these countries give effect to their commitments in law and practice, their *implementation* scores and CRGs may also be quite different in size from what they are now, their ranks as well. This can be expected to happen in the second half of the current decade.

3.2. What Influence Does 'Interest' Have on Scores?

What is the influence of adding notes of *interest* on (a) the implementation dimension and (b) CRG scores? Examples must suffice, with a focus on some of the following countries that were credited with more notes of interest than others:

- Argentina, Canada, Costa Rica, Nicaragua, Pakistan, Paraguay, the United Kingdom and Venezuela in the case of the two freedom of association and collective bargaining Conventions;
- Brazil, India, Pakistan and Thailand in the case of the elimination of all forms of forced labour;
- Kenya, Honduras and Romania in the case of Convention No. 138 concerning the abolition child labour. No country has yet been credited with interest under Convention No. 182 (nor with an expression of satisfaction for that matter); and
- Chile, Germany, India, Romania, Sweden and Turkey as far as the elimination of non-discrimination is concerned.

As regards (a) and choosing ranks for the illustration,[8] the improvement in 2000-4 overall implementation scores is highest in the case of Costa Rica and Sweden (18 ranks each), Argentina, Brazil, Germany (15 ranks each) and Romania (12 ranks). India improves its implementation score little, by merely four ranks.

As regards (b) 2000-4 CRGs, the implementation improvements feed through strongly for high ratifiers, less so for others. For example, Brazil's overall CRG improves by 29 ranks, Costa Rica's by 21 ranks, and Argentina's, Germany's and Romania's by 12 ranks. Being high ratifiers, these countries are scarcely or not at all afflicted by adherence gaps (see under 2000-4 CRG ranks 102, 61, 45, 43 and 7, respectively). Low ratifier India's CRG rank of 142 in 2000-4 is, as for implementation, a mere four steps higher with interest than without it; its persistently large adherence gap is mainly responsible for this.

3.3. Countries' Performance in Static and Dynamic Comparison

The light will now be trained on countries' general position regarding fundamental human rights in terms of 2000-4 average CRGs. To that end, I distinguish 'good' from 'medium' and 'poor' performers by applying the commonly used thresholds of up to 25%, 25-50% and more than 50% of the maximum non-achievement score, which is Sierra Leone's at 0.432 points. The thresholds are <0.108 points (good performers, not shaded), 0.108-0.216 points (medium performers, shaded lightly) and >0.216 points (poor performers, shaded strongly).

Under this static comparison, a mere 12 countries can be considered good performers (8%), 89 countries fall into the group of medium performers (56%) and

---

[8] The comparison is based on Table 2 of this contribution and Table 1 of Böhning, 2005a.

58 countries are poor performers (36%). This result, buttressed by many other findings of the *gap* system, explains why I have entitled my book "Labour rights in crisis". If one carries out the same kind of calculation for *gaps* in individual areas – freedom of association and collective bargaining, forced labour, child labour and discrimination – one finds a higher proportion of good performers (Böhning, 2005a). But it suffices for a country not to do well in one or two areas and it will fail to make the mark, as it were, at the overall level.

A more dynamic picture of the state of fundamental labour rights today can be obtained by examining how adherents and implementers performed since 1985. In the last few years, of course, countries have adhered more extensively to core labour standards. Table 3 shows that the 10 bottom-ranked adherents are no exception; there are even some among them who proceeded to ratifying a Convention or two. Their average scores decrease continuously, and the ratio of 'smaller' to 'larger' adherence gaps has been widening. It is interesting to note that China increasingly outscores the U.S. as far as adherence is concerned, and that the U.S. find themselves in the uncomfortable neighbourhood of countries often considered to be among the worst offenders in the field of human rights.

The picture changes for the worse if one considers implementation problems. The scores of the 10 worst implementers are listed in Table 4. One might expect extensive recent ratifiers not to be prominent among them; indeed, Table 4 contains only one: Turkey. But this country has been battling with implementation problems for a long time; and they appear not to have been attenuated by the sliding-scale time lags of its ratification record: Turkey entered the gap system with four ratification, added the 5th in 1993, the 6th and 7th in 1998 and Convention No. 138 in 2001. There are also two long-standing ratifiers among the worst implementers, Dominica and Algeria, and their scores tend to worsen rather than improve over time (which is a general phenomenon for long-standing ratifiers, see Böhning, 2005a and 2005b).

The several measurements incorporated in Table 4 convey the same sobering, even worrying, message that the implementation gaps of the worst implementers have generally worsened rather than improved in the last 20 years. The average size of their scores did get smaller between 1985-9 and 1990-94, but since then the trend has turned in the wrong direction. Most implementation gaps increased strongly in 1995-9 and grew still further in 2000-4. On the right side of the table change is expressed qualitatively, with eight 'larger' outweighing two 'smaller' implementation gaps by the end of the review period.

The huge average scores at the bottom of Table 4 suggest that, in 2000-4, 30% of the 10 worst implementers' laws and practices concerning fundamental human rights were not in accordance with the ideals that they had subscribed to and which they were supposed to give concrete effect to in law and in practice. Proportions were as high as 35% in the case of Turkey and 40% in the case of Guatemala, with a tendency for their implementation problems to grow as time went by. The ratification records of the 10 worst implementers vary somewhat but appear to have had comparatively little impact on their implementation ranks. Dominica, Algeria and Venezuela were high ratifiers throughout the review period, which renders their performance particularly worrisome. The Central

Table 3. Size of and Change in Adherence Gaps of the 10 Worst Adherents (normalized averages sorted by 2000-4 order of worst CRG performers).

| Country | 1985-9 | 1990-94 | 1995-9 | 2000-4 | Rank | Country | Changes in gaps | | | |
	(1)	(2)	(3)	(4)			(2 to 1)	(3 to 2)	(4 to 3)
Uganda	0.148	0.148	0.143	0.124	150	Uganda	same	smaller	smaller
Singapore	0.180	0.184	0.175	0.126	151	Singapore	larger	smaller	smaller
Qatar	0.218	0.216	0.196	0.137	152	Qatar	larger	smaller	smaller
VIETNAM	-	0.250	0.204	0.138	153	VIETNAM	-	smaller	smaller
Sao Tome & P.	0.182	0.150	0.136	0.144	154	Sao Tome & P.	smaller	smaller	larger
China	0.250	0.216	0.203	0.149	155	China	smaller	smaller	smaller
U.S.	0.250	0.221	0.209	0.164	156	U.S.	smaller	smaller	smaller
Oman	-	-	0.236	0.171	157	Oman	-	-	smaller
Myanmar	0.179	0.182	0.187	0.171	158	*Myanmar*	larger	larger	smaller
Lao P.D.R.	0.220	0.218	0.218	0.217	159	Lao PDR	smaller	same	smaller
Average	*0.203*	*0.198*	*0.191*	*0.154*		*Ratio smaller/*			
						larger	*4:3*	*7:1*	*9:1*

-Not applicable. Light and dark shading according to 2000-4 CRG scores, capital letters and italicizing of countries as per Table 2.

Table 4. Size of and Change in Implementation Gaps of the 10 Worst Implementers (normalized averages sorted by 2000-4 order of worst CRG performers).

| Country | 1985-9 | 1990-94 | 1995-9 | 2000-4 | Rank | Country | Changes in gaps | | |
	(1)	(2)	(3)	(4)			(2 to 1)	(3 to 2)	(4 to 3)
Dominica	0.099	0.213	0.175	0.267	150	Dominica	larger	smaller	larger
Central Afr. Republic	0.373	0.297	0.177	0.267	151	Central Afr. Republic	smaller	smaller	larger
Bangladesh	0.290	0.175	0.251	0.270	152	Bangladesh	smaller	larger	larger
Algeria	0.259	0.244	0.286	0.287	153	Algeria	smaller	larger	larger
Guinea	0.293	0.194	0.343	0.287	154	Guinea	smaller	larger	smaller
Bolivia	0.084	0.145	0.229	0.290	155	Bolivia	larger	larger	larger
Pakistan	0.392	0.347	0.338	0.294	156	Pakistan	smaller	smaller	smaller
Venezuela	0.213	0.160	0.293	0.310	157	Venezuela	smaller	larger	larger
TURKEY	0.160	0.145	0.183	0.348	158	TURKEY	smaller	larger	larger
Guatemala	0.210	0.240	0.398	0.401	159	Guatemala	larger	larger	larger
Average	*0.237*	*0.216*	*0.267*	*0.302*		*Ratio larger/ smaller*	*3:7*	*7:3*	*8:2*

-Not applicable. Dark shading according to 2000-4 CRG scores, capital letters and italicizing of countries as per Table 2.

African Republic, Bangladesh, Guinea, Pakistan and Guatemala were medium ratifiers until, respectively, 1999, 2000, 2002, 2000 and 1989, and thereafter became high ratifiers. Bolivia and Turkey moved from low to medium and high levels of ratification over the years.

If one examines *implementation* across the board, it becomes clear that there are unfortunately rather more countries with worsening than with improving scores (Böhning, 2005a). Furthermore, if one standardizes countries' implementation scores by the number of ratifications (Böhning, 2005b), the picture brightens only a little – in the area of forced labour and in the European region – but the prevailing impression is one of gloom.

4. Peeping into the Future

The two-dimensional index called *Core Rights Gaps* rests on sound theoretical foundations. Its constituent indicators are valid, transparent and replicable, and they measure countries' performance with identical yardsticks and objectivity. The gap system's results are currently held hostage by the recent spurt in ratifications in the sense that a third or more of the countries' implementation scores and CRGs are not, or not fully, up to date. But the time lags deriving from the ILO's reporting cycles and the working habits of the Committee of Experts will work themselves out of the system in the coming years. By the time the five-year averages of 2005-9 can be calculated, implementation gaps and CRGs will no longer be significantly affected by large-scale ratifications.

How can one be that optimistic? One can be. Because, even though 60 of the gap countries have not yet adhered to one or several of the Conventions that define the fundamental human rights in the labour field, a closer look shows that it is not very probable that many of them will proceed to ratifying the remaining core labour standards. First, 18 of them are extensive recent ratifiers. These countries will presumably have studied seriously the question whether to ratify the outstanding Conventions – and decided against them. Of course, they may change their governments or their minds. Second, quite a number of the non-ratifiers are traditionally reluctant to ratify international labour Conventions, notably countries in the Asian and Gulf regions. They are unlikely to turn into enthusiastic ratifiers any time soon. Third, it is unrealistic to expect a great many ratifications of one of the standards that to date has attracted least adherents, Convention No. 87. Countries such as China, India, Saudi Arabia and the U.S. are politically strongly opposed to ratification. The ratification prospects of the companion Convention, No. 98, are similarly bleak. Half of the 30 non-ratifiers of the two freedom of association and collective bargaining Conventions have actually been at the receiving end of CFA interim reports, which will scarcely have endeared them to the freedom of association and collective bargaining Conventions. Fourth, as regards the least ratified standard, Convention No. 138, insightful policies, a determination to put primary education high on the domestic agenda or fears of foreign boycotts of goods produced by their children may induce some developing countries or transition economies to adhere. The companion Convention, No. 182, is also likely to be ratified by several developing countries or transition economies that have not yet taken that step. But universal ratification is not on the horizon of either Convention. Fifth, the forced labour and non-discrimination Conventions are closest to universal adherence, which implies that one should not expect many future ratifications. In the case of Convention No. 105, Malaysia and Singapore took the unusual step of denouncing their ratification; and they are not likely to reverse that decision.

Therefore, excepting the two child labour Conventions, one can expect very few further ratifications by the current member States of the International Labour Organization. New member States will probably ratify core Conventions in most areas. But the group that I called 'extensive recent ratifiers' is a dying breed which will cease to play havoc with the new indicator system. It follows that the *gap* system has a future.

References

Adcock, R. and Collier, C. 2001. Measurement validity: a shared standard for qualitative and quantitative research. Am Pol Sci Rev 95(3): 529–546.
Böhning, W.R. 2005a. Labour rights in crisis: measuring the achievement of fundamental human rights in the world of work. Palgrave Macmillan, Basingstoke and New York.
Böhning, W.R. 2005b. Standardised proxies to measure the implementation of core labour standards. In: Eva Senghaas-Knobloch (ed) Welweit geltende arbeitsstandards in globalen strukturen: erfahrungen und einblicke. Lit Verlag, Münster, pp. 49–62.
ILO, CEACR, various years. Report of the Committee of Experts on the application of Conventions and Recommendations, general report and observations concerning particular countries. Report III (Part 4A), International Labour Conference, Geneva, (1985–2004).
ILO, various years. *Review of annual reports under the follow-up to the Declaration on Fundamental Principles and Rights at Work*, Part II, Compilation of annual reports by the International Labour Office (Geneva, ILO document GB.277/3/2, March 2000, and at each subsequent March session of the ILO Governing Body).
ILO 2003. Programme and budget for the biennium 2004–2005. ILO document GB.286/PFA/9, Geneva.
ILO 2006. ILO Programme implementation 2004–2005. ILO document GB.295/PFA/13, Geneva.

W. R. BÖHNING,
Formerly International Labour Office official; now private consultant

Chapter 9

Employment Protection in Industrialized Countries:
The Case for New Indicators*

GIUSEPPE BERTOLA,
European University Institute and University of Turin
TITO BOERI,
University of Bocconi, Milan
SANDRINE CAZES
International Labour Office

The poor employment performance of European countries compared with that of the U.S. is often attributed to the strictness of employment protection in Europe. Many believe that differences in labour market regulations play an important role in explaining international differences in labour market outcomes. This argument clearly has strong implications for policy design. If tight rules governing employment protection are to be blamed for poor labour market performance, then conservative governments may reduce restraints on the ability of firms to hire and fire (by weakening trade unions and labour market regulations for example). This controversial proposition has generated a considerable literature and much debate. Theoretical models show that employment protection does tend to have a constraining effect on both layoffs *and* hirings, job creation *and* destruction, unemployment inflows *and* outflows, with the extent to which one effect dominates the other depending on the values of the parameters. It follows that the role played by employment protection in determining aggregate labour market outcomes is mainly an empirical question. However, the available empirical evidence on the relationship between employment protection and labour market performance is based on highly imperfect measures of the strictness of employment protection legislation (EPL).[1] While considerable work – both theoretical and empirical – has been done on the subject, few studies have focused on how employment protection is measured. Previous research has circumvented measurement difficulties by using qualitative rankings of EPL stringency. But recent developments – notably ongoing reforms of employment protection in most countries and the expansion of non-standard forms of employment – have not only rendered existing information obsolete, they have also called into question the methodological basis of that empirical research.

---

* Reprinted from *International Labour Review*, Vol. 139 (2000), No. 1.

[1] For the purposes of this chapter, EPL is understood to refer to regulatory provisions that relate to "hiring and firing", particularly those governing unfair dismissals, termination of employment for economic reasons, severance payments, minimum notice periods, administrative authorization for dismissal, and prior consultations with trade union and/or labour administration representatives.

D. Kucera (ed.), Qualitative Indicators of Labour Standards, 237–252.
© 2007 by ILO.

While EPL rankings developed in the late 1980s are rather strongly correlated with employment stability in the 1980s, more recent evidence indicates that some innovative work is required to improve methods of measurement. What is needed is not only an update of EPL rankings to capture new legal provisions in the various countries, but also measures that reflect the increasing complexity of legal provisions in this area, their interactions and/or inconsistencies. Reforms of protective legislation have rarely addressed the whole set of relevant provisions but, more typically, only those applying to specific contractual types, e.g. by broadening the scope of some types of fixed-term contracts without reducing the protection afforded by contracts of unlimited duration. This increasing dualism of labour markets and institutional complexity (proliferation of different types of contract and ad hoc provisions) requires substantial revision of the methodology previously used to compute EPL rankings. Appropriate indicators should try to account not only for these various features of EPL, but also for their interactions – e.g. the fact that the increasing share of employment under fixed-term contract may also be a *consequence* of strict employment protection.

The purpose of this article is to highlight the need for new analytical and statistical tools for understanding and measuring labour market flexibility and performance. It opens with a short survey of existing theoretical and empirical work on the relationship between EPL and broad labour market performance indicators. It then illustrates some of the shortcomings of available measures of employment protection and suggests improvements, taking account of the increasing dualism of European labour markets (i.e. the existence of a large group of workers under fixed-term contracts alongside the protected segment of workers under regular contracts) and making better use of the limited available data on litigation and judicial decisions concerning individual dismissals. The strengths and weaknesses of existing measures are shown in the light of simple empirical evidence. The article concludes with reflections on how to move forward.

Existing Evidence on the Effect of Employment Protection

Measuring employment protection is a difficult task. Quantitative measures can be readily computed for some aspects like the number of months' notice required for individual and collective redundancies. But other aspects are more difficult to measure precisely, such as the willingness of labour courts to entertain law suits filed by fired workers or judicial interpretation of the notion of "just cause" for termination.

Such problems have been circumvented in previous work by taking advantage of the fact that even partial and qualitative indicators of EPL provisions make it possible – when such indicators are positively correlated with each other – to produce qualitatively unambiguous cross-country rankings of EPL. Work along these lines has found that, in the late-1980s, countries mandating longer notice periods also tended to specify larger redundancy payments and more complex procedures for authorization and implementation of collective dismissals. Such measures were also consistent with survey assessment indicators of EPL stringency, especially those derived from the European Community's 1985 survey of enterprises (see Emerson, 1988). Bertola (1990) used this evidence to draw up a ranked list of ten industrialized countries.

Grubb and Wells (1993) then developed rankings for a larger group of industrialized OECD countries on the basis of various aspects of the regulations governing individual dismissals under regular contracts and fixed-term contracts, and the regulations governing temporary work agencies. So far, rankings have only been produced on a cross-sectional basis (see Table 1 for a selection of such rankings).

Table 1. Ranking of Employment Protection Legislation Indicators by "Strictness".

Country	Maximum severance pay and notice period[1] 1993	OECD[2] 1989	International Organization of Employers (IOE)[3] 1985	Bertola 1985	Average ranking based on the four preceding columns[4] 1985-1993
U.S.	0.00	0.36*	0.4*	1.0	1
New Zealand	0.25	0.72*	0.4*	1.3*	2
Canada	1.25	1.65*	0.6*	2.0*	3
Australia	3.00	3.26*	0.9*	3.1*	4
Denmark	4.50	3.25	1.0	2.0	5
Switzerland	5.00	1.75	0.9*	3.2*	6
United Kingdom	6.00	2.25	0.5	4.0	7
Japan	1.00	3.71*	1.0*	5.0	8
Netherlands	4.00	7.25	2.5	3.0	9
Finland	6.00	10.50	1.0	5.5*	10
Norway	6.00	9.75	1.5	5.9*	11
Ireland	14.00	2.75	1.5	6.0*	12
Sweden	6.00	8.50	2.0	7.0	13
France	3.50	9.50	2.5	8.0	14
Germany	4.50	12.00	2.5	6.0	15
Austria	14.75	9.00	1.5	7.6*	16
Belgium	8.50	10.50	2.5	9.0	17
Greece	13.25	11.00	2.5*	9.1*	18
Portugal	17.00	12.50	2.0	9.5*	19
Spain	15.00	11.25	3.0	10.0*	20
Italy	13.00	14.25	3.0	10.0	21

* Figures are estimates of missing values, made by regression/extrapolation (see note 4 below).

[1] The sum of maximum notice and severance pay, in months (see Grubb and Wells, 1993).

[2] The average of OECD rankings of the strictness of protection for regular and fixed-term contract workers.

[3] The average of the IOE scorings of obstacles to termination or use of regular and fixed-term contracts on a scale from 1 to 3 (for details, see OECD, 1994a, pp. 73-74).

[4] This average ranking is the rank order of a weighted average of the indicators in the preceding columns. In the weighted average, the weight of each indicator is the inverse of the coefficient estimated when that indicator is regressed on the weighted average itself. The missing values for each indicator are estimated from these regressions. Mutually consistent estimates with these properties were obtained by an iterative procedure.

Source: OECD, 1994a.

This overview of existing work concentrates on the effects of employment protection on labour market adjustment – i.e. the processes of job and labour real-location [2] – as theory predicts that a given set of EPL provisions should affect the dynamic behaviour of employment rather than its average level. Accordingly, there are several important and interrelated issues that will not be addressed directly, such as the impact of EPL on the level of unemployment, labour force participation, productivity or efficiency (e.g. stable employment relationships can foster investments in job-specific human capital). However, such effects and related concerns must have motivated existing legislation, and should therefore be taken into account in any reform process.

Theoretical models clearly indicate that employment should be more stable and individual employment relationships more durable when EPL is stricter: given a constant (or any other) cyclical wage pattern, higher firing costs stabilize employment in downturns but also deter employers from hiring in upturns. More stringent EPL should therefore be associated with smoother dynamic employment patterns.[3] To the extent that firing costs prevent termination of existing employment relationships, sharp employment reduction is less likely in countries with stringent job security provisions. Yet lower turnover implies that new entrants to the labour market and individuals who happen to be unemployed at any given point in time are less likely to find employment and more likely to experience long-term unemployment.

Empirical work has explored these implications using the above-mentioned overall "rigidity ranks" as indicators of EPL, and a variety of cross-sectional indicators of labour market performance. That evidence is inconclusive though it does give some support to theroretical predictions concerning the behaviour of standard *macro-level indicators* of labour market performance. Thus, while aggregate employment and unemployment levels are not strongly correlated with cross-sectional indicators of EPL stringency, they do seem more stable when EPL is more stringent. The cyclical volatility of employment, for example, is much more pronounced in the relatively less regulated labour markets of the U.S. and the United Kingdom (since the 1980s) than it is in the countries of continental Europe, especially France (Bertola and Ichino, 1995). Markets where EPL is more stringent

---

[2] Following Davis and Haltiwanger (1992), job reallocation or turnover is defined as the sum of job creations and job destructions. In other words, job turnover at time t is the sum of all plant-level employment gains and losses that occur between (t-1) and t. Labour turnover measures the movement of individuals into and out of jobs over a given period and is defined as the sum of hirings and separations. Put another way, labour turnover at time t equals the number of persons who change their place of employment or employment status between t and (t-1).

[3] Yet, since EPL has contrasting effects on employers' propensity to hire and fire, its net effect on *longer-run* relationships between wage and employment levels is *a priori* ambiguous. It may increase or decrease average employment, depending on such subtle features of formal models as the functional form of labour demand functions, the persistence of labour demand fluctuations, and the extent to which future firing costs are discounted at hiring times. A general insight holds true: since higher turnover costs reduce both hiring and firing, their effect on average employment levels over periods when both hiring and firing occur is an order of magnitude lower than that on hiring and firing separately.

feature more stable employment and unemployment, but around levels which, in the long run, are not clearly correlated to the stringency of job security provisions. In formal empirical regressions, EPL indicators are statistically significant but their coefficient is small (Scarpetta, 1996).

Empirical studies have also looked into the effects of EPL on the stability of employment relationships from a *disaggregated perspective*, by applying various measures of such stability from the employees' and employers' points of view. Measures of labour turnover tend to be negatively related to EPL rankings. In the U.S. and Canada, for example, labour turnover is about twice as high as in most European countries.[4] Similarly, average job tenure is significantly longer in countries with more stringent EPL, such as Italy and France.[5] In other respects, however, the evidence does not readily conform to theoretical predictions. For example, if gross job turnover is taken as a rough proxy for labour market flexibility – and since stringent EPL reduces both hiring and firing – it is quite surprising to find that job turnover rates are very loosely related to EPL rankings (see Table 2). Most remarkably, not only are the estimates for Italy and France, at 21 and 24 per cent respectively, very high in absolute terms (one in every five jobs is either created or destroyed each year), but they are also extremely close to the estimates for the U.S. and Canada despite the much heavier regulation of dismissals in the European labour markets. However, EPL does appear more relevant if continuing establishments only are considered.

Some empirical work has also related labour market performance to the behaviour of quantitative EPL indicators over time (even though such indicators are a very partial measure of EPL, rankings are essentially cross-sectional by nature and cannot be used in time-series analysis). The results of such exercises are mixed. Lazear (1990) finds evidence of a positive relationship between EPL and unemployment, but Addison and Grosso (1996) find no significant evidence when using a similar but more precise set of data. This is not surprising: while theory predicts that a given set of EPL provisions should affect the dynamic behaviour (rather than the average level) of employment, changes in EPL provisions generally produce ambiguous effects which certainly differ depending on whether the changes are expected or not.[6]

In sum, empirical work provides mixed results in the evaluation of the influence of labour market regulation on labour market adjustment. Studies using "rigidity rankings" as indicators of EPL do not give clear-cut results. This suggests

---

[4] In the late 1980s the annual rates of labour turnover (the sum of separations and new hires during the sample period as a percentage of average employment levels) were respectively 126.4 and 92.6 for the U.S. and Canada, as against 58 for France, 62 for Germany and 68.1 for Italy (OECD, 1994b and 1996).

[5] Respectively 11.6 and 10.7 years, as against 6.7 in the U.S. (from Eurostat and OECD data).

[6] An unexpected relaxation of EPL, for example, might initially reduce employment if firms shed labour taking advantage of currently low firing costs but – fearing future firing costs – still implement restrained hiring policies in the expectation that EPL will be tightened again (Bertola and Ichino, 1995). Available information does not generally make it possible to disentangle these effects.

Table 2. Job Turnover: Average Annual Rates as a Percentage of Total Employment; Selected Countries.

	Canada 1983-91	France 1984-91	Germany 1983-90	Italy 1987-92	United Kingdom 1985-91	U.S. 1984-91	U.S. (manufacturing) 1984-88
Gross job gains	14.5	12.7	9.0	11.0	8.7	13.0	8.2
Openings	3.2	6.1	2.5	3.8	2.7	8.4	1.4
Expansions	11.2	6.6	6.5	7.3	6.0	4.6	6.7
Gross job losses	11.9	11.8	7.5	10.0	6.6	10.4	10.4
Closures	3.1	5.5	1.9	3.8	3.9	7.3	2.7
Contractions	8.8	6.3	5.6	6.2	2.7	3.1	7.7
Net employment change	2.6	0.9	1.5	1.0	2.1	2.6	−2.2
Net entry	0.1	0.6	0.6	0.0	−1.2	1.1	−1.3
Net expansions	2.4	0.3	0.9	1.1	3.3	1.5	−1.0
Job turnover	26.3	24.4	16.5	21.0	15.3	23.4	18.6
Continuing establishments	20.0	12.9	12.1	13.5	8.7	7.7	14.4

Notes: Net entry = openings − closures; Net expansion = expansions − contractions.

Source: OECD, 1996 and 1997, ch. 3.

that the link between theoretical and empirical results is tenuous and ambiguous – perhaps partly because of the elusive and complex nature of available information, and of the EPL concept itself.

The Need for New Measurement

Existing Indicators of Employment Protection Legislation

Existing measures produce various rankings of EPL – corresponding to different aspects of the regulations [7] – and then add them up via a "ranking of rankings" procedure; the idea of rankings is a good one because many aspects of employment protection are qualitative and difficult to measure, such as the distinction between fair and unfair dismissals, the consequences of unfair dismissal, etc. This method, however, requires detailed information on all countries in order to compute the

---

[7] So far only for individual dismissals. The OECD, however, is revising its EPL indicators to include regulations of collective redundancies (OECD, 1999).

ranking, which makes it difficult to update the information and evaluate changes in the tightness of employment protection over time. Moreover, existing EPL measures are based on institutional information dating back to the end of the 1980s, and no longer display cross-country co-variation with various aspects of labour market performance in line with the predictions of theoretical models.

For example, Bertola (1990) found a negative correlation between the variability of employment growth and job security rankings using data that ranged from the 1960s to the mid-1980s. This is consistent with theoretical predictions if the countries considered are similar in all respects other than EPL stringency (particularly in respect of the dynamic volatility of labour demand and wages). In Figure 1 (Graph 1), the downward sloping alignment of country-specific points indicates that stringent EPL is associated with low employment-growth variability across countries. Italy, for example, has the most stringent EPL (ranked 1) and low employment-growth variability (ranked 8). Over the whole period 1969-97 the empirical relationship is indeed negative but not very pronounced, as shown by the loose alignment of points in graph 1. For the sub-period 1969-86 (Graph 2) the evidence displayed is fully consistent with theoretical predictions and previous findings: when the countries considered experienced similar shocks (from the oil shocks to restrictive monetary policies), employment volatility was very significantly and negatively related to the stringency of EPL as measured in the mid-1980s. In the more recent 1985-97 period, however, the correlation is essentially absent (Graph 3). This quite possibly reflects more varied shocks across countries (for example, the obviously peculiar case of German unification). More importantly for our purposes, however, lack of correlation in the more recent period might also indicate that EPL rankings developed on the basis of late-1980s information are obsolete. Indeed, reforms in the 1970s were synchronized and consistent across countries, so the rankings were largely unaffected. But in the 1980s, and even more so in the 1990s, reforms may have changed the extent to which individual components of EPL co-vary with each other and, more significantly, they were much more country-specific. The United Kingdom, for example, moved from stringent EPL and strong unionization to a largely deregulated labour market (for a summary of recent changes in legislation, see Cazes, Boeri and Bertola, 1999).

Directions of Progress in Measurement

If available EPL rankings are obsolete, is it simply that the underlying indicators need updating or should they be completely rethought? Over the past 20 years, the institutional environment has grown increasingly complex. In the late 1980s and through the 1990s, European labour markets witnessed frequent reforms, but these were piecemeal in character. Job security provisions have generally remained in force for standard employment contracts, while less protected (part-time and temporary) forms of employment have been allowed in order to reduce overall EPL stringency. Understanding the role of nonstandard forms of employment is therefore crucial to assessing labour market performance and flexibility, particularly for cross-country comparisons. Saint-Paul (1997), for example, notes that the introduction of more flexible contracts should increase employment along a two-tiered

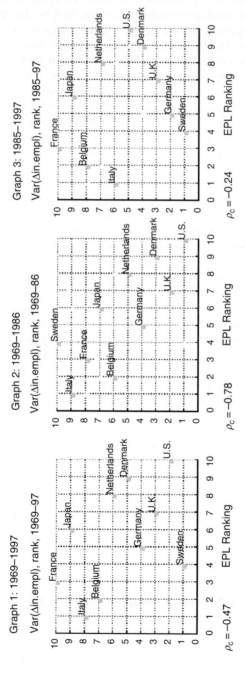

Figure 1. Relationship between EPL rankings and variability rankings of employment growth rates[1].

ρ_c = rank correlation.

[1] EPL rankings are based on late 1980s information (Bertola, 1990).

Source: OECD Economic Outlook database ("Total Dependent Employment'); data for Germany refer to west Germany until 1994, to the united Germany's growth rate thereafter.

adjustment path: as employers take advantage of new, more flexible hiring opportunities and, at the same time, hoard protected employees, employment increases
during the transition to the new steady state. Other sources of (costly) flexibility,
such as overtime, may also be exploited by employers to the extent that hiring and
firing are inhibited by EPL. In Europe, Abraham and Houseman (1994) find that
aggregate employment fluctuations are relatively subdued, but hours per worker
are more variable. The problem is that standard employment protection indicators
do not always capture the role of atypical forms of employment.

Moreover, there seem to be relevant links between EPL and other labour
market institutions, such as unemployment benefit schemes, wage-setting institutions, early retirement, pensions, etc. Some of these institutional provisions seem
substitutable for one another, while others are *complementary*. Labour market
institutions aim to protect workers from dismissal and wage loss and/or to provide
unemployment compensation to those who lose their job. Protection against job
loss is all the more desirable when only scant unemployment insurance is available,
and unemployment insurance is highly appreciated when weak job security provisions increase the risk of job loss. Indeed, in some countries job security – especially
case law favourable to employees – does appear to be inversely correlated to the
coverage and level of unemployment insurance (suggesting a trade-off between the
strictness of EPL and the unemployment benefit system, as in Denmark, Italy or
Spain, for example) or other adjustment tools such as early retirement
provisions (see also Auer, 2000). Conversely, compressed wage dispersion tends
to be associated with stronger employment security: quantitative firing restrictions could hardly be effective if wages were completely deregulated and employers could reduce them so as to make stable employment profitable to them, or to
induce voluntary quits. The limitation of employers' and workers' freedom to set
wages thus gives force to such constraints. As noted by Bertola and Rogerson
(1997), fluctuations in demand for labour are more likely to generate hiring and
firing when institutional features make it difficult or impossible for wages to
accommodate them. What is needed, therefore, is not only an update of EPL rankings, but new measures to capture the increasing complexity of legal provisions
and their interactions.

As already mentioned, many aspects of employment protection are qualitative. Ideally, one should try to develop monetary-equivalent measures of these
aspects; but translating laws and words into actual and expected costs is almost
impossible. Yet the following analysis of an important aspect of EPL that is particularly hard to measure, namely enforcement procedures, sheds some light on
possible directions for research into this broad area of interest.

Employment Protection Enforcement Procedures

Most EPL indicators are based on the legal constraints that apply in each country.
They are therefore ill-suited to tracking asymmetries across countries and over
time in the degree of enforcement of employment protection. Yet, there are
several important indications that such asymmetries may be more marked than

differences in regulations per se and that they may play a crucial role in the workings of labour markets, notably in determining labour market flows such as job losses and inflows into unemployment. Indeed, the role of the courts in interpreting the law may be strengthened by the increasing complexity of EPL. As discussed above, the fact that reforms of employment protection were piecemeal has amplified the *duality* of labour markets: on the one hand, the protection afforded by regular contracts remains undiminished and, on the other hand, widespread use is being made of non-regular contracts.[8] These new contracts and, more broadly, atypical forms of employment often lack a well-defined juridical status, and the process of defining "charters of rights" for atypical workers is still far from being completed. Given such institutional complexity and the legislative vacuum surrounding the rights of workers under new types of contracts, national administrations and labour courts objectively play a more determinant role in the enforcement of employment protection. Moreover, the indicator currently offering the closest approximation of judicial interpretation of EPL – namely an OECD indicator based on the notion of "difficulty of dismissals"[9] – is more closely related than other available indicators to job-termination probabilities and to the inflows of persons into unemployment.

Once it has been established that enforcement matters – and, in particular, that jurisprudence seems as important as (if not more important than) the nominal strictness of regulations per se – it still remains to be decided how to measure it properly. This is a complex task, since there is little information on the jurisprudence concerning termination of employment. Some data are often (though by no means always) available from administrative records on the cases brought before the competent tribunals and on judicial decisions. But like all administrative statistics, such data are affected by changes in regulations: their meaning changes along with the features they are supposed to measure. Such statistics may also be seriously affected by selection bias. For example, only relatively clear-cut cases may be taken to court, which would imply that data sampled from court records are not representative. However, even the limited and rough information available appears highly relevant to recent empirical evidence.[10]

---

[8] There are indications that this duality increases in proportion to the strictness of the protection of regular contracts. If one plots the share of employment under temporary contracts vs. measures for the protection of regular contracts in the countries which have reformed their EPL, one gets a strikingly positive association between the two. This suggests that countries which liberalized temporary contracts have experienced a growth of temporary employment that is proportional to the rigidity of employment protection for regular contracts (see Boeri, 1999).

[9] This indicator of EPL reflects a qualitative assessment of the strictness of legal definitions of unfair dismissal, the frequency of verdicts involving the reinstatement of employees, and the monetary compensations awarded in cases of unfair dismissal (the methodology is discussed in detail in Grubb and Wells, 1993).

[10] Other issues, such as data comparability or the exogeneity of jurisprudence – which is likely to be affected by cyclical and regional labour market conditions, the degree of unionization of the workforce and institutional features – are discussed in detail in Cazes, Boeri and Bertola (1999).

Preliminary Evidence on the Role of the Courts

Subject to the above caveats, Table 3 provides information on the number of cases brought before the courts and on the percentage of verdicts favourable to workers in selected industrialized countries. Standard indicators of the strictness of EPL and measures of the coverage of unemployment benefits are also reported in order to facilitate interpretation of the data. The most striking fact revealed by this table is the very wide cross-country variation in the number of cases brought to court. In Spain, one employee in 200 appealed to the courts in 1995 compared with one employee in 15,000 in Austria. There is also significant cross-country variation in the percentage of cases won by workers, with Spain and France at one extreme and Ireland at the other: in 1995, workers in Spain and France won 72 and 74 per cent of the cases respectively, as compared with less than 50 per cent in each of Canada and the U.S. and a mere 16 per cent in Ireland. Cross-country differences of this magnitude could be caused by a variety of factors, including simply inconsistencies in the coverage of statistics. Yet, it is tempting to try to make some inferences on economic factors which may also have played a role in cross-country variations in the incidence and outcomes of court cases concerning labour disputes. Significantly, the countries whose courts are the most frequently involved in labour disputes over termination of employment also tend to be those displaying the highest percentages of rulings favourable to employees.[11] As shown in Table 3, the likelihood of a favourable ruling seems to play an important role in inducing workers to take their cases to court, although this may also encourage employers to reach extra-judicial settlements – a possibility not captured by available statistics.

Other features of EPL enforcement that may explain cross-country variation in the incidence of court cases include the definition of unfair dismissal, applicable sanctions, and the cost of legal proceedings. Rather vague legal definitions of unfair dismissals, which give the courts broad discretion in interpreting regulations, may indeed be an important reason for the impressive caseloads of the French, German and Spanish courts, as highlighted by Table 3. In Germany, the Protection Against Dismissal Act, 1951, gave the labour courts much discretion to interpret existing regulations, in striking contrast with German legal tradition which more typically places strong restrictions on the discretionary power of judges (Berger, 1997). Indeed, labour court activity appears to have declined in more recent years, following amendments to this Act.[12] Similarly, in Spain the statutory definition of unfair dismissals was only expanded and clarified in 1997, allowing, inter alia, for economic, technological, organizational and cyclical factors to be considered as grounds for "justifiable dismissal". Before that date, the labour courts in Spain had more discretion than in other countries to determine

---

[11] Anecdotal evidence suggests that this also applies to Germany, with most of the cases won by workers, though it was not possible to collect statistics on judicial outcomes in this country.

[12] These amendments reduced the discretionary powers of the labour courts by establishing that the applicability of "social plans" (allowing for rather generous compensation of workers made redundant) were to be related to objective parameters like the size of firms and the number of employees affected by redundancies.

Table 3. Role of the Courts in the Enforcement of EPL, 1995.

	No. of cases brought before the courts/ employees (%)	Percentage of cases won by workers	Definition of unfair dismissal[1]	Extent of reinstatement[2]	Unemployment benefit coverage rate[3]
EU					
Austria	0.007	...	1	1	...
Denmark	0.004	...	0	1	85
France	0.510	74	1.5	0	44
Germany	0.510[4]	...	2	1.5	64
Ireland	0.110	16	0	1	69
Italy	0.050	51	0	2	19
Netherlands	...	...	1.5	1	38
Spain	0.545	72	2	0	29
United Kingdom	0.180	38	0	0	62
North America					
Canada[5]	0.080	48	0	1	...
U.S.	0.021[6]	48[7]	0	0.5	...
Oceania					
Australia	0.150	57	0	1.5	...
New Zealand	0.060	62	0	1	...

Notes: [1] From OECD, 1999: score is 0 when worker capability or redundancy of the job are adequate and sufficient grounds for dismissal; 1 when social considerations, age or job tenure must, when possible, influence the choice of which worker(s) to dismiss; 2 when a transfer and/or retraining to adapt the worker to different work must be attempted prior to dismissal; and 3 when worker capability cannot serve to justify dismissal.

[2] From OECD, 1999: the extent of reinstatement is based upon whether, after a finding of unfair dismissal, the employee has the option of reinstatement even when this goes against the wishes of the employer. The indicator is 1 when this option is rarely made available to the employee, 2 when it is made available fairly often, and 3 when it is always made available.

[3] Percentage of unemployed people reporting receipt of unemployment benefit in the EC Labour Force Survey (see OECD, 1994a, ch. 6).

[4] 1990 for Germany.

[5] Quebec only.

[6] 1991 for U.S..

[7] Based on a Bureau of National Affairs survey of plaintiff's awards regarding wrongful discharge from 1988 to 1995.

Sources: Australia, total claims finalized (Annual Report of the Industrial Relations Court of Australia); Austria, total claims filed (Ministry of Justice); France, total claims finalized (Ministry of Justice); Germany, total claims finalized (A.G. Statistics, Ministry of Justice); Ireland, total claims filed (The Employment Appeals Tribunal); Italy, total claims filed (ISTAT); New Zealand, total claims finalized (The Employment Tribunal); Quebec, total claims brought before the arbitrator (CNT); Spain, total claims finalized (Ministry of Labour and Social Affairs); United Kingdom, total claims filed (Employment Tribunals Service); U.S., total claims filed in the Federal courts (in Dunlop and Zack, 1997); OECD (Labour Force Statistics).

whether the conditions for an unfair dismissal were met. Unfortunately, available EPL rankings consider legal definitions in terms of a single dimension only, namely whether or not workers' capability is considered a valid ground for dismissal (third column of Table 3). Yet the foregoing observations suggest that the precision, transparency and consistency with which legislators define justified reasons for dismissal are very important.

The sanctions applicable to employers for unfair dismissals may also partly explain cross-country variations in the incidence of judicial proceedings. Tough sanctions, however, may have a twofold effect. On the one hand, they should incite workers to take legal action, but, on the other, they should also encourage employers to settle disputes out of court before workers take such action. The fourth column in Table 3 summarizes information on what may be the strongest deterrent to dismissal, namely the option offered to the employee to request reinstatement. In many countries, the employer may have the right to refuse reinstatement, choosing to pay compensation instead;[13] in other countries, both reinstatement and financial compensation may be awarded simultaneously. The information provided in the table, however, is based only on national regulations, whereas actual reinstatement depends on several other factors, such as the length of legal proceedings (if there are years of delay between the start of the proceedings and the verdict, reinstatement is unlikely), the size of the undertaking (being reinstated in a larger enterprise is easier than in a small one), and on the penalties faced by employers who do not reinstate a worker, i.e. the amount of the compensation (see Cazes, Boeri and Bertola, 1999, for details).

Finally, the coverage offered by unemployment insurance may have some influence over court rulings. The last column in Table 3 shows that countries with a high percentage of rulings favourable to workers tend to be characterized by a low coverage of unemployment benefits (beneficiaries over unemployed, according to the European Community's Labour Force Survey definitions). Conversely, in countries like Ireland and the United Kingdom, where courts are favourable to employees in significantly less than half of the cases, unemployment insurance covers a very high proportion of the unemployed. These are just hypotheses; more data would be needed to assess the correlation between these variables.

The foregoing observations suggest that there is much to learn from cross-country variations in the degree of involvement of the courts in labour disputes. Another relevant empirical issue is whether the predominance of judicial enforcement over legislated standards alters the effects of EPL and makes them subject to changes over time. For example, judges may feel that workers should be more heavily protected against dismissals during cyclical downturns than in buoyant labour market conditions. Such information can be obtained by analysing the time-series data on litigation and/or jurisprudence. Unfortunately this was possible only for two countries, namely Germany and Spain.

Figure 2 shows the number of closed labour court cases as a proportion of the labour force in Germany over the period 1970-93, together with the unemployment

---

[13] In Italy, for example, this choice depends on establishment size and on how the dispute is dealt with.

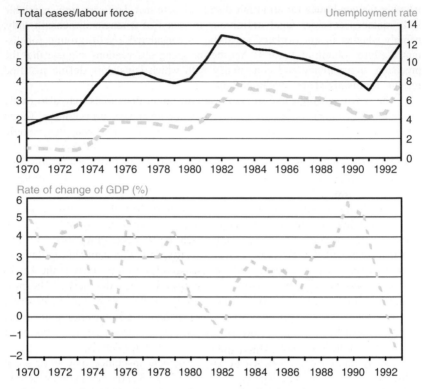

Figure 2. Labour Litigation, Unemployment and GDP Growth in Germany, 1970-93.

rate and the yearly growth rate of GDP. The striking fact is the very marked co-variation of the incidence of litigation and of unemployment. Cyclical conditions, captured by GDP growth rates, would seem to be relevant only insofar as they significantly affect unemployment.

Co-movements of indicators of litigation and unemployment can also be observed in Spain, especially when the focus is on cases settled in favour of employees (see Figure 3). This suggests that labour market conditions do indeed play an important role in the incidence and outcomes (more or less favourable to employees) of litigation. In other words, the evidence points to an endogeneity of jurisprudence which should perhaps be duly acknowledged when assessing the causal relationship between EPL and unemployment.

Concluding Remarks

The effects of EPL on employment flows, while fairly clear from a theoretical standpoint, are difficult to study in practice because of the complex and elusive nature of available information, and of the EPL concept itself. While assessing the

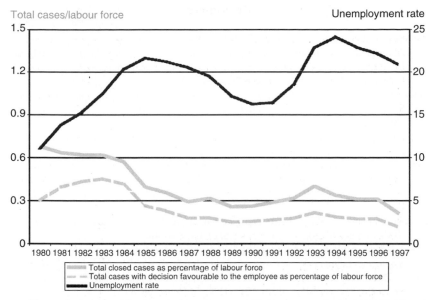

Figure 3. Labour Litigation, Jurisprudence and Unemployment in Spain, 1980-97.

impact of EPL will always remain a complex exercise, new measurement efforts are necessary, since existing indicators of protection are based on unsatisfactory information and capture neither the increasing complexity of legal provisions nor their interactions. Measurement issues cannot be avoided because they are central to the political debates and policies on labour market regulation and its reform. Against that background, this article has focused on an important and hitherto neglected aspect, namely enforcement procedures as a source of EPL heterogeneity across countries and over time.

How does this bear on the hotly debated policy issue of whether EPL may be blamed for the poor employment performance of certain European countries? In the light of ambiguous empirical results and measurement issues, policy recommendations should be formulated with caution, and should *not* be based on any of the indicators available to date. Available rankings of employment protection are too imperfect and imprecise to inform the debate on EPL reforms and cannot be used to monitor structural reforms in the labour market. Yet governments should try to exploit the meaningful linkages between EPL and other institutional features. For example, the negative correlation established between the strictness of employment protection and the coverage of unemployment insurance suggests that the extension of unemployment insurance coverage (which does not necessarily imply an extension of its duration!) could ease the pressure to remove protection.

In other words, there is no simple means of calculating relevant indicators and rankings. There is need for further research to find reliable means of capturing the complexity of the theoretical and empirical issues involved and thus providing a more solid basis for policy.

References

Abraham, Katharine G.; Houseman, Susan N. 1994. "Does employment protection inhibit labour market flexibility? Lessons from Germany, France, and Belgium", In Rebecca M. Blank (ed.): *Social protection versus economic flexibility: Is there a trade-off?* Chicago, IL, University of Chicago Press, pp. 59-93.

Addison, John T.; Grosso, Jean-Luc. 1996. "Job security provisions and employment: Revised estimates", in *Industrial Relations* (Cambridge, MA), Vol. 35, No. 4 (Oct.), pp. 585-603.

Auer, Peter. 2000. *Employment revival in Europe: Labour market success in Austria, Denmark, Ireland and the Netherlands.* Geneva, ILO.

Berger, Helge. 1997. *Regulation in Germany: Some stylized facts about its time path, causes, and consequences.* Paper prepared for the IMPE Conference on "Institutions, Markets and (Economic) Performance: Deregulation and its Consequences", Utrecht, 11-12 Dec.

Bertola, Giuseppe. 1990. "Job security, employment and wages", in *European Economic Review* (Amsterdam), Vol. 34, No. 4 (June), pp. 851-886.

——; Ichino, Andrea. 1995. "Crossing the river: A comparative perspective on Italian employment dynamics", in *Economic Policy* (Oxford), No. 21 (Oct.), pp. 359-420.

——; Rogerson, Richard. 1997. "Institutions and labor reallocation", in *European Economic Review* (Amsterdam), Vol. 41, No. 6 (June), pp. 1147-1171.

Boeri, Tito. 1999. "Enforcement of employment security regulations, on-the-job search and unemployment duration", in *European Economic Review* (Amsterdam), Vol. 43, No. 1 (Jan.), pp. 65-89.

Cazes, Sandrine; Boeri, Tito; Bertola, Giuseppe. 1999. *Employment protection and labour market adjustment in OECD countries: Evolving institutions and variable enforcement.* Employment and Training Papers, No. 48. Geneva, ILO.

Davis, Steven J.; Haltiwanger, John. 1992. "Gross job creation, gross job destruction and employment reallocation", in *Quarterly Journal of Economics* (Cambridge, MA), Vol. 107, No. 3 (Aug.), pp. 819-863.

Dunlop, John T.; Zack, Arnold. 1997. *Mediation and arbitration of employment disputes.* Jossey-Bass Conflict Resolution Series. San Francisco, CA, Jossey-Bass Inc.

Emerson, Michael. 1988. "Regulation or deregulation of the labour market: Policy regimes for the recruitment and dismissal of employees in the industrialised countries", in *European Economic Review* (Amsterdam), Vol. 32, No. 4 (Apr.), pp. 775-817.

Grubb, David; Wells, William. 1993. "Employment regulation and patterns of work in E.C. countries", in *OECD Economic Studies* (Paris), No. 21, pp. 7-58.

Lazear, Edward P. 1990. "Job security provisions and employment", in *Quarterly Journal of Economics* (Cambridge, MA), Vol. 55, No. 3 (Aug.), pp. 699-726.

OECD. 1999. *Employment Outlook.* Paris.

——. 1997. *Employment Outlook.* Paris.

——. 1996. *Employment Outlook.* Paris.

——. 1994a. *The OECD Jobs Study: Evidence and explanations. Part II: The adjustment potential of the labour market.* Paris.

——. 1994b. *Employment Outlook.* Paris.

Saint-Paul, Gilles. 1997. *Dual labour markets: A macroeconomic perspective.* Cambridge, MA, MIT Press.

Scarpetta, Stefano. 1996. "Assessing the role of labour market policies and institutional settings on unemployment: A cross-country study", in *OECD Economic Studies* (Paris), No. 26, pp. 43-98.

GIUSEPPE BERTOLA,
European University Institute and University of Turin
TITO BOERI,
University of Bocconi, Milan
SANDRINE CAZES,
International Labour Office

Chapter 10

Measuring Concealed Rights Violations:
The Case of Forced Labour*

PATRICK BELSER, MICHAËLLE DE COCK, AND FARHAD MEHRAN[1]
International Labour Office

Introduction

This chapter is about the measurement of rights violations that are concealed from the public and the authorities. We focus on one particular problem: the existence of cases of forced labour. Estimating forced labour serves not only to monitor and document de facto implementation of this core labour standard, but also to identify the relative magnitude of different forms of forced labour, to map violations according to geography, and ultimately to develop appropriate policies for eliminating forced labour in the future. Although some people feel that the number of forced labour victims does not matter (because one victim is one too many), we believe that better quantification helps to promote better implementation of rights, even when data and methods are less than perfect.

In this chapter we describe in detail how we have estimated the worldwide number of reported cases of forced labour during the period 1995-2004. Reported cases and number of victims have to be *estimated* because there are very few reliable national statistics and because, in a short period of time, it is impossible to collect *all* the reports that have been published on forced labour cases. This is why we have implemented a double-sampling procedure. In this procedure, two teams of researchers have collected – independently of each other – a sample of reported cases from any ILO and non-ILO source they could think of. These reports then went through a meticulous process of validation, in which the project supervisor checked whether the reports were indeed about forced labour as defined by the ILO and whether the reports indicated the date, geographical location, and the number of victims involved. The supervisor also checked the source and eliminated cases of double-counting within each team. The number of cases and victims found by each team, and the proportion of cases found by both teams, were then used to estimate the total number of reported cases and victims. This sampling procedure was adapted from a methodology called "capture-recapture" in the statistical literature.

---

* A different version of this chapter has previously been published as *ILO Minimum Estimate of Forced Labour in the World*, International Labour Office, Geneva, April 2005.
[1] With the assistance of Aurélie Hauchére, and of Olivier Annequin, Leila Dajani, Lisa Eichhorn, Giancarlo Fiorito, Akshay Garg, Haleh Mehran, Nitya Mohan and Dmitriy Poletaev.

D. Kucera (ed.), *Qualitative Indicators of Labour Standards*, 253–283.
© 2007 by ILO.

The chapter is organised as follows. The definition of forced labour formulated for the present statistical purpose is discussed in Section 1 where a typology of forced labour is also developed. The estimation methodology and the basic statistical units are presented in Section 2. The procedure used for collecting and validating the data are described in Section 3. The numerical results obtained are shown and discussed in Section 4. Finally, in section 5 we discuss the assumptions under which, the estimate of the number of reported victims during 1994-2005 is equal or larger than the average number of people in forced labour (both reported and unreported) at each given moment in time during that same period.

1. Forced Labour and its Main Forms

(a) Definitions

The ILO Forced Labour Convention, 1930 (No. 29), defines forced or compulsory labour as "all work or service which is exacted from any person under the menace of any penalty and for which the said person has not offered himself voluntarily" (Art. 2.1). The Convention provides for certain exceptions, in particular, with regard to military service for work of purely military character, normal civic obligations, work as a consequence of a conviction in a court of law and carried out under the control of a public authority, work in emergency cases such as wars or other calamities, and minor communal services (Art. 2.2). Subsequently the Abolition of Forced Labour Convention, 1957 (No. 105), specifies that forced labour can never be used for the purpose of economic development or as a means of political education, discrimination, labour discipline or punishment for having participated in strikes.

Other ILO Conventions rely on, or complement, the basic Forced Labour Convention No. 29. In particular, the Worst Forms of Child Labour Convention, 1999 (182), considers that the worst forms of child labour include, among others, "all forms of slavery or practices similar to slavery, such as the sale and trafficking of children, debt bondage and serfdom and forced or compulsory labour ..." (Art. 3). The Protection of Wages Convention, 1949 (No. 95), prohibits methods of payment that deprive workers of the genuine possibility of terminating their employment.

Forced labour, as defined by the ILO, is thus not just equivalent to poor working conditions or low wages. It represents a very serious restriction in human freedom and is to be treated by member States as a penal offence. It is the type of engagement that links the person to the "employer" which leads to forced labour, not the type of activity he or she is actually performing. A young man who cuts trees in the Amazon forest to pay back a fraudulent debt to his employer is in forced labour because of the fake debt that he has been trapped in, not because of the type of forestry activity he is conducting, however hard or hazardous the conditions of work in that activity. Similarly, a woman trafficked and forced into prostitution is in forced labour because of the menace under which she is working, not because of the sexual duties that her job demands or the legality or illegality of that particular occupation. In fact, the activity itself may not even be an economic activity in the sense of national accounts. An example is the situation of a child beggar who is forced to beg and return his or her daily collection to an "employer". According to economic statistics, begging is not an economic activity, even though it generates income. Yet this child beggar should be considered as a forced labourer, irrespective of the economic or non-economic nature of the activity of begging.

Embedded in the international definition of forced labour as formulated in Convention No. 29 are two essential criteria: the *menace of penalty* and the *involuntariness*. Accordingly, forced labour occurs when people are being subjected to psychological or physical coercion (the menace of a penalty) in order to perform some work that they would otherwise not have accepted at the prevailing conditions (the involuntariness). The penalty can take many forms: physical violence, death threats to the victim or a family member, confiscation of identity documents, or the denunciation to the police in the case of undocumented migrants. "Involuntariness" is most easily verified by examining the process by which the victim has entered into forced labour. Abductions and kidnapping clearly indicate involuntariness. In most cases, however, the mechanism is more subtle, involving deception or fraud to achieve the consent of victims. A person may decide to migrate voluntarily and end up in forced domestic work at destination with no reasonable possibility of returning or getting out of the engagement. Some young women may accept good job proposals only to find out later that they are being deceived and forced into prostitution. In principle, both the penalty and involuntariness criteria should be verified. Yet, in practice, if there is a menace of penalty one can often assume that there is also involuntariness.

(b) A Typology

A striking feature of forced labour is its heterogeneity. The ILO's 2001 Global Report called *Stopping Forced labour* identified no less than 8 different categories of forced labour: (1) "slavery and abductions"; (2) "compulsory participation in public works"; (3) "forced labour in agriculture and remote rural areas, with coercive recruitment practices"; (4) "domestic workers"; (5) "bonded labour"; (6) "forced labour exacted by the military"; (7) "forced labour as a result of trafficking"; and (8) "prison-linked forced labour". For statistical purposes, this categorisation is somewhat problematic, as these categories are not always mutually exclusive.

For the present purpose, the forced labour data has been regrouped into three main forms:

(1) state-imposed forced labour;
(2) forced commercial sexual exploitation;
(3) forced economic exploitation;

In this report, estimates will be developed on the number of reported cases and victims in each of the above three forms of forced labour, separately. In addition, estimates will be made for the number of cases and victims in forced labour as an outcome of human trafficking. The resulting typology is schematically shown in Figure 1. The content of each form is described in the subsequent sections.

State-imposed Forced Labour

The first category in our typology is state-imposed forced labour. The early international standards set by the ILO were designed to combat forms of forced labour which involved the direct responsibility of the state authorities. When Convention No. 29 on forced labour was adopted (1930), slavery had already been abolished in the last Latin American bastion for almost half a century. The main concern of the ILO was thus the practice of colonial authorities who forced women and men to work in plantations, mines or infrastructure development. By 1957, the year the ILO adopted Convention No. 105, another form of state-exacted forced labour was on top of the list of priorities: prison camps for political re-education. Millions of people were reportedly forced to work in the "gulags" of the former Soviet Union and in other socialist countries.

Nowadays, three main types of state-imposed forced labour, discussed at length in the Global Report of 2001, are singled out. The first type is forced labour exacted by the military, such as in Myanmar (ex-Burma) where the army has been reported to use forced labour in the construction of roads and military bases or for portering and detection of mines. Also included in this category is the forced recruitment of child soldiers or young adults by military or paramilitary groups. The second type of state-imposed forced labour is the compulsory participation in public works, a practice that mainly subsists in a few socialist or post-socialist countries, where children or adults have an obligation to work in sometimes harsh conditions. And finally, the last type of state-imposed forced labour is the practice of forced prison labour. According to ILO Conventions, forced prison labour under the supervision and control of a public authority is only allowed if it results from a conviction in a proper court of law, and if it is not used as a means of political education, discrimination, labour discipline or punishment for having participated in strikes.

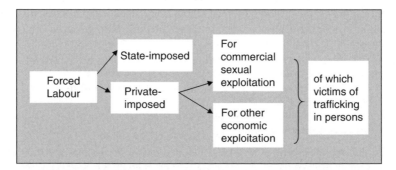

Figure 1. A typology of forced labour for statistical estimation.

Regarding forced prison labour, it is important to note that, according to ILO Convention No. 29, prisoners should not be forced to work for private individuals, companies or associations. Hence the practice of some industrialized countries to "rent out" prisoners to private companies or even to privatise prisons are problematic in this regard. If a prisoner is being forced to work under the menace of losing privileges, it should be counted as forced labour. In estimations made here, such forced labour is considered as state-exacted even if the prison is privatised. This is because the state is directly responsible for its prisoners, irrespective of the ownership or managerial arrangement of the prisons.

Forced Commercial Sexual Exploitation

While state-imposed forced labour continues to exist, new forms of forced labour imposed by private individuals, groups, or gangs, are now emerging. This is the case, in particular, of forced commercial sexual exploitation, especially forced prostitution. Victims of forced prostitution are often young migrant women with primary education or less. These women are attracted by traffickers in their countries of origin, who promise good jobs and high pay in destination countries. Proposed jobs typically include domestic workers or waitresses. Women often take a loan from the trafficker in order to pay for the visa and travel arrangements. Once in the country of destination, these women are asked to repay the loan by working as a prostitute and their passports are confiscated. In other cases, women and girls are simply abducted from the streets and forced into prostitution. In forced pornography, young women and men are being coerced into performing sexual acts for the production of sexually explicit pictures or films.

Forced Economic Exploitation

Forced economic exploitation has both modern and traditional forms, and includes practices such as slavery, serfdom and debt bondage. The League of Nations' *Slavery Convention* (1926) defines slavery as "the status or condition of a person over whom any or all of the powers attaching to the right of ownership are exercised". Serfdom is defined by the UN *Supplementary Convention on the Abolition of Slavery, the Slave Trade and Institutions and Practices Similar to Slavery* (1956) as "the condition or status of a tenant who is by law, custom or agreement bound to live and labour on land belonging to another person and to render some determinate service to such other person, whether for reward or not, and is not free to change his status". Debt bondage is defined in the same Convention as "the status or condition arising from a pledge by a debtor of his personal services or those of a person under his control as security for a debt, if the value of those services as reasonably assessed is not applied towards the liquidation of the debt or the length and nature of those services are not respectively limited and defined".

In South Asia, one form of forced economic exploitation is linked to the practice of bonded labour. A bonded labourer is a worker who has taken a loan from an employer and who is repaying the loan (with accumulated interests) through his labour. Implicitly or explicitly, the employer is retaining part of the worker's salary for the reimbursement and service of the debt – hence reducing the worker's pay. The bondage results from the fact that the worker is not free to leave the employer as long as the debt is not fully reimbursed. However, not all bonded labour should automatically be considered as forced labour. Indeed, a worker paying back a small wage advance with his labour may call himself a bonded labourer – even though the agreement is voluntary with clearly specified repayment terms. Thus, the criteria used in our estimate for identifying debt bondage include: (1) whether there is use of coercion or physical violence and/or (2) whether the length of the debt repayment is unlimited in time and whether the work of the debtor is not properly applied towards the liquidation of the debt (i.e. whether implicit interest rates are unreasonably high). Such bonded labour often takes place in a context of social discrimination.

Many other forms of forced economic exploitation exist, virtually everywhere in the world. Because they work in the sphere of private households, migrant domestic workers are particularly vulnerable. In the worst cases, their passports are confiscated, and they are maltreated by employers who restrict their movement and force them to work very long hours for low pay. In the Middle East, this has led to the problem of so-called "runaway maids" – young women who try to escape from their employers. In industrial countries, some employers work for embassies or international organizations and enjoy diplomatic immunity. Modern forms of forced labour also affect workers in other activities, often as a result of trafficking, deception and fraud. Just as in the case of forced commercial sexual exploitation, victims are being made false promises in their place of origin and realize only later that they have been deceived. They end up in situations of debt bondage in agriculture or other labour-intensive activities. Forced labour also occurs in illegal activities such a drug trafficking, burglaries, deforestation or begging (which is illegal in some countries). In the modern forms of forced economic exploitation, the existence of debt plays a central role. In some cases, the debt is known in advance but is manipulated by the employer to force the victim into unwanted work. In other cases, the debt is not known in advance, but is discovered when victims arrive at the place of destination, where they are being told that travel costs are higher than expected and must be repaid through work in a job different than the one originally promised. There are also cases of completely fictitious debts, invented by "employers" to extract forced labour.

Note that not all child labour is categorized as forced labour. For the purpose of this report, child labour is considered as forced labour either when there is coercion by someone other than the parents or when the child's activity is a direct result of the fact that the parents are themselves in forced labour.

Forced Labour as a Result of Trafficking in Persons

There is an increasing awareness that globalization has been accompanied by an important increase in human trafficking, sometimes called the "underside of globalization" (ILO, 2001). Given the growing importance of this problem, the measurement framework developed in this study provides for separate estimates of the number of reported victims of forced labour as a result of trafficking.

It is important to distinguish between trafficking and smuggling in human beings. Whereas the purpose of smuggling is the illegal crossing of borders, the aim of trafficking is the exploitation of people. According to the *UN Protocol to Prevent, Suppress, and Punish Trafficking in Persons, Especially Women and Children* (the so-called Palermo Protocol), trafficking in persons means "the recruitment, transportation, transfer, harbouring or receipt of persons, by means of the threat or use of force or other forms of coercion, of abduction, of fraud, of deception, of the abuse of power or of a position of vulnerability or of the giving or receiving of payments or benefits to achieve the consent of a person having control over another person for the purpose of exploitation". The document further specifies that, "exploitation" includes "forced labour or services, slavery, or practices similar to slavery" as well as "the exploitation of the prostitution of others or other forms of sexual exploitation" and "the removal of organs".

Human trafficking can take place within or across borders. An example of internal trafficking involves so-called "slave labourers" in Brazil. Casual workers are recruited in large cities by intermediaries called "gatos", who promise good pay for hard work. Workers are then transported into the Amazon forest and exploited by a group of armed people, who force them to work for little or no pay at all. For practical purposes, we have counted as cases of trafficking all cases of forced labour where victims have been recruited by an intermediary and moved to a place that is distinct from the place of recruitment.

2. Estimation Methodology

A natural method to derive global estimates of a phenomenon is to aggregate corresponding national estimates into regional and then global figures. This direct aggregation method is often preceded by preliminary steps to harmonize eventual differences in national concepts and definitions, and to impute for possible missing data. This approach has been adopted in broad terms by the ILO since the 1970s for deriving global estimates and projections of the economically active population (http://laborsta.ilo.org EAPEP data), and more recently for calculating global and regional estimates of unemployment (Schaible, 2000).

In the case of forced labour, however, reliable and widely accepted national estimates based on specialised data collection instruments, surveying directly the victims have yet to be developed. Available national estimates are often disparate, concerning one or two particular forms of forced labour, generally calculated on the basis of secondary information obtained by individual experts or non-governmental organizations for specific purposes. The underlying concept and methodology of these forced labour components are often undocumented and, in some cases, even the date or the time period to which they refer is unclear. Of course, there are also carefully made estimates with well documented methodologies. As part of the present project, a review has been made of a selected number of such methods (Fiorito, 2003). Overall, however, the data does not lend itself easily to the direct aggregation method described above. This scarcity of statistics is due to the fact that the exaction of forced labour is usually illicit, occurring in the underground economy, concealed from the public and the authorities.

(a) Reported Cases as the Basic Statistical Unit

In the absence of solid and widely accepted national estimates for many countries, we decided to estimate the number of reported cases of forced labour in the world. A reported case of forced labour is defined as a piece of information that contains at least the following four elements:

a = an activity recognized as a form of forced labour
x = a numerical figure indicating the number of persons in that activity
h = a geographical area where the activity is reported to have taken place
t = a date or a time period in which the persons were in that activity

In practice, of course, each of these elements may be reported with different degrees of precision. Indeed, there may be doubts about the nature of the activity as a form of forced labour. The numerical value may be an approximation. The reported area may be broader than the actual area to which the number refers. The reported time period may erroneously represent the date of the report rather than the date of the case. And many other ambiguities may arise in the process of identifying and recording a reported case. For validating the reported cases, two basic principles were established. First, the process used to validate a reported case should be, to the extent possible, replicable. Second, there must be sufficient reason to believe that the reported numerical figure represents actual people, i.e. persons who have been – or who could have been – identified and listed. This principle discards as reported cases, a numerical figure which is known to be an estimate or an extrapolation. For example, a police report with a mention that "on January 15, 2004, 10 women have been liberated from forced prostitution in a raid in Town X" is a reported case, while a police report with an indication that "it is estimated that 400–600 women are trafficked into prostitution every year in Town X" is an estimate which cannot be used in our capture–recapture methodology.

Two reported cases are considered as distinct if one or more of the four recorded elements (a, x, h, t) are distinct. It should be noted that the source of the information does not enter into consideration in establishing distinctions among reported cases. Thus, if the same information is reported both in the French journal *Le Monde* and the Pakistani monthly *The Herald*, the two reported cases are considered as one, and only one of them is accounted for this study. Furthermore, in determining identity or distinction, some allowances are made for rounding numbers, and differences in terms used and locations named. For example, the case of 387 children, victims of commercial sexual exploitation in Rondonia may be reported in a different document as a case involving around 400 children in North Western Brazil. Similarly, the case of 7,121 persons in forced prison labour may be reported elsewhere as 7,121 prisoners in forced rehabilitation camps. In each of these examples, it is clear that the reported cases are identical.

Because the procedure relies on the available visible information, cases of false identity may occur, i.e., declaring two reported cases as identical while they are in fact distinct. For example, one document may report the case of 100 freed workers from debt bondage in Utter Pradesh in April 2001, and another a seemingly identical case of 100 freed workers from debt bondage in 2001 in the same Indian state. If it is decided to neglect the precision of the month of April in one report, the two cases will mistakenly be considered as identical. The reverse (i.e., false distinction) may also occur, when two identical reports are falsely considered as distinct.

(b) Sampling of Reported Cases: The Capture–Recapture method

Complete enumeration of all reported cases of forced labour is an impossible task. The normal practice, when complete enumeration of a phenomenon is not possible or too costly, is to draw a random sample and generalise from the sample observations by means of special statistical techniques. Random sampling procedures, however, require a reliable sampling frame from which to draw the sample. No such sampling frame exists, or can reasonably be constructed for measuring forced labour at the global level. As an alternative to random sampling from sampling frames, we propose to use another sampling technique designed traditionally to estimate the abundance of animal populations (fish, birds, insects, etc.) and more recently applied also to estimate the abundance of elusive human populations such as the homeless or undocumented migrants. The method is called capture–recapture sampling and is briefly described in the following section.

In its simplest form and in the context of estimating the abundance of fish in a lake, the method consists of two parts: capture and recapture (Thompson, 1992). In the capture part, an initial sample of fish is drawn in a closed universe, their number counted, and each fish marked with a special ink–marker before being released back in the lake. After a short period of time, a second sample is independently obtained (the recapture part), and the number of fish with ink–marks and the number of without ink-marks are counted and noted. These numbers are then used to estimate the total number of fish in the lake with the following formula:

$$N = \frac{(n_1)(n_2)}{(n_{12})}$$

where n_1 is the number of fish captured, n_2 the number of fish recaptured, and n_{12} the number of fish captured twice. The argument goes as follows: If the second sample is representative of the fish population in the lake, the ratio of marked to unmarked fishes in that sample should be the same as in the fish population as a whole. The method also provides estimates of margins of errors, from which confidence intervals can be constructed (Jensen, 1898). More elaborate procedures are also available to deal with more than two catches and with capture probabilities varying from sample to sample, and detection probabilities from animal to animal (Norris et al., 1996).

A numerical illustration of the method is given below with fictive numbers using reported cases of forced labour as sampling units. Suppose that two teams of researchers are formed. Each team independently draws haphazardly a sample of

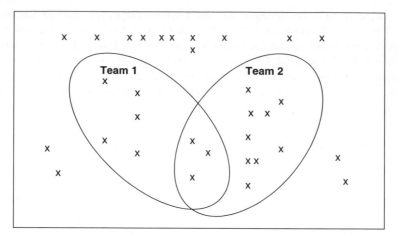

Figure 2. Illustration of capture–recapture.

reports on forced labour (each report is characterised by an x in Figure 2). Team 1 finds eight valid reported cases of forced labour, while Team 2 working independently finds twelve valid reported cases of forced labour. There are 3 reported cases which have been found by both teams. How can we estimate the total number of reported cases of forced labour in the universe? The answer is the following. In Team 2's draw (the recapture), the proportion of reports which were already captured by Team 1 is 3/12 or equivalently 25% of the total. If this proportion is also valid in the universe of reported cases then the question is: how many reported cases are there in total so that Team 1 captured 8 of them? The answer is 8/(0.25) = 32 reported cases. Since the two teams only captured together 17 distinct reported cases out of the total of 32, there are 15 existing reported cases which were not caught by any one of the two teams.

For the capture–recapture method to work, two basic conditions should be satisfied. First, the two teams should be working independently of each other and second, they should be sampling the reported cases on a random basis. In practice, of course, neither of these conditions are fully satisfied, but as reported later, attempts have been made to organize data collection and validation activities to be as close as possible to the underlying assumptions of the capture–recapture methodology. Furthermore, the calculation for the numerical illustration is based on the assumption that each reported case has the same probability of being captured by the two teams. In practice, however, this assumption may not be valid all the time, as some reported cases may be harder to find than others. There are statistical methods of dealing with this complication as cited earlier. In the present study, this aspect has been dealt with by stratifying the sample according to region and type of force labour. This in effect assumes that the probability of capture differs from one strata to another (for example state-imposed forced labour in Sub-Saharan Africa may have lower probability of capture than, say, commercial sexual exploitation in Industrialised countries), but is constant within strata.

In practice, the formula that we have used for computation is a modified version of the one used for the numerical illustration above. The modified version, which avoids the problem that arises when the number of common cases n_{12} is zero in one or more strata, is given by:

$$N = \frac{(n_1 + 1)(n_2 + 1) - 1}{(n_{12} + 1)}$$

(c) Estimating the Number of Reported Victims

Having estimated the total number of reported cases of forced labour, the total number of victims involved may be estimated by straightforward multiplication with the average number of victims per reported case. The average number of victims of forced labour in the reported cases may be calculated in at least three ways: on the basis of reported cases captured by Team 1, on the basis of reported cases (re)captured by Team 2, or on the basis of the combined set of reported cases capture by Team 1 and Team 2. In general, the third estimate based on both Team 1 and Team 2 data should be preferred as it uses a larger number of observations. It can be shown that the combined estimate necessarily lies between the Team 1 and Team 2 estimates.

If we go back to our numerical illustration and assume that there is an average of 65 victims in the 17 reports that were found by the teams, we can estimate the total number of reported victims by multiplying the estimated total number of reported cases (32) by the average number of victims per case (65). The result is thus 32 * 65 = 2,080. Another approach in estimating the total number of victims of forced labour is to frame the estimation problem in the context of sampling theory where a total is being estimated on the basis of a sample of observation units with known probabilities of selection (see Appendix 1).

3.   Constructing the Database

(a) Data Collection

The methodology adopted in this project requires two samples (the capture and recapture) to be drawn independently of each other, and identical probabilities of sample selection. These requirements have been implemented in practice by constituting two teams of researchers working with identical instructions and workloads, but independently of each other. Independence was enforced by physically placing the two teams at extreme parts of ILO Headquarters in Geneva and requesting them to avoid exchanging information on their findings and work methods. Each team had a total of six person-months of workload and access to similar equipments (Internet, ILO telephone and libraries, etc.). They received the same training with identical syllabus, covering ILO Conventions No. 29 and No. 105 on forced labour, and other related documents. Each team was instructed on the materials to look for and on the elements to enter in the database. Each team created its own database, with no access to the database of the other.

To facilitate the supervision of the work and the subsequent data validation process, each team was instructed to place in a special folder a hardcopy of the document from which the forced labour information was extracted. A unique identification code was given to each document which had to match the identification code of the corresponding record entered in the database. In addition to the source identification code, the following elements were considered as key and no record with blank information on any one of them would be entered into the database. The mandatory key fields were:

- Identification code of the source of information
- Country or geographic region
- Type of forced labour
- Numerical estimate of persons involved
- Reference date or time period of the estimate

No other limit was set on the nature of data that the researchers could collect. In fact, they were encouraged to also include, when relevant, qualitative information that may help to better understand forced labour. During their assignment, the two teams examined a wide range of sources of data in a multitude of languages (French, English, Spanish, Arabic, Portuguese, Russian and Hindi). Data sources that were explored by the two teams included the following broad categories:

- ILO (reports of supervisory body, national and regional studies, results of rapid assessment surveys)
- Other international organisations (qualitative studies, regional or thematic estimates, data compilations)
- Governments (national estimates, statistical reports, court and police reports)
- Trade Unions (data compilations, regional or thematic analyses, global estimates)
- Local NGO's (testimonies, case studies, reports of activities, local estimations, qualitative information)
- International NGO's (data compilations, regional or thematic analyses, global estimates)
- Academia (research papers, qualitative studies, quantitative estimations with methodologies)
- Media (testimonies, interviews, news in brief, global estimations, quotations)

Table 1 shows that more than 5,000 data on forced labour were identified from these sources. The geographical distribution by team is also shown below. It can be noticed that the total number of data collected by each team is about equal; Team 1 covered relatively more the industrialised countries, transition economies, and the Middle East and North Africa, while Team 2 concentrated more on Asia and the Pacific and Latin America and the Caribbean. The coverage of Sub-Sahara Africa was about even between the two teams. The 6 and 54 data items recorded under the general heading "world" refer to general information transcending several regions or pertaining to the world as a whole.

To contribute to the analysis of forced labour beyond mere estimation of its incidence, a framework was developed to collect, where possible, a maximum of

Table 1. Number of collected reports

Region	Team 1	Team 2
Asia and the Pacific	710	1,049
Industrialised countries	820	402
Latin America and Caribbean	290	578
Middle East and North Africa	200	110
Sub-Saharan Africa	298	224
Transition economies	230	140
World	6	54
Total	2,554	2,557

information on the nature and circumstance of forced labour and the characteristics of the persons involved. In addition to geographical information (country or region), the database includes information on the population category of the victims (children, women, indigenous, etc.), their status (freed, rehabilitated, etc.), the circumstance of entry into forced labour (trafficked in, trafficked out, etc.), the economic aspects (branch of economic activity, salary, etc), as well as information on indebtedness, confiscation of documents, violence and threats. The database also includes information on the nature of the recorded data, in particular, the date or time period of forced labour, whether the data refers to a headcount or an estimate, if it is a stock or a flow, if it is meant to be a minimum value or a maximum, etc. Finally, the database records full bibliographical information of the source including page number, the name of the researcher who entered the data and the date of data-entry.

(b) Data Validation

The data entered by each team into its respective database was subject to a four-step validation procedure. The first step in the validation process was to verify that the data entered into the database indeed concerns forced labour in the sense of the ILO Convention Nos. 29 and 105. Experience has shown that there is a general lack of precision in the vocabulary used with regard to forced labour and related situations. For example, undocumented migrants working for harsh employers are sometimes presented as being in a situation of forced labour, even though they may not work under any binding constraints. Conversely, there may be situations that are not explicitly referred to as forced labour in the reports, but under scrutiny could turn out to be in fact situations of forced labour. There are also situations such as sales of organ or trafficking children for purpose of adoption where the basic activity is not a work activity and therefore the classification as forced labour would be incorrect.

In practice, the following three general criteria have used for considering a person to be in forced labour:

- The person has entered into that activity against his or her will. The victim may have been kidnapped, menaced or deceived. Children sold in exchange for debts of their parents or victims of commercial sexual exploitation fall into this category.

- The person is retained in employment against his or her will. The person could have been retained physically (locked in a room, or working and living in a place permanently watched, or even guarded by armed personnel), or by other means such as confiscation of identity papers or holding back a part or the totality of wages.
- The person can only leave the job at great risk, such as menaces against the person or his or her family, or menaces of being denounced to the authorities.

It should be noted that the last two criteria are independent of the first. A person may have entered into a job voluntarily, but later retained by force. Data that did not meet the above criteria were discarded.

The second step in the validation procedure was to ensure that the data refer to the estimation period 1995-2004. Curiously, a significant number of publications describe events and data with no mention of dates or time periods. The main task of validation has therefore been to move through the various sources cited in the publications to find, if possible, a date or time-period that could be associated to the reported fact. A number of problems had to be confronted in this process. Often, there was no way of knowing whether the data in question referred to an annual flow of victims or to a total number of persons in forced labour at a given time. Some data in recent publications in fact relate to situations reported ten or fifteen years ago.

The third step in the validation process was to assess the reliability of the data. Not all that is written or published should be believed! Two basic principles were used in evaluating the data.

- First, the evaluation should relate to the primary source of the data, not just the reporting source. This principle implied sometimes a long exercise of moving from one reference or footnote to another to eventually discover the primary source. There were also surprises, for example, when discovering loops such as A citing B, B citing C, and C citing A! Such data were, of course, not validated.
- Secondly, the reliability of the data depends on the credibility of the original source. This principle was adopted as a shortcut to detailed analysis of sometimes unavailable information on the methodology used to obtain the data. Credibility was assessed on the basis of authorship. In the case of specific facts, all data first issued by identified individuals or institutions were considered as reliable. By contrast, all data reported with no mention of authorship or affiliation was discarded.

The fourth and final step in the validation process was the elimination of duplicated data *within* each team's database. This step did not concern duplications between teams, as these are essential to the capture-recapture methodology. Three types of duplications were most widespread:

- A source publishes information or an estimate on forced labour and the article is cited in a multitude of other studies. In the present validation process, two publications reporting the same number with the same primary source were considered as duplicates.

- Material published by a source is reproduced by another but with some minor or major distortions, for example, rounding the figure of 783 to 800, changing the date of say "July 2003" to "last year", or omitting the identity of "women and children" and referring simply as "victims of forced labour". These types of duplications were in general more difficult to identify, but they could often be detected by finding the original source.
- In the case of trafficking in persons for forced labour, duplications may occur when one person from a team finds the data recorded at the place of origin, and another member of the same team finds it for the place of destination. Such duplications were detected by matching the figures and the locations. Where duplications were found, the place-of-origin data were discarded, and the place-of-destination data maintained.

(c) The Final Database

The final output, after the validation process, is shown below in Table 2.

4.   Results and Sampling Errors

Using the double-sampling methodology and the validated output on reported cases shown in Table 2, we estimated forced labour by form for each geographical region. The results are shown in Table 3. The total estimated number of persons reported in forced labour over the last 10 years is 12.3 million people. Of this total, state-imposed forced labour is estimated to have involved about 2,490,000 persons, forced sexual exploitation affected 1,390,000 victims, and forced economic exploitation such as slavery, debt bondage or forced domestic labour involved an estimated 7,810,000 people. In addition, there were an estimated 610,000 people (not shown in Table 3) in forms of forced labour that could not be clearly identified.

Of the 12.3 million victims, 2.4 million were trafficked. Among these trafficked victims, 43% were in forced commercial sexual exploitation, 32% in forced economic exploitation, and 25% were trafficked for undetermined or mixed forms of forced labour. Concerning regional distribution, the bulk of reported forced

Table 2. Number of validated reported cases.

Region	Team 1	Team 2
Asia and the Pacific	193	272
Industrialised countries	306	258
Latin America and Caribbean	110	255
Middle East and North Africa	62	77
Sub-Saharan Africa	132	160
Transition economies	145	188
Total	948	1,210

Table 3. Forced labour estimates with capture-recapture.

Region	State-imposed	Sexual exploitation	Economic exploitation	Total (rounded)	of which Trafficked
Asia and the Pacific	2,186,000	902,000	5,964,000	9,490,000	1,360,000
Industrialised countries	19,000	200,000	84,000	360,000	270,000
Latin America and Caribbean	205,000	115,000	994,000	1,320,000	250,000
Middle East and North Africa	7,000	25,000	229,000	260,000	230,000
Sub-Saharan Africa	70,000	50,000	531,000	660,000	130,00
Transition economies	1,000	98,000	10,000	210,000	200,000
Total	2,488,000	1,390,000	7,812,000	12,300,000	2,440,000

labour was in Asia and the Pacific, with an estimated 9.5 million victims. This figure represents more than 77% of our total estimate. The region with the next highest number of reported victims is Latin America and the Caribbean with some 1.3 million victims, followed by Sub-Sahara Africa (660,000), the industrialised countries (360,000), Middle East and North Africa (260,000), and finally transition economies (210,000). When we put these numbers in relation to the size of the populations, Asia & the Pacific, Latin America & the Caribbean, and Sub-Sahara Africa remain the three regions with highest incidence with, respectively, 3, 2.5 and 1 victim of forced labour per 1,000 inhabitants. This is followed by the Middle East & North Africa (0.75/1,000), transition economies (0.5/1,000) and industrialised countries (0.3/1,000).

Regarding forms of forced labour within regions, we can observe that private-imposed economic exploitation dominates in the Middle East & North Africa (88%), Sub-Saharan African (80%), Latin America and the Caribbean (75%) and in Asia and the Pacific (63%). In these regions, the share of state-imposed forced labour does not exceed 20% and forced commercial sexual exploitation is about 10% of the total. In industrialised countries and transition economies the pattern of forced labour is somewhat different in that forced commercial sexual exploitation appears to be the dominant form of forced labour.

These estimates, like most estimates, are subject to sampling errors. This is due to the fact that only a sample of all reported cases of forced labour has been examined in the study. The capture-recapture methodology was designed to control the sampling errors and provide estimates of its extent. We have thus calculated the sampling error of the global estimate using standard formula given in Thompson (1992, p. 214, equation (6)). The results are shown in Table 4.

We can see that our global estimate of 12,300,000 reported victims is subject to a standard error of around 2,500,000. This represents a relative standard error of

Table 4. Estimates and standard errors.

	Estimated incidence	Standard error
By Region:		
Asia and the Pacific	9,500,000	1,900,000
Latin America and the Caribbean	1,300,000	300,000
Sub-Sahara Africa	660,000	160,000
Middle East and North Africa	260,000	80,000
Transition economies	210,000	70,000
Industrialised countries	360,000	100,000
By Form:		
State-imposed forced labour	2,500,000	530,000
Private-imposed, commercial sexual exploitation	1,400,000	310,000
Private-imposed, other economic exploitation	7,800,000	1,600,000
Mixed private-imposed forced labour	610,000	150,000
Trafficked forced labour	2,440,000	520,000
Total forced labour	12,300,000	2,500,000

about 20%, indicating a large rate of sampling error. The sampling error may be interpreted in terms of a confidence interval. Thus, the unknown true number of reported people in forced labour in the world, estimated from a set of sample data, is likely to be within an estimated range of roughly one standard error, which in the present context is equal to:

12,300,000 +/− 2,500,000

or

9,800,000 − 14,800,000

The level of confidence associated with this confidence interval is about 68%.

5.   From reported victims to total victims

In our project, the capture–recapture methodology is applied to reported cases of forced labour over the period 1995 to 2004. The resulting estimate, therefore, has to be interpreted as an estimate of the total number of reported victims who experienced forced labour at some time during the ten-year period 1995-2004. Although the main focus of the present paper is on the methodology to estimate the number of reported cases, we are also interested to know the total number of people (reported and unreported) who are currently in forced labour.

Can our methodology be used to obtain such an estimate? Figure 3 shows the relationship between flow and stock estimates. It shows that the total number of victims at each moment during 1995-2004 is equal to the total number of victims who experienced forced labour in that period (reported and unreported) multiplied by the average duration of forced labour as a proportion of the 10 years period.

Total number of victims of forced labour at a given time during 1995–2004
=
Total number of victims who experienced forced labour during 1995–2004
×
Average duration in forced labour as a fraction of the 10-year period 1995–2004

Figure 3. Relationship between stock and flow of forced labour.

Of course, because the unreported cases of forced labour will fall outside the scope of any direct method of estimation, including the capture–recapture methodology, they will have to be accounted for by indirect procedures.

As we already pointed out, we have used the capture– recapture methodology to estimate the total number of reported victims who experienced forced labour at some time during the ten-year period 1995-2004. The relationship between this flow estimate and the total number of people (reported and unreported) who are in forced labour at each moment in time during this period can be expressed as:

Total forced labour = Total reported + Total unreported

$$T_{stock} = \Sigma_h \, T_{flow \, h} \, \mu_h + \Sigma_h \, T_{flow \, h} \, \mu_h / r_h$$

where $T_{flow \, h}$ is the flow estimate of forced labour in stratum h given by the capture-recapture method described earlier, where μ_h denotes the average duration in forced labour as a proportion of the 10 year period in stratum h, and where r_h denotes the ratio of reported to unreported number of victims in stratum h. This can be rewritten as:

$$T_{stock} = \Sigma_h \, T_{flow \, h} \, \mu_h \, (1+1/r_h) = \Sigma_h \, T_{flow \, h} \, \mu_h / p_h$$

or

$$T_{stock} = N_h \, (\mu_h / p_h)$$

where total forced labour at one moment in time (T) is equal to our flow estimate (N) in stratum h multiplied by a ratio (μ_h / p_h) where μ_h is the average duration in forced labour as a proportion of the 10 years period in stratum h and where p_h is the proportion of reported victims in stratum h. We may call this ratio "the multiplier", as it represents the number by which we need to multiply the estimate from our capture-recapture to obtain an estimate of the total number of people in forced labour at each moment during 1995-2004.

A conservative assumption is that this "multiplier" is equal to at least 1. According to our estimates, trafficked victims typically remain in forced labour from 6 months to 2 years. At the same time, available studies from official sources, including law enforcement agencies, suggest that the proportion of reported cases is about 10 percent. The *Dutch National Rapporteur*, who conducts every year one of the most comprehensive empirical country-analysis on trafficking, reports 300 to 400 registered victims every year. According to Van Dijk (2002) from the BNRM, however, the true number of victims of trafficking is at least 3,500 people

– suggesting that the proportion of reported victims is about 10 percent. Similarly, the U.S. estimates that 18,000 to 20,000 people are trafficked annually into the U.S. (U.S. Government, 2003), but has only recorded 315 victims in the 20 prosecution cases that were opened during the fiscal year 2001-02 and has probably identified between 800 and 2,000 victims in the 128 open trafficking investigations.[2] This implies that the U.S. Government's overall estimate of trafficking is 10 to 20 times higher than the number of victims who have actually been identified. On the basis of these and other studies on the "dark figures" of crime statistics, it can be estimated that the "multiplier" roughly takes a value of about 1. Indeed, if trafficked victims spend an average of 1 year in forced labour and if only 10 percent of cases are reported, then:

$$\mu_h/p_h = (0.1/0.1) = 1$$

At the same time, we know that other forms of forced labour can have longer duration. Bonded labour in South Asia, for example, typically lasts longer than sex trafficking. Based on the data we collected and on a number of other studies, we have estimated that the average duration in bonded labour is about 5 years. If the proportion of reported cases was the same as for trafficking (i.e. an estimated 10 percent) our multiplier would take the value of 5. That is, we would have:

$$\mu_h/p_h = (0.5/0.1) = 5$$

This would imply that the capture-recapture substantially underestimates the number of people in bonded labour at each moment in time. However, in reality, the proportion of reported cases is likely to be substantially higher for bonded labour than for trafficking. In the case of trafficking for forced commercial sexual exploitation – not only is the duration of exploitation shorter and, hence, by definition less likely to be reported – but both the means of entering in the activity is illicit, with perpetrators risking severe penalties. Bonded labour, on the other hand, is not only longer, but also much more visible and in some instances openly justified on the basis of tradition with little risk for the "employers". Thus, while the duration in forced labour varies from one form of forced labour to another, the proportion of reported victims also varies from one form of forced labour to another. Generally, forced labour of short duration seems to be associated with lower probability of reported cases, while forced labour of long duration is also associated with higher probabilities of reported cases (as illustrated by the two cases of trafficking and bonded labour).

Assuming that there is continuous and monotone positive relationship between the probability of reported cases of forced labour and duration in forced labour, one can conclude by the mean value theorem that the expression of the stock of forced labour can be approximated by:

---

[2] This range is based on i) a maximum assumption that the ratio of victims per case is the same in investigated cases as in prosecuted cases (i.e. 315/20=15.7 victims); and ii) a minimum assumption that the average ratio of victims per case is the same as in prosecuted cases but discounting the exceptionally large case of *U.S. v. Kil Soo Lee*, which involved over 200 victims (i.e. 115/19=6 victims)

$$T_{stock} = \Sigma_h \, T_{flow \, h} \, \mu_h/p_h$$
$$= \Sigma_h \, T_{flow \, h} \, x/p \, (x)$$
$$= \Sigma_h \, T_{flow \, h} \, x/x$$
$$= \Sigma_h \, T_{flow \, h}$$

where x is the average duration in forced labour over all forms of forced labour and $p(x)$ is the probability for a case of average duration to be reported. If this assumption is true, the flow estimate from our capture-recapture is equal to the stock estimate, meaning that our global estimate of 12.3 million people reported in forced labour can also be interpreted as the estimated number of persons in forced labour in the world at any given time during 1995-2004. Because we believe that this assumption is a conservative one (as it implies that forced labour of longer duration is significantly more reported than short-term trafficking), we also believe that 12.3 million people in forced labour is a minimum estimation. It may well be that, at the moment when we are writing these lines, many more than 12.3 million people are being exploited in forced labour, hidden from the public and the authorities.

Conclusion

This chapter has described the methodology that we have used to estimate the total number of reported victims of forced labour during 1994-2004, and in the last section we have described how this estimate of reported cases can be used as a basis for estimating the total number of people – both reported and unreported – who are in forced labour at each moment in time during this period. The results were first published in the ILO's report *A Global Alliance Against Forced Labour* (ILO 2005) and the methodology was presented in more details in a separate technical document (Belser, De Cock, and Mehran, 2005). To our knowledge, this was the first global estimate on forced labour published along with the methodology used to produce it.

Beyond the global figure, our estimate has generated a number of findings, in particular that: 1) Asia is the continent with the most severe problem; 2) most forced labour is exacted by private agents and not by public authorities; 3) the majority of forced labour in the world is for the purpose of labour exploitation and not for sexual exploitation (although this represents a particularly gruesome form of exploitation); 4) human trafficking is just one of the many ways that people are drawn into forced labour. All these findings contribute to a better understanding and mapping of modern forced labour.

It has to be emphasized that this methodology is experimental and that there are, doubtless, many ways to improve forced labour statistics in the future. One concern is that although enough data was available to compute meaningful estimates by regions and by the main forms of forced labour, too little data was available to compute reliable country-estimates (margins of errors become very large when the quantity of data is insufficient). Thus, country-estimates are better generated through different methods. Another concern is that the methodology cannot be used in a straightforward way to measure trends in the actual incidence of forced labour. This is because it seems probable that in the future, as more and more attention will be given to problems of forced labour and human trafficking, the proportion of reported to actual cases of forced labour will increase. Thus, it will become difficult to separate changes in the rate of reporting from changes in the actual incidence of forced labour, especially if these changes vary for different regions and different forms of forced labour. Thus, monitoring trends may require different statistical methods. One possibility to assess the impact of policies and to estimate actual trends could be to estimate the number of arrests and prosecutions. Alternatively, we could collect information on the duration of forced labour spells from rescued victims. A significant reduction in duration could indicate an improvement in law enforcement.

Finally, we believe that the double sampling methodology based on "capture-recapture" that we have described in this paper can be used to estimate reported rights violations beyond the special case of forced labour. In fact, the capture-recapture approach can be used in theory with a large number of subjects and can be applied to constructing other indicators of labour standards, such as violations of trade union rights, or for the purpose of quantifying other concealed human rights violations.

References

Belser, Patrick, Michaëlle de Cock and Farhad Mehran 2005. ILO minimum estimate of forced labour in the world. International Labour Office, Geneva.

Dutch National Rapporteur on Trafficking in Human Beings. Various years. Trafficking in human beings. Bureau NRM, The Hague.

Fiorito, Giancarlo. 2003. Methodological compendium for the calculation of estimates of forced labour. Mimeograph, in-focus programme on promoting the declaration. ILO, Geneva.

International Labour Office. 2001. Stopping forced labour. Global report under the follow-up to the ILO declaration on fundamental principles and rights at work. ILO, Geneva.

International Labour Office. 2005. A global alliance against forced labour. Global report under the follow-up to the ILO declaration on fundamental principles and rights at work. ILO, Geneva.

Jensen, A.L. 1989. Confidence intervals for nearly unbiased estimators in single-mark and single-recapture experiments. Biometrics 45: 1233–1237.

Norris, James L. III and Kenneth H. Pollock. 1996. Nonparametric MLE under two closed capture–recapture models with heterogeneity. Biometrics 52: 639–649.

Schaible, Wes. 2000. Methods for producing world and regional estimates for selected key indicators of the labour market. ILO Employment Paper 2000/6.

Thompson, Steven K. 1992. Sampling. John Wiley & Sons, New York.

United Nations. 2000. Protocol to prevent, suppress, and punish trafficking in persons, especially women and children. Supplementing the United Nations convention against transnational organized crime, New York.

US Government. 2003. Assessment of US activities to combat trafficking in persons. Washington, DC.

Van Dijk, Essy. 2002. Mensenhandel in Nederland 1997–2000. KLPD/NRI, Zoetermeer.

Appendix 1

Once we have estimated the total number of reported cases of forced labour, it is possible to estimate the total number of victims of forced labour. We can frame the estimation problem in the context of sampling theory where a total is being estimated on the basis of a sample of observation units with known probabilities of selection. Here the observation units are the reported cases and the probability of selection in each strata is the probability of the report case being captured by the first team, and if not, by the second team. This formulation may be expressed in mathematical terms as follows. Let i denote a reported case of forced labour, and X_i the number of victims involved. Suppose there are in total N reported cases (N unknown). The corresponding total number of victims of reported forced labour, also unknown, is expressed by:

$$T = X_1 + ... + X_i + ... + X_N$$

The capture–recapture methodology gives a sample of n distinct reported cases, $n=n_1+n_2-n_{12}$, where n_1 is the number of reported cases found by Team 1, n_2 the number found by Team 2, and n_{12} the number in common. Let $x_1,..., x_n$ denote the corresponding number of reported victims. According to sampling theory, an estimate of T based on these observations is given by:

$$T = (x_1/\pi_1) + ... + (x_i/\pi_i) + ... + (x_n/\pi_n),$$

where π_i is the probability of selection of reported case i, i=1,2,...,n. Using the capture-recapture assumptions, this probability may be calculated to be equal to:

$$\pi_i = p_1 + q_1 p_2,$$

where p_1 is the probability that the reported case i is captured by Team 1, q_1 the probability that it is not, and p_2 the probability that it is captured (or recaptured) by Team 2. Under simple random sampling with fixed same size, these component probabilities can be further calculated as follows:

$$p_1 = n_1/N, \quad q_1=1-n_1/N, \quad \text{and} \quad p_2 = n_2/N$$

leading after simplification to:

$$\pi_i = n_1/N + n_2/N - (n_1 n_2)/N^2$$

Replacing the unknown value of N by its capture-recapture estimate, N, the estimated probability of selection obtained above can be re-expressed simply as:

$$\pi_i = n/N,$$

where $n=n_1+n_2-n_{12}$ and $N = (n_1 n_2)/n_{12}$. Finally, replacing π_i by its estimate π_i in the expression of T, we obtain after simplification the required estimate of the total number of victims of reported forced labour:

$$T = N x,$$

where N is the estimated total number of reported cases and x is the average number of victims per reported case found in the sample of distinct reported cases.

This result is identical to the calculation in Section 2 c). The main advantage of the present formulation is that it can be generalized in a straightforward manner to variables other than the number of victims, yet maintaining consistency between the different estimates. For example, to estimate the number of children in forced labour consistently with the estimate of the number of children trafficked into forced labour. Another advantage of this formal approach of estimation is its computational generality. Once the probabilities of selection are estimated and associated to each reported case in the sample, the calculation of different estimates will be based on the same form of a weighted sum of reported cases, the values of the x's changing depending on the phenomenon being estimated, but the weights themselves remaining constant. This format can be easily programmed for general computer application and ready to apply at any time on variables that may have not been envisaged initially but considered later in the analysis.

Appendix 2. List of Countries.

Regional Breakdown According to ILO's KILM (Key Indicators of Labour Market)

Developed (industrialized) economies

Major Europe
Austria
Belgium
Denmark
Finland
France
Germany
Germany, Federal Republic of (Western)
Greece
Iceland
Ireland
Italy
Luxembourg
Netherlands
Norway
Portugal
Spain
Sweden
Switzerland
Turkey
United Kingdom

Major non-Europe
Australia
Canada
Japan
New Zealand
U.S.

Other Europe
Andorra
Cyprus
Faeroe Islands
Gibraltar
Isle of Man
Liechtenstein
Malta
Monaco
San Marino

Other non-Europe
Greenland
St. Pierre and Miquelon

Transition economies

Baltic States
Estonia
Latvia
Lithuania

Central and Eastern Europe
Albania
Bosnia and Herzegovina
Bulgaria
Croatia
Czech Republic
Czechoslovakia
Germany, Former Democratic Republic of (Eastern)
Hungary
Poland
Romania
Serbia and Montenegro
Slovakia
Slovenia
The former Yugoslav Republic of Macedonia
Yugoslavia (Former)

Commonwealth of Independent States
Armenia

Azerbaijan
Belarus
Georgia
Kazakhstan
Kyrgyzstan
Republic of Moldova
Russian Federation
Tajikistan
Turkmenistan
Ukraine
Uzbekistan

Former USSR
USSR: before Sept. 1991

Asia and the Pacific

Eastern Asia
China
Hong Kong, China
Korea, Democratic People's Republic of
Korea, Republic of
Macau, China
Mongolia
Taiwan, China

Pacific
Melanesia
Fiji
New Caledonia
Papua New Guinea
Solomon Islands
Vanuatu
Micronesia
Guam
Kiribati
Marshall Islands
Nauru
Northern Mariana Islands
Pacific Islands (Trust Territory)
Polynesia
American Samoa
Cook Islands
French Polynesia
Niue
Samoa
Tokelau

Tonga
Tuvalu
Wallis and Futuna Islands

South-central Asia
Afghanistan
Bangladesh
Bhutan
India
Maldives
Nepal
Pakistan
Sri Lanka

South-eastern Asia
Brunei Darussalam
Cambodia
East Timor
Indonesia
Lao People's Democratic Republic
Malaysia
Malaysia: Peninsular Malaysia
Myanmar
Philippines
Singapore
Thailand
Viet Nam

Latin America and the Caribbean

Caribbean
Anguilla
Antigua and Barbuda
Aruba
Bahamas
Barbados
Belize
Bermuda
British Virgin Islands
Cayman Islands
Cuba
Dominica
Dominican Republic
Grenada
Guadeloupe
Guyana

Haiti
Jamaica
Martinique
Montserrat
Netherlands Antilles
Puerto Rico
Saint Kitts and Nevis
Saint Lucia
Saint Vincent and the Grenadines
Suriname
Trinidad and Tobago
Turks and Caicos Islands
U.S. Virgin Islands

Central America
Costa Rica
El Salvador
Guatemala
Honduras
Mexico
Nicaragua
Panama

Latin America
Argentina
Bolivia
Brazil
Chile
Colombia
Ecuador
Falkland Islands (Malvinas)
French Guiana
Paraguay
Peru
Uruguay
Venezuela

Sub-Saharan Africa

Eastern Africa
Burundi
Comoros
Eritrea
Ethiopia
Kenya
Madagascar

Malawi
Mauritius
Mozambique
Réunion
Rwanda
Seychelles
Tanzania, United Republic of
Uganda
Zambia
Zimbabwe

Middle Africa
Angola
Cameroon
Central African Republic
Chad
Congo
Congo, Democratic Republic of
Equatorial Guinea
Gabon
Sao Tome and Principe
Southern Africa
Botswana
Lesotho
Namibia
South Africa
Swaziland

Western Africa
Benin
Burkina Faso
Cape Verde
Côte d'Ivoire
Gambia
Ghana
Guinea
Guinea-Bissau
Liberia
Mali
Mauritania
Niger
Nigeria
Senegal
Sierra Leone
St. Helena
Togo

Middle East and North Africa

Middle East
Bahrain
Djibouti
Iran, Islamic Republic of
Iraq
Israel
Jordan
Kuwait
Lebanon
Oman
Qatar
Saudi Arabia
Somalia
Syrian Arab Republic
United Arab Emirates
West Bank and Gaza Strip
Yemen

North Africa
Algeria
Egypt
Libyan Arab Jamahiriya
Morocco
Sudan
Tunisia

PATRICK BELSER, MICHAËLLE DE COCK, AND FARHAD MEHRAN
International Labour Office

Author Index

Subject Index

Social Indicators Research Series

1. V. Møller (ed.): *Quality of Life in South Africa*. 1997   ISBN 0-7923-4797-8
2. G. Baechler: *Violence Through Environmental Discrimination*. Causes, Rwanda Arena, and Conflict Model. 1999   ISBN 0-7923-5495-8
3. P. Bowles and L.T. Woods (eds.): *Japan after the Economic Miracle*. In Search of New Directories. 1999   ISBN 0-7923-6031-1
4. E. Diener and D.R. Rahtz (eds.): *Advances in Quality of Life Theory and Research*. Volume I. 1999   ISBN 0-7923-6060-5
5. Kwong-leung Tang (ed.): *Social Development in Asia*. 2000
   ISBN 0-7923-6256-X
6. M.M. Beyerlein (ed.): *Work Teams: Past, Present and Future*. 2000
   ISBN 0-7923-6699-9
7. A. Ben-Arieh, N.H. Kaufman, A.B. Andrews, R. Goerge, B.J. Lee, J.L. Aber (eds.): *Measuring and Monitoring Children's Well-Being*. 2001
   ISBN 0-7923-6789-8
8. M.J. Sirgy: *Handbook of Quality-of-Life Research. An Ethical Marketing Perspective*. 2001   ISBN 1-4020-0172-X
9. G. Preyer and M. Bös (eds.): *Borderlines in a Globalized World*. New Perspectives in a Sociology of the World-System. 2002
   ISBN 1-4020-0515-6
10. V. Nikolic-Ristanovic: *Social Change, Gender and Violence: Post-communist and war affected societies*. 2002   ISBN 1-4020-0726-4
11. M.R. Hagerty, J. Vogel and V. Møller: *Assessing Quality of Life and Living Conditions to Guide National Policy*. 2002   ISBN 1-4020-0727-2
12. M.J. Sirgy: *The Psychology of Quality of Life*. 2002   ISBN 1-4020-0800-7
13. S. McBride, L. Dobuzinskis, M. Griffin Cohen and J. Busumtwi-Sam (eds.): *Global Instability. Uncertainty and new visions in political economy*. 2002
    ISBN 1-4020-0946-1
14. Doh. Chull Shin, C.P. Rutkowski and Chong-Min Park (eds.): *The Quality of Life in Korea*. Comparative and Dynamic Perspectives. 2003
    ISBN 1-4020-0947-X
15. W. Glatzer: *Rich and Poor*. Disparities, Perceptions, Concomitants. 2002
    ISBN 1-4020-1012-5
16. E. Gullone and R.A. Cummins (eds.): *The Universality of Subjective Wellbeing Indicators*. A Multi-disciplinary and Multi-national Perspective. 2002
    ISBN 1-4020-1044-3
17. B.D. Zumbo (ed.): *Advances in Quality of Life Research 2001*. 2003
    ISBN 1-4020-1100-8

18. J. Vogel, T. Theorell, S. Svallfors, H.-H. Noll and B. Christoph: *European Welfare Production*. Institutional Configuration and Distributional Outcome. 2003   ISBN 1-4020-1149-0

19. A.C. Michalos: *Essays on the Quality of Life*. 2003   ISBN 1-4020-1342-6

20. M.J. Sirgy, D. Rahtz and A.C. Samli (eds.): *Advances in Quality-of-Life Theory and Research*. 2003   ISBN 1-4020-1474-0

21. M. Fine-Davis, J. Fagnani, D. Giovannini, L. Højgaard and H. Clarke: *Fathers and Mothers: Dilemmas of the Work-Life Balance*. 2004
                                                                    ISBN 1-4020-1807-X

22. M.J. Sirgy, D.R. Rahtz and D.J. Lee (eds.): *Community Quality-of-Life Indicators*. Best Cases. 2004   ISBN 1-4020-2201-8

23. A. Dannerbeck, F. Casas, M. Sadurni and G. Coenders (eds.): *Quality-of-Life Research on Children and Adolescents*. 2004   ISBN 1-4020-2311-1

24. W. Glatzer, S. von Below and M. Stoffregen (eds.): *Challenges for Quality of Life in the Contemporary World*. 2004   ISBN 1-4020-2890-3

25. D.T.L. Shek, Y. Chan and P.S.N. Lee (eds.): *Quality of Life Research in Chinese, Western and Global Contexts*. 2005   ISBN 1-4020-3601-9

26. A.C. Michalos (ed.): *Citation Classics from Social Indicators Research*. The Most Cited Articles Edited and Introduced by Alex C. Michalos. 2005
                                                                    ISBN 1-4020-3722-8

27. A. Ben-Arieh and R.M. Goerge (eds.): *Indicators of Children's Well Being*. Understanding Their Role, Usage and Policy Influence. 2006
                                                                    ISBN 1-4020-4237-X

28. M.J. Sirgy, D. Rahtz and D. Swain (eds.): *Community Quality-of-Life Indicators*. Best Cases II. 2006   ISBN 1-4020-4624-3

29. R.J. Estes (ed.): *Advancing Quality of Life in a Turbulent World*. 2006
                                                                    ISBN 1-4020-5099-2

30. David Kucera (ed.): *Qualitative Indicators of Labour Standards*. Comparative Methods and Applications. 2007   ISBN 1-4020-5200-6